Laird Cregar

LAIRD CREGAR

A Hollywood Tragedy

Gregory William Mank

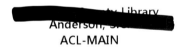

McFarland & Company, Inc., Publishers

Jefferson, North Carolina

Frontispiece: **Portrait, circa 1941.**

LIBRARY OF CONGRESS CATALOGUING-IN-PUBLICATION DATA

Names: Mank, Gregory W. author.
Title: Laird Cregar : a Hollywood tragedy / Gregory William Mank.
Description: Jefferson, North Carolina : McFarland & Company, Inc.,
Publishers, 2018. | Includes bibliographical references and index.
Identifiers: LCCN 2017048598 | ISBN 9780786449569
(illustrated case bound : acid free paper) ∞
Subjects: LCSH: Cregar, Laird, 1913–1944 | Actors—United States—Biography.
Classification: LCC PN2287.C6713 M36 2018 | DDC 791.4302/8092 [B] —dc23
LC record available at https://lccn.loc.gov/2017048598

BRITISH LIBRARY CATALOGUING DATA ARE AVAILABLE

ISBN (print) 978-0-7864-4956-9
ISBN (ebook) 978-1-4766-2844-8

Front cover: Laird Cregar as Jack the Ripper in *The Lodger*, 1944

Printed in the United States of America

*McFarland & Company, Inc., Publishers
Box 611, Jefferson, North Carolina 28640
www.mcfarlandpub.com*

For my Dad, the late William C. Mank—
who watched *The Lodger* with me when I was seven years old.

For the late Elizabeth Cregar Hayman—
who so deeply loved her "Uncle Sam."

For David Frankham—
who, inspired by Laird Cregar's performance as
The Lodger over 70 years ago, became an excellent actor.

For Ned Comstock, curator of USC's Performing Arts Library—
who's provided such great help with my research over
the past 30 years, especially on this book.

And, as always ... for Barbara.

Table of Contents

Acknowledgments

Although Laird Cregar died more than 70 years ago, I was determined that this long-in-the-works biography would depend on as many primary sources as possible. Many people, some no longer living, and many archives, some no longer in existence, have dynamically assisted.

Thanks, first of all, to Elizabeth Cregar Hayman, Laird Cregar's niece, who lived with him in Los Angeles when she was seven and eight years old and whose affectionate, insightful memories of her "Uncle Sam" proved invaluable. "Betsey" died in 2015 and I wish it had been possible to present this book to her with my most sincere gratitude.

DeWitt Bodeen, the writer of the 1942 classic *Cat People* and film historian extraordinaire, was a personal friend of Cregar, and, fortunately, a personal friend to me as well. Over the years, DeWitt had provided me with many stories and between-the-lines information about Cregar and the often sinister Hollywood of the World War II years. DeWitt died in 1988; it's hard to believe that almost 30 years have passed.

David Frankham, prolific actor and author of the superb memoir *Which One Is David?*, became an actor after being inspired by Cregar's portrayal in *The Lodger*. David arrived in Hollywood in the mid–1950s and collected many Cregar stories that he generously shared with me. His encouragement and friendship are much appreciated.

Julie Graham, Performing Arts curator at UCLA, made available Laird Cregar's legal file from 20th Century–Fox, an extraordinary source of information. Fox has reclaimed its papers from UCLA and I was fortunate to have had them to analyze when this window of opportunity existed.

Ned Comstock, Performing Arts curator at USC, Los Angeles, was, as always, a tremendous resource, providing all variety of information, as well as access to USC's John Brahm Archive—Brahm having directed Cregar's two best-remembered films, *The Lodger* and *Hangover Square*.

Kristine Krueger, of the National Film Information Service, Academy of Motion Picture Arts and Sciences, made available much important material, notably information from the Censorship Files (critical to analyze in the case of such "sex-horror" films as *The Lodger* and *Hangover Square*). She also found Gladys Hall's unpublished draft of the longest and (despite many fabrications) most candid interview Cregar ever gave.

The late Ellen Bailey, Pasadena Playhouse alumna and the Playhouse's Archive curator, cordially gave me entree to the archives, making it possible to document Cregar's various stage performances there before he made his mark in Hollywood.

R. David Schaaf, Philadelphia architect and historian, and my second cousin, located many sites associated with the Cregar family history in that city and accompanied me to them, notably on a high-spirited and multi-stop "pilgrimage" in November 2014.

G.D. Hamann of Filming Today Press produces a wonderful series of books on classic Hollywood stars, character actors and directors, providing a compilation of newspaper stories, interviews and film reviews from the period the subject of each book was active. The book he assembled on Cregar was of enormous help.

Over the past 40 years, various people who knew Laird Cregar gave me interviews. In addition to those already cited here: the late Charles Bennett, the late Henry Brandon, the late Fritz Feld, the late Undeen Darnell Hunter, the late Roger Kinzel, Faye Marlowe, the late Peggy Moran, the late Alan Napier, Peggy Stewart and Ned Wynn.

The Billy Rose Library for the Performing Arts at Lincoln Center, New York City, as always, has been a great source for material. A startling recent discovery, however: When I revisited the library in June 2016 to review the Cregar clippings file, as I had years before, the staff informed me that the entire file has been stolen.

Scott Gallinghouse and Frank Dello Stritto contributed valuable information from census files and various online newspaper archives; so did my son Christopher Mank, a Baltimore County research librarian.

Eileen Wolfberg, who diligently proofread this manuscript, and her husband Tom Jackson, both offered encouragement and good fellowship.

Thanks also to:

Ron Adams, Robert Connors, Dr. James T. Coughlin, David Del Valle, Jonathan Dixon, Scott Eyman, Denise Fetterley, Bruce Forsberg, Suzanne Foster (Winchester College, England), Martin Grams, Charles and Sherry Heard, Roger Hurlburt, the late Josephine Hutchinson, Cassandra Keith (the Episcopal Academy, Philadelphia), the late Kay Linaker, Tim and Donna Lucas, Leonard Maltin, Mark Martucci, Gavin Murrell (Montgomery Management, West Hollywood, California), Constantine Nasr, Bill Nelson, Doug and Kelley Norwine, James Robert Parish, Gary Don Rhodes, David J. Skal, Karl Thiede, Tom Weaver and Scott Wilson.

My appreciation is extended as well to the staffs of Eddie Brandt's Saturday Matinee, Celebrity Collectibles, Forest Lawn Memorial Park (Glendale) and the Woodlands (Philadelphia).

All source information as to interviews, cited books, newspapers and magazines, etc., can be found in the chapter endnotes.

There are several sources who provided important information regarding various topics, ranging from Cregar's sexuality to the costs, profits and losses on his films. These people have requested their contributions not be specified as to source, and I have respected their wishes.

Finally, my most personal and loving thanks to my wife Barbara, who shared with me so many of the research adventures that led to this book, and did so very much to make the book take final form. We've been a team in every way for over 45 years. I could never do it without you.

Author's Note

My fascination with Laird Cregar is almost lifelong. As such, I beg the reader's indulgence if this book begins and ends with uniquely personal stories.

My first memory of seeing Laird Cregar dates to about 1958; I was seven, playing in the living room with a compass my dad had brought back from World War II, and which I'd found in the attic. It was a Sunday afternoon, we turned on the TV, and there were the last five minutes or so of *The Lodger*. Cregar's Jack the Ripper was amok ... and in my child's eyes, looking right at me.

"Who's that actor?" I asked Dad.

"Laird Cregar," he answered immediately.

"Is he still alive?" I asked.

It was my usual question. A short time before, *Shock! Theater* had come to Balti-more, 11:15 p.m. on Saturday nights, presenting such legendary bogeymen as Bela Lugosi's Dracula, Boris Karloff's Frankenstein Monster and Lon Chaney, Jr.'s Wolf Man. When Dad stayed up late with me to watch *Shock!* I frequently asked if the actors we saw were living or dead.

"No," said Dad. "Laird Cregar died a long time ago."

What was the fascination? Part of it came from a single, unforgettable shot. As the Ripper rampaged across a catwalk in a Victorian theater, the shadows cast by the lights below rippled up and down his face and body, so he appeared to be a striped, zoomor-phic creature. I'd seen Chaney on *Shock! Theater* as a werewolf; Cregar's Jack the Ripper seemed a were-zebra.

"Look at him!" I remember exclaiming in awe.

At that age, I loved horror films and circuses. This monster looked as if he belonged in a circus ... or maybe had *escaped* from a circus ... or maybe the actor had a circus raging *inside* him. At any rate, he looked diabolic, and dangerous. I was hooked.

Over the next 15 years, a strange thing happened: Laird Cregar, via his old films, seemed to make guest appearances in my life at odd times ... seemingly haunting me, but in a friendly, affirmative way. One of Cregar's 16 films came on TV the week I grad-uated from high school; another, the night before I left for my freshman year at college. What little I learned about him made him all the more fascinating—that he was only 28 [*sic*] when he died, and that his final film, *Hangover Square*, was released after his death.

While attending Mount St. Mary's College in Maryland, I'd bought through the mail (from Larry Edmunds Bookshop in Hollywood, still thriving today) an original one-sheet poster for *Hangover Square* (cost: $17.50). It appealed to me both as Cregar memorabilia and for its generously dominant imagery of Linda Darnell, rapturously showing her thighs. The poster decorated my dormitory room for most of my four years at the Mount.

I could go on, but I'll jump ahead to 1973, when as a 22-year-old desperate to be a writer, I wrote a story about Cregar and submitted it to Leonard Maltin, who was destined for big things (*Entertainment Tonight* among them), and at that time publishing the magazine *Film Fan Monthly*. Leonard ran the story in that December's issue. James Robert Parish, prolific film book author, read the story and hired me as a research associate. I became a paid writer, modestly but legitimately.

Over 40 years later, I'm still working as a writer, having met fascinating people, visited wonderful places ... and owing a lot of the credit to Laird Cregar.

All the while, I've continued seeking information on the man, determined to write eventually as full, comprehensive and honest a Cregar biography as possible. As over 70 years have passed since his death, and I'm now over twice the age Cregar was when he died, I figured the time is now. It's been a challenge, as legends about his life and career abounded, some carved in stone by Cregar himself.

Here and there in the book, I interject brief accounts of my adventures in this admittedly odd quest, hoping they do not prove too disruptive to the narrative, and saving the strangest one for last.

Everyone in life should have passions, obsessions, fascinations ... happy, healthy ones that provide them great enjoyment. Researching Laird Cregar has been one of mine.

This book represents my most sincere gratitude to him.

Introduction: The Ripper Incarnate

Love is very close to hate.... Did you know that?
—Laird Cregar as Jack the Ripper, *The Lodger* (1944)

Boris Karloff used to talk about the fan letters he received from children who were moved to tears by his hapless Monster of *Frankenstein.* Bela Lugosi boasted that most of his fan mail came from women, aroused by his sexy vampire in *Dracula.*

In September 1944, Laird Cregar tells a reporter about a fan letter he's received from a 16-year-old girl in Canada[1] She wrote that she passionately dreams about him, creeping into her house at night with a long knife and, in a maniacal frenzy, butchering both her parents. She also asked him for an autographed picture.

The teenage girl had just seen Cregar as Jack the Ripper in *The Lodger.*

* * *

When *The Lodger* opened in January 1944 at Broadway's Roxy Theatre, Cregar appeared in person and received a five-minute ovation.[2] That summer, police had pursued a teenage Cregar stalker who, apprehended, hysterically threw herself out of a second floor window and broke a leg.[3] "Fan" letters had been pouring in from sadistic, self-righteous moviegoers who listed, in frighteningly precise detail, the various ways they'd enjoy killing him.[4]

There's no denying it. For 1944 audiences, Cregar's Ripper, to use a 21st-century colloquialism, is a rock star.

Laird Cregar (pronounced Cre-*gar*, as in ci-*gar*) is 31 years old, stands 6'3" and, after dieting off almost 100 pounds, weighs about 245. Come late summer, at the time he'd heard from the teenage girl with parent issues, Cregar's starring for his home studio 20th Century–Fox in *Hangover Square.* Like *The Lodger*, it's a sexed-up melodrama, at least for 1944. Cregar, top-billed for the first time, portrays a 1903 Jekyll-Hyde composer, destroyed by an evil vamp (alluringly played by Linda Darnell in silk panties and fishnet stockings). Joseph Breen, Production Code chief, is concerned about this lingerie, and has fired off a warning to the studio:

> Regarding Change No. 2, for Linda Darnell in *Hangover Square*, we call your attention that these panties should be changed in such a way as to obviate their apparent tightness in the crotch.[5]

There's a horrific heat wave, the temperature registers 104 degrees[6] on the *Hangover Square* soundstage, and fire is the film's motif. The macabre centerpiece: Cregar, having

1

strangled Darnell, costumes her corpse as a masked dummy, carries it through the streets and cremates the cadaver atop the towering Guy Fawkes bonfire.

Hangover Square will be one of the great horror films of the 1940s. Cregar, however, despises it. He'd refused to do the movie, at first taking a suspension,[7] caving in only after severe studio pressure. He fights bitterly with director John Brahm, who'd also directed *The Lodger*. "I *hate* Hollywood!"[8] he rages, terrified by his typecasting as a bat-shit crazy, sexually deranged ogre.

He wants to be, he desperately tells *Hangover Square* co-star George Sanders, "a beautiful man."[9] He fanatically plans to do so via a 500-calorie a day diet[10] and plastic surgery.[11]

It's a morbid obsession that's literally killing him.

*   *   *

It wasn't always this way.

In 1941, Cregar had delighted in becoming a sensation in Fox's *I Wake Up Screaming*, playing a 300-pound kink of a detective with lovelorn eyes and a silky flat voice, keeping a macabre shrine to a dead blonde. He slickly stole the *noir* thriller from the top-billed bodies beautiful of Betty Grable, Carole Landis and Victor Mature.

"[T]hat great big Cregar boy!" wrote *Photoplay* in its review. "Mama, turn the light on quick."[12]

Indeed, "Sammy" Cregar, as his friends call him (his birth name is Samuel Laird Cregar), had once reveled in his cinema flair for villainy … offbeat, sexually charged villainy. Off-screen, conversely, he was a gay Gargantua, his larger-than-life humor, affection and audacity at times skirting scandal:

- How many actors, much less one weighing 300 pounds, would attend a well-publicized Beverly Hills party dressed as a Mack Sennett Bathing Beauty … and wearing a blonde woman's wig?[13]
- How many, when their friend was ill, would take his place in a musical stage revue … dancing with chorus boys who weighed about one-third of what he did?[14]
- How many, at a Hollywood party mocking the 1942 Academy Awards, would receive an "Oscar" for "Best Female Impersonator of the Year" (for *The Black Swan*, in which he played a magnificently bewigged Capt. Henry Morgan), and then launch into a wickedly funny lampoon of Greer Garson … hilariously imitating the red-haired diva's long-winded Oscar acceptance speech for *Mrs. Miniver*?[15]

Gossip hounded him, and Cregar usually volleyed with a line from *Oscar Wilde*, the play that had launched his film colony fame in 1940: "It is perfectly monstrous the way people say things against one behind one's back that are absolutely and entirely true."

He'd always dreamed of being a full-fledged movie star, ever since he was a little boy in Philadelphia, practicing before a mirror making faces to present to his neighbors. He was terrific as the prissy, peppermint-gobbling villain in *This Gun for Hire*, and had played Satan himself in Ernst Lubitsch's romantic fantasy *Heaven Can Wait*—Lucifer, in Technicolor.

It was as Jack the Ripper that Laird Cregar fully pounced into stardom, slyly crafting a performance that the *New York Herald-Tribune* review called "a Krafft-Ebing case history of a sex maniac."[16] Cregar's Ripper conveyed a love for his dead brother that was not only homosexual, but incestuous; his scenes with leading lady Merle Oberon were tautly tense, and his delivery had the scent of necrophilia: "...when the evil is cut out of a beautiful thing, then only the beauty remains...."

Tragically, in the midst of the shooting of *The Lodger*, Laird's close friend David Bacon, star of the serial *The Masked Marvel*, had been murdered; like the Ripper, the killer had used a knife.[17] In the sordid murder's wake, complete with sagas of a male brothel-by-the-beach, Bacon's wife, Austrian singer Greta Keller, had suffered a miscarriage. Laird had taken her into his cottage high in Coldwater Canyon, and nursed her back to health.[18]

Had the personal impact of a real-life knife murderer on Cregar's powerhouse portrayal been *too* strong? Was Cregar's un-closeted Ripper *too* intense? If so, would audiences ever accept him on-screen as anyone *but* a raging psycho? If not, could he handle it?

For Laird Cregar is a very emotional man, hypersensitive, even for an actor. He laughs and cries easily. He'd brought both his beloved mother and aunt from Philadelphia, setting them up in fine style in Los Angeles. He'd hoped to adopt his niece Betsey, who turned eight while living with him in Beverly Hills, where he spoiled her like a princess; she calls him "Uncle Sam" and adores him.[19] She's back east now, he misses her terribly, and she cherishes the fact that he'd taught her to do a perfect cartwheel ... which he himself could perform, even at 340 pounds, with the grace of a circus acrobat.

Of course, most of the 85,000,000 World War II Americans who attend the movies weekly[20] don't know about Laird Cregar's cartwheels; to them, he's Jack the Ripper. Nor do they know that, as he fumes his way through *Hangover Square*, he's planned his "beautiful man" strategy, continuing to starve himself.

If Cregar's Ripper has creeped out audiences, the response of some of them, and of the Hollywood underbelly, has creeped him out as well. He's the victim of a vile whisper campaign, spread by an adversary—maybe his own studio?—portraying him as an out-of-control sexual degenerate, and calculated to destroy his career. This sordid slander, along with other recent events in his personal and professional life, has broken his heart. He retaliates

Laird Cregar's most celebrated performance: Jack the Ripper in *The Lodger*.

bitterly, self-destructively, seething and sweating through the hothouse traumas of *Hangover Square,* throwing frightening tantrums, haunted by the rumors, tormented by the fear that his giant body blocks him from ever truly entering Hollywood's Holy of Holies ... and taunted by an uncanny, long-lingering sense that he's going to die while he's still young.

Laird Cregar is hell-bent on going straight ... as an actor and a lover. Come *Hangover Square's* climax, Cregar's anti-hero sits at a piano, mournfully playing Bernard Herrmann's "Concerto Macabre," a towering fire hungrily roaring about him, the camera reverently tracking up and away to observe the Wagnerian fade-out inferno.

And on December 9, 1944, 60 days before *Hangover Square* will open in New York City, Laird Cregar, only 31 years old, suffers two heart attacks and dies.[21]

* * *

In retrospect, Laird Cregar's private, 12-days-before-Christmas funeral at Forest Lawn, Glendale, the film colony's all-star Limbo, had its quirks of high Hollywood Gothic. One of the pallbearers was Tom Neal, who will play the doomed hero of the *noir* classic *Detour* (1945), and who in 1965 will fatally shoot his wife Gail in the back of the head.[22] Reading the eulogy was Vincent Price, who immediately replaced Laird as Fox's top villain, inheriting the career Cregar might have had.[23]

His grave is up the hill from Forest Lawn's Great Mausoleum, in the section called Eventide. The simple marker is near the road, with words from Matthew's Gospel: *I Am with You Always.*[24]

Anguish, onscreen and off: Laird Cregar, starring, dieting and dying in *Hangover Square*.

Considering his screen roles, the words seem a nightmarish threat more than Biblical verse, something Laird might have leered at Victor Mature while hounding him in *I Wake Up Screaming.*

Inevitably, the ghost will rise ... and haunt film history.

* * *

As with many Hollywood tragedies, the truth depends on the agenda of whomever's telling the story.

For some, he's Saint Laird, martyr ... professionally anguished by his typecasting as a villain, personally tormented by his closeting as a homosexual, obsessively waging a gallant, pathetically doomed battle with 20th Century–Fox's almighty mogul Darryl F. Zanuck, bitterly vowing to bury his screen ogre image via crash dieting and plastic surgery, fatally dreaming of his resurrection as a transfigured "beautiful man." But the campaign went awry, the pet devils pounced, the dream became a manically self-destructive nightmare, and a 340-pound character star became a 235-pound corpse. Dead ... but dying while giving a defiant finger to Zanuck and the whalebone constrictions of 1944 Hollywood.

Others see it all differently: a classic show biz Death by Vanity. Cregar's pitiful self-crucifixion unfolds as a Hollywood Passion Play, with a dogmatic moral: Defy your studio, reveal your sexual "deviance," try to change your type, take for granted your fame, fortune and $1,500 weekly salary ... and you too can be dead at 31, a-moldering away at Forest Lawn.

There's middle ground, of course. And always there's the debate whether Laird, at the end of his life, wanted to be "a beautiful man" to attract a male or a female.

Whatever one chooses to believe, George Sanders, who acted with Cregar in three films, expressed it eloquently: Hollywood virtually "assassinated"[25] Laird Cregar.

Or did Cregar assassinate himself?

* * *

He's transcended his tragedy; indeed, the past 70 years have crystallized Cregar's place as one of the greatest of all Hollywood character actors. At a time when 1940s film acting was generally slick, compact and underplayed, Cregar was a spellbinder, a virtuoso. Only in his late 20s when fame came, he was, in his own words, an "oddity,"[26] a young, soulful actor with a quirky sense of humor, a treasure chest of acting tricks, and the curse of being trapped in a towering, obese body. The dramatic choices he made were decades ahead of his time; it was as if he were playing a sly game with sophisticated audiences, baiting them to catch on to his daring. His audacity made him unique in the buttoned-down Hollywood of the 1940s.

The Laird Cregar saga has various fascinating tendrils, themselves virtual melodrama. Among them is the presence of homosexuality in Hollywood in the 1940s, and the film colony's hypocrisy toward it. Another is the monolithic, sometimes sinister power of the studio system, and how it could nurture or smash talent. Both of these dark realities had an impact on Cregar, whose sensitivity, which so powerfully detonated on the screen, ultimately imploded in his life.

Researching this biography has had its bizarrely psychic edge, which the reader can decide to accept or reject. For now, however, just one story along those lines:

During Cregar's time at 20th Century–Fox, the ladies who operated the Fox telephone switch board worked Christmas Day. Cregar was one of the studio's very few celebrities who took time on that holiday to visit the ladies. In late December 1943, he was in New York for the upcoming opening of *The Lodger,* so he telephoned his greetings and promised he'd be with them for Christmas 1944. He died on December 9, 1944.

To the telephone operators' surprise, they discovered Christmas Day that Cregar, maybe sensing his approaching demise, had bought gifts for all of them, and had arranged for those gifts to be delivered to the studio.

"[H]e'll always be in our hearts every Christmas," said Nettie McLaughlin, chief phone operator at Fox. "He was a wonderful man."[27]

He was also a wonderful actor, and I hope this book will do him justice on both scores.

PART I

If You Try to Find Me, I Will Kill Myself

He is really not so ugly after all, provided, of course, that one shuts one's eyes, and does not look at him.
—Oscar Wilde, "The Birthday of the Infanta,"
A House of Pomegranates (1891)

1

Philadelphia

From my first day of consciousness, I wanted to be an actor.[1]
—Laird Cregar

Sedgwick Street is in West Mount Airy, a sector of Philadelphia whose rich history precedes the Revolutionary War.[2] The architecture is largely Victorian, and the stately three-story houses in Sedgwick's 600 block all date to 1906. Tall trees line the street. At night, the residents hear the whistles from trains running along the Schuylkill River.

In the summer of 1920, a little boy named "Sammy," who lived at 629 Sedgwick Street and who turned seven years old that July, had a favorite game he dearly loved. Rather than playing in nearby Carpenter's Woods, where children caught salamanders in the stream, or swimming in the Wissahickon Creek, where brave boys dived into "The Devil's Pool," he practiced "making faces" in the mirror. Then Sammy would knock on the neighbors' doors, asking them to play, "What's this face?" "My 'trapped rat' face was something, also my 'man-into-beast.' In Philadelphia, where I grew up, they thought I was mad!"[3]

The "man-into-beast" face surely had inspiration. On March 28, 1920, the John Barrymore film *Dr. Jekyll and Mr. Hyde* had premiered in New York City. Barrymore, who'd based his Hyde on a red tarantula at the Bronx Zoo, performed his terrifying transformation into Hyde largely without makeup. Critics hailed his sensational performance as almost preternatural, and Philadelphia was proud: John Barrymore was its native son.

It's doubtful that Sammy Cregar's widowed mother allowed her youngest son to see the racy, horrifying *Dr. Jekyll and Mr. Hyde*, but he heard about it and about Barrymore, who became his idol. Sammy ardently pursued his "What's this face?" game. If the neighbors applauded, he beamed, bowed and, like Alice's White Rabbit, ran away, frenetic. No time... No time...

Whatever the reception, warm or cold, he knew one thing: He had to be an actor.

"There have been times, though," Laird Cregar said ruefully 20 years later, on contract to 20th Century–Fox in Hollywood, "when I've wished my ambition wasn't so firmly fixed."[4]

* * *

*Maybe the quirk, the fact that villainy is my special forte—
although I hate to be symbolized such—comes from being a
direct descendant of John Wilkes Booth. He was a "Ham," and
so am I.[5]—Laird Cregar*

He claimed it was destiny that his screen infamy traced back to Good Friday, April 14, 1865. On that night of a full moon, John Wilkes Booth fatally shot Abraham Lincoln, leapt from the stage left balcony onto the stage of Ford's Theatre and, a "ham" even this fateful night, struck an absurd "villain" pose[6] as he waved a dagger and cried, "Sic semper tyrannis!"

As Laird once explained it, Booth's mother was his great-great-grandmother. On another occasion, he claimed that his great-great-grandmother was Ann Booth, the *wife* of John Wilkes Booth. No Booth biographies mention such a woman, and most historians doubt that the assassin ever married.[7]

Perhaps suffice to write that, on more than one occasion, Laird Cregar admitted that his "everpresent friend" was "Dishonesty."[8]

Laird related that one of his "maternal forebears"[9] was William Marshall, who designed the murals for London's Drury Lane Theatre. Playing up the villainy ancestry, he also said that another "Marshall" was the "special confidante"[10] of Oliver Cromwell, the Puritan fanatic who scuttled the theater during the reign of Charles I.

Maybe.

At any rate, it's possible to trace the family back to post–Civil War days[11]: Laird's father, Edward Mathews Cregar, was born in Philadelphia on December 29, 1868.[12] He was the son of Benjamin Cregar, a dry goods merchant, and his wife Sarah. By 1880, 54-year-old Benjamin and 45-year-old Sarah were living at 2215 Venango Street in Philadelphia with their four children: 27-year-old Robert (a dry goods cashier), 17-year-old William, 11-year-old Edward, and 5-year-old Emily. Also sharing the house: 74-year-old mother-in-law Ann Louise Phillips, 53-year-old brother-in-law William Phillips, 42-year-old sister-in-law Charlotte Phillips, and a 28-year-old servant and cook, Sarah Moore.

Ten years later, Benjamin and Sarah were still living on Venango

Never camera-shy: Samuel Laird Cregar, aspiring actor and sailor, at age 5.

Street, and the three brothers were making their marks in distinctly different fashion. Robert still worked in the family's dry goods business. William was a noted genealogist, living for a time in Annapolis, Maryland, contributing research to the Anne Arundel Courthouse. Edward was a rising cricket star. Cricket was enormously popular in Philadelphia, and it was the era of "the gentleman cricketers," wealthy men who could devote themselves to the game without requiring the salary of a full-time job. Edward wasn't a member of this rarified society—he was a tailor—but he was a valued and popular player, quickly making his mark as a member of the Tioga Club.

Then tragedy struck. On Saturday, December 13, 1890, the evening edition of *The Critic*, a Washington, D.C., newspaper, gave front page coverage to a death in northeast Philadelphia:

> GROUND UNDER THE WHEELS
>   A Philadelphian Meets Death in a Horrible Manner.
>   Philadelphia, December 13—William Francis Cregar of 2215 Venango Street, was killed last night near Holmesburg Junction by a fall from the New York and Washington passenger train....[13]

The Critic ghoulishly described William's mysterious demise with purple prose and gory detail:

> The exact nature of his fall, be it merely accidental or of a suicidal nature, is a point in doubt. The train had just passed the station at Holmesburg Junction, when it was discovered that Cregar had in some manner fallen under the wheels, where he was ground into fragments. The train was immediately stopped, and everyone ran to the rescue, but it was too late, for the man had been killed instantly. His head was completely severed from his body, as were also both his legs, while the body was so badly mashed and cut as to have lost its shape entirely.
>   In his pockets were found a card case, from which was obtained his name and address; knife, keys, some small change and an accident insurance policy for $6000, good for one day and dated December 12, 1890. This policy leads to the theory of suicide, though the nature of the fall is more that of accident....

The Critic wrote that there had been nothing "peculiar" about William's actions on the train, and that he'd "sat quietly reading a magazine all the way from New York." Railroad officials thought perhaps that as the train slackened speed at Holmesburg Junction, William, maybe hoping to take a streetcar to his home, slipped between the steps and fell to the tracks. There, as *The Critic* reminded its readers, he "was ground to pieces."

Besides devoting such vivid description to the mangled corpse, *The Critic* also provided a physical description of William Cregar in life: "Cregar was about 40 years old and was a very large man, being fully six feet tall and weighing about 300 pounds. He was dressed in a dark business suit, with a light overcoat. The whole case is a mystery to both the police and the railroad officials."

William Cregar was, in fact, only 28, but like his yet-unborn nephew, who would also be "fully six feet tall" and would weigh "about 300 pounds," he looked older.

William F. Cregar's funeral took place on Tuesday, December 16, 1890, at Philadelphia's Church of the Resurrection. The next day, the coroner's jury announced a verdict of "accidental death,"[14] opining that Cregar was "thrown from a train." In March 1891, Benjamin and Sarah Cregar sued the Pennsylvania Railroad Company for negligence, asking for $20,000 damages (which would be approximately $525,000 in 2017), claiming that William "was thrown from a fast train coming from New York, was left lying near

6705 Cresheim Road, Mount Airy, Philadelphia. Laird Cregar was born in this house on July 28, 1913 (author's photograph, 2014).

the track and subsequently run over and killed."[15] While no report of settlement has been found, one can presume that, based on the coroner's jury verdict, William Cregar's survivors received at least part of this sum. William's life insurance policy likely paid off as well. The family's social position assuredly rose accordingly.

Edward Cregar, handsome with blonde hair and a mustache, turned 32 in the year 1900. He was still a tailor, but had magnified his fame as a Philadelphia cricket star. The games were events, and thousands of young ladies, described by the *Philadelphia Inquirer* as "visions of loveliness," arrived in horse-drawn carriages to cheer their favorite players.

One such vision, a very tall one, was named Elizabeth Bloomfield Smith.

She was 20 years old in 1900, the daughter of magistrate Frank Smith and his wife Eugenia. Elizabeth, nicknamed Bess, was an auburn-haired Amazon who, at over six feet tall, loomed over most of her suitors. She had a weight problem, but nevertheless was glamorous in the well-corseted, bonnet-wearing Lillian Russell fashion of the turn of the century.

In 1900, the socially prominent Smith family lived at 3915 Woodland Avenue, high on a hill on the west bank of the Schuylkill River.[16] The Smith house neighbored the

Woodlands, a magnificent estate and a marvel of 18th-century American architecture, purchased by Philadelphia lawyer Andrew Hamilton in 1735. The Woodlands boasted a manor house, carriage house, greenhouses and 10,000 species of plants, and its 600 acres rambled far down the hill, all the way to Gray's Ferry on the Schuylkill. In 1840, a large part of the estate had become a cemetery, vying for desirability with Laurel Hill Cemetery across the river. Among those buried at the Woodlands by 1900: artist Rembrandt Peale, nursing pioneer Alice Fisher, Naval hero Commodore David Porter (who captured the first British warship in the War of 1812), circus mogul "General" Rufus Welch (who brought to the U.S. the first three giraffes from Africa) and various Civil War generals. Also interred at the Woodlands: the tragic William F. Cregar.

Bess loved the richly atmospheric charms of 1900 Philadelphia; over 40 years later, after her youngest son had earned her a modest celebrity of her own, she'd write a never-published book, *Make Me a Child Again*, expressing her nostalgia for gaslit Philadelphia. She was close to her 18-year-old sister Eugenia, known as Nean, rather a plain Jane and thin as a rail. If Eugenia envied Elizabeth her assurance, swagger and beauty, "Bess" envied "Nean" her metabolism.

As Edward Cregar scored in cricket, he'd see Miss Smith, the towering beauty,

The six strapping Cregar brothers, circa 1915. From left: Edward, Robert, John, William, Marshall and two-year-old Laird.

strolling with her parasol by the sidelines, or standing as she watched from her open carriage.

Wednesday, December 2, 1903: Elizabeth Bloomfield Smith married Edward Mathews Cregar at St. Mary's Protestant Episcopal Church in Philadelphia.[17] The newlyweds moved into the Cregar ancestral house at 2215 Venango Street.

Thursday, September 8, 1904: Nine months and six days after the couple's wedding, their first son, Edward Mathews Cregar II, was born and named after his father.

Friday, April 6, 1906: A second Cregar boy was born. It became a Cregar tradition to name a child after an ancestor, but Edward and Elizabeth, for whatever reason, bypassed Edward's father Benjamin, who'd died less than three months before. They named the boy Robert Phillips Cregar, after Benjamin's brother.

Monday, December 16, 1907: A third Cregar boy was born, and again, not named for Benjamin. At the time, John Barton King was the cricket batsman-bowler superstar of Philadelphia. The name of the third son: John Barton King Cregar.

February 1908: Frank Smith, Elizabeth's father, died. The funeral took place at Edward and Elizabeth's new home, 908 Farragut Terrace.

Monday, July 6, 1908: The Philadelphia Cricket Club, having traveled to the British

7201 Boyer Street, Mount Airy. Edward M. Cregar died here in 1916 (author's photograph, 2014).

Isles, played its first game there in Cardiff. Coaching the team: Edward Mathews Cregar. The Young Philadelphians went on to play in such cities as Dublin, Belfast and Canterbury. John Barton King, then 35, set a bowling record not bettered until 1958, and while the Philadelphians won four and lost six in their "first-class" matches, they did their city proud. Edward Cregar came home a hero.

October 1908: Sarah Cregar, Edward's mother, died.

Thursday, July 8, 1909: The fourth son of Edward and Elizabeth was born, and named for his unfortunate uncle, William Francis Cregar, who'd been dead for over 18 years.

Monday, February 13, 1911: The fifth son, Marshall Bloomfield Cregar, was born, named after John Marshall (1775–1835), fourth Chief Justice of the United States, to whom the family claimed ancestry.

1913: The Cregar family was living at 6705 Cresheim Road in Mount Airy. The area was known as Pelham, a colony of Philadelphia well-to-dos who'd created their own rural world in the Cresheim Valley, outside the big city. Pelham had its own bank, where a family could place their silver and jewelry in the neighborhood vault while away on vacation. It had its own garage, where the mechanics knew the whimsicalities of the Ford Model T and the Stutz Bearcat.

It was in that house on Monday, July 28, 1913, at 4:30 a.m., that Dr. Josephus Ullom, of 24 Carpenter Street, delivered the sixth and last of the sons of Edward and Elizabeth.[18] His name: Samuel Laird Cregar.

*   *   *

It was a colorful year for the arts.

For the movies, 1913 was a year of "firsts."[19] The Keystone comedy *A Noise from the Deep*, starring Mabel Normand and Fatty Arbuckle, featured the cinema's first pie in the face. Lon Chaney played his first cinema hunchback, Barnacle Bill, in *The Sea Urchin*. Universal released the first "exploitation" feature, *Traffic in Souls*, a saga of prostitution, and Cecil B. DeMille began shooting the first feature-length movie filmed in Hollywood, *The Squaw Man*.

In the New York theater, Mary Pickford and Lillian Gish co-starred in *The Good Little Devil*, and Pauline Frederick was an alluring Potiphar's Wife in the Biblical spectacle *Joseph and his Brethren*. "When Irish Eyes Are Smiling" and "You Made Me Love You" were among the popular songs of 1913. Da Vinci's *Mona Lisa* returned to the Louvre after its theft two years previously. And curiously, Laird Cregar's birth year also saw the publication of a best-selling novel by Marie Belloc-Lowndes: *The Lodger*, based on Jack the Ripper, who in 1888, 25 years before, had slaughtered five Whitechapel prostitutes and escaped capture.

"Sammy" wasn't quite seven months old when *The Philadelphia Inquirer* ran this page one headline (Wednesday, February 11, 1914):

SECOND ATTEMPT TO KIDNAP SON OF E.M. CREGAR
> Boy on Way to School with Chum Accosted by Man
> Lads Run Home While Stranger Flees into Woods. Police Institute Search.
> Parents of Germantown children who are required to walk to school unescorted are wrought up over the strange actions of a man who is believed to be bent upon spiriting away boys, and whose motive is a mystery.

What are believed to have been two deliberate attempts at kidnaping sons of Edward M. Cregar, the noted cricketer, whose home is at 6810 Quincy Street, Pelham, have occurred within a week and a rigid search for a suspect is being conducted.

Note that the Cregar family had moved from Cresheim Road to Quincy Street, barely a block away. *The Inquirer* reported that seven-year-old Robert Cregar and his "chum," seven-year-old neighbor Graham Ayres, were on their way to the Charles W. Henry School at Greene and Carpenter Streets on the morning of February 10, when a man "intercepted" them and "invited Robert to go to a candy store with him." They ran home and "pantingly related" the news to Aunt Eugenia, who lived with her sister's family. "Aunt Nean" sent the boys back to school with a nurse and phoned the Germantown police. The *Inquirer* continued:

Man Seen Entering Woods
   As the lads were on their way to school for the second time the man who had accosted them was seen entering Carpenter's Woods. When the police learned this the woods were searched, but no trace of the man could be found.
   The supposed attempt at kidnaping has aroused the Germantown police because of what is also believed to have been an attempt to kidnap another of the Cregar children.

Indeed, only the previous Tuesday, Aunt Eugenia took Marshall to a Germantown theater where the boy, not quite three, suddenly "disappeared." It took half an hour for Eugenia to find Marshall, held by a man at Germantown and Chelten Avenues. When the man saw Eugenia storming after him, he "dropped" the boy and fled.

Edward Cregar told the police that he believed that someone was intent on, as the *Inquirer* expressed it, "spiriting away one of his six sons." Additionally, Eugenia said that, two weeks before, she'd seen "a man peering through a parlor window." She called Edward, who gave chase, but the man escaped.

It's tempting to write that this predator would prophesy the type of creepy roles later played by Laird Cregar; however, as vile as he'd be on screen, Laird never played a pedophile. At any rate, the six Cregar boys escaped kidnaping.

Sunday, June 6, 1915: William (almost six), Marshall (four) and Samuel (almost two) were baptized at Grace Episcopal Church. Designed by noted Philadelphia architect Charles M. Burns and built in 1888, this beautiful church is on the National Registry of Historic Places and one of the architectural talismans of Mount Airy.

The Cregar family was prospering. They moved to 7201 Boyer Street, neighboring Grace Episcopal Church, in an area known as Gowen Estates, designed as a spectacular, one-upmanship challenge to Pelham. Life appeared very promising for the family.

Then tragedy struck again.

Saturday, May 6, 1916: Edward Mathews Cregar died at the house on Boyer Street. He was only 47. Cause of death: cancer of the throat.[20] *The Philadelphia Inquirer* listed the death as "Suddenly," although Edward had been ill for several months, and his death was reportedly "a surprise and shock to his many friends." The viewing was at the family home and the funeral took place at Grace Episcopal Church on Tuesday, May 9, at 2:15 p.m.

Burial was private at the Woodlands. Elizabeth Cregar came home to Mount Airy, a 36-year-old widow with six husky boys to feed. Edward had left some money, enough at least to keep up appearances; nevertheless, she'd have to find a job. Meanwhile, her

The grave of Edward M. Cregar, the Woodlands, Philadelphia (author's photograph, 2014).

very devoted sister Eugenia made a great sacrifice: About to marry, she broke her engagement, volunteering to stay home with the boys as Elizabeth went to work.

"Bess" probably foresaw herself buried one day with Edward, overlooking the Schuylkill, and records at the Woodlands note that Edward Cregar's grave was eight feet deep, allowing another coffin to be placed upon it eventually, likely Elizabeth's.[21]

She was, of course, then unaware of the enormous changes her youngest son would eventually bring to her life.

*   *   *

Late November 2014. I join my second cousin, R. David Schaaf, a noted Philadelphia architect and historian, on what we call "The Laird Cregar Tour." David lives in the Mount Airy area; in fact, the old Cregar home on Sedgwick Street is a stone's throw from his own house.

We see Laird's birthplace, and most of his childhood homes, austere and impressive in the sunshine. The homes appear well-kept, although no occupants are in evidence; a cat lounges on the porch of the house on Cresheim. Nothing conjures up a husky little boy's ghost, running about and making faces.

The home of his grandparents on Venango Street is now an empty lot, although most of the houses on that street still survive. An old factory stands down the street, many of its glass panes shattered.

The sky clouds up mid-afternoon as we reach the Woodlands Cemetery. We have a map and information, provided by email from the cemetery's office, and surprisingly quickly we find the grave marker of Laird's father, Edward Mathews Cregar. It's an impressive monument and, although 98 years old, looks almost new ... a worthy tribute to a man who, as a star cricketer, once made Philadelphia proud. (I also notice that it bears an incorrect birthdate.) We take a look at the nearby Carriage House, and proceed to try to find the 1890 grave of the tragic William F. Cregar, located in another part of the cemetery.

We find the area, but not the 124-year-old grave. Perpetual care isn't what it used to be in what was once the grandest of Philadelphia cemeteries; a number of the markers in this sector have fallen down, while others are so faded as to be unreadable. I wonder how many decades it's been since anyone visited William Cregar's grave; for that matter, how many years since anyone paid tribute at his noted brother's.

The afternoon grows colder and darker. The view of the Schuylkill River isn't as lovely as I'd expected. A jogger runs through the lonely cemetery and an Amtrak train passes between the river and the Woodlands, sounding its horn.

*   *   *

A picture taken about the time of Edward's death shows the six Cregar boys, formally posing. Sammy, the youngest, has a Buster Brown hairdo and sailor suit, and appears totally at ease before a camera.

Not yet three years old when his father died, Sammy surely had few memories of Edward Mathews Cregar. He'd deeply miss having a father, and the loss likely contributed to his lifelong fear of an early death. Strangely, in later years, Laird Cregar would basically resurrect his father, casting him as a significant player in the fiction he weaved about his tortuous rise to fame.

2

The "Secret Heart" Thing

Dishonesty is a quality which sometimes, particularly for actors, is extremely useful.[1]—Laird Cregar

At the age of five, Samuel Laird Cregar was already in show business ... sort of. He became impresario of his own Mount Airy neighborhood circus, offering his little friends jobs as clowns—if they paid him their small change for the privilege.

"I usually played the giant," Laird remembered, "for even then I was pretty big."[2]

He also began writing plays, his true passion. The writing hobby provided escape as well. Sammy Cregar was an emotional child, whose weight drew taunts and beatings from other boys. His early "artistic" bent didn't help, and after gaining fame, Laird admitted the bullying, if rather jocularly. "They used to gang up on me," he'd laugh, "so it came out even."[3]

Still, there were traumas, and he eventually dramatized his own early life in a bizarre rewrite that invites analysis. For example, Laird claimed that, when he was about eight, circa 1924, his father took him to England and enrolled him at Winchester College, founded in 1382 and at the same Hampshire location for over 600 years.[4]

In fact, Laird was born in 1913, so he was 11 in 1924 ... and his father had been dead for eight years. Nowhere in Winchester's records is there a listing of Samuel Laird Cregar.

"We do find that people often claim to have attended Winchester when they actually went to school somewhere else," the school's archivist Suzanne Foster wrote to me after searching the rosters, "so Mr. Cregar is in good company."[5]

Laird's story went on that, while at Winchester, he served as a page boy at Stratford-upon-Avon, Shakespeare's birthplace, then the home of the Shakespeare Memorial Theatre.[6] This is unlikely, as there is no ship's record of Samuel Laird Cregar having ever sailed to England.

Then there was Laird's claim that, after his father died suddenly (ten years or more after he actually *did* die), the well-off Widow Cregar brought her youngest boy back from England and sent him to the famed Episcopal Academy of Philadelphia, founded in 1785. There young Laird acted in (and even wrote, he said) the school plays.[7] However, Episcopal Academy archivist Cassandra Keith reviewed the school's meticulously kept records. As for noted actors, she confirmed that Lionel Barrymore had entered Episcopal Academy when he was eight, attending from February 14 to June 30, 1887; she also ascertained that John Carradine was an alumnus, entering at age ten on June 7, 1916, and attending through January 6, 1919. But there's no record of Samuel Laird Cregar in the Episcopal Academy archives.[8]

What really was happening? Laird's mother, whom he hero-worshipped and described, significantly, as "one of those completely charming women who never faced reality in her life,"[9] had found work in the basement at Wanamaker's, Philadelphia's 12-story Florentine marvel, complete with the marble Grand Court and the Wanamaker Organ, imported from the 1904 St. Louis World's Fair.

Laird hailed his mother as "a remarkable woman"[10] who worked her way up at Wanamaker's to head buyer. The 1920 census, which lists the Cregar family living at 629 Sedgwick Street in Mount Airy, confirms Laird's story: Elizabeth, who told the census reporter that she was 38 (knocking off two years), was now "Head" of the family, and listed as "a department store manager." The oldest boy, Edward, had left school and, at age 15, was a bonds salesman. The other five sons were all attending public schools, while Aunt Eugenia loyally kept the house and raised the six-boy brood.

Turning ten in 1923, Sam was a handful. Elizabeth Cregar had special affection for her youngest boy, and Gladys Hall, after a lengthy 1942 interview with Laird in which he let a few facts mix with fancy, offered this prose:

> [W]hat appeared to be a shapeless bolster trundled into the room where Mrs. Cregar sat at her sewing. From the billowing depths of sheets and pillow-slips an incongruously reedy voice piped, "I am the Sheik of Araby!"
>
> Mrs. Cregar regarded this ten-year-old youngest of her six Herculean sons with compassion. Poor child, he so wanted to be an actor. One day he was the Sheik of Araby; the next day, Genghis Khan, and so on. But actors were shaped, so to speak, after the fashion of John Gilbert, blade-like. How could this bouncing boy with the appetite of a young bull-elephant hope for a career on stage or screen?[11]

"Sam was different from his brothers," remembered his niece, Elizabeth Hayman. "He was moody and tempered with a quiet innocence. He broke rules, talked back and made up outrageous stories that he believed as gospel truths."[12]

Sometimes, he tripped up over his own rampant fictions. In the interview with Gladys Hall, Laird admitted that he'd attended Roo-

The Cregar boys, circa 1919. Edward stands center; John stands rear left; Robert stands rear right. Front, left to right: Marshall, William and Laird, who was still fond of sailor suits.

sevelt School in Germantown ... although he quickly alluded to having previously attended Winchester and the Episcopal Academy, claiming that Roosevelt's "school theatricals were beneath one who had raised his voice among the Stratford-on-Avon Players." Theodore Roosevelt Junior High School made the National Register of Historic Places in 1988 and survives today as an elementary school in urban-challenged Germantown. As Laird recalled his alma mater:

> [W]hen, for a mid-term offering, I was cast as Bluebeard, equipped with a broad wooden scimitar, painted blue, with which I was to kill off my "wives," named, nauseously, "School Spirit," "Public Health," and such, whereupon "Truth" was to come in and kill me, I ran away. I had a quarter in

629 Sedgwick Street, Mount Airy, where the Cregar family lived in 1920 (author's photograph, 2014).

my pocket, my clothes in a cardboard box and my everpresent friend, Dishonesty, to keep me company.[13]

There were reasons other than dramatic arrogance for Laird to have run away. He was 15, had no family faith in his ambition, and was a target for mockery, due to his size, his artistic passions and, at this age, maybe for his emerging sexuality. He took steerage on a boat for Miami, figuring his mother would be searching for him to drag him home. Before leaving the boat in Miami, Laird claimed he wrote a note and pinned it to his pillow: "If you try to find me, I will kill myself."[14]

If he were fibbing about the note, it was a very disturbing fib.

July 28, 1929: Samuel Laird Cregar turned 16. He worked as a dishwasher in Miami, and then headed cross-country for his natural destination: Hollywood.

Based on best evidence, Cregar arrived in Hollywood in the fall of 1929. The HOLLYWOODLAND sign on Mount Lee was six years old, and its 4,000 light bulbs burned all night. The top box office stars were Lon Chaney and Clara Bow. The first Academy Awards banquet had taken place, and Paramount's *Wings* won Best Picture. It was a colorful season, and sound was making and breaking careers.

"I rented a tent in the backyard of a private house,"[15] said Laird years later. "I walked, daily, two miles to a bathroom and ten times that number of miles to the studios."

Hyperbole? Probably. In fact, one might be tempted to dismiss altogether Laird's account of his 1929 Hollywood adventure, but for a few specifics that give the story credibility. He claimed that Fred Datig, a Paramount casting director who "was very kind to me," got him onto the studio lot, where he was considered for a role in *Young Eagles*, starring Buddy Rogers and directed by William Wellman. It was an airplane saga follow-up to Wellman's *Wings*, in which Rogers had also starred. Laird said he failed to land a role because his build was "more that of a pelican than an eagle."[16]

Police soon nabbed Laird, tracking him down at his mother's request. It was one of many such misadventures, and Laird later said his size "cast its behemoth of a shadow" over his dream:

> Pleasingly plump as a child, the pleasingly plump developed into the frighteningly fat. Between the ages of 16 and 18, it gave me a terrific inferiority, and I suffered. But, bluntly, not enough to cause me to stop eating. Moreover, it was my lack of appeal for girls that troubled me, not a fear that my girth would handicap me in the theater.
>
> For acting, was, with me, what I call the "Secret Heart" thing. That is to say, there are some people who hope they will achieve their ambition, but are by no means sure.... I never doubted for a moment that I would be a success in the theater. I knew in my heart that, irrespective of dimensions, I had what it takes. I *really* knew.[17]

For an obese 16-year-old plagued by "terrific inferiority," feeling wholly unattractive, and possibly frightened by sexual longings that in 1930 were rated "unnatural," the faith in his dream was all that Sammy Cregar really had.

The 1930 census found the Cregar family at 6222 Greene Street in Mount Airy, Philadelphia. Elizabeth was no longer working, but Edward, now 26, was a manager at a broker's office; Robert, 23, was a paper supplies salesman; William, 20, was a bonds trader. John, 22, had apparently left home, and neither Marshall, then 19, nor Samuel, then 17, were listed as working.[18] Aunt Eugenia was still faithfully keeping house.

Laird claimed he sold books in a shop in Philadelphia by day and worked as a bouncer in a night club by night. Elizabeth eventually began managing several tea houses in Philadelphia ... "And mismanaged them so completely," said Laird, "that they all failed at the same time, and were sold out by the sheriff."[19]

Before Elizabeth forfeited her tea room franchise, Laird fell in love ... and trauma ensued. The lady was named Marie Leary, and 80 years later, Marie's daughter "Betsey" (as everyone called her), remembered her unusual bond with her "Uncle Sam":

> In the early 1930s, times were very hard, so my mother left high school and went to work as a waitress in Elizabeth Cregar's tea house in Philadelphia. My mother was a very pretty woman, very dark hair; in fact, my grandmother used to say we were "Black Irish," because Mom almost looked Spanish. Dark-skinned, dark-haired, and that's what my grandmother said: "Dark Irish, before all those Scandinavians came over and invaded Ireland!"
>
> Well, my mom dated Sam ... and then he made the mistake of introducing her to his brother William [laughs]. Mother used to tell me, "The minute I saw your father, I was in love.... The minute I saw him, I knew that he was going to be my husband."[20]

Broken-hearted, Sam ran away, hitchhiking to Hollywood ... again. This time, his contact was Merritt Hulburd, Paramount's story editor, who'd known the Cregar family back east. Laird recalled that Hulburd was "charming," but the only job he could provide Laird at Paramount was as a laborer, $4 a day, tearing down sets. "It was a pleasure," said Laird, "to demolish, thoroughly and savagely, the make-believe world from which I was excluded."[21]

But there were lay-off periods, and eventually, police arrested him for vagrancy. He came home to Philadelphia. On February 4, 1934, Elizabeth Cregar, daughter of William and his wife Marie, was born, named for her proud grandmother.[22] Laird was delighted but, considering he'd been in love with Marie, had complex feelings that would last the rest of his life.

Laird as a schoolboy ... but at what school?

"He thought I should have been *his* daughter,"[23] recalled Betsey. Indeed, Laird greeted Betsey's imminent birth in both a dramatic and adventurous way: He became a cadet in the Merchant Marine.[24]

The first arrival date in the archives is February 22, 1934, the ship was the SS *Manhattan*,[25] and listed in the crew is Samuel Cregar, age 20, born in Pennsylvania. The contact he listed was his mother Elizabeth, who in the wake of her failing tea room enterprise was now living at 704 North 20th Street in Philadelphia, near the historic Eastern State Penitentiary.

Launched December 5, 1931, the SS *Manhattan* was a $21,000,000, 24,189-ton luxury liner that sailed back and forth from New York to Hamburg. As such, cadet Cregar would have observed the growing pangs of Nazi Germany. A picture survives of Sam Cregar, Merchant Marine cadet, standing on board with several fellow crewmen, husky but not fat, flashing a large smile and boasting what decades later one might call JFK handsomeness. In March, Laird arrived again in New York on the *Manhattan*; he sailed on different ships to

Samuel Laird Cregar, center, as a Merchant Marine cadet, circa 1934.

San Francisco, Los Angeles, San Diego, Havana and the Panama Canal. The last recorded New York arrival: February 27, 1935.

Samuel Laird Cregar abandoned the Merchant Marine after a year's service. He was 21 years old. For a while, his trail again becomes cold.

* * *

"America's First Repertory Theatre"
—slogan of the Hedgerow Theatre, Pennsylvania

The Hedgerow Theatre, located in Rose Valley, Pennsylvania, began in 1923, based in an old mill house built in 1840 and operated by New York director-actor Jasper Deeter (1893–1972). Deeter, after decades of theater work, would finally make his film debut: When *The Blob* (1958) was filmed at Valley Forge Studios in Phoenixville, Pennsylvania, he played a Civilian Defense Volunteer.

Hedgerow is still operating in 2017, producing about two dozen plays a year; its website lists among the actors who played there Ann Harding, Richard Basehart and Keanu Reeves.

Back home, Samuel Laird Cregar finally made definite headway dramatically by joining Hedgerow, working there the summers of 1935 and 1936. He dreamed of heading west to study playwriting at another theater that was already legendary ... and only 16 miles from Hollywood.

* * *

"The Athens of the West"—George Bernard Shaw,
regarding Pasadena and its playhouse

The story goes that Gilmor Brown, who founded the Pasadena Playhouse in 1917 and headed it until his death in 1960, haunts the theater. The late Ellen Bailey, a Playhouse alumna and former devoted archivist, was a believer:

> Gilmor Brown's ghost is still here, and shows up from time to time. Once, a director was rehearsing on the Playhouse's main stage. A scene wasn't going as it should. Suddenly a large lamp light fell onto the stage. "All right, Gilmor," said the director. "I'll fix it!"
> A very strange thing ... the light booth, way in the back, up a stairway.... No one goes up there other than the lighting and sound person. Well, they found someone had changed the set-up in the booth. They locked the door, stationed an usher to guard it ... and the set-up was changed again! Gilmor's ghost plays games!
> Not long ago, at a dress rehearsal, a three-legged table fell over, a drawer opened ... and out came a picture of Gilmor![26]

Paranormal groups, visiting the Playhouse, support the accounts of the ghost.

In 1937, the Pasadena Playhouse was in its twentieth year. Located at 39 South El Molino Avenue, it offered fare both traditional and wildly experimental. Admirer George Bernard Shaw likened it to the ancient Greek rites honoring Dionysus. In a 1935 Midsummer Festival, the Playhouse presented all of Shakespeare's "Chronicle" plays on the main stage of its Spanish Colonial Revival style theater; in the summer of 1936, it followed with the Bard's "Graeco-Roman" plays. It was the first time Shakespeare's works had received such a showcase in the United States, and in March of 1937, the California assembly, properly impressed, passed a unanimous resolution bestowing upon the Pasadena Playhouse the honorary title of the State Theater of California.[27]

Robert Taylor, Frances Dee, Tyrone Power, Gloria Stuart and Randolph Scott were among the stars who'd acted there. A pre-fame John Carradine had played the title role in *Richard III* in the 1935 Shakespeare festival, roaring, "My kingdom for a horse!" The trainees worked for no money and many lodged in old houses that basically served as dormitories along El Molino Avenue.

Cregar, aware of the Pasadena Playhouse, desperately wanted to attend, but had no family resources to get him there. He appealed his cause to the Philadelphia Rotary Club.[28] The Rotarians in 1936 primarily benefitted orphans and students seeking legal and medical careers. Gaining an audience, Laird launched into his appeal, pleading for money to advance his dramatic hopes.

The Rotarians, fondly remembering Edward Mathews Cregar, Laird's cricket star father, decided to favor him. The club presented him a $400 loan and Laird went west, describing himself as "a 300-pound Civic project."

3

A Grotesque

I am, after all, a grotesque. That is, an actor who doesn't fit readily into parts. I am too big, too tall, too heavy. I don't look like an actor. If I wanted to act, I would have to find plays I could act.[1]—Laird Cregar

Hollywood, 1937. It was a classic year for the movies, especially ones with tragic endings.

Both the Academy Awards' Best Actor and Best Actress that year perished in their Oscar-winning performances: Spencer Tracy drowned in *Captains Courageous* and Luise Rainer succumbed after a locust invasion in *The Good Earth.* Garbo died of consumption in *Camille;* Fredric March drowned himself in *A Star Is Born.* Even a cartoon star died, temporarily: Walt Disney's Snow White, laid out in her crystal casket before the prince's kiss resurrected her.

The year's #1 box office star amidst all this cinematic misery: Shirley Temple.

Ironically, 1937 was also a year of shocking deaths in the film capital. January 2: Ross Alexander, Warner Bros. star, fatally shot himself in the head, 13 months after his wife Aleta had committed suicide in a similar way. January 23: Marie Prevost, former Mack Sennett "Bathing Beauty," was found dead in her Hollywood apartment, a victim of alcoholism, the legs of the two-day-dead corpse nibbled on by her pet dachshund (who'd apparently tried to awaken her). June 7: Jean Harlow, MGM's "Blonde Bombshell," died at 26 from kidney failure. June 25: Colin Clive, Henry Frankenstein of Universal's *Frankenstein* and *Bride of Frankenstein*, died at 37 from alcoholism and consumption. December 21: Ted Healy, comic actor and former head of the Three Stooges, died at 41 after a violent beating outside Hollywood's Trocadero night club, only days after the birth of his son.

There was considerable heartbreak, and, in the eyes of some, a sinister undercurrent. Vincent Price, who would arrive in Hollywood the following year and was destined to cross paths with Laird in some very curious ways, quickly detected it.

"If there's a power of good," said Price in later years, "it follows that there must be a power of evil. And I've seen evil. Years ago, Hollywood used to be one of the most evil places on Earth. No, I'm not joking."[2]

* * *

If sack and sugar be a fault, God help the wicked!
—Falstaff, Shakespeare's *Henry IV*

26

In the late 1930s, the world still had a fascination for what's now known as "morbid obesity." The fattest of the fat often survived in circuses and freak shows.

During the late Depression, Ringling Brothers and Barnum and Bailey Circus offered the legendary Dolly Dimples (1901–1982), hailed as "The World's Most Beautiful Fat Lady." Dolly sang, did impressions (including Kate Smith, naturally) and at her peak weighed 588 pounds. Her height: 4 feet, 11 inches. Obesity even had a faithful following in burlesque. In 1937, Youpel's New "Club Gay" in Chicago offered BEEF TRUST, featuring "The Beefy Darlings"[3]:

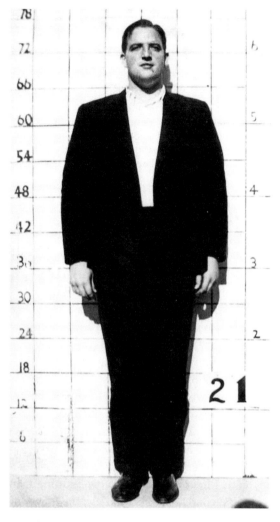

Laird Cregar, Pasadena Playhouse student, standing at the height chart (courtesy the Pasadena Playhouse Archives).

> None Under
> 250 pounds
> Presented by
> Tiny Gorman
> MC
> Bull of the Herd
> 3 Floor Shows Nightly
> 1,000 LBS. OF BEEF

In the movies, the only male dramatic star who was truly fat[4] was Charles Laughton, who'd been in full bloom when he won the 1933 Best Actor Academy Award for the British-produced *The Private Life of Henry VIII*. It's interesting, however, that when Laughton delivered a trio of his most acclaimed performances—Javert in 20th Century's *Les Miserables*, Ruggles the butler in Paramount's *Ruggles of Red Gap* and Capt. Bligh in MGM's *Mutiny on the Bounty*, all in 1935—he played all three roles after a severe diet. Laughton, miserable while dieting, quickly packed the pounds back on. It was actually part of his appeal as a "heavy heavy," suggesting to his audience a multitude of self-indulgent sins.

Nothing seemed sinful about the Laird Cregar who'd arrived at the Pasadena Playhouse. He was a 23-year-old giant ... 6 feet, 3 inches, when the average man's height was 5 feet, 9 inches, and weighing approximately 300 pounds when most scales didn't register over 250. He was never sloppy in his weight, carrying it as his mother did—with elegance, and almost a swagger. While evidence shows he considered himself unattractive, he was actually quite handsome, with striking hazel eyes and a very expressive smile. He could (and did) recite Byronic verse; he was also both very strong (he could lift a car off the ground by its bumper) and remarkably graceful, a marvelous dancer who avoided only a rumba ("I wiggle too much"[5]). Privately moody at times, he was characteristically full of humor, energy and affection.

One man who quickly befriended Laird was DeWitt Bodeen, who in 1937 was a 29-year old aspiring playwright. In 1942, Bodeen would write the script for the *noir* horror classic, *Cat People.*

> I knew Laird Cregar quite well.... He always had a weight problem. Sometimes he'd actually starve himself for a week until he looked like a leading man. Once he started eating, he took on the proportions of a character actor.... Everybody called him "Sammy" Cregar, and he was well-read, and had a true dramatic flair for acting.
> Of course, nobody wants to be a big fat man ... especially a young big fat man![6]

It's peculiar that Laird described himself as "a grotesque." Granted, times have changed; a literature professor of 2017 describing Quasimodo as "a grotesque" would face charges of judgmental insensitivity. But in 1944, when Laird used this term, it was still strong language, even in the theatrical way he'd employed it.

Perhaps he thought he was being realistic in his theatrical jargon. Or maybe the heckling and taunting he'd suffered as a boy had left a deeper scar than he wanted to admit.

Laird arrived at Pasadena during a colorful era. There were such young hopefuls as Victor Mature (who had so little money that he lived in a tent pitched in a friend's backyard), Robert Preston (then known by his real name of Robert Preston Meservey, and totally unaware of the singing and dancing skills he'd display so triumphantly in the 1957 Broadway hit *The Music Man*) and Dana Andrews (who met both his first and second wives at the Playhouse). Hollywood character actors Victor Jory and Onslow Stevens were Pasadena mainstays.

There was no course in playwriting at the Playhouse, so ever-resilient Laird decided to pursue acting. There was, of course, a problem: his height and weight. They weren't his only handicaps. "My voice was bad," Laird remembered. "Thin and high, it gave the eerie effect of a rabbit's voice issuing from an elephant, and could not be heard from the second row."[7] Fortunately, the Playhouse had a world-class vocal coach named Belle Kennedy:

> Hour after hour she'd keep me in the empty theater, reciting over and over such nonsense as, "How now the brown cow" and "The rain in Spain still stains." When she finished with me, she promised I could be heard anywhere within a radius of a mile, should I so choose.[8]

Laird made his Pasadena Playhouse debut as a "first-nighter" and a member of the ensemble in *Limelight Swing*, presented on June 9, 1937.[9] It was on that morning that Jean Harlow's funeral, "a spectacle,"[10] had taken place at Forest Lawn, Glendale, the most grandiose wake Hollywood had seen to that time. As if totally upstaged by the Harlow funeral, the play seems to have left no trace, and no program survives in the Playhouse archives.

The Pasadena Playhouse decided that the 1937 Third Annual Midsummer Drama Festival would be "The Great Story of the Great Southwest," presenting "The Spaniards, the Aztecs, the Mexicans, the missions, the gringo, the early Californian, the miner, and the Indian...."[11] One of the seven plays[12] was an original: *Miracle of the Swallows* by Ramon Romero. The play, against the background of San Juan Capistrano, the "Jewel of the Missions," told the story of the title miracle as well as presenting the California

The Pasadena Playhouse (author's photograph, 2011).

earthquake of 1812. There was one problem with this pageant: Gilmor Brown, desperately needing a seventh play, had engaged Romero to write *Miracle of the Swallows* in a hurry, and Romero, as noted in his 1981 obituary, "managed to stay a few words ahead of the actors who were rehearsing each scene as it was written."[13]

Laird landed the role of Pedro Fages (1734–1794), Spanish-born explorer, soldier and the military governor of "Las Californias." His nickname was "The Bear," based on his hunting bears near San Luis Obispo. He and his explorers were the first Europeans to see the Sacramento River Delta, the Central Valley of California and the Sierra Nevada mountains after climbing Mount Diablo.

Miracle of the Swallows opened on July 5, 1937, a pageantry with a cast of over 60 players, plus 11 "neophyte children," two dozen dancers and a band of musicians. Among the cast: Victor Mature played Hypolite Bouchard, the Argentine pirate who plundered Mission San Juan Capistrano; and George Bessolo, who became George Reeves, TV's Superman, was one of five "caballeros." Romero later admitted "It was a miracle in itself that the play was completed in time for the curtain to rise."[14] Father Arthur J. Hutchinson, pastor of San Juan Capistrano, attended the play's first matinee and blessed the cast behind the stage. As the *Los Angeles Times* reported:

> It was a strange company. They were clad in war paint and feathers, in Spanish finery of green, yellow and red, in the solemn gray of priests, in the gaudy trappings of pirates. One of them was a murderer. Another was a wanton woman. But a famous priest, robed all in black, raised his hands and blessed and thanked them all, while the whir of swallows' wings sounded over their heads....[15]

Despite the blessing, the *New York Times* blasted *Miracle of the Swallows* as "the low point of the festival in every respect."[16]

July 1, 1937   Thirteen

494th Production of the Pasadena Playhouse, now in its 20th Year

PASADENA PLAYHOUSE ASSOCIATION
Gilmor Brown, Supervising Director   Charles F. Prickett, General Manager
STATE THEATRE OF CALIFORNIA
Member of the National Theatre Conference of America

Presents

"MIRACLE OF THE SWALLOWS"
By RAMON ROMERO
GILMOR BROWN, Supervising Director
Directors—WILLIAM WILLIAMS, LENORE SHANEWISE, FRANK FOWLER
Assisted by—RAY ARVEDSON
RITA GLOVER, Art Director   FRED C. HUXLEY, Technical Director
FRANCES McCUNE, Production Manager   FAIRFAX P. WALKUP, Costume Director

OPENING DATE—JULY 5, 1937

AUTHOR'S NOTE
MOST OF THE CHARACTERS AND INCIDENTS USED IN THIS PLAY ARE HISTORICALLY TRUE, BUT IN ORDER TO EMBRACE THE GLORY OF THE MISSIONS AS WELL AS THEIR RUIN, THE AUTHOR HAS TELESCOPED DATES OF CERTAIN HAPPENINGS SO THAT THE DRAMATIC CONTINUITY OF THE PLAY MAY NOT BE HAMPERED. THE PLAY STRIVES TO COMBINE THE ROMANTIC LEGENDS OF CAPISTRANO WITH THE POLITICAL FORCES RESPONSIBLE FOR THE DOWNFALL OF THE MISSION'S AUTHORITY.

CHARACTERS
LOUISA	JUNE EVANS
LOLA	EMILIE JOHNSON
JOSEPHINA	MAUDE GEORGE
JUANA	LOLA MONTERO
PADRE JOSEF BARONA	EARL GUNN
MANUEL	ROBERT GILLETTE
MENDOZA	HARRY BLOOM
AURELIO	WESLEY MEREDITH
MARIA	DOROTHY WEGMAN
PADRES	HENRY HINDS, GEORGE READING, BERT JOHANNES
PADRE GERONIMO BOSCANA	JAMES WESTERFIELD
DONA EULALIA FAGES	VIRGINIA LYKINS
PEDRO FAGES	LAIRD CREGAR
ANA	CATHERINE FELTUS
PEDRITO FAGES	TOM SEIDEL
MAGDALENA	JOAN WHEELER
AUGUSTIN	STEVAN DARRELL
NEOPHYTES	NICIAS RECKAS, CLAUDE WISBERG, VALERIE KEITH, MARGO SNYDER, JOE HELGESEN, FERNANDO TORRES, E. MARIE BULLIS, JOHN LANSING WALSH, THAD SHARRETS, ANN CLAREY, MELCENA LAFOLLETTE, ELLIN DUNNING.
JORDAN	RICHARD WILLIAMS
JOSE ECHEANDIA	VICTOR N. ZIMMERMAN
PANCHO	PETER VESELICH
JUAN	GUSTAVE TWEER
RELIEF GUARD	IAN McDONALD
TEOFILO	CHARLES WOOD
MULE-TRAIN DRIVER	NICIAS RECKAS
GOVERNOR JOSE ARRILLAGA	HERBERT THAYER
SAILORS	ROBERT WILLEY, ROBERT F. STEVENS, FREDERICK SMITH, BARTON BOOTH, BENSON GREENE
LIEUTENANT PACHECO	SIDNEY SANNER
PRESIDENTE TAPIS	HOUSELEY STEVENSON
VALLEJO	LAURENCE VAN MOURICK
SENORA VALLEJO	MARGUERITE SNYDER
PIO PICO	JAMES CROW
SENORA PICO	ELYNORE DOLKART
CABALLEROS	JACK NOBLE, HECTOR OFFENBACH, GEORGE BESSOLO, GUSTAVE SCHIRMER, RALPH TWEER
HYPOLITE BOUCHARD	VICTOR MATURE
MATEO	SHIRO TAKAHISA
PEDRO	RICHARD CARPENTIER
KAYA	CARMEN MORALES
ALVEREZ	ROBERT HOOD
SALAT	GEORGE TYRONE
NEOPHYTE CHILDREN	JO MUSACCHIA, BILLY SCOTT, MARY LEE JONES, NANCY ANN KNETTLE, LEMYART KNETTLE, HARVEY KNETTLE, JOHN EPPOLITO, NANCY SNYDER, GEORGE SNYDER, ERNEST CARLSON, PATRICIA CALLAHAN.
DANCERS	CARMEN, JACQUE POLEY, MARTHA SHAW, GWEN HORN, NELL WEBB, MEG WYLLIE, GENE KNUDSEN, MARY ALICE WRIXON, CHRISTINA WELLES, LORRAINE KELLEY, ESTHER FROMM, RUTH JONES, LUCY GALLEGOS, FLORENTINA VALADEZ, RUBY GALLEGOS, BENITA ESPAZA, MARY PORRAS, CONSUELO OREGUERA, FELICITAS HERNANDEZ, MAGGE HERNANDEZ, RAMONA GARCES, VICTORIA VALADEZ, ALVINA MITCHEL, KATHLEEN HINCKLEY.
MUSICIANS	STELLA RAE, PATRICIA CORELLI, OLA LORRAINE, NATURIDAD VACIO

Continued on page 15

The Pasadena Playhouse program for *Miracle of the Swallows,* **1937 (courtesy the Pasadena Playhouse Archives).**

Meanwhile, Laird had received advice from Thomas Browne Henry, one of the Playhouse's directors and later a prolific film and TV actor, perhaps best remembered as the U.S. general trying to defeat the giant monster from Venus in Ray Harryhausen's *20 Million Miles to Earth* (1957). According to Laird,

> [Henry] told me, "Don't ever lose a pound of weight, Laird. It may take you longer to get there but, when you do, you'll be the only one of your kind." Prior to that palatable advice, I had made sporadic attempts at dieting. Now, I went back, with gusto, to my two huge steaks, with all the trimmings, for dinner, and to my favorite bedtime "snack," a huge hunk of roast beef, rare....[17]

Of course, these feasts depended on Laird's financial situation, which was often too precarious for such epicurean indulgence. At any rate, as he continued:

> At the same time, I began to develop what I call my "Thin Man" personality. Which means, simply, that I dismiss all consciousness of physical bulk from my mind, move quickly, talk quickly, think quickly, abolish lethargy, and become a man mountain of action.

His goal as to how he saw himself—surely expressed with tongue at least partly in cheek—was as "a deer, fleet and quivering."[18]

Before fully becoming fleet and quivering, and after spending a chunk of his Rotary Club scholarship on steaks and rare roast beef, Laird went home to Philadelphia and appeared in three Federal Theatre productions: as "a mate" in both Eugene O'Neill's *Bound East for Cardiff* and *The Moon of the Caribbees*, and as "Stand-Up Steadfastly Snat" in *A Moral Entertainment*.[19] The plays, presented at Bryn Mawr's Goodhart Hall for the Federal Theatre, provided fine experience, but scarcely paid Laird enough money to buy food.

He began hitchhiking from Philadelphia to New York to audition for plays. With no money for a hotel room, he tried sleeping in Grand Central Station. "They moved me off the benches there, so I sneaked into the Savarin Restaurant, where I spent two nights sleeping on the marble floor after it had been swept and scrubbed. I was hidden by the piled-up tables and chairs!"[20]

Laird soon was sporting the captain's cap and gold brocades of a movie house usher, orating "Immediate seating in the balcony!" outside Broadway's 3,664-seat Paramount Theatre. "They wanted somebody," reminisced Laird, "whose size would command an instant authority over the crowds queuing up outside."[21] One day, he managed to sneak Claudette Colbert into the Paramount, unnoticed by the sidewalk horde, and the star gratefully awarded her gallant young usher with a special autograph.[22]

From the Paramount Theatre, Laird worked behind a counter at Gimbels, where he met another glamorous star: Kay Francis,[23] to whom he sold linens. Back and forth he went, from New York to Philadelphia,[24] later citing such survival jobs as a night shift worker at a woolen mill, where he washed fleece in vats, and laboring at a rubber boots factory, where he loused up the bookkeeping.

Laird also claimed that his ominous size won him an usher-bouncer job at an all-night theater in Philadelphia that showed "smokers" (i.e., "adult" films). Later, when he played the psycho detective in *I Wake Up Screaming,* the film had a scene take place in a similar grindhouse in Times Square, where Victor Mature and Betty Grable watch *Flames of Passion.* Laird suggested to 20th Century–Fox that he double-dip as technical advisor for the sequence.

*   *   *

On October 4, 1938, William Cregar, the fourth of Elizabeth's sons, died, the victim of a rheumatic heart, at Philadelphia's Jewish Hospital.[25] He had been a broker and was only 29 years old. William was survived by his wife Marie and four-year-old daughter Betsey, on whom Laird doted.

After many New York rejections, Laird pooled his meager resources, headed west and cast his fate again with the Pasadena Playhouse. He'd arrive in 1939, Hollywood's Glory Year. In January alone, 20th Century–Fox premiered *Jesse James*, RKO *Gunga Din* and Universal *Son of Frankenstein*. John Ford had recently finished *Stagecoach*. MGM's *The Wizard of Oz*, Paramount's *Beau Geste*, Samuel Goldwyn's *Wuthering Heights* and David O. Selznick's *Gone With the Wind* were all in production.

For Laird, however, there was no glory to be found. Indeed, he'd call 1939 his "Nightmare Year."[26]

4

Life in a Sedan

I was desperate and had to do something. A young married couple I knew at the Pasadena Playhouse had a one-room apartment in Hollywood. They offered to let me sleep on the davenport, but instead I slept for months on the back seat of their sedan. Cramped, it's true, but I slept. Food was a matter of one meal a day—dinner. This was because I helped a friend write some lyrics for a song and nightly he bought me my big meal.[1]—Laird Cregar

In 1939, the arena of Hollywood villainy, which Laird Cregar was fated to enter, offered epic wickedness worthy of the greatest year of the movies.

In *Jesse James*, John Carradine, as Bob Ford, shot Tyrone Power's Jesse in the back, the coward's hands trembling as he fired. In *Son of Frankenstein*, Boris Karloff's Monster almost threw a little boy into a boiling sulfur pit but, always a sympathetic creature, couldn't bear to do it. In *Beau Geste*, Brian Donlevy, as the scar-faced Sgt. Markoff, profanely propped up the dead bodies of his Foreign Legionnaires on the parapets of Fort Zinderneuf, making attacking Arabs think he had an inexhaustible army.

"The rest of the bullets you stop won't hurt as much as that first one," Donlevy's Markoff jokes to a corpse.

Screen villainy was a profitable, if peculiar, life. Outside a theater showing *Jesse James*, a little boy recognized Carradine "and the son of a bitch kicked me in the shin!"[2] When Karloff mailed out autographed pictures of himself after *Son of Frankenstein*, 500 fans sent them back, demanding a picture of him as the Monster.[3] And on the *Beau Geste* location in Buttercup Valley, west of Yuma, Donlevy was so "in character" as the terrible Markoff that, come his death scene, Ray Milland, who despised him, intentionally missed his under-costume shield and stabbed Donlevy in the armpit with a bayonet.[4] He nearly bled to death.

"Brian didn't appreciate it," said Donlevy's widow Lillian.[5]

Villains were among the 300,000 people to whom the film industry issued checks in 1939.[6] For a few days, Laird Cregar worked in that industry, receiving a pittance. During 1939, "Hollywood's greatest year," he almost starved to death.

Laird's first Pasadena Playhouse appearance upon his return from Philadelphia: *The Shoemaker's Holiday*, which opened January 18, 1939. It was a bawdy Elizabethan comedy by Thomas Dekker; Laird played Cornwall.

February 21, 1939: Where the Blue Begins opened at the Playhouse, based on Christopher Morley's fantasy. The play called for the actors to pretend to be dogs. *Variety* critiqued:

> Pasadenans have discovered they're barking up the wrong trees. First nighters weren't so sure they laughed in the right places.... Just what is the proper behavior for auditors viewing a stage full of amateur actors acting like dogs and yipping at each other is not to be found in any of the etiquette books.... To carry out the deception, each actor wears a wig to indicate the hound he portrays. Characters are programmed as Mrs. Spaniel, Mr. Poodle, Miss Airedale and other such piffle.[7]

Laird's role: "Dane," presumably a Great Dane. "It's just too silly," wrote *Variety*.

March 7: Laird played Lt. "Lace Drawers" Rogers in the Pasadena Playhouse's *Brother Rat,* the comedy about Virginia Military Institute cadets that had been a 1936 Broadway hit and a 1938 Warner Bros. film. The director was Vic-

Infamous Hollywood villains of 1939 (clockwise from top right): John Carradine as Bob Ford in *Jesse James*; Brian Donlevy as Sgt. Markoff in *Beau Geste*; Boris Karloff as the Monster in *Son of Frankenstein*.

tor Jory, fresh from his terrifying Injun Joe in Selznick's *The Adventures of Tom Saw-yer.*

April 18: Laird played Capt. Stewart in the Playhouse's *To Quito and Back*, a comedy by Oscar-winning screenwriter Ben Hecht, concerning a New York author who runs away from civilization to the primitive world of Quito, South America. Victor Mature played Zamiano, leader of the revolutionaries.

May 2: The Pasadena Playhouse presented *The Great American Family* by Robert Chapin and Charley King, based on a novel written by *Los Angeles Times* columnist Lee Shippey. It was a "homey" play about Mr. and Mrs. Gregory Seymour, writers who hope to produce the great American novel, but keep having babies, requiring them to crank out literary potboilers. Eventually they realize that while they never penned the great American novel, they did produce the great American family. Shippey later wrote:

> Laird Cregar was an intellectual who went into acting largely because he wished to know the the-ater from the inside. He had the same inexplicable gift for doing the right thing on the stage that Babe Ruth had for hitting a baseball, but it was more than mere muscular reflex. Laird was a reader and a thinker and essentially a human being desirous of rising to the highest standards, personally and professionally. He loved the theater so that he understood it instinctively and spontaneously. He was just as big spiritually as he was physically.[8]

Frank Ferguson (prolific film character actor, whom many film buffs will remember as Mr. McDougal in 1948's *Abbott and Costello Meet Frankenstein*) directed the play *and* portrayed Gregory Seymour; Mary Todd played his wife Sylvie. Laird's role: Mr. Perkins, a real estate agent. As Shippey wrote:

> At that time there was only a small part in the first scene for a real estate man but Laird was glad to get it—and it was almost entirely due to his superb acting that the play started with a bang which made all the bored Hollywood scouts sit up and get interested. The audience began laugh-ing at his first speech and never stopped.[9]

Variety was moderate in its review: "[W]ith some more work on a few of the scenes and a professional cast, it might stand a moderate chance on Broadway."[10] But it praised Frank Ferguson, and listed Laird first in a group of supporting players who "stand out." *The Great American Family* set a Pasadena Playhouse record, running 42 consecutive performances. Shippey recalled:

> [W]ithin two weeks, 18 different New York producers were bidding for it—but all had the idea that it would have to be revised so that the real estate man could be carried all through it.... [I]n its simplicity and spontaneity, and some intangible feeling that Cregar gave it by his fine perform-ance, it was a knockout.[11]

The authors signed with Homer Curran, West Coast impresario, so that they could do any necessary rewrites before going to New York. A professional cast assumed the key roles: James Bell played Gregory Seymour and Carol Goodner took on the role of his wife Sylvie. Naturally, Shippey retained Laird as Mr. Perkins, and the play was set to try out in Santa Barbara, San Francisco and Los Angeles, prior to Broadway. "We had visions," recalled Shippey, "of wealth and fame."[12]

Meanwhile, Laird carried on at the Pasadena Playhouse:

May 25: He played Jason Foster in *Petticoat Fever*.

546th Production of the Pasadena Playhouse, now in its 22nd year

PASADENA PLAYHOUSE ASSOCIATION

Gilmor Brown, Supervising Director   Charles F. Prickett, General Manager

STATE THEATRE OF CALIFORNIA

An educational, non-profit organization, incorporated under the laws of this state, devoted to the interests and advancement of the American theatre.
Member of the National Theatre Conference
Presents

"THE GREAT AMERICAN FAMILY"
By Lee Shippey
Dramatized by Robert F. Chapin and Charley King from the novel of the same name.
GILMOR BROWN, Supervising Director

FRANK FERGUSON, Director   FRED C. HUXLEY, Technical Director
FRANCES McCUNE, Production Manager   RITA GLOVER, Art Director

OPENING DATE—MAY 2, 1939
Characters in Order of Appearance

MR. PERKINS	LAIRD CREGAR
GREGORY SEYMOUR	FRANK FERGUSON
SYLVIE SEYMOUR	MARY TODD
DR. GILLESPIE	GENE LOVE
MRS. MAGUIRE	LISA LAWRENCE
HANK (Younger)	JOHN LONG
CHUCK (Younger)	RICHARD BARRETT
JOHN (Younger)	BILLY EPP
FRANK (Younger)	JACKIE FOYIL
GRISETTE	HERSELF
POSTMAN	FRANK ROLLINGER
TINA GONZALES	LUCIA SCIARRINO
JUAN GONZALES	DOMINGO RAMIREZ de ARELLANO
HANK	ROBERT WILLEY
CHUCK	WARD WOOD
SYLVIA	BARBARA PITZER
FRANK	THOMAS RUCKER
JOHN	GEORGE GREENE
HELEN	DORIS BRENN
FORREST JONES	IRVING JUDSON
DRIVER	CHALMERS PAULSON
DRIVER'S HELPER	ROBERT HANCOCK
MARION GALE	MARGARET KENDALL
MRS. GALE	JULIA GAGE
MRS. FITCH	LEOLINE SOMMER
DELIVERY BOY	PIERRE HATHAWAY
MRS. WILLIS	VIRGINIA LYKINS
FIRST WOMAN	ELLA CRANE
SECOND WOMAN	VIOLA GILBERG
RADIO ANNOUNCER	CHALMERS PAULSON
MILKMAN	MARVIN ALTER

(PROGRAM—Continued on Page 6)

PHYSICAL THERAPY AND X-RAY . . .

COLONIC IRRIGATIONS: For eliminating toxins; for relieving constipation.
CABINET BATHS and MASSAGE: For reducing weight; for building vitality.
ULTRA-VIOLET and INFRA RED: For a Vitamin "D" Tonic and treatment of skin diseases.
GALVANISM: For hay fever and sinus complications.
DIATHERMY
SHORT WAVE: For relieving arthritic conditions and muscular soreness; stomach and liver disorders.
DIET: Special attention given to individual's particular needs.

Special Rates for Colonic Treatments

Dr. Maurice L. Lachman, D.C., Ph.S.

Private Practice	199 S. El Molino	Pasadena
for Twenty Years	SY. 6-6411	

•5•

Program, *The Great American Family,* Pasadena Playhouse, 1939 (courtesy the Pasadena Playhouse Archives).

June 26: He portrayed Burbage in *Elizabeth the Queen,* part of a Maxwell Anderson midsummer festival.[13]

July 10: Laird played the Reverend Phineas McQueston in Maxwell Anderson's *The Wingless Victory.*[14] The tragedy play took place in 1800 Salem, and Laird's Rev. McQueston was a frightful, wicked clergyman, who goes lecherously and hysterically toxic after his brother, seagoing captain Nathaniel, brings home a Malayan beauty named Oparre as his wife. The play ended tempestuously, *à la Medea.*

It was a richly villainous role, and Laird played it to the hilt—and apparently beyond it. Guest reviewer John Russell McCarthy of the *San Mateo Tribune* called *The Wingless Victory* one of Anderson's "most difficult plays," adding:

> *The Wingless Victory* approaches melodrama to within, say, half an inch. There are points where it slinks and snarls over the line. Laird Cregar, as the Reverend Phineas McQueston, helps to hold the play on the drama side through the first scene. But in scene II those leers of his are definitely melo. The audience ceases to shiver and hate him; the audience begins to practice leers too, and tiny sneers; here and there we heard a chuckle. Even a New England clergyman, it seems, can be too wicked to be credible.[15]

Meanwhile, Laird was set to open in the pre–Broadway try-out of *The Great American Family*. It had a preview in Santa Barbara in early August, and the *Los Angeles Times* report was favorable, despite several "despites":

> Despite an evident first-night nervousness during the opening scenes, the laughs came so regularly that they drowned out many a line.... Despite the laughs, which must have deeply gratified the three authors, who were all present, and despite the capable acting of the principals, and excellent work of the nine child actors, the play is still somewhat unwieldy.... Nonetheless, this audience liked it just as it is, and the Pasadena record stands.... Excellent comedy was provided by Laird Cregar as Mr. Perkins, the real estate man....[16]

Laird almost never made it to San Francisco ... for Hell hath no fury like an upstaged leading lady. Carol Goodner was a New York City–born actress who'd worked mostly in British films and excelled at playing vamps. The mother in *The Great American Family* was a change-of-pace role for her, but she wasn't happy. As Shippey remembered, Goodner "was so jealous of the hit Cregar made that she did her best to have him tossed out of the show."[17] Goodner got the director on her side, Shippey fought to keep Laird in the play, and Shippey won ... but, as he wrote, "the director made [Laird] tone down his part so that it didn't give the play the kickoff it had had before."[18]

August 14: *The Great American Family* opened at the Curran Theatre. "A white pullet, a black goat and a flock of clever kids stole the show" wrote *Variety*; the critique not only angered Goodner, but had typed her name as "Goorned."[19] One of those "clever kids" in the cast was 16-year-old Peggy Stewart, destined to become a popular star of Republic westerns and serials. Peggy became fast friends with Laird:

> Laird was a wonderful man—just wonderful! My mom had come out from Atlanta to be with me, because I was only 16, and Laird taught her about "the birds and the bees"—his version of "the birds and the bees" [laughs]. My mom was pretty naïve, at that time, so this was an eye-opener for her!
>
> We were together much of the time, the three of us, and when we got to San Francisco, it was so much fun, because Laird and I would get on the trolley car, go to Fisherman's Wharf, get cracked crab and cold nectarines, and take them back to the hotel room to eat them! It was the first time I'd played the Curran Theatre, and I remember Laird telling me on stage, "Now don't look up." Of course, I did—I had to after that! And there was a balcony, and another balcony, and your head would be straight back, looking up at those scary, spooky balconies!
>
> I thought Laird was excellent ... just excellent.[20]

Peggy Stewart's recollection is significant, as it was the first documentation of Laird's homosexuality. While she remembered that he was casually candid about it, and apparently humorous, she also recalls there was no flamboyance or effeminacy about him. Oddly, while he was open with Peggy and her mother, he'd not revealed his predilection to his own family.

As the story will show, Laird Cregar's sexuality was complicated.

To the shock of all who'd held high hopes for it, *The Great American Family* floun-

Carol Goodner tried to have Laird Cregar fired from the West Coast try-out of *The Great American Family*. She's seen here with Monty Woolley in Broadway's *The Man Who Came to Dinner* (1939).

dered, overwhelmed by such San Francisco attractions as the *Folies Bergere* and a revival of the sex melodrama *White Cargo*. The flop was fine with Carol Goodner, who'd proved a virago, trying to break her contract to accept an offer from George Kaufman and Moss Hart for their new Broadway play *The Man Who Came to Dinner*. The role, ironically: Lorraine Sheldon, the vampy bitch actress.

The Great American Family closed in two weeks, leaving Laird stranded in San Francisco. Less than two months later, on October 16, 1939, Goodner slinked onstage for the triumphant Broadway opening night of *The Man Who Came to Dinner*.

Laird, broke, desperate, and back in Hollywood, was trying again to crash the movies.

*   *   *

It's "Dynamite May" Robson in **Granny Get Your Gun**
—trailer quote from *Granny Get Your Gun*

Several of Laird's Pasadena Playhouse confreres had made good. Robert Preston signed with Paramount, landing co-starring parts in the studio's two big epics of 1939, Cecil B. DeMille's *Union Pacific* and William A. Wellman's *Beau Geste*. Victor Mature made his film debut in Hal Roach's racy *The Housekeeper's Daughter*. George Reeves had also entered films, playing Stuart, one of the Tarleton twins, in Selznick's *Gone with the Wind*.

Laird's size would immediately slate him as a potential screen villain. On October 16, 1939, George Phair, in his "Retakes" column in *Variety*, made up a "Hollywood Heavies" football team. The roster:

- Center: Basil Rathbone
- Left Guard: Brian Donlevy
- Right Guard: Edward Arnold
- Left Tackle: Boris Karloff
- Right Tackle: Bela Lugosi
- Left End: John Carradine
- Right End: Humphrey Bogart
- Quarterback: Peter Lorre
- Left Half: Akim Tamiroff
- Right Half: Claude Rains
- Fullback: Orson Welles

Aware of Welles' RKO contract that eventually led to him producing, directing, co-writing and starring in *Citizen Kane*, Phair added, "P.S. Orson is also head coach, captain, dean, prexy, chair of the board of trustees, and cheer leader."

Laird, of course, not only wasn't on the team ... he wasn't even in the stadium.

Meanwhile, on Wednesday, October 11, 1939, Warner Bros. had begun shooting *Granny Get Your Gun*, a 56-minute "B" curio based on Erle Stanley Gardner's Perry Mason story "The Case of the Dangerous Dowager" ... but which wrote Perry Mason out of the script! The stars were venerable oldsters May Robson (as a rip-roarin' grandmother who straps on a six-shooter) and Harry Davenport (as her smitten lawyer). The combined age of the two stars: 154.

Directed by George Amy, usually an ace Warners' editor, *Granny Get Your Gun*

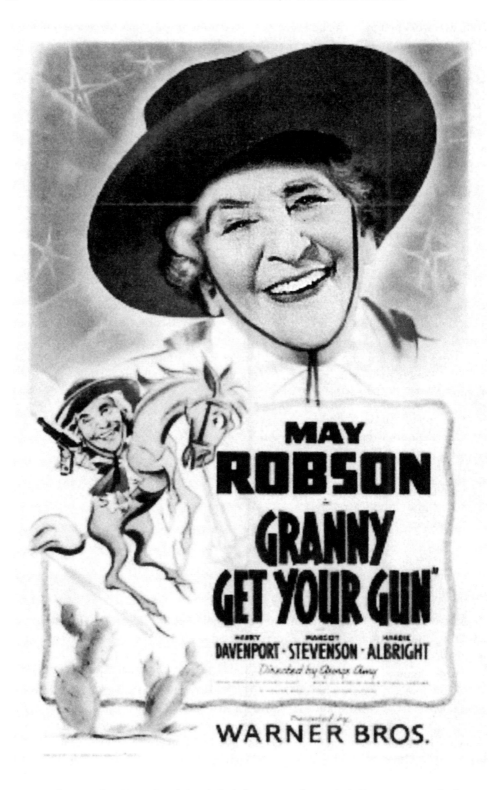

In *Granny Get Your Gun* (1940), Laird appeared very briefly as a court clerk.

gave a glimpse of Laird as a court clerk, holding a Bible, sharing this dialogue with Miss Robson:

> CREGAR: Raise your right hand. Do you solemnly swear to tell the truth, the whole truth and nothing but the truth, so help you God?
> ROBSON: Yes I do.
> CREGAR: State your name.
> ROBSON: Minerva Hildegarde Hatton. The "Hildegarde" for an old Swedish aunt of mine.
> CREGAR: Hmm. Be seated.

The rest of the time, Laird silently takes notes. He receives no billing.

Warners completed *Granny Get Your Gun* on October 25, 1939, and released it February 10, 1940. Its negative cost: $98,000. (Average cost of a feature film in 1940: $300,000.[21]) Gladys McArdle, "manageress" of the Owl Theatre in Lebanon, Kansas, posted this opening-night ad: "All grandmothers admitted free, if you bring a gun. Toy pistols, air guns, revolvers, rifles, shot guns, automatics, Tommy guns, cannons, anti-aircraft guns—anything, just so long as it's a gun."[22]

A car full of grandmothers showed up, the leader carrying a shotgun. Another had a six-shooter wrapped in newspaper ("I haven't got a permit to carry a gun," she explained). Others brought "everything from toy guns to rifles," and the Owl Theatre enjoyed "a lot of extra business from grandfathers, children and grandchildren who came to see that nobody shot grandmother." *Showmen's Trade Review* reported that the stunt was "Attempted with no casualties."[23]

* * *

Yes, Mr. Thistlebottom!
—the first of Cregar's few lines in *Oh, Johnny, How You Can Love!*

Laird's next film bit came at Universal City, the hallowed grounds of Karloff's Frankenstein Monster and Lugosi's Count Dracula—although, by 1939, the lot's top star was 17-year-old songbird Deanna Durbin. *Oh, Johnny, How You Can Love!*, a 63-minute musical far below Durbin's standards, began shooting on November 24, 1939, with a budget of $94,000.[24]

The film starred Tom Brown as a salesman who travels in a truck, Peggy Moran (destined to be leading lady of Universal's *The Mummy's Hand* in 1940) as an eloping runaway heiress, and Allen Jenkins as a derby-wearing bank robber called "Ed the Weasel." Betty Jane Rhodes sang the popular title song and Donald Meek, best-remembered as the whiskey drummer in 1939's *Stagecoach,* was Mr. Thistlebottom, who wears a cowboy suit and a toupee (the wig blown off by fireworks in the climax). When the brakes fail on his truck, Brown, Moran and Jenkins take quarters at Meek's auto court. We briefly glimpse Laird as a smilin' lug of a mechanic; interestingly, Meek addresses him as "Sam" as he asks him to fix the brakes.

"Yes, Mr. Thistlebottom!" smiles Laird, sporting a mechanic's uniform and cap. A little later, during a night-time community sing-along and while Brown and Moran smooch in the woods, Jenkins' hoodlum underlings "Doc" (Joseph Dowling) and "Lefty" (Horace McMahon) arrive. They toot their horn, Laird crawls out from under the truck, and they have this dialogue, Laird grinning all the while:

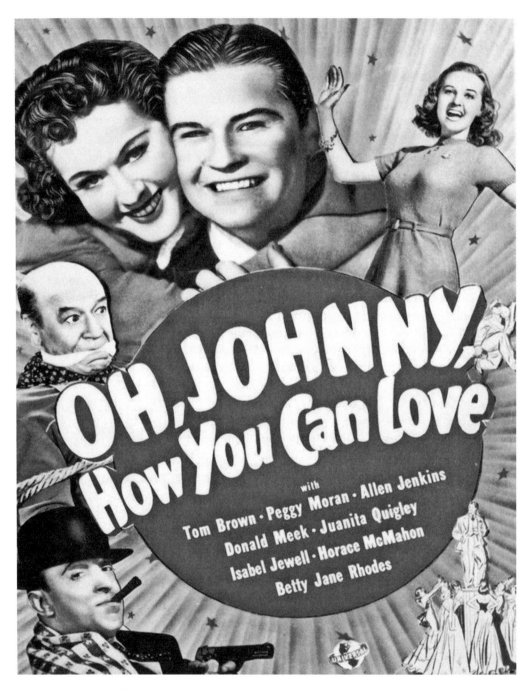

Oh, Johnny, How You Can Love! **provided Laird with the bit role of Sam, the mechanic.**

DOWLING: When that truck come in?
CREGAR: This evenin'.
DOWLING: Who was drivin' it?
CREGAR: A fella.
DOWLING: A dopey-looking fella in a derby? About 40?
CREGAR: Nope. Nice-lookin' young fella. There was a dopey-lookin' guy with him, though.

DOWLING: Yeah?
McMAHON: Yeah?
CREGAR: A girl too. Swell-looking girl.... Said they'd take a cabin for the night.

Despite adverse weather, director Charles Lamont (who'd later direct many of Universal's Abbott and Costello comedies) completed *Oh, Johnny, How You Can Love!* early on the afternoon of December 9. "This company worked 14 days and five nights," reported Martin Murphy in his Universal weekly production report, "plus a second unit for one day and night, and five days pre-production shooting on chases and backgrounds—all summed up, a rather long shooting period for a program picture." The final cost: $100,000 ($6000 over budget).

March 15, 1940: A *Variety* critic attended *Oh, Johnny, How You Can Love!* (which Laird later jocularly described as "a Universal opera"[25]) at the Hollywood Pantages. His next-day review: "Purely destined for the bottom rung of dualers, *Oh, Johnny* kills 63 minutes of running time and will serve its purpose."[26] The bit provided Laird no on-screen billing and did nothing to relieve his financial woes. In fact, he later grimly recalled the date of Tuesday, December 5, 1939, while *Oh, Johnny, How You Can Love!* was still shooting, as the precise day he feared he'd eventually literally starve to death.[27] It was then that the married couple he knew at the Pasadena Playhouse allowed him to sleep in their convertible sedan, and Laird later recounted the grim episode, quite humorously:

> It was a serious problem to keep warm and sleep in the seat of a canvas-topped car.... At first the cop on the beat thought it was a gag, but after he found out I made a practice of sleeping there he called the sergeant about it. Half a dozen times during the period a squad car drove up and urged me to move on.
> "Where?" I'd ask them.
> "Dunno," they'd say, "but it just ain't right."
> The next night I'd be there still, and because they couldn't think of what to do with a guy my size, they finally left me alone.[28]

It sounds like the type of fanciful tale Cregar would tell after achieving success. However, in 1993, I interviewed Peggy Moran and asked if by chance she had any memory of Laird Cregar from *Oh, Johnny, How You Can Love!* Her response surprised me:

> Oh, and how! I remember driving in a truck with him! There was a young guy in the music department at Universal named Arnold Schwarzwald, and his best friend at the time, they used to call Sammy ... Sammy Cregar. Arnold kind of liked me, and I'd go out with him, and he always brought Sammy along! Sammy was a nobody then, a very nice, humble, simple guy, and I heard he was living in a car. And I remember, when we were driving in that truck, that he told me about his one ambition in life.
> It was to play Oscar Wilde![29]

5

Oscar Wilde

We are all in the gutter, but some of us are looking at the stars.[1]
—Oscar Wilde

Fifty-six years ago, a vandal stole the flying angel's testicles.[2]

The naked, castrated angel adorns the tomb of Oscar Fingal O'Flahertie Wills Wilde (1854–1900) in the Pere Lachaise Cemetery in the hills above Paris. Wilde's noble shade keeps company there with such fellow legends as Edith Piaf, Alice B. Toklas and the Doors' Jim Morrison. Artist Jacob Epstein designed the tomb. Many had argued that the sybarite Wilde deserved no tomb at all ... and certainly not with an angel who evoked the Assyrian figures of the British Museum.[3]

In 1961, the angel's manhood went missing. The story goes that, for a time, the manager of Pere Lachaise used them as a paperweight. At any rate, they remain lost, and in 2000, multimedia artist Leon Johnson provided Wilde's guardian angel, as way of a replacement, with a silver prosthesis.

Genitalia notwithstanding, Oscar Wilde's tomb, for over 100 years, has been a potent tourist draw. Indeed, a tradition arose: The pilgrims, applying heavy lipstick, kissed the tomb, leaving their mouth marks. In July 2011, Bernard V. Kleinman of White Plains, New York, visited Pere Lachaise Cemetery with his wife, and wrote to the *New York Times*:

> Of all the graves we visited, the one for Oscar Wilde was the most disappointing ... defaced with graffiti of all kinds. While the graves of other artists were ready accessible (like those of Modigliani or Gertrude Stein), none were so egregiously treated.[4]

The shrine eventually became so "drooled and kissed over"[5] that, in 2011, the French and Irish authorities paid approximately $60,000 to restore it and erect a seven-foot-tall plate glass wall.[6] The tomb could be seen, but not kissed.

Twenty-three years before the vandalism, on October 10, 1938, *Oscar Wilde*, a play by Leslie and Sewell Stokes, opened at Broadway's Fulton Theatre. The star was Robert Morley, who'd played the title role in London. Brooks Atkinson, esteemed critic of the *New York Times*, wrote in his Sunday column:

> Oscar Wilde was prosecuted under the moral code on April 27, 1895 ... his career was destroyed and he died five years later. The atmosphere in which he was prosecuted was as abnormal as he was; it was furious with rancor and rapacity, for the custodians of morality grow sadistic when the pack is aroused.... In a play laconically entitled *Oscar Wilde* and brilliantly acted by Robert Morley, Leslie and Sewell Stokes have exhumed the main facts in the story of Wilde's five years of anguish....[7]

A triumph for Morley, *Oscar Wilde* ran 247 performances, a controversial hit. The account of Wilde's "perversion" was sensational drama, but for some, deeply disturbing. "I left the theater feeling ashamed to have seen such a play," Spencer Tracy told Ed Sullivan (then a major columnist). "I felt sort of unclean, because to a normal person the topic is almost obscene."[8] In his opening night review of *Oscar Wilde*, Brooks Atkinson wrote:

> Despite the merit of Mr. Morley's acting and of the production, the Messrs. Stokes' play merely confirms the conviction that Wilde suffered enough in the last five terrible years of his life. The world had no charity for him when he was alive. In view of the brilliant things he wrote, perhaps the world can afford to be charitable now and let his tired bones lie quietly.[9]

Out in California, however, Laird Cregar, living in a car, had decided this was no time for Wilde's "tired bones" to "lie quietly." He realized he'd found his dream role. It was time not for a peaceful interment, but a magnificent resurrection.

> Every actor not of normal size and shape, I perceived, *must make his own break.* This being so, I had to make mine. I had been going on the assumption that, because I knew I had what it takes, others would be aware of it, too. Now I realized that I would have to force the knowledge on them, with a bludgeon, if necessary.
> *Oscar Wilde*, it came to me, must be the bludgeon used.[10]

* * *

As Laird was homeless in Los Angeles, the 1940 census listed Samuel Laird Cregar living at 5308 Wayne Avenue in Philadelphia, with his mother Elizabeth, Aunt Eugenia and brothers Robert and John. Robert was now a retail linen salesman, John, an office furniture salesman. Laird's profession, according to the census: none.

Epic, heartbreaking foppery: Laird Cregar as Oscar Wilde.

The Cregar home, Wayne Avenue, Philadelphia. Laird's mother, aunt and two of his brothers lived here in 1940. That year's census listed it also as Laird's address, as he had no permanent address in Los Angeles (author's photograph, 2014).

The census also reveals that Laird's eldest brother Edward was living in North Hollywood with his wife and seven-year-old stepdaughter, and employed as a manager in the oil industry. There's no indication that Edward did (or didn't) provide Laird any assistance at this crucial time.

The Cregar family was keeping the light burning for the prodigal son to come home to Philadelphia, but Laird had a plan. The dream had formed, obsessively: Somehow, he had to play Oscar Wilde. He knew he had the audacity, the flamboyance and the girth to pull it off.

In 1940, this dream was virtually all he had.

Actor Henry Brandon is best remembered as evil Barnaby in Laurel and Hardy's 1934 *Babes in Toyland* (he played the geezer villain when he was only 22!). He knew Laird from the Pasadena Playhouse and remembered taking a pre-fame Laird to dinner one night—"and he ate a whole loaf of bread and an entire bowl of butter before the main meal came." Brandon recalled:

> "Sammy" Cregar realized he was born to play Oscar Wilde. He put the play in his pocket, and wherever he was invited where there were more than two people, he'd take the play out and start reading it, hoping to attract a producer who believed in him and the play. The idea worked with my friend, "Blackie" O'Neal....[11]

In 1940, Charles "Blackie" O'Neal was a 36-year-old scrapper from North Carolina who'd studied literature at the University of Iowa. He was a handsome man; his son Ryan, born in 1941 and who grew up to star in *Love Story* (1970), resembles him. "Blackie" had been supporting himself as a bank clerk, a horse groomer and a telephone repairman, since he had yet to win distinction as an actor and writer. "Blackie didn't have a nickel himself," remembered Brandon, "but he went out, raised the money and got a major production mounted in Los Angeles."

Oscar Wilde, of course, could easily crash and burn: an all-male play about "the love that dare not speak its name," starring a complete unknown. A little theater production would have been the safest venue, but O'Neal bravely went for broke, hoping this freak play with a freak star would prove a novel attraction in darkly closeted Hollywood.

O'Neal enlisted his cohorts. He convinced 33-year-old Arthur Hutchinson, a former ice cream manufacturer, to co-produce *Oscar Wilde*. Hutchinson set himself up as president of Los Angeles' Stage League, and one of his first tasks was to take $100 of the desperately raised capital-to-date and fly east to get signed permission to produce the play on the West Coast.[12]

As director, O'Neal engaged 43-year-old Arthur Ripley,[13] whose film career dated to 1916 ... producer, director, writer, cinematographer, editor, gag man and director for Mack Sennett. As of 1940, however, Ripley had never directed a stage play. So O'Neal heroically persevered, with a co-producer who'd never produced, a director who'd never staged a play, and a "star" who'd been living, and perhaps still was living, in a sedan.

Thursday, April 11, 1940: "Cregar as *Wilde*," headlined *Variety*, noting the play would premiere April 22 at the El Capitan Theatre, 6838 Hollywood Boulevard. Opening in 1926, with Spanish Colonial exterior and East Indian interior, the El Capitan had housed many plays, including the April 1939 hit engagement of *Of Mice and Men*, starring Wallace Ford and Lon Chaney, Jr. (whose success in the play won him the role of Lennie in the film version later that year). By April 1940, the theatre had seen better days. O'Neal arranged to book the house for *Oscar Wilde* on a modest rental.[14]

Everyone, including Laird, agreed to work for scale. There were no "name actors" in the play. Few had any film experience. George Pembroke, who played Carson, the Irish attorney who brilliantly secured Wilde's conviction, was a bit player in films; he'd recently appeared in the 1940 Republic serial *Drums of Fu Manchu*, starring Henry Brandon as the title fiend. Pasadena Playhouse alumnus Howard Johnson, who played Charlie Parker, the effeminate groomsman with whom Wilde has a fateful assignation, had appeared at Hollywood's Musart Theatre the previous season as the psychotic Dan in *Night Must Fall*.

In preparing the program, O'Neal camouflaged the production's bizarre evolution, while Laird added fictional flourishes that became part of his legend:

> Laird Cregar, who plays the title role of *Oscar Wilde*, was sent abroad to England where he acquired his education and experienced his first taste of the theatre at Stratford-on-Avon.... By chance producers O'Neal and Hutchinson heard Cregar in a private reading of the play early this year.... In Laird Cregar they see one of the most promising young character actors of the stage today.[15]

Monday night, April 22, 1940: It was the opening night of *Oscar Wilde. Gone with the Wind* was playing at the Carthay Circle Theatre, *Rebecca* at the Four Star Theatre,

Deanna Durbin's *It's a Date* at the Pantages and RKO Hillstreet Theatres. On stage at the Biltmore in downtown Los Angeles, Raymond Massey was flopping in *Abe Lincoln in Illinois*, despite his success in the Broadway play and the RKO film version.

The advertisement for *Oscar Wilde* in that day's *Variety* promised, "Introducing the Stage's newest character star, LAIRD CREGAR."[16]

In retrospect, the most interesting alternate attraction that night, in regard to Cregar, was at the Paramount Theatre, which offered a Universal double bill: *Black Friday* and *The House of the Seven Gables*. The former starred Boris Karloff and Bela Lugosi, into whose horror arena Laird would eventually enter. The latter starred George Sanders, who would co-star with Laird in three films, including his traumatic final one, and Vincent Price, who was two years older and one inch taller than Laird. Price had won stage stardom in 1935 in *Victoria Regina*, co-starring with Helen Hayes in both London and New York. He was currently cast as Joseph Smith, founder of the Mormon religion, in *Brigham Young*, which was shooting at 20th Century–Fox.[17]

Within only six months of this night, Price would be billed below Cregar at Fox.

*   *   *

You see, I happen to like people better than principles. And I like people with no principles better than anything else in the world!—Laird Cregar as Oscar Wilde

Blackie O'Neal had done his job heroically well. The El Capitan wasn't full, but it was, as *Variety* reported, "liberally sprinkled" with "picture folk."[18] The major Los Angeles critics had come too.

Laird had been electrifying in rehearsals. He'd delivered the Wilde epigrams with a comic timing that almost called for rim shots. His piece-by-piece breakdown on the witness stand had been nearly painful to watch. His final scene of decay was heartrending. Be he smoking a perfumed cigarette, enjoying an olive, or weeping over his downfall, he *was* Oscar Wilde.

It was the biggest night of Laird Cregar's life to date. A Hollywood audience would literally be sitting at his feet, seeing him in his dream role. The irony was all too perfect: *Oscar Wilde* was indeed his "bludgeon," an "unclean," "obscene" play; producers had rejected Laird because of his weight and perhaps his homosexuality, and now here he was, with both attributes serving him nobly in this title role. Backstage, he might have exulted in this wonderful chance, expressing his gratitude to the faithful O'Neal for daring to provide it.

What he did instead was shocking. As 8:40 p.m. arrived, Laird closed his dressing room door and refused to come out—until he received a new contract and $100 more per week.[19]

O'Neal was outraged. He'd risked everything he owned and more to produce *Oscar Wilde*. Facing personal and professional ruin, O'Neal responded understandably: He broke through the dressing room door and attacked his star.

"Blackie was a tough little Irishman," said Henry Brandon, "and he *went* for Cregar ... the stagehands had to pull Blackie off of him!"

As the first night audience waited, unaware of the melodrama erupting backstage, O'Neal, restrained by the crew, weighed his options. He could announce to the first-nighters and critics Laird's unforgivable behavior, forever destroying Cregar's chance for a career. Yet it was O'Neal who'd believed in Laird Cregar; if the star went under, the producer would surely drown with him. There was nothing he could do.

Laird got his new contract with the promise of $100 more a week.

The question: Why, on this night of all nights, did Laird behave so arrogantly? Egomania, perhaps; he was only 26 years old, and believed himself on the threshold of fame he'd passionately desired all of his life. One might also suggest he was suddenly terrified, and the money demand a ruse to escape what he saw as the shock of a dream coming true. However, as Henry Brandon said: "Sammy was a genius, with that selfishness that goes with genius ... and he was frenetic. I think he sensed he wasn't going to live very long, and he had to get everything in what little time he had." In this case, Laird was eager for not only fame and glory, but for compensation. Considering his psychic sense of his too-short life, it was, while unpardonable, maybe at least understandable.

The actors took their places. The house lights dimmed. The curtain rose on *Oscar Wilde*.

* * *

> *What is this picture I behold? Hylas and Hyacinthus have returned to earth!*
> *The flower of Grecian boyhood is here to welcome my homecoming. Too wonderful!*
> —Laird Cregar's entrance lines as Oscar Wilde

Act I, Scene i: The terrace of a hotel in Algiers. Lord Alfred Douglas is vacationing, sharing quarters with Oscar Wilde, who calls Douglas "Bosie." A letter arrives from Douglas' father, the Marquis of Queensbury, who warns: "I strongly disapprove of your intimacy with this man Wilde.... If I catch you again with that man I will make a public scandal in a way you little dream of...."

Wilde's unruffled reply: "It is perfectly monstrous the way people say things against one behind one's back that are absolutely and entirely true."

Act I, Scene ii: A Private Room at a Restaurant. Wilde's *The Importance of Being Earnest* has just opened triumphantly. Wilde celebrates by dining with Charlie Parker, an illiterate Cockney teen, his hair "plastered in a lovelock on his forehead"; in today's jargon, he'd be called "flaming." Wilde tells Charlie he'll provide him one of the best seats to *The Importance of Being Earnest* whenever he likes. Charlie isn't sure he'll understand the play.

> PARKER (*confidentially*): Between you and me, I ain't 'ad much edgecation.
> WILDE: Really, Charlie, I should never have guessed....

The orchestra plays "You Should See Me Dance the Polka."[20] "Delicious tune!" says Wilde, and he and Charlie dance together out of the room.

Act I, Scene iii: The study of Wilde's home in Chelsea. It's shortly after midnight. Wilde ("wearing an elaborate dressing gown") tells Frank Harris (his friend and later biographer) that the Marquis of Queensbury has sent a card to Wilde at his club, reading, "Oscar Wilde posing as sodomite." Wilde has decided to sue for criminal libel, despite

Harris' warning that a trial will create "a scandal for a dirty-minded world to lick its lips over."

Act II, Scene i: The Queensbury Trial at the Old Bailey. Mr. E.H. Carson, Q.C., attorney for the Marquis of Queensbury, questions Wilde, who for a time, smoothly banters. Then Carson begins listing the names of young men with whom Wilde has had private dinners. One was a servant named Walter Grainger.

> CARSON: Did you ever kiss him?
> WILDE: Oh dear no. He was a peculiarly plain boy. He was, unfortunately, extremely ugly. I pitied him for it.
> CARSON: Was that the reason why you did not kiss him?

Wilde, trapped, begins to unravel.

Act II, Scene ii: The Old Bailey. Charlie Parker tells the court of his many dates with Wilde, laughing that when he last saw Wilde, Wilde told him, "You're looking as pretty as ever." Wilde, "haggard and worn," takes the stand, and explains:

> The love that dare not speak its name in this century is such a great affection of an elder for a younger man.... It is that deep, spiritual affection that is as pure as it is perfect. It dictates and pervades great works of art like those of Shakespeare and Michelangelo.... It is in this century misunderstood ... and on account of it I am placed where I am now. It is beautiful, it is fine, it is the noblest form of affection. There is nothing unnatural about it....

The judge's response: "It is the worst case that I have ever tried. That you, Wilde, have been the center of a circle of extensive corruption of the most hideous kind among young men it is impossible to doubt." The sentence: imprisonment and hard labor for two years.

Act III, Scene i: Wilde's ghostly, dust-covered study, two years later. Wilde returns home from prison. His friends Eustace and Dijon are waiting for him, but not Lord Douglas. Wilde announces that he's changing his name to "Sebastian Melmoth" and will enter a Catholic retreat for six months to begin his life and work anew. He talks of having read Dante's *Inferno* in prison: "You see—I was in hell too." Harris arrives with a letter from the Catholic retreat; Wilde reads it, and crumples it in his hands. "They won't receive me. Even they won't receive me. [*He sinks into a chair.*] I thought my punishment was ended. It has just begun...." He buries his face in his hands and sobs.

Act III, Scene ii: Outside a Paris café. Oscar Wilde is in exile, drinking absinthe, bloated, gibbering, decaying ... dying. He's haunted by his prison time: "[D]id you know that when I was arrested, the police let the reporters come to the cell and stare at me? As if I had been a monster on show...." He's had a reunion with Lord Alfred Douglas, whose family had kept him from seeing Wilde. Wilde speaks emotionally, and gives a final soliloquy: "Sh! This is a dream. I am telling one of my stories, and all the stars have come out to listen."

Wilde tells a story of Jesus returning to Nazareth, a place so changed that he didn't recognize his own city. "The Nazareth where He had lived was full of lamentations and tears," says Wilde; "this city was filled with outbursts of laughter and song...." He sees a young man following a woman: "The face of the woman was the face of an idol," says Wilde, "and the eyes of the young man were bright with lust." Jesus asks the man why he follows the woman.

"But I was blind once, and you gave me my sight," says the young man. "At what else should I look?"

Jesus then asks the painted woman, "Is there no other way to walk save the way of sin?"

"But you forgave me my sins," says the woman, "and the way is a pleasant way."

As Laird Cregar's Oscar Wilde climaxed this beautifully bitter soliloquy, tears ran down his face[21]:

> When Jesus had passed out of the city, He saw, seated by the roadside, a young man who was weeping. He went towards him, touched the long locks of his hair, and said to him: "Why are you weeping?" The young man looked up, recognized Him, and made answer:
>
> "But I was dead once, and you raised me from the dead. What else should I do but weep?"

Wilde tries to stand, but is too drunk. "I have had my hand on the moon," he says. "What is the use of trying to rise a little way from the ground!" Lord Alfred Douglas hands the waiter some money to give to Wilde and leaves.

The program for *Oscar Wilde*, El Capitan Theatre, Hollywood, 1940.

The orchestra begins playing "You Should See Me Dance the Polka," and Wilde remembers the song from the first night he'd dined with Charlie Parker. As the script writes, he "bursts into a horrible laugh."

The waiter gives him the money from Douglas. Cregar's Wilde turns to the empty chair and, in his delirium, speaks to Douglas, as if he's still there: "Thank you, Bosie. Thank you."

Curtain.

*   *   *

It was as if the audience at the El Capitan had witnessed an unholy miracle: Oscar Wilde's ghost had arisen from his angel-with-phallus-decorated grave in Paris, taking possession of a 26-year-old L.A. vagrant and happily serving as the "bludgeon" he'd needed to strike Hollywood right between the eyes. The opening night audience stood and cheered, a thunderous reception reported as "unbelievable" and "extravagant."[22]

Laird Cregar stood in the lights, bowed time and again, and like Oscar Wilde in Act III, he wept.[23]

PART II

The Lion of the Hour

The world was my oyster but I used the wrong fork. —Oscar Wilde

6

Success

Oscar Wilde ... was all I needed. The show, although it didn't make much money, was an artistic success and critics lauded my performance. Hollywood studios, which would not let me past the gate before, now lionized me.... From a half-starved actor, I became a star overnight. It's a grand feeling.[1]—Laird Cregar

The reviews the morning of April 23, 1940, after *Oscar Wilde*'s opening night, were raves. Edwin Schallert wrote in the *Los Angeles Times*:

A new stage personality was introduced to audiences last night at El Capitan Theatre. Laird Cregar, unknown to most of those who witnessed the Coast production of *Oscar Wilde*, scored a sensational success in the title role...

Assuredly he achieves a splendidly drawn characterization at virtually every stage. My only personal objection would be that emotion seemed overstressed toward the close, but the applause and bravos of the audience might even serve to confute that "testimony."

In *The Hollywood Citizen-News*, James Francis Crow critiqued:

It is a personal triumph for Laird Cregar.... [A]t the final curtain, there was an ovation for the entire company, and a special ovation for Cregar himself.... Cregar is a tall and massive man, but he portrays the exquisite Wilde with almost feminine delicacy and flourish in the early sequences, and creates some quite terrifying moments of melodrama in the scenes of Wilde's degradation....

Virginia Wright, in her *Los Angeles Daily News* headline, said it all: "LAIRD CREGAR, A NEW STAR, EMERGES IN *OSCAR WILDE*."

Overnight, Laird Cregar was Hollywood's 300-pound *enfant terrible*; Wilde resurrected, a fey, freak attraction with the crackerjack timing of a burlesque comic and the dramatic fireworks of a great tragedian. He was a "grotesque," as Laird would have expressed it, but a grotesque with star quality, taking bows and living the dream.

Initially, there was one problem for *Oscar Wilde*: box office, or lack of it. "Wilde, $3500, Dismal in L.A.," headlined *Variety*, noting: "Despite excellent notices," audiences were shying away from the "all male cast."[2] Although Hollywood was a worldly town, many ticket buyers were wary, perhaps fearing their presence at such a play would be an admission of prurience, or even perversity, and week two took in only $2500.[3] (By comparison, the second week's take for *Of Mice and Men* at the El Capitan the previous year had been $11,000.[4])

Come week three, however, and business spiked. Maurice Evans had opened at the Biltmore in Shakespeare's *Richard II*, and as *Variety* would report, "Bard of Avon is vying with the psychopathy of *Oscar Wilde* and the sprightliness of a revue [*Meet the People*] for Los Angeles audiences."[5] The El Capitan had become a temple of lavender decadence, and Laird its high priest.

Meanwhile:

Monday, May 6, 1940: Louella Parsons reported in the *Los Angeles Examiner* that the powers at MGM "have their eye on Laird Cregar, who is such a hit in the local presentation of *Oscar Wilde*, for a long-term contract."

Wednesday, May 8: Warner Bros. tested Laird for *The Letter*, starring Bette Davis and directed by William Wyler. As Laird remembered:

> Bette was kind to me. She came to see me in *Oscar Wilde*, and visited me backstage after the performance. She insisted that I make a test with her for a part in *The Letter*. The role was unsuited to me and the test was horrible. But no matter. Bette's gesture was that beautiful, inordinate thing that one actor sometimes does for another.[6]

The test was for the plum role of Howard Joyce, the lawyer who defends Davis for murder and falls under her spell. (It would have been a bad fit for Laird, but was ideal for Warner contractee James Stephenson, who ultimately won the part and received a Best Supporting Actor Oscar nomination.)

Also May 8: Laird was guest of honor at the Authors Club Luncheon at the Hollywood Athletic Club.[7] The same day, a feature on Laird appeared in the L.A. *Evening Herald Express*. W.E. Oliver wrote:

> One of those stories that brightens the eye of the old trouper, lights the face of the stage neophyte with hope, and gives the playgoer a glow is the case of Laird Cregar ... the 23-year-old [sic] youth from Philadelphia who created such a sensational effect on the first night audience of *Oscar Wilde*, and has been repeating it each night.

Note that Laird had trimmed three years off his age. Oliver reported Laird's struggles, repeated his claims about his Philadelphia family that went back "14 generations," wrote that the Cregar family "has supplied 83 bishops," and included the Ann Booth (wife of John Wilkes) saga.

> He has ambitions to do Falstaff, a life of Goldsmith, and Mahomet. He also plans to write, produce and act his own shows.... He believes the theatre is never dead for those who really want to find life in it and adds, "I would have been prepared to go on starving until I got my chance. It's not being heroic. If you want to act, you are just that way."

Friday, May 9: Harry Crocker, in his "Behind the Makeup" column in the *Los Angeles Examiner*, wrote, "Laird Cregar gives one of the best performances I have seen on the Coast. He IS Oscar Wilde."

Meanwhile, the third week

Laird's elegant Oscar Wilde.

of *Oscar Wilde* took in $6000, and because of the shoestring budget, *Variety* noted that "spells plenty profit."[8]

As he considered film offers, Laird carried on at the El Capitan, extravagantly earning his increased *Oscar Wilde* salary, wringing himself out into near-exhaustion at every performance. DeWitt Bodeen saw *Oscar Wilde* in both New York and Hollywood, and remembered that Laird was "very frequently just as good as Morley."[9] Peggy Stewart, who'd so enjoyed Laird on and offstage in *The Great American Family*, came to see the play. "Of course, Laird was just marvelous as Oscar Wilde. He just chewed it up! I went backstage to say 'Hi' to him—oh, it was so much fun!"[10] Henry Brandon saw *Oscar Wilde* time and again: "God, to watch Sammy on the stage! Blackie O'Neal's wife Patricia and I used to sit, night after night, in the back of the theater, just to watch him create, just to watch the fantastic new things he brought to the play. Every night, it was a different performance.... He was brilliant."[11]

As Brandon recalled, after every show, Laird welcomed any and all admirers from the audience to his dressing room. He wore a robe after the marathon performance, the back of the robe peculiarly pulled up and placed over his head, "like a monk's cowl," as Brandon described it. The costume suggested both a boxer after a championship bout and a holy man at peace after battling the Devil. Thusly did Laird accept his due from the awe-struck.

"Sammy was a chameleon," chuckled Brandon. "After playing Oscar Wilde on stage, he'd become another person backstage. The most wonderful, sweet, darling man, hum-

Laird as Oscar Wilde, with Howard Johnson as Charlie Parker.

ble, grateful for every little word of praise. It was almost a better performance than the one he'd given on the stage!"

Oscar Wilde tallied $4500 in its fourth week,[12] and fell to $3700 in its fifth.[13] Meanwhile, there was a surprise announcement: Laird had bought the rights to *Roman Holiday*, to become a Broadway musical comedy, with Laird as Emperor Nero ... and co-starring Ethel Merman![14] Maybe *Roman Holiday* was an impetuous pipe dream on Laird's part, or more likely, a move to make both the *Oscar Wilde* producers and the film studios believe he had options. At any rate, no play titled *Roman Holiday* ever played Broadway; the 1953 film *Roman Holiday,* for which Audrey Hepburn won an Oscar, was an entirely different property.

Perhaps the greatest thrill for Laird came when John Barrymore—by 1940, the ruins of John Barrymore—came to see *Oscar Wilde.* On May 23, Barrymore had returned to Hollywood, after debasing himself in the Broadway comedy *My Dear Children,* and was set to report to Fox to humiliate himself further in a lame comedy titled *The Great Profile.*[15] (Ironically, Fox provided Barrymore the star bungalow recently vacated by Shirley Temple, still decorated with dolls and stuffed animals.[16]) Laird's boyhood idol was extravagant in his praise.[17] Laird was so proud that, once again, he wept.

Come its sixth and final week, *Oscar Wilde* eked out a mere $2000.[18] The play closed Saturday night, June 1, 1940, set to reopen in two weeks in San Francisco. Two days later, *Variety* reported that Charles O'Neal had sold his interest in the production to Arthur Hutchinson.[19] Relations between "Blackie" and Laird hadn't improved since the opening night debacle. While Hutchinson had dreams of touring the play nationally and opening in New York, O'Neal suspected that Laird's commitment to *Oscar Wilde* would evaporate once the film offers became definite.

Indeed, during the two-week layoff for *Oscar Wilde,* Laird considered his movie options. 20th Century–Fox made a tempting offer, but again, Laird dickered—insisting that, for his screen test, he play several characters, to display his versatility and dissuade potential typecasting. Such a demand was a risk.

Fox acquiesced.

* * *

Thursday, June 13, 1940: *Variety* wrote:

Cregar Up for Pair
   Laird Cregar will be tested today by 20th-Fox for roles in *The Californian* and *Down to the Sea in Ships,* both on the summer shooting sked.

"I tested for an ancient padre, a sea captain, and a dashing Spanish Don,"[20] Laird recalled. The padre and the Don were part and parcel of *The Californian,* a remake of Douglas Fairbanks' 1920 *The Mark of Zorro,* with Fox's top male draw Tyrone Power set as Zorro and Linda Darnell his co-star. The ancient padre was Fra Felipe, a Friar Tuck type that was a natural for chubby, frog-voiced Eugene Pallette, who'd played Tuck in Warners' 1938 *The Adventures of Robin Hood*—and who ultimately played Felipe.

More colorful was Laird's test for the role of "dashing" Capt. Esteban Pasquale, the villain, who dies fighting Zorro in a crowd-pleasing sword duel.[21] It's unlikely that Laird worked with Power in the test—superstars almost never tested with unknowns—but he was pumped up anyway. Indeed, the test of an amazingly agile, 300-pound Laird, leaping, lunging and sprinting with sword in hand, was the talk of 20th Century–Fox. It became an attraction in its own right; directors would ask to see the test to enjoy the spectacle. Rouben Mamoulian, who'd direct *The Californian,* now seriously considered Laird for Pasquale.

As for the sea captain, the test was for *Down to the Sea in Ships,* with Laird playing grizzled Capt. Bering Joy, who takes his grandson on a whaling expedition. The 26-year-old actor amazed everyone by how convincingly he suggested advancing age; if *The Californian* displayed his flair, *Down to the Sea in Ships* showed off his dimension.

He'd knocked the trio of tests out of the park. Nat Goldstone, one of the 50 agents who called Laird the morning after *Oscar Wilde*'s opening night, or so Laird claimed, opened negotiations for a contract with 20th Century–Fox.

* * *

"Oscar Wilde, that unhappy hedonist ... relived his span on the stage of the Curran last evening in one of the most nerve-wracking yet exciting evenings first-nighters have experienced in many years."—Wood Soanes, *The Oakland Tribune,* June 18, 1940

Monday, June 17: Oscar Wilde opened at the Curran Theatre in San Francisco for a two-week run. Laird was back in the theatre where *The Great American Family* had died such an ignoble death. His Oscar Wilde was in full bloom before first-nighters including Walter Huston, Ina Claire and Elsa Maxwell.[22]

Wood Soanes, reviewing the play in *The Oakland Tribune* on June 18, warned his readers that the play was "at once horrendous and compelling," and praised "the complete understanding and histrionic flair of Laird Cregar, an American novice in the theater." The critic wrote that "from the first scene, it was Oscar Wilde and not Laird Cregar who was on view":

> [I]t was possible to see not only the exhibitionist in Wilde as he pranced around Algiers, the lion of the hour, but to discern that, beneath his hollow-sounding unction and his infectious merriment, having the soul of a lonely, troubled man, somewhat embittered at the world, accepting its plaudits but conscious that it lacked understanding of him.

Soanes, zeroing in on Laird's Wilde as a "lonely figure," offered insight that's politically incorrect today, but was likely the prevailing 1940 attitude toward the subject of homosexuality:

> Hugh Walpole explained something of this in *Roman Fountain* when he discussed Michelangelo, observing: "I do not doubt that his nature was homosexual, as was Leonardo's and El Greco's; he was only the worse for that in that he was a lonely man. All men are lonely, but those with a twisted sexual nature are loneliest of all; which does not mean they are not happy. Only, in their experience, they are by themselves."

The critic had not only focused on the play *Oscar Wilde,* but on the personality of Laird Cregar, whose private behavior the next four and a half years, for all his rashness, revealed his own terror of loneliness.

Despite the reviews, *Oscar Wilde* was not a box office hit in San Francisco. It closed at the Curran Saturday night, June 29, and Laird headed back to Hollywood to review his Fox contract.

For a time, Arthur Hutchinson and Arthur Ripley insisted they'd launch a northwest and Midwest tour of *Oscar Wilde*, and a New York City re-opening, with "first call" on Laird's services. However, they were being naïve if they believed they'd ever get their star back, or thought Fox would release him.

"[I]f anyone is asking me," wrote Wood Soanes, aware of the delicate situation as the play shuttered in San Francisco, "Cregar certainly owes [Hutchinson] something for the chance to display his wares. Cregar will never be a leading man, but he can give actors of the Charles Laughton type a good deal of trouble because he has sincerity, diligence, and a definite flair for characterizations."[23]

The beleaguered Hutchinson meanwhile gave up all hopes of reviving *Oscar Wilde*.[24] The adventures and misadventures of producing the play eventually cost Hutchinson and Arthur Ripley $45,000.[25] Hutchinson's dramatic career ended and he faded from celebrity. Ripley went on to direct *Thunder Road* (1958), become UCLA's first professor of cinema, and found the UCLA Film Center. He died on February 13, 1961, age 64.

As for "Blackie" O'Neal, who truly made *Oscar Wilde* happen for Laird Cregar: In 1943, he co-wrote (with DeWitt Bodeen) Val Lewton's remarkably morbid *The Seventh Victim* (1943), focusing on an ex–devil worshipper who hangs herself. Other writing credits included *Cry of the Werewolf* (1944) and *The Alligator People* (1959), as well as scripts for TV's *The Untouchables* and *Lassie*. As an actor, O'Neal became the leading player of the Old Globe Shakespearean Repertory Theatre in San Diego.

O'Neal's greatest exposure came on the night of April 2, 1974, when he escorted his granddaughter Tatum O'Neal, a Best Supporting Actress nominee for *Paper Moon*, to the Oscars. Ryan O'Neal was apparently not present, and when Tatum won, the gray, bearded, bespectacled, 70-year-old "Blackie" went to the stage with her. After Tatum's brief acceptance speech, "Blackie" said a few grateful words himself, which were inaudible. The audience wondered who he was. When Andrew Sarris of *The Village Voice* covered Tatum's victory, he alluded to *Lolita*: "Who was that Humbert Humbert with her?"[26]

Charles O'Neal died on August 29, 1996, in Los Angeles, at age 92.

* * *

Laird Cregar had won stardom via one of the strangest ways an actor could in 1940: an outlandish yet sympathetic portrayal of a gay man. *Oscar Wilde*[27] had been a dream come true for him, the benefits perhaps even greater than he'd dared hope. It had been a dizzying three months, going from living in a car to a 20th Century–Fox contract and praise from his boyhood idol, John Barrymore.

He was only 26. The future as an actor seemed limitless.

7

The Rabbit with the Glass Teeth

We have another 23-year-old genius in our midst, it seems. His name is Laird Cregar.... Darryl Zanuck has built great hopes on this amazing young actor, who looks ten years older than he is and who is exceptionally bulky and tall. He would never be able to be a romantic hero, but he certainly has a brilliant future as a character actor, which seems odd with his juvenile years...
                        —Louella Parsons, *Los Angeles Examiner*, July 4, 1940

A photograph survives from 1934, showing Darryl F. Zanuck on safari in Africa.[1] The mustached, buck-toothed, five-foot-six Zanuck, dressed *à la* Hemingway's Great White Hunter, proudly poses with his giant rifle beside a rhinoceros he's shot to death. Sitting and smiling atop the rhino's corpse: Zanuck's gracious, long-suffering wife Virginia, who accompanied her spouse into the jungle while she was three months pregnant.

Sometimes a picture is truly worth a thousand words.

Turning 38 in 1940, Darryl Francis Zanuck, of Wahoo, Nebraska, was Hollywood's youngest mogul, reigning at 20th Century–Fox, 10201 West Pico Boulevard in Westwood. His was the power and the glory, an empire boasting such assets as Betty Grable's legs, Tyrone Power's profile and a sprawling back lot with sets evoking virtually every locale in the world, all protected by the fifth largest police force in Southern California.[2] His legendary mantra: "Don't say yes until I finish talking!"[3]

Zanuck was a dynamo who habitually swung a polo mallet, and who'd defined two major studios. From 1931 to 1933, he had been executive producer at Warner Bros., developing the gutsy, Big City style so much a part of classics such as *The Public Enemy* (1931) and *42nd Street* (1933). In March 1933, Zanuck had been Hollywood's hero of the hour: All the studios, spooked by the Depression, had instituted emergency salary cuts, and after weeks of weathering the storm, all began paying back the withheld money—except Warners. Zanuck walked out. He never looked back. He co-founded (with Joseph Schenck) 20th Century Pictures, producing such blockbusters as *The House of Rothschild* (1934) and *Les Miserables* (1935), merging in 1935 with Fox Studios, creating 20th Century–Fox and developing a new corporate identity: Shirley Temple vehicles, Technicolor musicals and enough historical epics to inspire some jokers to refer to the studio as 19th Century–Fox.

Yet for all his brilliance as a showman and his machismo as a personality, Zanuck wasn't always a popular man. Henry Fonda called him "Darryl F. Fuck-It-All Zanuck."[4] Alice Faye, who despised Zanuck, referred to 20th Century–Fox as "Penitentiary Fox."[5]

An aerial view of the 20th Century–Fox lot, circa 1939. The area in the middle of this picture, the old golf course, would later feature the exterior sets for *The Lodger* and *Hangover Square*, Laird's final two films.

Glenn Langan, who'd appear in Laird Cregar's final film *Hangover Square*, joked that he'd always liked Zanuck "due to my inbred love of animals!"[6]

But consider Zanuck's top 20th Century–Fox product:

The Prisoner of Shark Island (1936): The saga of Dr. Samuel Mudd, directed by John Ford. The film features the best-ever cinema recreation of Lincoln's assassination, then segues into a religious-style pageantry: Mudd (Warner Baxter), suffering Hell at Fort Jefferson Prison in the Dry Tortugas, agonized by a Lucifer of a jail sergeant (John Carradine). The climax: an apocalyptic tropical storm.

In Old Chicago (1938): Americana about the O'Leary family, directed by Henry King and starring Zanuck's super-discovery Tyrone Power. Alice Faye sang the title song and did a can-can, Alice Brady won a Best Supporting Actress Oscar as the O'Leary matriarch, and the climax was the 1871 Chicago fire, complete with a cattle stampede that tramples villain Brian Donlevy. The film earned a Best Picture Oscar nomination.

Alexander's Ragtime Band (1938): The star trio of *In Old Chicago*—Power, Faye and Don Ameche—go from the 1915 Barbary Coast to 1937 Carnegie Hall, without any signs of aging. Directed by Henry King, the show offers 30 Irving Berlin tunes, including

Ethel Merman belting out "Pack Up Your Sins and Go to the Devil." It received an Oscar nomination for Best Picture and an Oscar for Best Score.

Jesse James (1939): A Technicolor super-western, starring Tyrone Power as Jesse and Henry Fonda as Frank James, directed by Henry King. Location shooting in Pineville, Missouri; dastardly villainy from Brian Donlevy (who blows up Jesse's mother, played by Jane Darwell) and John Carradine (who, as Bob Ford, shoots Jesse in the back). The one flaw: The breathtaking scene of two horses diving off a cliff into a river, shot in the Ozarks, killed both horses.

Drums Along the Mohawk (1939): John Ford's first Technicolor film, with Claudette Colbert and Henry Fonda as a Revolutionary War Adam and Eve. The serpent: John Carradine as a one-eyed Tory who leads a climactic night attack against the settlers' fort with demonic "savages" (an oddity for Ford, considering his later noble depictions of American Indians). Providing the pastoral, Garden of Eden scenery: Cedar Breaks, 11,000 feet high in the mountains of Utah.

Kay Linaker, a *Drums Along the Mohawk* cast member, recalled the company's sobriquet for Zanuck: "the Rabbit with the Glass Teeth."[7] (He had shiny buck teeth, and apparently some people thought he looked like a rabbit.) Whatever animal he evoked, Zanuck was a powerhouse, and from 1933 through 1939, Fox was number two in fiscal profits, behind only almighty MGM. Fox's 1939 profit: $4,200,000,[8] equivalent to $71.8 million in 2017 dollars.

On January 24, 1940, 20th Century–Fox had premiered *The Grapes of Wrath*, based on John Steinbeck's novel, at Broadway's Rivoli Theatre. *The New York Times* hailed it as "magnificent" and "a testament to the power of the screen."[9] It remains visceral, haunting and inspiring; Henry Fonda as Tom Joad, Jane Darwell as Ma Joad and John Carradine as Casy the preacher are all superb, and John Ford directed brilliantly. It was Zanuck's greatest triumph to that date, a mix of the social cause activism he'd sparked at Warner Bros., and the epic sweep he'd masterminded at Fox. The man was at the height of his powers.

There was also the dark side. Zanuck was a legendary seducer,[10] infamous for his 4:00 p.m. casting couch breaks with an aspiring starlet *du jour*. In fact, in 1940[11] 20th Century–Fox, in its way, was the most sinister of Hollywood studios, headed by a sybarite screamer, and backed up by his giant police force.

Still, the sybarite was a master at making movies. The destiny of many relied on the power of Darryl F. Zanuck. As of July 1940, Laird Cregar's did too.

> Laird Cregar Given Two Spots by 20th
> When Laird Cregar, recruited from legit, checks in at 20th Fox this week to start his first screen termer, he will find two assignments awaiting him. First he goes into *The Californian* with Tyrone Power and Linda Darnell, then plays Lord Gooseberry in *Hudson Bay Company* [*Variety*, July 8, 1940].

Monday night, July 1, 1940: Laird, back in Hollywood, celebrated, significantly. He returned to the El Capitan Theatre, where he'd won stardom as Oscar Wilde, as a member of the opening night audience of *Good-bye to Love*, starring Joan Blondell and Patric Knowles. Also at the performance: Dick Powell (Blondell's husband at the time), Ida Lupino (whose mother, Connie Emerald, was in the cast) and Louis Hayward (Lupino's husband at the time).

Zanuck clearly perceived Laird the same way Paramount had promoted Charles Laughton in the pre–Code 1930s: an off-beat, heavyweight, eccentric talent, ready to spring startling surprises on movie audiences. Meanwhile, Fox welcomed Laird, although he'd yet to sign his contract officially. He was like a kid in a candy shop. Laird met Tyrone Power and Linda Darnell, rehearsing their big Spanish dance for *The Californian*, in which he was to co-star. The dashingly handsome Power was gracious and fun, and Laird quickly became friends with him. He basically fell in love at first sight with the amazingly beautiful 16-year-old Darnell. Laird found it endearing that her family still called her "Tweedles," and that she'd come to Hollywood from her native Texas with a pet rooster named Weedy.[12] He greatly looked forward to making his Fox debut with these two friendly, charming stars.

There was plenty to see and enjoy. Fox was producing *Down Argentine Way*, a Technicolor musical starring Betty Grable and Don Ameche. Laird, who loved music, visited the soundstage, meeting the vivacious Grable and affable Ameche, and watching Nick Castle choreographing the acrobatic Nicholas Brothers. Carmen Miranda, one of the stars of the film, was actually in New York, playing the Versailles Room, where Fox filmed her numbers for the movie.

There was the Fox back lot[13]: the lake that the studio had dug for *In Old Chicago*, the six acres of "1871 Chicago" atop a hill northeast of the Fox main gate (Chicago had appeared to burn in that film, but the set actually didn't), the western "Tombstone Street" from *The Cisco Kid* (1931), the "Colonial Home" from Shirley Temple's *The Little Colonel* (1935), "The Permanent Garden" from *Zoo in Budapest* (1933), the "New England Square" from Will Rogers' *David Harum* (1934), "The Algeria Street" from *Under Two Flags* (1936). There was also an annex, the original William Fox Studio, located in Hollywood at Sunset Boulevard and Western Avenue, where Theda Bara had vamped.

One of the most interesting fixtures of Fox for Laird was his "competition," a character actor often described by the press as "cadaverous." In fact, Laird said, perhaps jocularly, that this man's presence was one of the reasons he signed with the studio.

"At the time, there was only one other character man, John Carradine, under contract, and, of course, we two couldn't ever vie for roles!"[14]

> There seems to be a trend toward reformation in these parts. Brian Donlevy, the toughest sergeant that ever infested the Foreign Legion, sees the evil of his ways in *The Great McGinty*. Peter Lorre, Bela Lugosi and Boris Karloff are about to mingle harmoniously with Kay Kyser in *You'll Find Out*. Someday John Carradine will break out with a lullaby, and the Millennium will be just around the corner [George E. Phair, in his "Retakes" column, *Variety*, July 23, 1940].

Like Laird, John Carradine had also won "fame" on Hollywood Boulevard, although not in a theater.

In 1930, Carradine had paraded at night in cloak and a battered Homburg hat, roaring Shakespeare, a mix of classical actor and carnival geek.[15] He was then basically a vagrant, like Laird had later been (although there's no record of him ever having lived in a car). Fox had signed Carradine to a seven-year contract after his wild-eyed villainy in 1936's *The Prisoner of Shark Island*; the studio knew it had done right when Carradine, leaving the premiere at Grauman's Chinese Theatre, was booed by the crowd, causing his bride of six weeks, Ardanelle, to burst into tears.

He was a fine actor, although his hard drinking and eccentricity flared up time and

John Carradine (left), Fox's top villain, and Tyrone Power, Fox's top hero, at the Stork Club in New York City, circa 1940.

again. Carradine arrived at premieres in his own Duesenberg, sporting a top hat, cape and cane. He recited Shakespeare at any opportunity. While on location up in Cedar Breaks for *Drums Along the Mohawk*, Carradine classically entertained at the nightly bonfire, once performing a streamlined *Macbeth*, playing Macbeth, Lady Macbeth and all the other major roles ... superbly.

"John was magnificent," remembered Kay Linaker. "I never heard anybody do 'Tomorrow and tomorrow and tomorrow' as well until I heard Ian McKellen do it."[16]

Although Carradine had won his fame as a villain, his brilliant *Grapes of Wrath* performance—as a Christ symbol, no less—persuaded Zanuck to reserve the actor for Fox's top productions. Come 1940, Carradine was receiving $1000 per week, 40 weeks a year at Fox.[17] He lived in North Hollywood with Ardanelle and sons Bruce and John (later David), but often escaped domesticity to cavort with the man who was his (and Cregar's) idol, John Barrymore. Among their frivolities: at-sea orgies with cronies such as Errol Flynn, accompanied by a posse of drunken whores, as Flynn remembered, "puking their guts up all over the place."[18]

Carradine welcomed Laird Cregar to Fox. Their careers would soon spin off in directions that were both wildly different and strangely similar.

*   *   *

[T]he artist shall furnish, at his own expense, all of the wardrobe used or worn by him in the portrayal of the roles or parts portrayed by him hereunder, except costumes for roles or parts known as costume parts, which are not possessed by the artist. All clothing, haberdashery, hats and shoes furnished and used by the artist shall be of conservative and first-class style and cut, of the highest mode and taste, and shall be procured from the best tailors and merchants, to the end that the artist shall maintain an excellent reputation for being well-dressed at all times, both on and off the screen, and that the roles and parts portrayed by him shall receive an interpretation and portrayal suitable to the best type of motion picture productions. Any costumes, apparel or other articles paid for or furnished by the producer shall be returned promptly to the producer, upon demand.[19]
—Clause 19 of Laird Cregar's 20th Century–Fox contract

Monday, July 22, 1940: Laird finally signed his seven-year Fox contract. It provided salary steps that, for a novice, were quite extravagant:

- First six months, 20 out of 26 weeks: $500 per week
- Second six months, 20 out of 26 weeks: $600 per week
- Second year: 40 out of 52 weeks: $750 per week
- Third year, 40 out of 52 weeks: $1000 per week
- Fourth year, 40 out of 52 weeks: $1250 per week
- Fifth year, 40 out of 52 weeks: $1500 per week
- Sixth year, 40 out of 52 weeks: $2000 per week
- Seventh year, 40 out of 52 weeks: $2500 per week

Compare this to John Carradine's contract, which had started at $200 per week in 1936, and was set to escalate to $1,750 per week come 1942.[20]

Laird's contract ran 21 pages and had 32 clauses, including the *de rigueur* "morals clause," which the erstwhile "Oscar Wilde" had to accept:

SEVENTEENTH: That the artist shall perform the services herein contracted for in the manner that shall be conducive to the best interests of the producer ... and if the artist shall conduct himself, either while rendering such services to the producer or in his private life in such a manner as to commit an offense involving moral turpitude under Federal, state or local laws or ordinances, or shall conduct himself in a manner that shall offend against decency, morality or social proprieties, or shall cause him to be held in public ridicule, scorn or contempt, or that shall cause public scandal ... the producer may, at its option and upon one (1) week's notice to the artist, terminate this contact and the employment hereby created.

Then there was the "deformity and disfigurement" clause:

EIGHTEENTH: That if the artist shall suffer any permanent facial or other physical injury, deformity or disfigurement, materially detracting from his appearance or ability to perform ... or if, by reason of mental, physical or other disability, the artist shall be incapacitated from fully performing and complying with the terms and conditions hereof ... the producer shall have the right and option, in addition to any other rights or remedies granted to it herein, to terminate this agreement....

Notary public Gladys Kenny affixed her signature and seal to the Laird Cregar contract on July 23, and George Wasson of the Fox legal department approved it July 31. Meanwhile, per the contract, Laird bought a new wardrobe of "first-class style and cut." Due to his perilous weight (and as later revealed by at least two catty female reporters), he usually wore a girdle to improve his tailoring.[21]

Meanwhile, on July 22, the same day Laird signed the contract, he surprised Fox with a stipulation of his own. He presented the studio with a list of eight plays[22] he'd completed writing, or was at work on, with brief synopses:

- *The Star Beneath the Fathoms*: A play concerning the lives of cadets on a German school ship.
- *The Glamorous Guinea Pig*: A farce about a girl who resents being experimented upon by relatives and turns the tables.
- *Winter Comes But Once*: A drama about an illegitimate son of a great American poet.
- *Two Tickets—Paid*: A murder story about a boy who pays the penalty for an unsuspected crime in lieu of the actual crime.
- *Beggars Can Be Choosers*: The story of a man and his wife affected by the consequences of the First World War.
- *The Life Beyond*: A metaphysical exploration into the life beyond.
- *Kid Stuff*: An idea for a musical comedy based on the same lines as *Babes in Arms*.
- *Right About Face*: A completed musical revue written in collaboration with Arnold Schwarzwald.

Laird wrote, "The ownership of these properties is to remain with me and is to be excluded from our contract."

He left a line for the 20th Century–Fox Film Corp. to sign the agreement. The legal department drew a large X through the line.

Laird quickly suffered a major disappointment, and one that quickly gave him a dose of the cruel realities of Hollywood: Basil Rathbone landed the role of Pasquale in *The Californian*, now retitled *The Mark of Zorro*. For the villain in a swashbuckler such as this one, no one was better suited. Director Rouben Mamoulian selected Rathbone, who, of course, would splendidly wage the sword duel with Power.

Laird probably enjoyed the later gossip about Rathbone's embarrassment during *The Mark of Zorro*: During the duel, and on a day that Rathbone had invited friends to the set, Power misjudged his aim in the choreographed duel, and his sword whipped off Rathbone's wig.[23]

Hudson Bay Company, meanwhile, remained on the Fox schedule. Twelve different writers over almost four years had tackled the story of Pierre Esprit Radisson and Medard Chouart des Groseilliers (aka "Gooseberry"), 17th-century fur traders whose adventures led to the British settling Western Canada.[24] Laird was still set for "Gooseberry," and the name said it all: a jolly giant in a beard and coonskin cap.

And as fate would have it, rather than act with Tyrone Power and Linda Darnell, he'd work in *Hudson's Bay Company*, with a man who was possibly the most selfish actor in 1940 Hollywood: Paul Muni.

8

Gooseberry the Great

"His eyes rolling, his massive chest heaving, Cregar enacts Gooseberry, the man who butts opponents with his head and bends prison bars as if they were Lady Hamilton's corset stays."

—Carl Combs, review of *Hudson's Bay*,
Hollywood Citizen-News, January 16, 1941

Warner Bros. had proclaimed him as "Mr. Paul Muni."

He'd latched onto the idea that great actors played great men—hence, his Oscar for *The Story of Louis Pasteur* (1936) and his New York Film Critics Award for *The Life of Emile Zola* (1937). Ironically, the Muni performance that dates best is *Scarface* (United Artists, 1932), in which he played the Capone-esque title role as a livid beast (in love with his sister). The same year, he'd starred in Warners' *I Am a Fugitive from a Chain Gang*, becoming one of that gutsy studio's legendary stars.

Muni was an alumnus of the Yiddish Art Theatre, a Broadway star ... and a terror to work with. In his memoir *Star Maker*, Warner producer Hal Wallis remembered:

[Muni] was a great actor, a private, withdrawn man who became considerably larger than life on the screen. His wife, Bella, strongly influenced him. When he worked, she stood behind the camera where Muni could see her. If she thought some element in his performance was wrong, she shook her head, Muni froze, and the whole scene would have to be redone. When Mrs. Muni nodded her head yes, we could all relax. Only because he was such a fine actor did we tolerate this very eccentric behavior.[1]

Josephine Hutchinson experienced the up-close-and-personal wrath of Muni as his leading lady in *The Story of Louis Pasteur*:

One day, when there were many visitors on the soundstage, we were playing a scene in which I was to rush up to Muni and embrace him. I did, and he stopped, pointed to his beard, and shouted, "This doesn't grow on me! You've ruined my makeup!" He stomped off to the makeup room and I was left on the set with egg on my face, feeling perfectly awful. Well, Clay Campbell, the makeup man, told me later, "You didn't hurt his makeup. He just didn't like the way he was playing the scene, and that was a good excuse to get off the stage and start again." Yet, Muni was such a perfectionist, he could be almost endearing....[2]

Bette Davis didn't find Muni endearing when they co-starred in Warners' *Juarez* (1939), he in the title role, she as Empress Carlota. In an October 22, 1938, memo to Muni from Hal Wallis, Wallis actually thanks Muni "for your willingness to permit us to co-star Bette Davis with you in *Juarez*. I want you to know that we appreciate very much your graciousness in acceding to this request."[3]

Muni took a leave of absence from Warner Bros. to star in Maxwell Anderson's play *Key Largo*, which opened on Broadway November 27, 1939. (He played King McCloud, Humphrey Bogart's role in the 1948 film version.) After 105 New York performances, *Key Largo* came to Los Angeles, opening May 20, 1940, for a week's run "to disappointing returns."[4] Muni headlined *Key Largo* at the Biltmore Theatre at the same time that Laird Cregar was starring as *Oscar Wilde* at the El Capitan.

Muni had hoped to star for Warners in *The Life of Beethoven*; instead, the studio offered him *High Sierra*, the saga of doomed hoodlum Roy "Mad Dog" Earle. Muni ultimately stormed out of the studio, and *Variety* headlined on July 24, 1940: "Muni Balks at Toting Guns, Quits Warners." (George Raft rejected *High Sierra* too, and Humphrey Bogart played "Mad Dog" Earle ... and greatly boosted his stardom.)

Meanwhile, Zanuck had considered Don Ameche, Henry Fonda and Dean Jagger (who'd played the title role in Fox's 1940 *Brigham Young*) for *Hudson Bay Company*'s lead role of Radisson. Also testing: Vincent Price, who'd appeared in *Brigham Young* as Mormon founder-martyr Joseph Smith. Then playing stock in Maine, Price returned to Hollywood, thrilled, as he put it, "to test for the best part I've ever been offered."[5] Price's height and muscular build would have made him ideal for the Radisson role.

Friday night, July 26, 1940: Four days after Laird had signed his Fox contract and two days before he celebrated his 27th birthday, a troupe of 36, including Laird and director Irving Pichel (well-remembered by Universal horror fans for his portrayal of Sandor, the evil servant of Gloria Holden in 1936's *Dracula's Daughter*) left by train for McCall, Idaho, to film outdoor scenes for *Hudson's Bay Company*.[6] The technical crew was already on location. The leading role was still not cast.

Wednesday night, July 31: Fox released the big news: Paul Muni had signed to star in *Hudson's Bay Company*. The *New York Times* reported: "Fox sent the script to Muni to read five days ago, and the actor demanded revision of his role. He and the scenarists have worked on it since, and the deal was concluded tonight."[7]

What Muni demanded, of course, was a beefing-up of his part—notably speeches. Shooting officially began Monday, August 19.[8] That same week, director George Abbott, who'd optioned Laird's play *The Glamorous Guinea Pig*, slated the show for New York production in the fall.[9]

It appeared that Laird would become a movie character actor and a Broadway playwright simultaneously.

*   *   *

Where they get the rope strong enough to hang me? That's what I'd like to know!
—Laird Cregar as Gooseberry, *Hudson's Bay*

Hudson's Bay (as it was retitled) would emerge as an $869,600 hybrid: half Muni biopic, half Fox historical saga. It also plays as a black-and-white storybook ode to Canada's wilderness: a fort stockade, glistening in snow; canoes, gliding along a sparkling lake; valleys and timber, presented in 1940 state-of-the-art rear projection. And it serves as a racist rant against the Indians, portrayed as brandy-crazed heathens. In fact, *Hudson's Bay* climaxes as Indians wipe out *other* Indians after a villain gets them wild on alcohol.

Unfortunately, we don't *see* this, we only hear about it. Presenting the action sequence would have derailed Muni's speeches. More on this later.

Most of all, *Hudson's Bay* is about actors, some at their best, others their worst. Lovely Gene Tierney (in her second film), as Lady Barbara of the English court, is all simper and flounce; John Sutton, Lord Edward Crewe, Lady Barbara's true love (and the third member of the fur-hunting trio, with Muni and Laird), is handsome and convincing; Sutton deserved a better career. Dashing Vincent Price, who'd lost out on the lead, has a nice consolation prize as King Charles II, resplendent in long curled wig, hat with plume, dainty mustache, and what appears to be lipstick. The *Los Angeles Times* review of *Hudson's Bay* aptly describes him as "spectacular."[10]

Left to right: Paul Muni, John Sutton and Laird Cregar, looming as the giant Gooseberry in *Hudson's Bay.*

The unsung stars of *Hudson's Bay*: the snow machines. Daily, these contraptions pulverized 40 tons of ice; the crew then sprayed the ice through hoses, effectively glistening the late-summer Los Angeles exteriors.

Yet upstaging even the snow machines was *Hudson's Bay*'s over-the-top byplay of Muni and Laird. As Pierre and Gooseberry, they revel in being "rogues"—making faces, pouring on impossibly thick accents, bellowing with laughter and, in the final shot of the film, actually dancing away together, arm in arm. *Hudson's B*ay was basically a "buddy movie," and Laird's "buddy" was an Oscar-winning star who knew every trick in the book for camera-hogging, upstaging and making his co-stars miserable.

Indeed, Muni in *Hudson's Bay* must be seen (and heard) to be believed. "Talk, talk, talk. You never heard so much talk,"[11] *Hollywood Citizen-News* critic Carl Combs marveled after seeing *Hudson's Bay*. Muni's Radisson soliloquizes about God. About Canada. About beavers. Sometimes he sings. Having demanded these speeches during the script revision period, Muni not only declaims them (one of them a remarkable two-and-a-quarter minutes long), he *responds* to these speeches, mugging, winking and popping his eyes as he considers what he just said. Now and then, the camera moves away from Muni to watch some other actor beholding him, and then quickly gets back to the star.

In his "Lights! Camera! Action!" column in the Los Angeles *Evening Herald Examiner*, Harrison Carroll wrote about a *Hudson's Bay* ball scene, in the court of King Charles II, filmed on one of Fox's largest soundstages: "The shot is where Paul Muni, John Sutton and the towering Laird Cregar create a sensation by appearing before the king dressed in the animal skin costumes of trappers." He continued:

> They present a strange spectacle as they enter the ballroom. Cregar, standing 6 foot 3 and weighing 315 pounds, looks like a giant beside Muni, whose small stature always is a source of surprise to visitors on the set. On the screen he looks like a man of average height or better. Actually, he is only 5 feet 8 and weighs about 150 pounds. Sutton, the other member of the trio, is taller than Muni, but he, too, is dwarfed by the massive Cregar.
>
> To complete the contrast to the elegant ladies and gentlemen of the court, both Muni and Cregar are wearing beards. The setup is perfect for comedy and director Pichel loses no time in getting the first laugh as the three trappers curtsy to their sponsor, the bewigged and dandified Nigel Bruce. One of the ladies, tiny Frances Leslie, looks up from her position on bended knee, gets a glimpse of Cregar and topples over backward. It's the movie's old reliable, the pratfall. It never fails to get a laugh from the audience.
>
> To top it, Cregar bends over, lifts the girl in the air and sets her down on her feet.[12]

This last bit didn't make it into the final print. Maybe that was because, as Carroll reported, Muni was with "his wife, who always is on the sidelines when he works before the camera."

Indeed, one can imagine Bella Muni, watching in horror as she realized her serial scene-stealer spouse had, in Laird Cregar, run into a massive brick wall. The effect of Muni and Cregar in *Hudson's Bay* is that of a diminutive Gypsy, holding a giant dancing bear on a chain. The Gypsy, aware the audience's eyes go to the bear, chews up the scenery; the dancing bear chews up the Gypsy. As *Photoplay* wrote: "There is, Twentieth believes, another star in the making in *Hudson's Bay*. This is Laird Cregar.... He is big as a blimp, a character actor and yet only twenty-odd in years. Muni is technically the star of *Hudson's Bay*, but the bets are all on Cregar stealing it...."[13]

As Muni hammed it up in his Yiddish Art Theatre-turned-exalted Movie Star way, Laird matched every bit of his bravado, and then some. Retakes were hopeless; for all of Bella Muni's furious head-shaking, nothing muted Laird's trumpeting presence. Naturally, some of Laird's best moments were when he was on-screen *without* Muni. In the London sequence, for example, Laird's Gooseberry sticks his head out of a coach and gleefully unleashes a harrowing war whoop, scaring the hell out of the coach driver. Later, in a British hall, he sees a bust of a woman's bare-breasted torso. Perusing the statue, he regards the head and the breasts, sees no arms and legs, and sadly shakes his head and sighs, "Poor lady!"

Wednesday, October 2: Shooting of *Hudson's Bay* wrapped.[14] Zanuck already knew the film had troubles, and on October 4, Lamar Trotti, the film's scenarist, was at work on a revised opening.[15]

Meanwhile, Laird was enjoying himself. Among the cast *of Hudson's Bay* he found a special friend and admirer in Gene Tierney. He also savored the press coverage. "Not since John Barrymore in his palmiest days has any actor given out such unorthodox interviews as Laird Cregar," wrote Louella Parsons in her October 6 column. "Fan mag writers are beating a path to the dressing room of this young actor...." One asked him what kind of woman he liked best. Laird's reply: "It really doesn't matter, as long as she is very bad-tempered. Also, I like vividly painted nails and red hair. It helps, too, if she is conspicuously dressed. What man likes to be seen with a mouse?"

Cal York of *Photoplay* took umbrage at Laird's remark, and volleyed: "For that matter, Laird (do you mind if we call you Laird?), what woman likes to be courted by an elephant?"[16]

After *Hudson's Bay*, Zanuck had planned to star Laird with Tyrone Power in *Down to the Sea in Ships*, in the role he'd tested for, Capt. Bering Joy. A special effects crew had been shooting around Monterey to capture background shots and sea weather.[17]

However, Zanuck indefinitely postponed *Down to the Sea in Ships.* Instead, he cast Laird in *Western Union*, a Technicolor outdoors spectacle based on a Zane Grey novel. His role: Charlie, a grizzled frontiersman who had been scalped, lived to tell about it, and shows off his scalped pate to his pals.

Laird joined Robert Young, Randolph Scott, Dean Jagger, Brenda Joyce (later replaced by Virginia Gilmore), John Carradine, Slim Summerville and the rest of the company, under Fritz Lang's direction, in Kanab City, Utah. They stayed at the Parry Lodge, the quarters for several of Fox's on-location productions of that era.[18] Considering Carradine's lusty recitations of Shakespeare, Laird's resounding renditions of Byronic verse, and Fritz Lang's characteristic screaming tantrums, the Parry Lodge was a very lively locale during early October 1940. In 2017, a signed portrait of Laird is still among the many autographed pictures hanging on the lodge's wall: "To the Parry Lodge, with most sincere regard, Laird Cregar."

Monday, October 14: Columnist Jimmie Fidler wrote, "Mr. Cregar, currently playing a comic cowboy in *Western Union*, is handicapped by the decision of studio bosses that he must not ride a horse. After viewing first-day rushes, they feared that audiences, instead of laughing, would call the Humane Society...."[19]

The same day: Harrison Carroll reported that Laird was working on *Hudson's Bay,* which had begun reshooting, and *Western Union* simultaneously, and was "being shuttled back and forth in a chartered plane" from Kanab to Hollywood. This couldn't go on indefinitely, and on October 18, *The Hollywood Reporter* noted that Fox had removed

Laird from *Western Union* so he could concentrate on the added scenes for *Hudson's Bay*, expected to go "for two weeks or more."

"Additional scenes have been ordered," claimed the *Reporter*, "to get more of Paul Muni into the story which, as first filmed, has him coming in when it is about 1/3 over."

For Hollywood insiders, the report read as a smoke screen: Rumors had spread that Laird had swiped *Hudson's Bay* from under Muni's nose, and now Muni was demanding extensive retakes and added scenes to recapture dominance. Zanuck only had a one-film commitment with Muni, but realized it was bad business to present any star at a disadvantage. It would also be unfortunate if the gossips claimed Zanuck had thrown the film to his new contractee while sabotaging a major star.

Laird had acted in only a few scenes of *Western Union*, so Fox scrapped his footage and offered his role to George "Gabby" Hayes.[20] However, Hayes was ill and so, by the end of October, Victor Kilian (who won attention 36 years later as "The Fernwood Flasher" on TV's *Mary Hartman, Mary Hartman*) took the part of Charlie, presumably cut down in the final release.

So *Hudson's Bay* was back in production, to protect Muni from Laird's larceny. The new opening had Muni enter two minutes and 15 seconds into the picture (Laird behind him), bursting into the Albany quarters of the snooty governor (Frederick Wor-

Laird Cregar as Gooseberry, Nigel Bruce as Prince Rupert, Vincent Price as King Charles and Virginia Field as Nell Gwynn in *Hudson's Bay*.

lock) and getting the governor's attention by throwing a knife at his feet. There followed a free-for-all, as Muni's Radisson pulled off the governor's wig, and Laird's Gooseberry bumped the governor's soldiers with his giant belly. Yet even with the new donnybrook beat-'em-up opening, the revised film was in trouble: Within 15 minutes, Muni nearly talked and mugged the film into an early death.

Inevitably, the film emerged as a patchwork. Rouben Mamoulian, between assignments, directed a few shots, and there were two top cameramen, Peverell Marley and George Barnes. (The latter would win the 1940 Best Cinematography Oscar for *Rebecca.*)

Reporter Lucie Neville, visiting the *Hudson's Bay* set, filed a fascinating report on 20th Century–Fox-by-night, writing that coffee was "almost everywhere a light is burning," and describing the film's exterior on the bank of the back lot lake, "crusted with tons of shaved ice":

> Driving through ghost towns, along the streets of "Old Chicago" or what was Czechoslovakia in *Four Sons*, you can park within a block of Hudson's Bay. Director Irving Pichel and a dozen assistants are on a barge anchored off-shore. The cameraman's focused on the dock, where a gang of fur-stealing redskins are loading bales in canoes, making a fast getaway. Most of them can't swim, and the sidelines are betting that the canoe paddled by two fat boys, called Jelly-Belly and Chief Budweiser, is going to spill. It doesn't, but just as they yell "Cut!" another canoe tips and the braves come up spitting water....[21]

In Wardrobe, Ms. Neville found four night-shift wardrobe girls, "washing hose and girdles," and beheld on racks everything from Betty Grable's "diamond-necked blue evening gown" for *Tin Pan Alley*, to Jane Darwell's "padded undersuit and limp lavender cotton tights" for her role as the circus fat lady in *Chad Hanna*. As for Laird, Neville found him enjoying "a double order of frankfurters" and "having mustard-in-the-beard trouble." She noted that the crew called him "Junior," and that at a later dinner break, Laird "had the hard-boiled egg market cornered." As Neville described the middle-of-the-night dinner: "With the long wooden benches and tables in the open, it looks like a cross between a Sunday School picnic and the first Thanksgiving. The Indians have shucked their wigs, the trappers their hot fur caps...."

So *Hudson's Bay* wrapped up ... again. In the final version, there was another scene-stealer: About 25 minutes into the film, where the heroes enter an Indian village with snow-covered teepees, a dog in the master shot, squats and pees. Presumably nobody noticed during the shooting or in the rushes.

*   *   *

Laird was making many friends. Among them were 26-year-old Bob Wright and 25-year-old Chet Forrest, songwriters and life partners who'd be together personally and professionally for 72 years. Their talent for adapting classical music had well-served such MGM films as *Rosalie* (1937) and *Sweethearts* (1938); they'd receive a 1940 Best Song Oscar nomination for "It's a Blue World" in Columbia's *Music in My Heart.*[22]

On Friday, November 15, 1940, Laird was a first-nighter at *Thank You, Columbus!*, a musical revue with songs by Wright and Forrest. Also at the Hollywood Playhouse for the opening: Greer Garson, Lana Turner, Eleanor Powell, Melvyn Douglas and wife Helen Gahagan, and directors Ernst Lubitsch and Josef von Sternberg. The show lasted only eight days. Wright and Forrest would fare much better in their most celebrated collaboration: Broadway's *Kismet*, for which they would win the 1954 Best Musical Tony Award.

Another close friend was Tom Neal,[23] a brooding mix of brains, brawn, dark hand-someness and what one of his three wives would later call "insane jealousy." The world remembers Neal for basically three things: (1) starring in PRC's delirious noir *Detour* (1945), as the ill-fated sap who picks up (and kills) psycho *femme fatale* Ann Savage, (2) beating up and disfiguring Franchot Tone over Barbara Payton in a real-life 1951 love triangle that became one of Hollywood's all-time lip-smacking scandals, and (3) his 1965 conviction for involuntary manslaughter after fatally shooting his wife Gail in the head in their Palm Springs home.

Twenty-six years old in 1940, Neal had played in about 20 features and short subjects, often uncredited. There will be more about Neal later, but for now, here's a 1965 courtroom quote from him, after his lawyer asked if he'd said anything after shooting his wife.

"Yes," said Neal. "'Talitha cumi,' which is interpreted as, 'Fair maiden arise, for thou art whole.'"[24]

He must have been an interesting chum, even back in 1940.

*　*　*

In December, before *Hudson's Bay*'s previews, Fox picked up Laird's option, raising his salary to $600 per week. He took a plane to New York, where production of his play *The Glamorous Guinea Pig* had derailed. Laird campaigned to find a producer, without success.

There was, however, another reason for his trip. The Cregar family black sheep–prodigal son headed to the family home in Philadelphia, a manic Santa Claus, joyfully announcing an early Christmas present: He would personally set up his mother Bess and Aunt Nean, then living on Wayne Avenue, in a new life in Los Angeles. They'd both share in his giant success. Laird later dramatized the event for Hedda Hopper, claiming that they made a final visit to his birthplace on Cresheim Road:

> Mother and my aunt went back to look at the house before they came out to this coast. They leaned against the iron palings of the garden fence, and tears filled their eyes. Then my mother said it seemed as if a wind blew through the doorway and up the stairs and filled the deserted hallways—a great wind of life and children's laughter. And she heard the voices of all the people she'd loved and lived with....[25]

*　*　*

The old Cregar house, 5308 Wayne Avenue, where the family was living in 1940, now survives in an area of intense poverty, and has been broken up into apartments. Two unfortunate-looking men, both smelling strongly of alcohol, enter and depart the house as I stand there with my camera. They're cordial, intrigued by my interest, and have no problem with me snapping pictures of their residence.

A neighboring house had been divided into two homes; one of the halves has been demolished, and the result looks like what it basically is: a half-a-house. A young man walks by. "Bet you wanna use that camera to take a picture of the half-a-house!" he laughs.

None of the folks I chat with has ever heard of Laird Cregar.

* * *

Nineteen forty was a joyous Yuletide for Laird, and he received a special gift: *Weekly Variety*'s review of *Hudson's Bay,* published on Christmas Day. "Zanuck takes another sideswipe at history and comes off second best again," began the review, panning Muni's "long speech after long speech" that "reduce the little action that is there in the first place." However, *Variety* hailed Laird as "a huge giant of a man, a character player for whom there is a distinct and important niche waiting. He combines the characteristics (generally speaking) of Laughton, Jannings and the French Harry Baur. As Muni's major domo here he doggone near walks off with a number of the important scenes...."

With one film, Laird Cregar had come close to fulfilling a lifelong dream. He made sure that his mother, aunt and loved ones would be sharing in his glory.

9

He-Goat Lucifer

From now on, the calendar of the bullring will be figured as "B.G." and "A.G."—
"Before Gallardo," and "After Gallardo." I, Curro, say it!
                                                        —Laird Cregar, *Blood and Sand*

Wednesday, January 1, 1941: Laird attended a New Year's Day cocktail party hosted, significantly, by his Fox "rival," John Carradine.[1]

Among the guests was Blanche Yurka, who must have fascinated Carradine and Laird: Both men were John Barrymore idolaters, and Ms. Yurka had played Queen Gertrude to Barrymore's incestuous Hamlet on Broadway in 1922. Also present at the party was a man with whom Laird would form an unusual friendship: George Sanders. The Russian-born, British-raised actor, also under contract to Fox, was as cynical about the film colony as Laird was punch-drunk about it.

"The only thing that keeps me from killing most of the people in Hollywood," Sanders would purr, "is the fear of being jailed."[2]

Wednesday, January 15: *Hudson's Bay* opened at Hollywood's Grauman's Chinese Theatre, with decorative flowers representing snow for the event. The film would earn a respectable $1.39 million in worldwide rentals, and turn a decent profit of $88,500. For Laird, the film was a triumph, as this January 19 review in *Albuquerque Journal* attested:

> More notable, we think, than Mr. Muni's return to the screen is the appearance of Laird Cregar as his pal. A huge man-mountain of a fellow, he lumbers through the film with high good humor and puts just the right, perfect touch on all his acting. He steals the picture, if we must be direct about the matter.[3]

Seventy-six years later, the revelation of *Hudson's Bay* still is Laird Cregar—a bearded romper stomper, bellowing his way to fame with colorful vivacity and remarkable assurance in his first major film performance. For Los Angeles audiences who'd seen him as Oscar Wilde, the transformation must have been amazing.

In retrospect, *Hudson's Bay* is intriguing as it's the only film in which Laird Cregar and Vincent Price appeared together. They stand out in the picture with a flair and presence no one else in the cast matches. Indeed, while *Hudson's Bay* was generally considered Laird's triumph, Harrison Carroll opined in the *Evening Herald Express*, "Vincent Price, as King Charles, gives Muni a close race for the acting honors, though he hasn't one-tenth the footage of the star."[4] Aware that Price had tested for Muni's Radisson role, it's easy to imagine Price and Laird starring together in this "buddy movie," and the rousing chemistry these two giants would have generated with their towering bodies and talent.

A gregarious man, Vincent Price, then wed to actress Edith Barrett (their son Barrett was born during the shooting of *Hudson's Bay*), naturally befriended Laird, but they were never close pals. Price was a slender, more handsome and even taller version of Cregar. Inevitably a rivalry ensued, even if neither man actively pursued it, and would flare up over the next several years in some strikingly strange ways. On February 10, Harrison Carroll reported, "Giant Laird Cregar is after 20th Century–Fox to let him go east and produce a play. If the deal goes through, he'll also star in it. Patrick Hamilton is the author. The title is *Gaslight* and the hero is a professor of psychology who deliberately sets out to drive his wife insane."[5] It was a very "hot" property: *Angel Street* had opened in London in December 1938, and had become the acclaimed 1940 British film *Gaslight*. The play *Angel Street* would eventually open on Broadway in December 1941, and prove a giant hit. Enjoying a triumph as the evil Mr. Manningham: Vincent Price.

*   *   *

"Here it is almost a month past Christmas, and Laird Cregar is
still wondering how to get into the sweater Gene Tierney knitted for him."
—Jimmie Fidler, January 15, 1941

On December 17, Louella Parsons wrote that Fox would film *Sioux City*, a Technicolor spectacle starring Randolph Scott and Cregar, the latter as Chief Rain-in-the-Face. Parsons claimed that Laird would lose 70 pounds to play the role, but *Variety*'s George E. Phair nevertheless joked, "Laird Cregar, the heap big paleface in *Sioux City*, will make heap big Injuns look like singer midgets...."[6] It was never produced.

Instead, in his next film, Laird Cregar got to play Oscar Wilde ... sort of. A Spanish Oscar Wilde. Gone rancid ... and from Hell.

*   *   *

"When 340-pound Laird Cregar came home with his hair dyed black
for *Blood and Sand*, his mother took one look at him and screamed:
'What have they done to my BABY?!!'"—Jimmie Fidler, February 27, 1941

Blood and Sand, directed by Rouben Mamoulian in a style perched between Bizet's *Carmen* and a Catholic funeral High Mass, shot in sumptuous, Oscar-winning Technicolor, was an all-stops-pulled remake of the 1922 silent Rudolph Valentino tragedy. Indeed, in 1940s Hollywood cinema, there's no other movie quite like it.

Tyrone Power (in bangs) tackled the Valentino role of doomed bullfighter Juan Gallardo. Linda Darnell, as his faithful wife Carmen, looked so beatific that when she prayed to a statue of the Virgin Mary, it was hardly a surprise that the statue spoke back to her. And there was Rita Hayworth as temptress Dona Sol, slinking through the film with demonically red hair and a smile prophetic of a Hammer Films vampire babe.

Notably, *Blood and Sand* was also an All Saint's Day for the featured players: Nazimova as Power's long-suffering mother; Anthony Quinn as Manolo, Power's lusty rival

Blood and Sand: **Tyrone Power (seated), J. Carrol Naish (tending to Power), John Carradine (standing and looking at Laird), Monty Banks (boutonniere), Pedro de Cordoba (tall, light suit) and Laird Cregar (seated at right).**

in the bullring and the boudoir; J. Carrol Naish as Garabato, a has-been toreador who becomes Power's servant; and John Carradine as Nacional, Power's conscience, who looks like a clean-shaven Christ, and after receiving a fatal goring, dies worthy of one, arms stretched out at his side, lying under a cross in crucified fashion: "I've dragged myself through the blood and sand of a thousand arenas!" sighs Carradine.

The Devil in this sexed-up Passion Play: Laird Cregar as Natalio Curro, a toxically fey and fickle fanboy critic of matadors, whose passionate screams as Power drives a sword into the bull's skull garishly reveal his fantasies. It would be a remarkably audacious performance.

Blood and Sand was Fox's first big production of 1941, and Mamoulian was indeed the man for it. "Mamoo," as he was nicknamed, reveled in stylistics, as evidenced by his 1931 *Dr. Jekyll and Mr. Hyde* and 1932's *Love Me Tonight*, both from pre–Code Paramount; more recently, he'd joined Fox, giving *The Mark of Zorro* a wonderful swashbuckling sweep. An admirer of Laird since seeing his Fox screen test, Mamoulian was enthused about directing him.

Early January found Mamoulian and his troupe in Mexico City, coping with extras who demanded siestas, while Darryl Zanuck, in Hollywood, considered casting the role of Dona Sol. (Among the contenders: Hedy Lamarr, whom MGM refused to loan out; Carole Landis, who balked at dying her blonde hair red for the role; Lynn Bari, who ended up cast as Encarnacion, Juan's selfish sister.) The company stayed south of the border for three weeks, shooting bullfights and atmosphere and bringing home the footage. Additionally, Laird came home with a reputation. Harrison Carroll wrote in his column: "Three-hundred-pound Laird Cregar is far from being unwieldy. Lying flat on his back, he can do a flip-up, landing on his feet.... And he is as strong as an ox. Ask some of the lads who tried to clown around with him on the *Blood and Sand* location."[7]

Blood and Sand began filming in Hollywood on February 3. Rita Hayworth was finally cast as Dona Sol the following week, borrowed from Columbia. Mamoulian let his actors loose, calling for flamboyance, and the character players, particularly, enjoyed the unleashing. However, Laird was the only one so gleeful that he'd perform cartwheels as he made his way to and from the *Blood and Sand* soundstage. He was in his glory ... but, as always, defiant. On February 13, Lew Schreiber of Fox's legal department wrote this memo to department head George Wasson:

> Laird Cregar has made a claim for two days' salary for making tests in connection with a role he is going to play in one of the forthcoming pictures. We are still going on the assumption that we do not pay for tests, publicity stills, wardrobe fittings, etc., to anyone making $500 or over. I checked with Metro and Paramount, who advise that they do not pay for tests, etc., to anyone making $500 or over, but Warner Bros advise that they do. I think it is a good idea to inject this into all contracts in the future, so that we will not get any kick-back. I understand that Paramount are [*sic*] doing this now on their long term contracts.[8]

It seemed a rather pushy claim against a studio that was committed to building him as a major player. Apparently, Laird lost the battle.

*   *   *

> "Rouben Mamoulian decked 300-pound Laird Cregar out in scarlet in *Blood and Sand*. As a result he broke the Technicolor exposure meter on his first take."
> —Harry Crocker, "Behind the Makeup," *Los Angeles Examiner*, March 8, 1941

We first behold Laird's Curro in *Blood and Sand*'s splashy opening: It's night, a Flamenco with castanets is dancing on a table, and the crowd is celebrating the most recent victory of Naish's matador Garabato—who boasts that, during his 19 years in the arena, he's killed 2,912 bulls, and been gored 67 times. "*Ole!*" cheer the celebrants.

"With my hand on my heart," says Laird, "I, Curro, declare all nations of the earth should come and admire toreros like Garabato! Oh, they may have ships, they may have gold, but they have no man like this!"

What animal does Laird suggest as Curro? A bull? A swine? An iguana? All of the above? At any rate, the crowd begins debating: Who was the greatest bullfighter of all? Among them is the teenage son of the now-dead Gallardo, played with fire by Rex Downing, his movie character fated to grow up to be Tyrone Power. The boy insists his father was the most wondrous of bullfighters: "He belonged to the slaughterhouse, not the bull ring," says Curro scornfully. "I was there the day he was killed. He trembled like a leaf! He had *cats in his belly*!"

The young Gallardo smashes a bottle of wine over Curro's head. A riot breaks out. *Blood and Sand* is on its way.

Ten years pass. Juan Gallardo is a rising matador. Naish's Garabato, dissipated and broken, is his servant. As the incredibly photogenic Power ritualistically dresses for his battle with the bull, Laird's Curro, all-eyes, gazes upon him, hailing him as "a saint—the first man of the world!" Gallardo reminds Curro of their first meeting and the bottle of wine they "split"; Curro claims the scar he bears is "my most prized possession." And as Laird exits the scene, the 300-pound-plus actor grabs a matador's cape and, in a surprise bit, performs a dazzlingly executed swirl, over his head!

Mamoulian, meanwhile, approached his Technicolor extravaganza with 16 spray guns of different colored paints, creating the film's varied palette look:

> *Blood and Sand,* about a bullfighter's career, was based on the work of Spanish painters: in the market scenes I used the style of Sorolla; in the luxurious house of the bullfighter's mistress, Dona Sol, Velasquez; in the chapel and the infirmary, El Greco. Anti-realism, of course; El Greco couldn't have passed a first-grade examination in anatomy. I had a crucifix which I sprayed blue and gray and green, and I sprayed the set with spray shadows when I couldn't do it with light....[9]

It's in the barbaric bullfighting scenes, however, that *Blood and Sand* is at its savage, sensual best. Laird roosts in the ringside sun, in straw hat and carnation, and purrs gossip about the *amours* of Rita Hayworth's siren, Dona Sol: "What I could tell you about that one would fill a whole book—*several* books. If this is death in the afternoon, she is death in the evening!"

In the arena, Mamoulian cleverly cuts back and forth from Hayworth's Dona Sol to Laird's Curro, each one passionately eyeballing Power. As for the Old Master influences, *Blood and Sand* now evokes Goya: the spectacle of his bullfight paintings, as well as the perversity of his devils, witches and monsters. The bullring is a Technicolor Kingdom of Hell, Laird is Goya's He-Goat Lucifer, and Hayworth is one of the artist's witches ... her rigid, toothy smile suggesting that the witch is wearing a beautiful mask.

"I tell you, he is the greatest of the great...!" Laird Cregar, crazed with passion, as Curro in *Blood and Sand.*

Even the innocent bull seems a demonic monster, with devil horns. "*Ole!*" bellows Curro.

Blasts of trumpets, bloodthirsty cries from the mob, Power driving his sword into the bull's head ... hysteria. A woman passionately screams, and there's an intense close-up of a sweaty, wild-eyed Laird, giving the impression that Curro, in his passion for Gallardo, is reaching a sexual climax. "I tell you he's the greatest of the great!" shrieks Curro. "The first man of the world!"

Writing in the *San Francisco Chronicle,* March 11, 1941, Jimmie Fidler joked that

20th Century has been unable to find a satisfactory stand-in for 340-pound Laird Cregar, so cameramen on his pictures, anxious to save time "setting up," resort to many expedients.

Yesterday, John Carradine, thinnest man on the screen, but about Cregar's height, came on the *Blood and Sand* set and was accosted by a cameraman with: "Will you stand in for Mr. Cregar a moment?" Carradine obliged. "Now, a foot to the right," said the lensman. Carradine moved over. "Two feet to the left," next instructed the cameraman. Again Carradine obeyed. "Thanks," said the photographer. "Ready for Mr. Cregar!"

Laird's best moment comes near the end of *Blood and Sand*. As Power's besotted Gallardo toppled, Laird's venomous Curro joyfully castrated him in his column. This sets the stage for Curro holding court one night in an outdoor café, sitting at a table, smoking a cigarette, slandering Gallardo … unaware that Gallardo is listening behind him:

> LAIRD: I understand Gallardo has one more contract to fulfill…. I predict he will make his exit in a cloud of rotten oranges and dead cats! … The trouble with Gallardo is he has cats in his belly…. His father was the same way. Like father, like son.
> POWER (*as Laird timidly turns around*): That's the second time you've said things about my father. As for you, you've probably never been baptized. Well, I baptize you now!
> (*Pouring a bottle of wine into Laird's sputtering face*)
> I christen you liar!—and your second name is swine!

The film ends in spectacular tragedy: a bull gores Power … he dies … a forgiving Linda Darnell gives him a final kiss. Trumpets. Cheers. There's a farewell panorama of the hellish bullring, with Hayworth throwing flowers to Quinn, and Cregar screaming, "Manolo is the greatest of the great! The first man of the world!" The Technicolor fade-out shot: blood on the sand.

The later part of the shooting of *Blood and Sand* offered its own real-life troubles. The worst: On March 15, 1941, Anthony Quinn's two-and-a-half-year-old son Christopher wandered from the Quinn home on DeMille Drive in Los Feliz (Quinn was then married to Cecil B. DeMille's daughter, actress Katherine DeMille), walked to W.C. Fields' nearby home, reached in the pond for a toy sailboat, fell in and drowned. Quinn, taken from the *Blood and Sand* set to the death site, fought the rest of his life to deal with this terrible tragedy.[10]

Additionally, Laird caught the measles. The contagious nature of the illness caused Fox to shoot around him at great expense, while the other cast members began daily check-ups to make sure they had no symptoms. Eventually Power caught the flu, and production shut down entirely.[11]

Shooting of *Blood and Sand* finally wrapped on April 8. Zanuck, who'd fought with Mamoulian throughout the shoot, so admired the final cut that he decided to release the film without a preview, and set release for late May. Laird's daring performance had sufficient subtlety to elude the censors. He'd created a character unmatched in lavender decadence since Charles Laughton's Nero had feasted his eyes on Amazons killing pygmies in DeMille's 1932 pre–Code *The Sign of the Cross*.

Laird was quite proud of himself.

* * *

"Laird Cregar is such a good actor that he doesn't have to care whether
Jack Oakie calls him "Lard" Cregar or not….—Louella Parsons, May 23, 1941

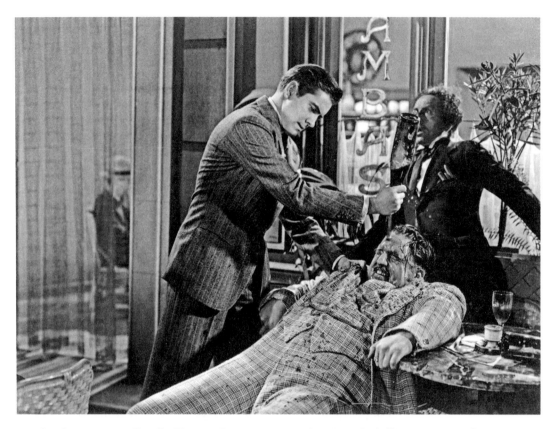

"I christen you liar!"—Tyrone Power pours wine into Laird's sputtering face in an audience-pleasing moment in *Blood and Sand*.

The measles had caused Laird to forfeit the role of William "Willie" Boulton in *Moon Over Miami*, a Fox Technicolor musical starring Don Ameche, Betty Grable, Robert Cummings and Carole Landis. Sixty-one-year-old George Lessey replaced him.

Monday, April 14: Laird visited Warner Bros. to test for the title role in *The Man Who Came to Dinner*. The comedy had opened on Broadway in 1939, with Monty Woolley triumphing as the acid-tongued Sheridan Whiteside—a dipped-in-acid lampoon of critic Alexander Woollcott. Laird was one of the candidates for the plum role in the film version, along with Cary Grant, John Barrymore, Charles Laughton, Fredric March and Woolley, who, despite his success in the play, seemed the dark horse, due to his rather open homosexuality.[12] For Laird to have been in the running with those established stars for such a juicy part, when he himself had only one released film at this time to his credit, was an honor in itself.

"I understand that Laird Cregar made a test that was sensational," wrote Ken Morgan in his "Hollywood Keyhole" column, "but that lack of drawing power in his name is a disadvantage when the final decision is being made."[13] Warner producer Hal Wallis later claimed that Laird's test was "overblown and extravagant,"[14] and Woolley eventually won the screen role.

At any rate, despite the lost chances, Laird was having a hell of a great time in the spring of 1941.

10

The Saint Bernard

"Laird Cregar was always like a big St. Bernard, who couldn't understand why you didn't want him in your lap."[1]—DeWitt Bodeen

He was Hollywood's Oscar Wilde, with touches of St. Bernard and famed female impersonator Julian Eltinge.

"Sammy" Cregar had arrived. Riotously. He wrote songs with ribald lyrics, and sang them ... loudly. Everyone wanted him at their parties. He played "Indications," a more athletic form of Charades, so wildly and enthusiastically that he had virtually no competition, and was so soaked after a round that he brought a change of clothes when he played. He performed outlandish impressions. And he consistently made the columns and the parties.

Friday, April 18, 1941: Louella Parsons reported that Laird had been at the Mocambo on two different nights and with two different redheads: Gloria Hawkins and Cathy Lewis.

Then, a little over a week later and within a marathon 48 hours, Laird made an indelible impression on the movie colony:

Saturday night, April 26: The 20th Century–Fox Studio Club hosted its second annual Spring Fiesta at the Biltmore Bowl.[2] Milton Berle was emcee, Carmen Miranda and Glenn Miller's Band were the star acts, Abbott and Costello, Virginia O'Brien, the Nicholas Brothers, the Merry Macs, Ella Logan and Jose Pablo and his Rumba Band were also on hand, and studio decorator Thomas Little spectacularly filled the Bowl with flowers. Among those in attendance: Darryl Zanuck and his wife Virginia, Tyrone Power and wife Annabella, Betty Grable and date George Raft, Jack Benny, George Burns, Ilona Massey, Cesar Romero, Carole Landis, Don Ameche and more than 1,100 "merry makers."[3]

None suspected the spectacle they'd behold as the night's finale: Berle and Laird dancing a wicked rumba in full drag *à la* Miranda.[4] Their satirical song (with lyrics by Mack Gordon) took aim at the studio's bosses. The crowd roared at the dueling Mirandas, a hilarious burlesque that was, as the *Hollywood Citizen-News* reported, "something to be remembered, even in Hollywood, land of superlatives."[5]

Sunday, April 27: Milton Berle, less than 24 hours after the previous night's frolic, hosted the Mack Sennett Bathing Party at the Beverly Hills Hotel Sand and Pool Club.[6] This time, Laird showed up among the 400 guests as a "Bathing Beauty"—wearing a blonde woman's wig and old-time red-and white-striped bathing suit. He joined Berle,

Joan Davis and Billy Gilbert, singing "Down By the Old Mill Stream." He jumped off a diving board, creating a splash worthy of a whale. The big show, however, was the custard pie fight. Reportedly, Judy Garland received the first pie in the face, and then joined "throwers" Linda Darnell, Carole Landis, Ann Miller, Joan Davis, Bonita Granville and Patti McCarty. The "receivers": Errol Flynn, Buster Keaton, Billy Gilbert, Parkyakarkus, Milton Berle and Laird. Considering Laird's continuing crush on Linda Darnell, one hopes she managed to hit Laird with a pie.

Personally judging the contest was Mack Sennett himself. It all climaxed with the Keystone Cops trying to break up the pie fight and receiving, according to the *Hollywood Citizen-News*, a "furious bombardment themselves."[7] The party, which also included tennis, clowns and comedy diving, was, all agreed, "riotous."[8]

Laird Cregar was a Hollywood madman ... in a happy, healthy way. Of course, the drag sideshows sparked the already rampant rumors about his sexual predilection. Zanuck and the Fox forces urged the columnists to dispel such chatter. Laird's pal Henry Brandon remembered:

> Sammy had a little boyfriend who was a dancer in a musical in Hollywood. One night, the boyfriend was sick, so Sammy went on for him, and he was in the chorus—and he was a star at

Laird as a "Bathing Beauty" with friend at the Mack Sennett Beach Party, April 1941.

the time! I happened to be in the theater that night, and I couldn't believe my eyes! And he was incredibly graceful, floating like a balloon; still, it was incongruous to see this great fat man among those little chorus boys.

Well, Zanuck found out about it, and put his foot down with a *bang!*[9]

And this brings us to a significant point: By this time, Laird reportedly had a male lover.

It's indicative of the early 1940s that information on this mysterious man survives only in fragmentary shreds. Brandon referred to "Sammy's little boyfriend" as "a dancer," either not remembering his name, or not wanting to provide it.

Oscar Wilde's description of homosexuality as "the love that dare not speak its name" seems to apply to this "boyfriend" whose name, in retrospect, no one dared to speak, nor, based on later developments, wanted to.

Laird walked the tightrope: In a sense, his in-drag camp seemed to convey an out-of-the-closet mischief that society would accept ... the act of a clown. On the other hand, he knew the necessity of playing the game, and the studio refereed this sensitive situation.

For example, on May 26, columnist John Truesdell reported that Laird was ardently wooing LaVerne Andrews of the Andrews Sisters. LaVerne was the oldest of the trio, always stage left in the lineup and considered by many the least attractive. The columnist described Laird as "310 pounds of quivering romance."[10]

"Quivering," perhaps, but it probably wasn't due to LaVerne.

May 28: *Blood and Sand*, all 125 minutes and $1,115,200 of it, opened in Los Angeles at Grauman's Chinese Theatre and Loew's State Theatre, complete with a lushly dramatic score by Alfred Newman, a giant advertising campaign and even a supporting feature, *The Cowboy and the Blonde* (George Montgomery and Mary Beth Hughes). Harrison Carroll called *Blood and Sand* "a spectacular moving picture production.... Darryl Zanuck obviously has spared no expense to make this film his studio's most lavish offering of the year."[11]

As for Laird, Carroll found him "clever," while Carl Combs of the *Hollywood Citizen-News* wrote that he was "in good form" as "the effete bullring critic."[12] In an era when the word "homosexual" was rarely printed in a newspaper, few critics zeroed in on the unique aspect of his portrayal of Curro, although the performance made him more notorious in Hollywood circles.

Blood and Sand earned giant worldwide rentals of $2.7 million, tallied a hefty profit of $662,500, and would win a Best Color Cinematography Academy Award for Ernest Palmer and Ray Rennahan. It became Laird's personal favorite of all his films, and advanced his close friendship with Tyrone Power, who said of Laird: "His weight is unimportant, for his dignity of bearing, his courtly manner and air of breeding give him the shape and semblance of elegance. To which his amazingly adult mind adds its charm. He is a highly civilized human being, Laird, with a warm and generous heart."[13]

It was an eloquent testimonial, but subject to its own slicing and dicing by the Hollywood gossips. Power himself, despite his marriage to Annabella, was rumored to be bisexual.[14]

Meanwhile, Laird was at work on a new picture. On Monday, May 12, Fox began

Trade advertisement for *Charley's Aunt.*

shooting *Charley's Aunt*, with radio superstar Jack Benny. Zanuck had high hopes for the Brandon Thomas comedy about Babbs Babberly, an Oxford student who masquerades in drag as his college pal's wealthy aunt from Brazil ("where the nuts come from"). The play had premiered in New York in 1893, and had enjoyed a 1940 hit Broadway revival, starring Jose Ferrer.

Charley's Aunt was the type of racy, slightly risqué entertainment Fox hoped would help turn the tide after the studio had lost a half-million dollars in fiscal 1940.[15] (*Brigham Young* itself had a loss of $582,900.) Directing was the plump and raucous Archie Mayo, formerly of Warner Bros., where his résumé included directing John Barrymore in *Svengali* (1931) and Leslie Howard, Bette Davis and Humphrey Bogart in *The Petrified Forest* (1936).

Laird's role: Sir Francis Chesney, of the British Army in India, a penniless aristocrat and the father of Jack (James Ellison), one of Babbs' roommates. Publicity ran rampant that Laird, at age 24, was playing the father of Ellison, who was 28. In fact, Laird was 27 and Ellison was 31, but it was still a nice thespic trick for Laird, who played his "mature" part in a silver mane and gray mustache.

Kay Francis, to whom Laird had once sold linens in Gimbels, played the "real" Charley's aunt, Donna Lucia; Richard Haydn was Charley; Anne Baxter and Arleen

Edmund Gwenn (left) and Laird (right) vie for the affections of Jack Benny in *Charley's Aunt*.

Whelan were comically coy as Amy and Kitty, the ingénues; and sharing the screen with Laird were two ghosts of Christmas Past and Future: 53-year-old Reginald Owen (Scrooge in MGM's 1938 *A Christmas Carol*) as Oxford's doddering Mr. Redcliffe, and 63-year-old Edmund Gwenn (destined to win an Oscar as Kris Kringle in Fox's 1947 *Miracle on 34th Street*) as Spettigue, who pursues Benny (who's disguised in old lady dress and wig).

It's amazing to watch Laird, young enough to be the son of Gwenn, Owen *and* the 47-year-old Benny, and easily holding his own with all three of them. One of the best (and most risqué) laughs comes when Laird's Sir Francis, who's made up his mind to propose to the wealthy aunt to save his family's finances, gets his first good look at Donna Lucia. He stands there, holding his cane at an erect, jaunty angle. After Benny lowers his fan from his face, Laird's face crumbles ... and his cane drops in his hand so it almost disappears! Also priceless is Laird's vocal response: "I thought you said she was only 90," he says *sotto voce* to Ellison.

In a scene in the garden, Laird's Sir Francis proposes to Benny's Donna Lucia. Sir Francis has brought a bottle of whiskey to bolster his courage, Laird and Benny battle for the bottle, the whiskey spills, Benny licks the whiskey off the table, and Laird masterfully carries on, proposing to his "flowerette": "Now that I've found this little flowerette, I want it to be with me always. I want it to walk by my side. To see the Taj Mahal.

8659 Holloway Plaza Drive, West Hollywood. This house was Laird's home after he achieved movie fame.

To be kissed by the tropical moon.... I want no more words. Donna Lucia ... will you be my little flowerette? Will you be my wife?"

To vie for attention with Jack Benny, while the comedy star lapped up whiskey off a table, was no small achievement. Laird carried it off with high style.

During *Charley's Aunt*, Laird became ill. In June, he entered Good Samaritan Hospital and had his appendix removed. In late June, Jack Benny, Archie Mayo and a Fox technical crew came to Good Samaritan to record dialogue for *Charley's Aunt*, as Laird was indefinitely stricken.[16] He left the hospital, but on July 9, Louella Parsons reported that Laird was hospitalized for a second operation, having returned to work too quickly. Harrison Carroll later wrote: "Did you know that the Cregar appendectomy scar is the darndest in Hollywood? 14 inches long. Surgeons had to cut over a parabola of fat."[17]

Meanwhile, Helen Hayes wanted Laird to co-star with her in Maxwell Anderson's new play, *Candle in the Wind*,[18] which would open on Broadway on October 22, 1941. Fox said no. Louis Borell got the part.

As Laird launched at Fox, he set up quarters at 8659 Holloway Plaza Drive in West Hollywood, south of the Sunset Strip, close to where Santa Monica Boulevard runs into Sunset Boulevard.[19] The area was a colony of handsome bungalows, built in 1937 and 1938, and Laird would walk up the hill to the Strip and such night clubs as the Trocadero, the Mocambo, Ciro's and the Club Gala, amazing everyone with his robust dancing. A short way east on Santa Monica Boulevard was Barney's Beanery, one of Laird's favorite hangouts.

*   *   *

In 2017, a Laird Cregar fan, wanting to make a pilgrimage to his old West Hollywood environs, could parlay the visit into a "ghost tour," with various neighboring sites related to tragic personalities and scandal. Barney's Beanery, 8447 Santa Monica Boulevard, still exists, one of a chain of "gastropubs" of the same name. Even before Laird's time, Barney's Beanery had been a favorite dining spot for Clara Bow, John Barrymore and Jean Harlow; long after his death, it won notoriety as the locale where Jim Morrison allegedly pissed on the bar, and where Janis Joplin had drinks the night before her fatal overdose. The original Barney's Beanery had a reputedly anti-gay manager, who posted a sign above the bar, "FAGOTS [sic]—STAY OUT." Sources differ as to whether the sign was on display in Laird's day.[20]

Perhaps of more fascination for some, are the deaths that took place in this area. Ken Schessler's excellent source book This Is Hollywood *relates a number of the more sensational.*

- *8563 Holloway Drive: Sal Mineo was knifed to death in his apartment's parking lot in 1976.*
- *1221 N. King's Road: Jack Cassidy burned to death in his apartment in 1977.*
- *1227½ N. Sweetzer: actress Karen Kupcinet was found naked and strangled in her apartment in 1963.*
- *8495 Fountain Avenue: Dorothy Dandridge died in her apartment of a drug overdose in 1965.*

- *8787 Shoreham Drive: Art Linkletter's daughter Diane, plagued by drugs, jumped to her death from her sixth floor apartment in 1969.*[21]

As for Laird's old house: 8659 Holloway Plaza Drive is now the quarters of Fuse Lighting.

*   *   *

Laird was on the rise. All he needed was a role that would fully unleash his theatricality and imagination. In his next film, he found it: Ed Cornell, the insane detective of *I Wake Up Screaming*.

11

I Wake Up Screaming
with Laird Cregar

I'll follow you into your grave! I'll write my name on your tombstone!
—Laird Cregar as Ed Cornell, *I Wake Up Screaming*

In 1940s Hollywood, the genre of *noir* fully blossomed, like a fragrant, man-eating plant. Film scholars love debating what *noir* is or isn't, but basically, like pornography, you know it when you see it ... you know it when you *sense* it.

The Maltese Falcon, directed at Warner Bros. in 1941 by John Huston, is a great (*the* greatest?) *noir*: Bogart's amoral Sam Spade; Mary Astor's sighing *femme fatale* Brigid O'Shaughnessy; Peter Lorre's gardenia-scented Joel Cairo; and, of course, Sydney Greenstreet's chortling "Fat Man." One of Greenstreet's best moments: giving his "gunsel," the teary-eyed Elisha Cook, Jr., a subtle but sassy pat on his ass.

In top-shelf *noirs*, there's a talisman, a fetish object. *The Maltese Falcon* had the Falcon itself: 12 inches tall, five inches wide, and weighing 45 pounds. In November 2013, it went up for auction in the Bonhams–Turner Classic Movies "What Dreams Are Made Of" auction. The winning bid: $4,085,000 (including a buyer's premium of $585,000).[1]

One fancifully wonders: What other fetish paraphernalia might go on the block at a fantasy auction for *noir* disciples? Barbara Stanwyck's blonde wig and ankle bracelet, which adorned her in Paramount's *Double Indemnity*? Clifton Webb's shotgun, with which he blasted off a woman's face in 20th Century–Fox's *Laura*? Tom Neal's phone cord, with which he strangled Ann Savage in PRC's *Detour*?

On July 21, 1941, three days after Warner Bros. completed *The Maltese Falcon*, Fox began shooting a *noir,* perfumed with perversion. The sensually teasing title: *I Wake Up Screaming*. It featured *noir*'s King Kink: Laird Cregar as Ed Cornell, a psycho detective who keeps his apartment a tabernacle to Vicky, a murdered blonde glamour girl. Playing the blonde was Carole Landis, a later Hollywood suicide, and her large, lush portrait hangs iconically on Cornell's wall, like a gothic crucifix above a profane altar.

The portrait of the smiling-from-the-grave Landis might be *noir*'s creepiest prop. Laird's Cornell is definitely *noir's* creepiest performance.

* * *

"Scene 273: Some political censor boards may delete the underlined word
in Cornell's speech, 'Did you ever read *The Sex Life of the Butterfly...?*'"
—Production Code Administration letter to 20th Century–Fox
regarding *I Wake Up Screaming*, July 24, 1941

Darryl Zanuck, tackling Steve Fisher's pulp novel *I Wake Up Screaming*, blueprinted the film as it was as a book—a racy sex melodrama. Perhaps thinking sex melodrama was too close to home in Hollywood, Zanuck ordered scenarist Dwight Taylor to change the setting from the film capital to New York City. There was also a title change: *Hot Spot*. The "hot spot" in such magazines as *Black Mask* (which often published Fisher's stories) meant a suspect was heading for execution; however, the name clearly had *double entendre* sexual connotation. It would remain the film's working title into its previews; *I Wake Up Screaming* would be an eleventh-hour switch.

Fisher had provided this description of Ed Cornell in the novel, as related by the story's first-person narrator, who suffers under the detective's sadistic interrogation:

> He was about thirty. He had red hair and thin white skin and red eyebrows and blue eyes. He looked sick. He looked like a corpse. His clothes didn't fit him. He wore a derby. Nobody in California wore a derby but Ed Cornell wore one. He was a misfit. But the rest of them thought he was smart. He was frail, gray-faced and bitter. He was possessed with a macabre humor. His voice was nasal. You'd think he was crying. He might have had T.B. He looked like he couldn't stand up in a wind. He was thin and his face was gaunt. He kept lighting cigarettes and flicking the lit matches in my face.[2]

The description was an inside joke: It lampooned Cornell Woolrich,[3] the famed and prolific crime writer, whose works later inspired such films as Hitchcock's *Rear Window* (1954) and Truffaut's *The Bride Wore Black* (1968). Fisher knew Woolrich, who was a homosexual (his 1930 Hollywood marriage to Violet Virginia Blackton lasted three months and was annulled), and lived with his mother at the Hotel Marseilles in New York. Woolrich's response to this horrific homage is unknown.

Based on the "gaunt" description and the line, "He looked like a corpse," Cornell seemed a fine role for Laird's Fox "rival" John Carradine. It would have been fun to hear what the skeletal actor might have done with a nasal "You'd think he was crying" delivery. However, Zanuck decided to go for bulk with Cornell—indeed, he'd originally cast Charles Laughton.[4] Laughton's pre–Code antics as Nero in *The Sign of the Cross* and Dr. Moreau in *Island of Lost Souls* (both for Paramount in 1932) made him a natural for the part, and his triumph in RKO's *The Hunchback of Note Dame* (1939) was fresh in moviegoers' minds.

Alice Faye initially landed the change-of-pace role as Jill, the heroine and sister of the slain Vicky. However, Zanuck replaced Faye with Betty Grable, new queen of the Fox lot, and Hollywood's "Girl with the Million Dollar Legs." The film would also showcase Carole Landis, whose soubriquets eventually included "The 'Ping' Girl," "The Blonde Bomber" and "The Chest," as Vicky, the slain beauty. The two blondes had already played sisters in Fox's big Technicolor musical of the summer, *Moon Over Miami*.

The male lead: Victor Mature, Laird's Pasadena Playhouse acquaintance, back in Hollywood after a run in Broadway's *Lady in the Dark* with Gertrude Lawrence. The

"Hunk of Man," as his publicity proclaimed him, played *I Wake Up Screaming*'s Frankie Christopher, hotshot Manhattan promoter who touts Landis from a waitress to a celebrity glamour girl. There was promotion a-plenty in starring Mature and Landis: They'd cavorted together in loincloths, battling dinosaurs in Hal Roach's *One Million B.C.* (1940). Why Laughton left *I Wake Up Screaming* isn't clear; perhaps he feared Zanuck would be all too eager to exalt Grable, Mature and Landis, and indeed, all three would "oomph" under H. Bruce "Lucky" Humberstone's super-slick direction. After Laughton's departure, Laird got the part.

Laird Cregar as Ed Cornell in *I Wake Up Screaming.*

Aware of the role's potential, Laird prepared properly: He joined real cops on patrol and in a station house. At one point, during a grilling interrogation, the police suddenly vacated the room, leaving Laird with the suspect, who promptly pulled a gun on him—at which time, the police came back into the room, roaring with laughter. The "suspect" was a fellow cop.[5]

At any rate, Laird's major preparation came from his richly macabre imagination. Indeed, after *I Wake Up Screaming*, his career, and life, would never be the same.

* * *

> When I get all my evidence together, I'm gonna have you tied up like a pig
> in a slaughterhouse!—Laird Cregar to Victor Mature, *I Wake Up Screaming*

Monday, July 21, 1941: *I Wake Up Screaming* began shooting under the title of *Hot Spot*. Betty Grable would wear a bathing suit and Carole Landis a negligee, both items of attire screened and passed by the Production Code Administration.

And a new type of screen villain was amok at 20th Century–Fox.

Yes, beware of Laird's Ed Cornell ... a psycho detective with dreamy eyes, a sick smile and a voice like a lovesick whale, aptly described by *noir* expert Eddie Muller as "300 pounds of sexual perversion."[6] Bristling with an insane lust for the dead Landis, Laird's Cornell took demonic possession of the melodrama, stirring up the temperaments of the film's three official stars. As Sidney Skolsky would report in the *Hollywood Citizen-News*:

> The set of *Hot Spot* is aptly named, with Betty Grable and Carole Landis feuding, Laird Cregar acting almost as much as he does in the commissary, and Victor Mature being Victor Mature.
> Just what Betty is angry with Carole about and vice versa is not known, but the girls do not speak to each other ... it might even end in a nice hair-pulling match, with a cameraman handy.

Cregar has the role of his film career ... and he should wrap up the picture and walk away with it. He is a good actor, although I do wish he wouldn't act so furiously when the camera isn't looking.

Mature, that "hunk of man," has returned to Hollywood a star. But Mature isn't satisfied.... In fact, he is receiving the same salary, $250 a week that he got before he went to Broadway and became a matinee idol.

"I could," said Mature, "get a couple a thousand dollars a week just to stroll through a department store and attract the girls who would rush to get my autograph."[7]

To protect his stars, Zanuck originally filmed a scene in which department store clerk Grable sang the song "Daddy." It clearly didn't belong, ended up on the cutting room floor, and retakes changed Jill's job from singing clerk to stenographer. Also, there was a pool scene (Frankie takes Jill to the Lido Plunge for a late night swim, shot at L.A.'s Venice Plunge), so that Grable could show her legs and Mature flaunt his physique. This stayed in the release print, although Grable felt it patronizing: "I loathed that scene!" she later said.[8]

The star trio had reason for jitters: Laird, as Sidney Skolsky wrote, was truly snaring *I Wake Up Screaming*. Apparently, Mature came to terms with Laird's stealing the show, saying, "He has the tread of a great cat."[9] The two blondes were less forthcoming: Laird was upstaging Betty Grable's "Million Dollar Legs" and Carole Landis's "Ping." As Hedda Hopper would write, "Laird Cregar's disgustingly evil performance is so good in *Hot Spot* that he dims the light of Betty Grable and Carole Landis, and those blondes are mighty hard to dim."[10]

*   *   *

You're a pretty cocky fella, Frankie. You've had your own way a long time.
First with Vicky Lynn, and now with her sister!
—Laird Cregar to Victor Mature, I Wake Up Screaming

In a startling introduction, Cornell's just a shadow, almost Oz-like, looming behind the glare of the light as the cops interrogate Mature. We first actually see him in *noir*-ish flashback, leering wolfishly at waitress Landis one night through a restaurant window. The film returns to the present, and Grable, having described that voyeur at the window, demands to see the head detective. Into the light comes Laird's Cornell ... the Big Bad Wolf that Grable and the audience had seen at the restaurant. He enters through the chain-fenced wall of the interrogation sweatbox, like an overheated animal emerging from a cage. "All right, all right," he grins at Grable, who looks at him aghast. "I'm a Peeping Tom!"

Thereafter, Laird haunts *I Wake Up Screaming*, like Javert in a pulp rip-off of *Les Misérables*. The macabre cop ghoulishly pops up everywhere, notably in Mature's bedroom, where he sits in the middle of the night, watching his nemesis sleep. The accouterments are perfect: a screen painting of a black leopard looms above him; a framed picture of Carole Landis smiles beside him; and a flashing hotel sign outside the window nightmarishly lights him. "First time I ever had a bad dream with my eyes open," says Mature.

Later in the film, Laird asks Mature for a ride uptown, and spends the ride teasingly tying a shoestring noose around his finger:

LAIRD: I could arrest you today ... but you might get some smart mouthpiece and get off with life instead of the chair. I won't be satisfied until I'm sure it's the chair!

"It sticks in their throats—especially when they're hung!" Laird ties a string noose to taunt Victor Mature in *I Wake Up Screaming*.

MATURE: You're a gay dog, Cornell. You make me feel as if I'm driving a hearse.

LAIRD: Oh, I know your type—I've seen hundreds of them. I don't scare you enough to make you commit suicide, but I worry you just the same. And when the day comes, they all act different. Some scream, a few faint, some light a cigarette and try a wisecrack. But it sticks in their throats ... especially when they're hung!

For 1941, the sex content of *I Wake Up Screaming* is surprising. Elisha Cook, Jr., as Harry Williams, the desk clerk at the apartment house where the Lynn sisters lived, takes it upon himself to pack the dead Vicky's possessions. He tells Jill he wanted to help, but the immediate impression (based on Grable's shocked expression, and the fact that Cook is playing the part) is that the clerk wanted to get his hands on Vicky's lingerie. When Mature and Grable hide from the police, they make out in an all-night theater, showing what's inferred to be an adult film (*Flames of Passion*).

Laird dominates all. And when Cornell mentions he's read *The Sex Life of a Butterfly* (yes, the word *Sex* made it into the film, despite censor worry), it's no big surprise; it was probably the only tome he could find one night while prowling a library, seeking a book with *Sex* in the title.

I Wake Up Screaming crackles. This is the same haunted New York City of misfits and perverts that Val Lewton would present in his RKO horror *noir Cat People* (1942), where a panther screams at night in the Central Park Zoo, "like a woman." Laird's Ed Cornell stalks the same shadowy Manhattan menagerie in his big flat feet as Simone

Simon's "Cat Woman" does in her high heels. A memorable close-up of Mature, prophetic of *Cat People*, captures him in a startling lighting effect that makes it appear he's in a cage. That's where Cornell wants him ... but the trap, of course, will boomerang. Cornell belongs in a cage ... he ends up in the cage.

And what a cage.

When the real murderer is revealed to be Elisha Cook's Harry, and Mature learns that Laird knew this all the time, Mature vengefully goes to his persecutor's apartment. He finds it a shrine to the murdered Landis, filled with her glamour glossies. As Mature hides, Laird enters gingerly with fresh flowers to place under her huge portrait. Mature reveals himself, Laird hysterically spins around with what must have been his "trapped rat" face as a boy, and begins a soliloquy: how Landis' beauty awed him while she was still a waitress; how he timidly followed her home from the restaurant at night, trying to get up the nerve to talk to her; how he finally got his chance on New Year's Eve when two louts got fresh, and he protected her. When the blonde seemed "really grateful," his thoughts soon shot to matrimony, and the detective created this sick sacristy of an apartment. "I intended," says Laird, with a tender, awful smile, "to surprise her...."

But Mature's plans took her away from him, and Cornell—transformed by Laird's artistry from a monstrous ogre to a lovelorn lost soul—kills himself. Suicide, of course, was a Breen Office no-no, and the Production Code Administration had written to Fox:

Ouch! Betty Grable has just hit Laird, saving Victor Mature from his clutches in *I Wake Up Screaming*.

In regard to the suicide of Cornell ... it has been the policy of the Production Code Administration to advise against suicides, as being bad theater and usually extremely distasteful to audiences. Realizing that you are playing this finish for some sort of suspense, we still wish to suggest to you that it would be better to leave the audience thinking that Cornell might have died of a heart attack, rather than definitely pointing up that he had taken poison.[11]

Zanuck defied Joseph Breen on this point. Laird's Cornell not only dies of self-poisoning, but does so looking at a framed portrait of Landis on his desk. The Production Code let it slide. Perhaps they agreed, off the record, that suicide, the gravest of mortal sins, was the only demise worthy of such an epic creep as Ed Cornell.

I Wake Up Screaming uses two music themes repeatedly: Alfred Newman's brassy "Street Scene" and Harold Arlen's "Over the Rainbow," from MGM's *The Wizard of Oz*. The latter, in a twisted, winsome way, suits Cregar's Cornell; one can imagine him playing Judy Garland's "Over the Rainbow" all night long as he sits alone in his morbid temple of an apartment ... a vestal virgin, paying solitary homage to the dead Vicky Lynn.

Curiously, in describing his lovelorn Ed Cornell, Laird used the expression "hag-ridden,"[12] an archaic adjective, defined as "tormented, as by a witch." Indeed, in *I Wake Up Screaming*, Cornell, for all his creepiness, is more touching than Landis' vapid, witchy Vicky, who's enchanted and possessed him. In a portrayal decades ahead of its time in Hollywood, Laird's Cornell is a bottom feeder, a parasite on the underbelly of sexual predators, a sick cop, a lonely, solitary sinner ... but he's also, really and truly, *I Wake Up Screaming*'s most sympathetic soul.

Via one haunting, unforgettably vile performance, Laird Cregar was finding his own *noir* niche: Hollywood's hag-ridden patron saint of perverts.

Meanwhile, in his personal life, he began a heterosexual romance. The lady's name was Peggy Stack, and she was the blonde, beautiful, 25-year-old daughter of playwright Guy Bolton and soprano Marguerite Namara.[13] While one might suspect that Peggy was Laird's "beard," their relationship would last, off and on, for the next several years, and even approach marriage.

July 31: While *I Wake Up Screaming* was in production, Peggy was Laird's date at the gala premiere of *Charley's Aunt* at Grauman's Chinese Theatre. "*Charley* Preview Draws Swankiest Crowd in Years," headlined *Variety* the next morning. Among the other celebrities attending from the film were Jack Benny, Kay Francis, James Ellison, Arleen Whelan and Richard Haydn. Also present: Darryl Zanuck and his wife Virginia, Robert Taylor and Barbara Stanwyck, George Burns and Gracie Allen, Bob Hope and his wife Dolores, Ronald Reagan and wife Jane Wyman, Carmen Miranda, Edgar Bergen, Rosalind Russell and Mary Livingstone (Mrs. Jack Benny). There were an estimated 7,500 people in the theater, the forecourt, the bleachers, the street and on rooftops, with 125 police to keep order. Disaster nearly struck when 30 teenagers climbed the electric signboard, risking "grave danger of electrocution"; police "eased" them down from their perch. As James Francis Crow wrote in the *Hollywood Citizen-News*: "[A] more serious mishap was John Carradine's arrival late. The lobby was empty and the doors were closed, and he didn't have his cape, or even his cane. It was probably the only bad entrance that Carradine ever made."[14]

The *Citizen-News* also reported that the film drew "roars of laughter," claimed

Benny was "priceless," and wrote, "Highly effective as the deluded suitors are Laird Cregar and Edmund Gwenn."

Charley's Aunt had a production tab of $889,300, would earn worldwide rentals of $2.27 million, and tally a fat profit of $722,800.

I Wake Up Screaming continued shooting, wrapping up August 26, 1941. In his eagerness to play Cornell, Laird, following two surgeries, had returned to work too early. His stomach muscles had mended improperly[15] and the result was a ventral hernia, which can cause periodic bowel blockage, nausea and vomiting. It was the beginning of over three years of severe stomach trouble that would eventually lead to tragic consequences.

Meanwhile, Laird was enjoying a star-making role, a $750 weekly salary and a pretty girlfriend whom he took out jitterbugging. What he wanted most, however, after his own erratic upbringing, was a family life. He'd thought often of his late brother William's daughter Betsey, then seven years old, and his dream that, had life been different, she might have been his own daughter.

In the summer of '41, while playing his scenes in *I Wake Up Screaming*—ogling Carole Landis, and committing suicide—Laird, who turned 28 during the film's shooting, came home each night to an approximation of that dream come true:

He'd sent for Betsey, and she was living at his home.

PART III

Betsey

"The only thing my Uncle Sam wanted was our love."
—Elizabeth Cregar Hayman, Laird Cregar's niece

12

Seven Years Old in Hollywood

"My 'Uncle Sam' was just magnificent!"[1]—Elizabeth Cregar Hayman, 2012

Betsey Cregar had seen her "Uncle Sam" now and then in Philadelphia, during his years of struggle, and he'd always showered her with gifts and affection. Now, having already set up his mother and Aunt Nean in Los Angeles, Laird sent for Betsey. "Send her out to me, just for a couple months, just for the summer," he said to Marie, Betsey's mom. Marie had remarried and the family was struggling, so she gave her blessing. As Betsey remembered the trip west:

> My train trip with my grandmother was phenomenal. She had come to visit her other sons, she and my Aunt Eugenia ... "Nean," we used to call her. My grandmother was about six feet tall, and as she got older, she got very heavy. She was always a great lady, and even after she'd lost her husband and had been left with six boys to raise, she'd kept her graciousness—she never lost that. She always had that attitude ... like she was who she was!
>
> Now, my Aunt Eugenia was totally opposite. Aunt Nean was 5'7" or 5'8" and she was skinny as a rail. To look at them together, it was hysterical ... this great huge woman, and this slim woman beside her! Nean was really the caretaker—she took care of the boys, she took care of my grandmother, she cooked, she cleaned, and she did everything, both in Philadelphia and later in California.
>
> So my grandmother and Aunt Nean took me on the train. I had never gone that far on a train—the most I think I'd ever ridden was a trolley car [laughs]! I couldn't believe that you slept on the train, and got fed on the train. So it was quite a wonderful adventure.

As Betsey vividly remembered, Laird was at the station in Los Angeles to greet the train, and had a big surprise awaiting her:

> Oh! I got off the train, and Uncle Sam was there. He was 6'3", and he was 300 pounds, and he was absolutely *huge*—I had to look straight up at him! He picked me up, and *threw* me up in the air, and I felt like I was *flying* in the air! He was awe-striking for me, he was just magnificent, and hugged me and took me home!
>
> So he was there to greet us ... and I couldn't believe what he did. It was afternoon when we arrived in California, and I was really tired. I can remember how tired I was, but [laughs], Uncle Sam said, "Betsey, you can't go to bed yet."
> "Well, I'm so tired!"
> "You can't go to bed!" he kept saying.
> Well, he had a dinner party that night ... for this little seven-year-old girl! He invited Tom Neal, neighbors ... he wanted to introduce me to all these people. It was incredibly nice, but as a little kid [laughs], I do remember being just super-tired!

As Betsey recalled, her life was suddenly "a fairy tale": "Anything I wanted, I could get. Absolutely anything." Laird was eager to show her off at Fox, and also wanted to make an impression on her as to the work he did:

100

Betsey Cregar with her Uncle Sam.

The first time I saw him in costume, my grandmother said, "We're going to meet your Uncle Sam for lunch over at the studio." So we go, and I look up, and here comes this giant man in a suede jacket with fringe, and he had a beard and a fur hat, and high boots—he'd dressed up in his *Hudson's Bay* costume and makeup [laughs]! He came strolling over to the table, he started to reach for me, I backed up.... I was scared to death!

"It's me!" he said.

So that was my introduction to studio life and how it worked, and he took me to the studio so many times.

As Betsey laughingly recalled, her Uncle Sam enjoyed a favorite joke on unsuspecting guests:

If we were having dinner and there were guests there who didn't know his sense of humor, or were just acquaintances, Uncle Sam had what looked like a giant soup spoon. The bowl of the spoon was as big as your hand, and the stem of the spoon was at least a foot and a half long. Because he was a big man, everyone knew he had an appetite. Well, he'd sit everyone down together, and they would serve soup, and he would take this spoon, and start eating [laughs]! And everybody at the table was just awestruck! Then, of course, he'd put it down and eat with a normal spoon. He had a good sense of humor!

Naturally, Betsey began mixing with the celebrities, and found them all very nice:

Tyrone Power? I was at his home. He and his wife, Annabella, were lovely people, and they had a beautiful swimming pool—which was all that mattered to me [laughs]! Cesar Romero was a very sweet man—he took me by the hand at the studio and showed me the set lights, and how they worked. Linda Darnell was very nice. Even though I was only seven, I used to watch the way my Uncle Sam looked at her, and thought, "Hmmmm!"

As for Uncle Sam and his own fame, people always asked for his autograph, and he was a perfect gentleman. An absolute gentleman. If someone stopped him and asked, "Can I have your autograph?" he'd say, "Of course." He always had time, which I thought was nice.

And so the fairy tale life went on—not for a single summer, as originally planned, but for over a year. More of Betsey's memories follow later in the book, and her time with her Uncle Sam was enchanting, and unforgettable: "He was always child-like at heart ... he really was. A great guy. As far as taking over the role that my father left behind, he was just wonderful. I felt so loved, and so wanted."

So Laird came home from a day on *I Wake Up Screaming* to a family he loved pampering. He gave joyously.

13

The Man Who Shouldn't Have Come to Dinner

I may vomit!—Laird Cregar's opening line as Sheridan Whiteside
in *The Man Who Came to Dinner*

Laird was certainly eager to return to the stage, and knew what part he wanted to play. Ever since Warners had bypassed him for the title role in *The Man Who Came to Dinner*, Laird was determined to show just how brilliant he could be as Sheridan Whiteside.

After wrapping up *I Wake Up Screaming*, Laird arranged to star at the El Capitan, home of his *Oscar Wilde* triumph, in *The Man Who Came to Dinner*. He decided he'd make himself up to resemble Alexander Woollcott, the inspiration for Whiteside, wearing glasses and a mustache.

Monday, September 8, 1941: Rehearsals began. His leading ladies were Rose Hobart, who'd played Muriel, the "good girl" of 1931's *Dr. Jekyll and Mr. Hyde*, and would play Maggie, Whiteside's secretary; and blonde Doris Nolan, remembered as Katharine Hepburn's lah-de-dah sister in 1938's *Holiday*, who'd portray vainglorious actress Lorraine Sheldon. Also in the cast were two young actors destined for TV success: Hugh Beaumont (Ward Cleaver of *Leave It to Beaver*) as the male ingénue and Sid Melton (Charley Halper of *Make Room for Daddy*) as the Harpo Marx–inspired "Banjo." Also of note in the cast, professionally and personally, was Renie Riano, 42-year-old character actress,[1] who played Miss Preen, Whiteside's long-suffering nurse, and whom he describes as having "the touch of a sex-starved cobra."

Also September 8: Sidney Skolsky wrote in his column that Laird was still dating Peggy Stack.

Friday, September 12: RKO's *Joan of Paris* began shooting. Michele Morgan starred in the title role as a self-sacrificing French barmaid, devoted to Joan of Arc; her heroism saves Paul Henreid and his RAF crew. Both Morgan and Henreid were making their U.S. film debuts. Laird, on loan from Fox, played Herr Funk, the Gestapo chieftain who pursues them.

Monday, September 15: Harrison Carroll reported that Laird and Renie Riano (14 years his senior) were together at a night spot called Tin Pan Alley.

Tuesday, September 16: Louella Parsons described Renie as "the big boy's new big moment"; also on the 16th, *Variety*'s Alta Durant, in her "Gab" column, wrote that Laird had "guested Renie Riano at Leone's last eve...."

Friday, September 19: Opening night of *The Man Who Came to Dinner* at the El Capitan. Perhaps Renie Riano had sensed Laird was more devoted to Peggy Stack; maybe she sensed he was using both her and Peggy as "beards," and wanted revenge; or maybe she felt it was just her risqué sense of humor. At any rate, she sent an opening night "gag gift" to Laird: a giant phallus, made of flowers. The press, of course, couldn't describe it, but Harrison Carroll wrote that "the most sheepish florist in town" delivered it, and that "it got a howl backstage."[2]

The first night audience, including Tyrone Power and his wife Annabella, roared at the play. *Variety* gave a rave review:

> Laird Cregar scores a tremendous personal triumph.... To the role of the perverse, irascible fellow who falls on his back and remains bound to a wheelchair in a middle-class home in the Midwest, Cregar brings a vitality and poise that has not been bettered by any other actor in these parts, including Alexander Woollcott. He portrays the character exactly as he was drawn by Moss Hart

Laird Cregar as Sheridan Whiteside in *The Man Who Came to Dinner*, El Capitan Theater, September 1941.

Laird as Herr Funk, Gestapo chief, in *Joan of Paris*.

and George S. Kaufman, a compound of bitter, egocentric brilliance, of colossal selfishness and barbed wit, with a saving percentage of sentiment.[3]

Taking in a performance: Monty Woolley himself, who was then enacting his Broadway role in the Warners Bros. film version, co-starring with Bette Davis and Ann Sheridan. Woolley's critique of Laird's Sheridan Whiteside: "It's more Wilde than Woolley!"[4]

The greatest accolade came from Laird's hero: John Barrymore. The Great Profile, or what was left of him, had seen *Oscar Wilde* and praised Laird's performance; now he came to see *The Man Who Came to Dinner*, and wrote Laird a fan letter. It came on Barrymore's personal stationery, bearing his self-created coat of arms: a serpent wearing a crown.

Laird, my Boy—
   I said it to the Masquers, and there is no possible reason why I shouldn't repeat it to you—I may jest about the absurdities of life, but—Acting is a sacred subject to me and I say this in deadly earnestness:
   You are one of the truly great young actors our stage has produced in the last ten years.
   I have watched with vast enjoyment your work in *Oscar Wilde* and *The Man Who Came to Dinner* and saw with delight and humility—the quality that makes great actors.

Believe me
Most sincerely
John Barrymore[5]

Laird could hardly have been prouder. Such praise from Barrymore—his childhood idol! Barrymore was in epic decline, of course, living in his decaying Bella Vista estate above Beverly Hills, making a fool of himself weekly on Rudy Vallee's radio show. At the time of *The Man Who Came to Dinner*, he'd just finished RKO's *Playmates*, in which he and bandleader Kay Kyser played themselves. It would be Barrymore's final film.

Yet for Laird, nothing could erode Barrymore's glory, and the letter was his prized possession. He had 20th Century–Fox photograph it and add it to his picture file. Laird had met Barrymore, yet such was his awe of the man that he'd shied away from him. Now, in gratitude for the praise, Laird decided to host a party for his idol. His co-hostess would be his mother. Perhaps, Laird thought, he too could become one of the Bundy Drive Boys, along with Errol Flynn, W.C. Fields, John Carradine, Thomas Mitchell and Anthony Quinn, rallying around Barrymore at the 419 North Bundy Drive studio of artist John Decker. Maybe, like Carradine, he'd sit at nights with Barrymore in Bella Vista, and they would read *Hamlet* aloud together...

The night of the party came. Barrymore failed to appear. The guests became hungry, restless and started drinking. Laird and Elizabeth Cregar feared the worst: Barrymore wouldn't show up!

Actually, worse than that happened: Barrymore *did* show up.

He was slovenly dressed, filthy, and obviously plastered. Barrymore, only about 5'8", gazed up at his host, as if marveling at a tall mountain. Then he turned to Mrs. Cregar.

"Madame," said Barrymore, pointing up at Laird, "that must have been *some fuck*!"[6]

Then he turned to Laird, and pointed up at Mrs. Cregar.

"I never knew," wheezed Barrymore, "that they piled *shit* that *high*!"[7]

The saga of this disastrous evening comes passed down in various forms; most present it as hilarious, but for Laird, it was devastating. To be insulted profanely this way by the man he'd hero-worshipped almost all his life was painful enough; worse, Barrymore had coarsely mocked his beloved mother. Elizabeth Cregar, a strong, positive woman, wasn't about to have her week (or probably even her night) ruined, even by John Barrymore, but her sensitive son was a different story.

The next day, Laird took refuge in his studio dressing room, where Bob Neff, his stand-in, heard him sobbing like a broken-hearted child.[8]

14

Quaking Like Jelly

"Suggestion for a food ad: John (Before) Carradine and Laird (After) Cregar."
—George E. Phair, "Retakes," *Variety*, September 30, 1941

Laird resumed his exhausting pace: playing the vile Gestapo chief Funk in RKO's *Joan of Paris* by day and the hilarious Sheridan Whiteside at the El Capitan by night. Laird gave Herr Funk (which he pronounced in the film as "Foonk") an elegant twist: "I tried to give the impression of wishing I had been born a Frenchman," said Laird of the role, "playing up the admiration of French culture and peeling grapes with a little silver knife."[1]

Again, Laird provided the role more than he admitted. The climax of *Joan of Paris*, stirringly directed by Robert Stevenson, was a chase through the City of Lights' sewers. Herr Funk has arrested Michele Morgan's Joan, forcing her to lead him and his storm troopers to the escaping RAF flyers. Morgan's svelte, cat-eyed heroine bravely makes her way through the sewers, wearing her beret, black high heels and a sashed raincoat, appearing almost swashbuckling; Laird's fat, piggy-eyed villain effetely follows, wearing his top hat, tux and black coat, looking timid and queasy. It's the propaganda message Hollywood loved to deliver: the Enemy is not only a monster, but a perverted monster. Joan leads the villains on a wild goose chase; thanks to her, the flyers escape via a waiting speedboat:

LAIRD (*to his soldiers*): Stop them, you imbeciles!
MORGAN (*triumphantly*): You can't stop them, Herr Funk. They have beaten you!
   (*He viciously slaps her face*)
MORGAN: Just as France will beat you....

Come the denouement, and Funk, the monstrous devil, sends Joan, the self-sacrificing angel, to the firing squad. Angelic voices sing, the RAF planes fly overhead, and Laird Cregar wraps up another out-of-the-closet performance. *The New York Times* opined, "Laird Cregar's performance as the head of the Paris secret police, while a bit too elaborately epicene, is nevertheless properly repulsive."[2]

Charles Bennett, who co-scripted *Joan of Paris*, was a 42-year-old Britisher who'd risen to film prominence via his collaborations with Alfred Hitchcock. At 92 years old in 1992, calling himself "the world's oldest living writer," he recalled:

I loved *Joan of Paris*, and Laird Cregar was charming—absolutely charming. We became very close friends. He came up many, many times to my house in Coldwater Canyon; I have a bar—a very good one—and he'd come up and have drinks.
  Of course, everyone knew he was homosexual; nevertheless, I liked him immensely.[3]

Gallant heroine and sissy villain: Michele Morgan and Laird Cregar in the climax of _Joan of Paris_.

RKO prepared *Joan of Paris* for an early 1942 release. Meanwhile:

Thursday, October 2: *Variety* reported on page one that Paramount was negotiating with Fox to borrow Laird for the "comedy heavy spot" in *This Gun for Hire*.

Friday, October 3: George Phair of *Variety* struck again: "If Hollywood had a football team, the choices for guards would be Laird Cregar and Sydney Greenstreet, who total 600 pounds on the hoof."

Monday, October 13: In the *Evening Herald Examiner*, Harrison Carroll wrote, "Evidently, Laird Cregar must be giving quite a performance as a Gestapo agent in *Joan of Paris*. Paul Henreid, star of the picture, says that, whenever he plays a scene with Cregar, he feels as if he is acting with rocks in his hands."

Friday, October 17: As *The Man Who Came to Dinner* played its final weekend, Laird guest starred with Betty Grable and Victor Mature on Louella Parsons' *Hollywood Premiere* radio show, promoting *I Wake Up Screaming*. After the 7:00 p.m. broadcast, he rushed to the El Capitan for the play's evening performance.

On the same day, *Variety* reviewed *I Wake Up Screaming*:

> Laird Cregar is the picture. He follows Mature with a grim singleness of purpose that projects itself from the screen. It is like Inspector Javert in *Les Miserables*, dogging the footsteps of Jean Valjean. But Inspector Javert followed on through grim undeviating sense of duty. Laird Cregar follows on in grim, undeviating inward passion. The sheer theater of his presence as he is discovered unexpectedly in the corner of Mature's room carries tremendous impact. The turgid clouds within him seem to loom through the show. And this is a swell show for anybody's money.[4]

Also on October 17, Harrison Carroll wrote that Laird and buddy Milton Berle had collaborated on the lyrics for a song titled "Would It Make Any Difference to You?" "The tune's already sold too," wrote Carroll.

Saturday, October 18: *The Man Who Came to Dinner* closed after four weeks, having taken in an estimated and excellent $40,000.[5] Laird wished he could have headlined it longer, but Fox recalled him. As for the relationship with Renie Riano, it ended with the run of the play. She went on to a prolific career; one of her typical roles was the shrewish Maggie in Monogram's *Jiggs and Maggie* film series of the late 1940s, based on George McManus's *Bringing Up Father* comic strip. Renie Riano died in 1971.

By the way, during the run of *The Man Who Came to Dinner*, Betty Grable attended a performance. Whatever she might have felt about Laird stealing *I Wake Up Screaming*, Betty, after returning from a visit to New York to see the hit plays, told Hedda Hopper that the best performance she'd seen this season was Laird's Sheridan Whiteside.[6]

*   *   *

> *"This Gun for Hire* has an amusing freak in bad guy Laird Cregar,
> nattily, effeminately huge, with a fondness for peppermints."
> —Ethan Mordden, *The Hollywood Studios*[7]

Monday, October 27: On the same date that Paramount began shooting *This Gun for Hire*, with Laird as the film's "arch-fiend,"[8] the actor, back from a brief New York vacation, attended the opening night of the musical *They Can't Get You Down* at Hollywood's Music Box Theatre. Hedda Hopper observed first nighters Mickey Rooney ("itching to get up on the stage"), Judy Garland and Laird ... the last, as Hopper reported, having such fun that he moved up to the front row.[9]

He'd have fun on *This Gun for Hire* too.

One of the best-remembered *noirs* of the 1940s, *This Gun for Hire*, based on the Graham Greene story and directed by Frank Tuttle, starred a curious quartet: Peekaboo Blonde Veronica Lake (fresh from her sexpot splash in Paramount's *I Wanted Wings*) as Ellen Graham, undercover investigator; Robert Preston (16 years before his triumph in Broadway's *The Music Man*) as Michael Crane, detective; Laird Cregar as Willard Gates, sissified Fifth Columnist; and Alan Ladd, his blond hair dyed dark (and direct from his death scene in *Joan of Paris* in which he played "Baby," one of Paul Henreid's men) as Philip Raven, a gunman hired and betrayed by Gates.

"I tried to give my character, a Fifth Columnist, a comedy twist," said Laird. "I played the brave lines with a touch of fear—there is always something ludicrous about a big man who is afraid."[10]

Laird and Ladd's first scene together is a gem: Gates paying off Raven in a diner (in marked bills, to assure Raven's arrest). Laird is a slick dude: mustached, prissy, his hair plastered down as if to suggest a toupee, flirting with the waitress; Ladd's Raven is a photogenic slab of ice. Laird, eating ice cream, is jittery with the gunman, and, losing his bravado, whispers a question:

> LAIRD (*quivering*): Raven.... How do you feel, when you're doing ... (*showing the newspaper murder headlines*) ... this?
> LADD (*deadpan*): I feel fine.

Laird, almost trembling, devours a spoonful of ice cream.

The film sparks, a melodrama shot on the eve of the U.S. entry into war ... taut, tense, sexy. One of Laird's best shots: lounging in bed in a train car, wearing silk pajamas, eating peppermints, and reading a book titled *Paris Nights*. Willard Gates is heterosexual: Described by one of his chorus girls as "that fat wolf," he manages a Los Angeles night club with a harem of leggy chorus girls, and merrily leers at Lake (an investigator, posing as a showgirl) as she auditions for him, performing magic tricks as she lip-syncs "Now You See Me, Now You Don't" (dubbed by Martha Mears).

Laird, aware that Lake is in pursuit, invites the heroine to his house high in the Hollywood Hills on a stormy night, where his chauffeur, Tommy (Marc Lawrence), plans to toss the bound beauty into the reservoir. "Such a lovely body," winces Willard. "It's revolting!"

Ladd's Raven comes to her rescue. Laird, clearly with tongue in cheek, claimed he disliked the Willard role because the character was "a mammoth man who is afraid of violence. You've no idea how much physical work it requires of a large man to quake like jelly!"[11] Obviously, he had a ball. A candid shot shows him playfully hoisting Veronica Lake in his arms; he masterfully delivers both the menace and the comedy, a splendidly sinister *noir* clown.

As Marc Lawrence remembered of *This Gun for Hire*: "Oh God, Laird was a barrel of talent. He was a joyous actor to watch. Laird had such richness of spirit; he just bounced all over the place! He was really something. Hell, when word got out that Laird was doing a scene, everyone on or near the lot showed up to watch...."[12] Among the celebrities Lawrence remembered in Laird's fan club: Marlene Dietrich.

Of course, Raven saves Ellen, and the climax is terrific: Raven forcing Laird's Gates to take him into the holy of holies of Gates' boss, played by 77-year-old Tully Marshall, a wizened mummy in a wheelchair, producing poison gas to aid the Japanese. (The film wrapped up the day before Pearl Harbor; six days of retakes would give it a World War II flavoring.) Laird has been Marshall's stooge, and has a blood-sweating, showcase death scene: Ladd shoots him, and Laird falls, hits the floor and rolls down several steps ... a quaking glob of jelly to the last. Ladd, shot by police, pays for his own sins shortly thereafter.

The script by Albert Maltz (later one of the Hollywood Ten) and W.R. Burnett *(Little Caesar, The Asphalt Jungle)* was suspenseful; the cinematography by John Seitz (who later filmed *Double Indemnity, The Lost Weekend* and *Sunset Blvd.,* with Oscar nominations for each) was superb. Paramount, aware it had a dynamite attraction, prepared a major spring release campaign for *This Gun for Hire.*

Incidentally, during the shoot, Laird, playing a scene with Veronica Lake, did something he very rarely did: He forgot his lines. The company roared when he looked at Lake and said, "You're a very intriguing girl and I can't think what else I was to say to you, but I'm sure it was a perfectly charming speech."[13]

In a little over 12 months, Laird had acted in six pictures. Meanwhile:

Saturday, November 8: Hedda Hopper, observing Laird's rising fortunes, wrote in her column, "If that boy keeps on, he's going to be Lord Hollywood—and give Orson a run for his money."[14]

Wednesday, November 12: I Wake Up Screaming opened at Grauman's Chinese Theater and Loew's State Theatres. The incongruous supporting feature: *Small Town Deb,* starring Jane Withers.

Thursday, November 13: George E. Phair wrote in *Variety,* "Secret ambition— To see Laird Cregar sliding down a banister."

Friday, November 14: The Washington Post, reviewing *I Wake Up Screaming,* wrote, "[I]t is Mr. Cregar who steals the picture.... [H]e plays with his prospective victim like a giant, purring cat with a midget mouse."[15]

Saturday, November 29: The Baltimore Sun, critiquing *I Wake Up Screaming,* reported, "[T]he chief honors go to Mr. Cregar," and continued the anthropomorphic comparisons: "Mr. Cregar lurks in the shadows and has all the qualities of a hungry tiger in repose."[16]

I Wake Up Screaming was a solid hit. Produced at a cost of $462,500, it reaped worldwide rentals of $1,491,500 and tallied an Ed Cornell–size profit of $574,100.

"An amusing freak": Laird as Willard Gates, villain of *This Gun for Hire.*

Laird was a sensation.

It called for a celebration, and Laird and his family moved into 621 North Palm Drive in Beverly Hills, "an old-fashioned, brick house, Tudor style," remembered Betsey, "and beautiful inside."[17] It remained Laird's joy to spoil the family. His mother had a Kerry Blue dog named Paddy, and Laird and Betsey often played with Paddy in the yard

Laird, Veronica Lake and Robert Preston, between scenes on *This Gun for Hire*.

on Palm Drive. Laird saw to it that all his loved ones got attention and pampering. Betsey recalled:

> My grandmother wanted to share the spotlight with her son, and she made sure that she made every tea, luncheon and event that she could. She got famous for her hats ... there was an article in one of the newspapers about "'Bess' Cregar and Her Hats" [laughs]!

Laird and Gene Tierney, taking a stroll during the production of *Rings on Her Fingers*.

> An aside: My grandmother used to listen to the radio at night while sitting up in her bed. My Aunt Nean would always bring me in to say goodnight to her before I went to sleep. And my grandmother would be sitting up in bed—and this is the honest-to-God truth—with a dozen donuts on the bed, listening to the radio, and eating every one of those donuts [laughs]! Yes, she was a very large lady!

Christmas was approaching. Unfortunately, so was Pearl Harbor.

*   *   *

"It is my profound and sincere conviction that this picture will be a flop!"[18]
—Darryl F. Zanuck, ending a late night conference
with Rouben Mamoulian preparing *Rings on Her Fingers*

Paramount was still completing *This Gun for Hire* when Laird returned to Fox for *Rings on Her Fingers*, set to start shooting December 3. The basic story: Susan Miller (Gene Tierney), a gum-chewing honey who sells girdles in a department store, dreams of a life of glamor. Her beauty entices a duo of elegant swindlers: Laird as Warren and Spring Byington (27 years older than Laird) as Mrs. Maybelle Worthington. As Laird tells Tierney: "You see, nature played a little trick on us: We should have been born with blue blood, so we have devoted our entire life to correcting this ... biological error.... We are merely bees that take a little nectar from the flowers that have so much. And you too can have some!"

The larcenous pair see sexy Susan as man-bait, enlist her to seduce and marry a millionaire so they can share in the wealth, and head for Catalina Island. Susan, masquerading as "Linda Worthington," casts her siren spell on Henry Fonda's John Wheeler, who, unbeknownst to Susan-Linda, really isn't wealthy at all, but a $65-a-week accountant. Naturally, she falls for him, even after learning the truth. Warren and Maybelle are foiled.

Almost everything about *Rings on Her Fingers* was doomed. The project was a rip-off of Paramount's *The Lady Eve* (1941), written and directed by Preston Sturges; that film had also starred Fonda, but opposite Barbara Stanwyck. Additionally, it was a punishment picture for Rouben Mamoulian, whom Zanuck hadn't forgiven for his costly indulgences on *Blood and Sand*, despite that film's box office success. Zanuck raged: "Let it be understood, once and for all ... that this picture is considered by me and our company as a *cheater*. By that I mean that we are to cut corners in every conceivable direction and get out of it a splendid top bracket 'A' picture...."[19]

The first week of December: The *Rings on Her Fingers* company headed for Catalina Island to start shooting. There Warren, masquerading as a limping sea captain, was to sell Wheeler a yacht that, of course, Warren didn't actually own, thereby sapping Wheeler of his life's savings. The yacht Fox hired for the shoot was the *Bali*, John Carradine's schooner. As things evolved, the company got the services of both the *Bali* and its cadaverous skipper, who wore his yachting cap at a jaunty angle and saw the trip as a vacation to indulge. Mamoulian, in his diary, described Carradine as "quoting Shakespeare and gulping straight Cutty Sark."[20]

Sunday, December 7: Weather had delayed shooting, so Mamoulian and the company were working this Sunday on the *Bali* as news reported that the Japanese had attacked Pearl Harbor. "Evacuate," came the order.

Rings on Her Fingers resumed in a Hollywood at war, with blackouts in L.A. and severe apprehension about a West Coast attack. Laird, the true screwball in this lame screwball comedy, strutted about in riding breeches in one scene; in another, he sang "Blow the Man Down." On December 15, Harrison Carroll wrote:

> Wait until you see Laird Cregar in a bathing suit in *Rings on Her Fingers.* The 25-year-old [sic] character actor is so huge, close to 300 pounds, that 20th Century–Fox couldn't find a garment to fit him in the local stores. They are having three suits specially made.
>   Incidentally, Cregar is a good swimmer and does a neat dive off a ten-foot board.

Laird's big moment comes when, sporting his bathing suit (with shirt), and afraid Fonda will recognize him as the bogus "captain" who sold him the yacht, he leaps into a swimming pool. He eventually emerges, running from bush to bush, hiding behind them as a little dog yips at him. Despite his size, Laird is remarkably fleet-footed, and the spectacle is perhaps the funniest scene of *Rings on Her Fingers.*

"It's a peerless part," Laird sportingly said of Warren, "one of those once-in-a-lifetime roles that permits an actor to go hammy in the story."[21] It was puffery. *Rings on Her Fingers* was an unhappy shoot: Fonda and Tierney failed to hit it off, Mamoulian considered the picture "the least important of my films," and Laird was

Pearl Harbor Day: Gene Tierney (left), Spring Byington, Henry Fonda and Laird, working on *Rings on Her Fingers* on John Carradine's yacht *Bali* at Catalina Island.

restlessly temperamental. Just as *Oscar Wilde*'s opening night had stirred up his arrogance, so had his recent success in *I Wake Up Screaming*. He was depressed, dissatisfied with this picture and, while he enjoyed working with Gene Tierney, he didn't care for a line she had to address to him: "You're all stomach. There isn't any room for a heart."

He was fearful of typecasting: *Joan of Paris* and *This Gun for Hire*, set for release in 1942, would present him as a villain; so would *Rings on Her Fingers*; and so would, to an extent, *Ten Gentlemen from West Point*, in which he'd play a heroic but sadistic commandant, and was soon to start shooting. And he wasn't well. His weight was ballooning after temporary diets. The ventral hernia was painful; he'd learned he'd require another operation to repair it. And, perhaps most thorny, there was his love life, with its conflicts between his "little boyfriend" and Peggy Stack. The pressure was mounting, privately and professionally.

A Jekyll-Hyde personality was emerging: Would Laird Cregar be full of fun and "richness of spirit"? Would he be defiant and temperamental? Mamoulian, who'd so enjoyed working with Laird in *Blood and Sand*, found the split personality disturbing on *Rings on Her Fingers* and wrote in his diary, "Laird Cregar goes fuming again—If he proceeds like this he will be impossible to handle within one year."[22]

*   *   *

"I remember my only Christmas with my Uncle Sam, in 1941. Absolutely anything I wanted, I could get. I had seen in a magazine a doll, and had said to my grandmother, whom I called Nana, "Oh, that's such a beautiful doll, Nana!" She said, "Let me look." It was a Bride doll ... and for Christmas, I got the Bride doll! Anything I saw or wanted, it was just, presto!—there it was."—Betsey Cregar Hayman

Yuletide, 1941: The Cregar family celebrated on Palm Drive. Laird made sure his mother, Aunt Nean and Betsey had everything they desired, and was careful not to show his anxiety at home. He also attended a Yuletide party at the Saltair Avenue home of Tyrone and Annabella Power. As night came, the drinking increased, and the party became rowdy. Hedda Hopper reported that an anonymous lout approached Laird by the Powers' pool. "Let's see how you do as a *float!*"[23] said the lout ... at which time he pushed Laird in.

It wasn't an unusual joke to play on an unsuspecting victim in pool-happy Hollywood. Leading men, comics and even glamour girls, in all their finery, often found themselves splashing into the deep end at many such soirees, to raucous laughter. All in fun ... sort of.

But Laird's splash drew a different type of cruel laughter. This was a 300-pounder in the pool, a heavy "heavy" ... who'd come to fame as Oscar Wilde ... who, with the release of *I Wake Up Screaming*, was the cinema's pin-up boy for perverts. He wasn't only Hollywood's new "Fat Man You Love to Hate." He was, in some vicious gossipers' eyes, Hollywood's new "Fat Queer You Love to Hate" who played sex creeps in the movies, and who lived with his mother.

The problem wasn't that the laughing guests saw him this way; it was that, based on his behavior to come, Laird Cregar would increasingly come to see himself this way.

He was a self-proclaimed "grotesque," but at 28 years old, hypersensitive under the humor, constantly surrounded by handsome men and beautiful women, his peculiar shade of celebrity was beginning to pale and to pall.

Laird's dream had been to become a Hollywood star. He was becoming, in his own mind, some freakish mutation of it. The nightmare aspects of his Hollywood fame were already in evidence.

15

Riding the Cannon

I am a soldier, not a schoolmarm. I am not here to wet-nurse a parcel
of popinjays with spelling books and chalk dust!
—Laird Cregar as Major Sam Carter, *Ten Gentlemen from West Point*

New Year's, 1942: Milton Berle hosted a costume party, dressed as Father Time, complete with white robe, an hourglass, a scythe and a fake beard. Columnist Bill Wickersham, reporting the frolic, noted that Laird Cregar was costumed as the 1942 New Year, but was cagey about the details. The inference: Laird had dressed up in drag as *Mother* Time.[1]

The guests were to masquerade as "any personage who made the front page during the past year." The party took a ribald spike as Berle provided scripts from old vaudeville acts, casting males in the female roles, and vice versa ... a natural for Laird. Among the revelers were Anthony Quinn and his wife Katherine, who'd lost their son in 1941, and who surely hoped for a better year.

The war, of course, dominated everything. On New Year's Day, James Stewart was promoted from corporal to second lieutenant; the same day, Dorothy Lamour began an eight-week tour that sold $25,000,000 worth of war bonds.[2] Santa Anita Race Track would soon close, and studios would cut back on location shooting, wanting to limit crowds in case of an attack. Blackouts continued in Los Angeles. So did rationing. A popular joke in Hollywood was that the glamour girls were in a dither, because the government's demand for rubber was causing a panic run on girdles.[3]

Laird, age 28, perilously overweight and suffering hernia trouble, was hardly likely to enter the military. Nor was his Fox "rival," John Carradine, who, 35 years old and married with two sons, tried to enlist anyway. He was rejected, allegedly due to bad teeth. "I'm not going to *bite* the Japs to death!"[4] protested the 4-F actor.

After Pearl Harbor, Carradine had joined Coast Guard patrol duty, sailing his yacht *Bali* 12 hours a night with a six-person crew.[5] Meanwhile, Laird made his own contribution to the war effort: He joined the cast of Fox's *Ten Gentlemen from West Point*, a saga of the founding of the military academy. The historical propaganda co-starred George Montgomery and Maureen O'Hara, and was directed by Henry Hathaway. Laird's fictional role: Major Sam Carter, part villain, part hero, who hopes to break the West Point cadets with discipline and torture.

Originally, Fox had set Randolph Scott to play Carter; with Laird's casting, the role took on a much more ogre-like nature. At first, Major Carter seems a mutation of

Charles Laughton's Captain Bligh, grossly fat and stretched giant-size on a rack. He even has a scar on his left cheek, rather like Brian Donlevy's Sgt. Markoff in *Beau Geste*. (The makeup department made the scar a subtle one, only obvious in some shots.) As Laird's major addresses the cadets:

> They call you gentlemen cadets. Allow me to be very frank with you. It is my opinion that all of you put together wouldn't add up to one soldier. Soldiers are made on the frontier, with blood and sweat, under fire. The entire idea of this academy is, in my opinion, political humbug and waste. But, as I have been appointed acting commandant, in Col. Williams' absence, I plan to perform my duties to the letter of the law.... If you choose to remain here, it is my duty to teach you soldiering. My way!

Laird's major was, quite literally, a ball-buster: He sadistically disciplined cadets by forcing them to "ride the cannon," the men straddling the muzzles as horses pulled the cannon, galloping over the fields and hills. He mellows, after the cadets climactically save him from Tecumseh's bloodthirsty Indians, via classroom-trained military strategy—using trees as catapults in a night battle, firing off fireballs of leaves at the fleeing Indians. Carter becomes a believer, and the film ends with a montage of West Point heroes, climaxing with a shot of Gen. Douglas MacArthur and a rousing blast of "The Caissons Go Rolling Along."

"The major in *Ten Gentlemen from West Point*," said Laird, "had to be played straight as it was written, a man who stands with a cigar in the corner of his mouth and his feet apart, barking orders at the top of his lungs."[6]

Fox built a replica of early West Point at Sherwood Forest, far west in the San Fernando Valley; in some shots, Lake Sherwood is visible, below the hills. Two of his friends landed small roles as cadets, possibly partially to his influence. Tom Neal had an uncredited part so small his cadet character didn't have a name. The other friend was David Bacon, a wealthy Massachusetts blueblood, playing Shippen, a cadet eager to atone for his uncle Benedict Arnold. Bacon somehow landed this quite good part (he even has a

Laird as Major Sam Carter in *Ten Gentlemen from West Point*.

Tom Neal, Laird and David Bacon (standing right) play cards between scenes of *Ten Gentlemen from West Point*. Laird claimed he knew 50 different card games. The seated man at right is unidentified.

dramatic death scene, as Laird's Major Carter keeps vigil at his bedside) although (1) he had no previous film experience, and (2) he wasn't supposed to be in California, due to a suspended sentence he'd received several years previously for contributing to the delinquency of a minor.[7] His friendship with Laird would eventually have sordid consequences.

Laird, of course, would prove fun to watch in *Ten Gentlemen from West Point*, but his youth, weight and tendency to gnash the scenery worked against the portrayal's credibility. As the *New York Times* commented when the film opened in June, "As the martinet major, Laird Cregar gives a good impression of a theatrical villain, but he never impresses one as a hard-bitten old campaigner."[8]

Also, during *Ten Gentlemen from West Point*, Laird suffered a widely reported embarrassment: He leaned back on a chair in his star trailer and capsized the portable dressing room.[9] Assistant director Abe Steinberg and "several other men" ran to his rescue.

Meanwhile, Laird's "rival" John Carradine was working at the old Fox Studio on Sunset Boulevard, playing a ham actor posing as a bogeyman (with an eye patch) in *Whispering Ghosts*. The "B" comedy starred Laird's crony Milton Berle and was directed by Alfred Werker. Carradine's big scene: rehearsing to play a "Frog Man" and acting like a bullfrog. Teaming up with Carradine in *Whispering Ghosts*: Laird's old "flame," Renie Riano.

Laird, at Fox for a year and a half, was earning $750 per week; Carradine, at the studio for six years, was receiving $1300 per week. However, in January, Fox dropped Carradine's option for his seventh year at the studio, which would have boosted his weekly pay to $1750.[10] He departed the lot, vowing he'd open on Broadway in *Richard III* in April (he didn't), and began freelancing in Hollywood. By December 1942, Universal would announce a campaign to build Carradine as a horror star. Laird, observing John Carradine's career twister of 1942, would take warning.

Twentieth Century–Fox easily could have afforded to keep Carradine on contract: The studio's 1941 profit was a walloping $4.9 million, after the half-million-dollar loss of 1940. This placed Fox fourth among the Big Four: MGM ($11 million), Paramount ($9.2 million) and Warner Bros. ($5.5 million), but well ahead of Universal ($2.7 million), Columbia ($600,000) and RKO (which had lost almost $600,000).[11] Fox's big hits of the year: *How Green Was My Valley*, directed by John Ford, and *A Yank in the R.A.F.*, starring Tyrone Power and Betty Grable.

Friday, January 9, 1942: The *Evening Herald Express* reported that Laird, who had

Fruits of stardom: Laird in his convertible.

ballooned in weight, would have to lose 50 pounds before undergoing his stomach surgery.

Monday, January 12: Sidney Skolsky, of the *Hollywood Citizen-News*, wrote that Fox would now pay half the cost of Laird's clothes. "He insisted on this," wrote Skolsky, "because Cregar, who weighs over 300 pounds, needs twice the amount of material for clothes, and his suits cost him twice as much."

Wednesday, January 14: Harrison Carroll, in the *Evening Herald Express*, wrote that Laird and his eldest brother Edward had bought a mine in the Sierras that produces "waltomonite, which the star says is used in the hardening of steel." (This might have been another of Laird's tall tales. There's no such word as waltomonite.)

Friday, January 16: Carole Lombard died in a plane crash while returning from a bond tour. World War II had quickly made its tragic mark on Hollywood.

Friday, January 30: Harry Crocker, of the *Los Angeles Examiner*, wrote that he'd visited Laird on *Ten Gentlemen from West Point* and said, "I hear that you have just had a large melon named after you. Were you flattered or flattened?"

Laird's reply: "It merely made me hungry."

Wednesday, February 4: Betsey Cregar turned eight. "I had a beautiful birthday

621 North Palm Drive, Beverly Hills, California. Laird lived here 1941 until late summer 1942. (Photo taken by author in 2016.)

party on Palm Drive," she recalled, "and got anything and everything I wanted!"[12] Meanwhile, Betsey was attending a prestigious school, with a very famous classmate:

> My grandmother had said, "Well, while you're here, you're going to school," and she enrolled me in Westlake School for Girls, where Shirley Temple attended. At that time, the game of marbles was big, and everybody had a bag of marbles. I'd met Shirley Temple on the playground, and her bag of marbles was huge. I mean, she had so many marbles! And I only had a few. So ... I decided to help myself to some of Shirley's marbles [laughs] ... and the teacher caught me!
>
> My teacher said, "What are you doing?" And what could I do—I said, "I was taking some marbles." Well, my grandmother was absolutely mortified! They called her, and she came to the school, and she said to the teacher, "I want you to call Shirley here so my granddaughter can apologize to Shirley and give her back her marbles. I want to see it." So they got Shirley out of class and I had to go up to her and say, "I am very sorry, Shirley. Here are your marbles."
>
> Shirley couldn't have cared less! She said, "Oh, it's okay!"

Meanwhile, Laird was still dealing with his hernia troubles and the complications from his surgery the previous summer. He was also coping with the endless barrage of "fat" jokes. "When Laird Cregar recovers fully from his recent operation," quipped Edith Gwynn in her February 24, 1942, "Rambling Reporter" column in *The Hollywood Reporter*, "there'll be enough rubber in the girdle he has to wear to tire a couple of cars."

Thursday, February 26: It was Oscar night at the Biltmore Bowl. The Best Picture of the Year Oscar went to Fox's *How Green Was My Valley*, which defeated (among eight other competitors) RKO's *Citizen Kane*. Darryl F. Zanuck, now a lieutenant colonel, proudly accepted the award, as he did for absent John Ford. Now a lieutenant commander, Ford defeated, among other Best Director nominees, *Kane*'s Orson Welles. Fox collected other Oscars that night, including a special joke Oscar for Jack Benny for *Charley's Aunt*: an Oscar in a wig and skirt with a cigar in its mouth.

There were five nominees for Best Supporting Actor: Walter Brennan for Warners' *Sergeant York*, Charles Coburn for RKO's *The Devil and Miss Jones*, Donald Crisp for *How Green Was My Valley*, James Gleason for Columbia's *Here Comes Mr. Jordan* and Sydney Greenstreet for Warners' *The Maltese Falcon*. The winner was Crisp, also in military uniform; the 59-year-old Crisp was a captain in 62-year-old Lewis Stone's station wagon brigade for evacuating civilians in case of an air raid.[13] It sounded like a joke emcee Bob Hope might have quipped, but it was true.

Laird certainly should have been

Laird at home in Beverly Hills with his dog Paddy.

among the nominees; in all of his 1941 film releases, he gave an Oscar-worthy perform-ance, especially *I Wake Up Screaming*. Indeed, it would have been fun if the annals of Oscar history had Laird's Cornell competing with Greenstreet's Fat Man for Academy honors. At any rate, neither would have had too much of a chance against Crisp, whose patriarch portrayal in *How Green Was My Valley* was, while very admirable, the type of sentimental characterization the Oscars loved to honor, especially now that it was wartime.

It's interesting that Cregar and Greenstreet won Hollywood prominence at almost exactly the same time. There was no real rivalry, as Laird was at Fox and Greenstreet at Warner Bros. Greenstreet, who'd turned 62 in 1941, gave the impression that a life of vice and sinful indulgence had led to his epic corpulence (although he'd actually been obese since his mid-20s).[14] Laird, who'd turned 28 in 1941, had an edge with moviegoers: He was already a sinister fat man, even at his young age.

Imagine what 30-plus years would do to him!

*   *   *

Meanwhile, Laird had a new friend with a scandalous past.

Twenty-five-year-old Van Johnson had come to Hollywood from New York and the ensemble of *Pal Joey*, where he'd received attention not only for his red-headed good looks, but for his promiscuous homosexuality; he had been, as later documented, "notorious on Broadway."[15] In early 1942, Johnson played a cub reporter in Warners' *Murder in the Big House* before joining MGM, where he'd quickly become one of World War II's biggest stars. One of Johnson's first and most ardent fans was Betsey Cregar, who was thrilled when her Uncle Sam invited Van to the Palm Drive house for a dinner party:

> Oh, I thought Van Johnson was a god. I also thought he'd pay more attention to me at that dinner party! I was crushed, and Uncle Sam was very sweet. He said, "Now, you have to be patient. You're only eight years old. When you grow up a little bit, things will change. You will be so beautiful, no one will be able to resist you." So [laughs], that kind of appeased me, for the moment!

If the rumors were true, Laird was having an affair with a man about to become the most adored male star in World War II Hollywood.

16

Swashbuckler

Your fulminations, my lords and gentlemen, are full of bilge and blather!
—Laird Cregar as Capt. Henry Morgan in *The Black Swan*

Laird Cregar's life remained a whirlwind.

Tuesday, March 3, 1942: Edith Gwynn's "Rambling Reporter" column in *The Hollywood Reporter* noted, "Laird Cregar has been showing the town to Diana Barrymore." John Barrymore's daughter (who turned 21 the day this notice appeared) had come to Hollywood as a Universal Studios attraction. Apparently Laird held no animosity toward the Barrymore family, despite the disaster that had occurred at the party he'd hosted for "The Great Profile."

Tuesday, March 17: Laird was the guest star on the Bob Hope radio show. His fee was $600, and under the terms of his Fox contract, he had to split the sum with the studio.[1] On the same date, Louella Parsons wrote in the *Los Angeles Examiner*: "Laird Cregar is negotiating with Bennett Cerf of Random House for Patrick Hamilton's novel, *Hangover Square*—a story of psychological murder. He will produce it first as a play and later as the movie." (Fox would buy the property at Laird's request. Two years would pass before its calamitous production.)

Laird got away for a brief vacation in New York City, staying at the Algonquin Hotel. He read a play by William Saroyan entitled *Jim Dandy* and said he was considering the title role. He also told the press that George Kaufman and Samson Raphaelson had "plays on the fire," either of which would have a juicy part for him.[2]

During his stay, he gave an interview to the *New York Times*:

I have learned three very important things in my life. First, dishonesty is a quality which sometimes, particularly for actors, is extremely useful. Second, I have found that a policy of non-resistance with directors works wonders. And third, I once had a weight phobia until Thomas Browne Henry of the Pasadena Playhouse told me not to lose a pound of weight, but instead to develop a thin man's personality—something which I have cultivated assiduously ever since.[3]

He also made this rather telling observation: "Hollywood is a strange place that sweeps you up to success long before you are actually ready for it."

Thursday, April 16: Joan of Paris opened at Los Angeles' Carthay Circle Theatre. *Los Angeles Examiner* critic Neil Rau wrote that Laird's "polished villainy has such hate-provoking power that you need not be ashamed if you are riled to the hissing stage."[4]

Sunday, April 19: Columnist Harold Heffernan, writing about the careers children originally had foreseen for their classmates who became movie stars, revealed what profession Laird's school chums had prophesied for him: a ballet dancer.[5]

Thursday, April 23: Rings on Her Fingers opened at Broadway's Roxy Theatre. *The New York Times'* review sniped that the comedy-romance had "all the gossamer grace of a hodcarriers' ball" and that "Laird Cregar floats about the screen like a buoyant elephant."[6]

Incidentally, *Rings on Her Fingers* would fulfill Darryl Zanuck's prediction that it would be a "flop": It lost $14,100.

*   *   *

> "In his role as Henry Morgan (the pirate) in *The Black Swan*, Laird Cregar wore costumes that cost a total of $22,000, used up 47 yards of cloth, and weighed between 40 and 55 pounds each. (Cregar is 125 lbs. heavier and six inches taller than the real Henry Morgan was, and was paid more money for his work in the picture than the fabulously wealthy pirate left when he died.)"
> —Feg Murray, "Seein' Stars in Hollywood," August 16, 1942

What actor doesn't love to play pirate king? *The Black Swan*, based on the Rafael Sabatini novel and directed by Henry King, was Fox's Technicolor present to Tyrone Power, as "Jamie Boy," red-caped scourge of the seas. Having started shooting April 20, it came complete with resplendently lovely Maureen O'Hara as Jamie's true love Lady Margaret and a terrific featured cast: Thomas Mitchell as Tommy Blue, Jamie's boozy second-in-command; George Sanders as Capt. Billy Leech, a villain in red wig and beard and an epic leer; Anthony Quinn as Wogan, Leech's second-in-command, in black eye patch; and George Zucco as Lord Denby, Lady Margaret's father.

Then there was Laird's rip-roaring Capt. Henry Morgan, one of his you-have-to-see-it-and-hear-it to-believe-it performances. He suggests a roaring, swashbuckling walrus, dressed as Puss in Boots, and wearing what looks like a long costume wig left at Fox by Theda Bara.

"The minute that drooling traitor sets his nose into Maracaibo," bellows Laird's magnificent Morgan, "I am taking his innards out, and stringing them to the tops of his masts!"

It was Maureen O'Hara's second film with Laird (after *Ten Gentlemen from West Point*). O'Hara told Rudy Behlmer on the *Black Swan*

Laird as Capt. Henry Morgan in *The Black Swan*.

DVD commentary track how much she enjoyed Laird and his performance as the historical Capt. Henry Morgan: "Well, [Laird] was a historical character himself! He wasn't overweight, he was just a big, big man. And he was big in every department—big in ability, big in charm, good humor, fun ... wonderful to work with! He was just big in every way.... [W]ith Laird you'd chitchat and gossip and laugh and have a wonderful time."

Laird also was becoming fast friends with George Sanders, who had very few friends, by his own choosing. One of George's other rare pals was Alan Napier, the 6'5" British actor who later gained fame as Alfred the butler on TV's *Batman* series. As Napier remembered, "In the vernacular, George was a first-class shit ... arrogant, heartless, totally self-interested and indulgent with delusions of grandeur as to his intellectual superiority.... He would have been very comfortable as an 18th-century English rake, with a large estate to squander...."[7]

Still, Napier was friendly with Sanders, due to his "marvelously ingenious and perverse sense of humor, and a boyish enthusiasm about his 'projects.'" The projects included building balsa planes the two men would set flying at Laguna Beach. Sanders once called Napier in the middle of the night, offering this insight: "Nape, it just occurred to me that Darryl Zanuck is worth his weight in balsa."[8]

Sanders' red beard and wig in *The Black Swan* delighted him; in such a disguise, George Barrows could double Sanders,[9] especially in the swordplay sequences, while George slept on the set or made up new, vile names for Zanuck. Sanders' irreverence greatly amused Laird, who was himself characteristically defiant. Significantly, they became friendly, and Laird had a blast on *The Black Swan*, also enjoying his ongoing camaraderie with Power and O'Hara.

Betsey Cregar visited the *Black Swan* set and marveled at the special effects, using 18-foot-long ships with 16-foot-tall masts:

> The battle that they did on "the ocean," that looked so real? It was done in a pond on the Fox back lot with small ships. It was incredible what they did with those ships.... They'd guide them from the shore across the water, and you'd see, as in the movie, the two ships coming together for battle, and then the technical director would set off the explosion ... all done on the pond! It was really fun to watch. I had no idea that was how they did things. I thought they blew up real ships![10]

The Black Swan's cost would run to $1,493,800, Leon Shamroy's Technicolor cinematography would win an Oscar, and the cast played with schoolboy high spirits. The sensations included Sanders dribbling wine over a bound female captive, a bare-chested Power stretched on a rope rack, Power suggestively telling O'Hara "I always sample a bottle of wine before I buy it," Power and O'Hara sharing a ship's bed (while he keeps his pants on under the sheets, but not his shirt), a black dancer gyrating with no brassiere under her costume, and a death scene that likely delighted Zanuck: Run through by Power, Sanders' Billy Leech lunges, turns, reveals to the audience the hero's sword sticking out his back, and lumbers off-screen to perish.

Even with all the sex and spectacle, Laird's Capt. Henry Morgan pirated away his share of scenes. There is, for example, the moment he sticks his finger under his long, curly wig to scratch his head. All in all, his Capt. Henry Morgan comes off as an almost operatic creation, proclaiming such full-blooded lines as:

Jamie Waring—where is that toad of a man? ... Don't mess around, fetch the deserter from his hiding! He left Port Royal with Denby's puling child in the sack. Stole her out of her home, like a Red Indian. I am sitting in me new wig as Lord of Jamaica, when a hundred foaming parents come clattering and howling for me life's blood.... I cracked a dozen skulls and fought me way to the waterfront, with the whole of Jamaica heaving stones at me, and hid myself in a stinking load of trout. Hoisted sail that night, and for three days I have been chewing raw fish! Well, don't gape at me—fetch me some ale before I blow away to dust!

It was on *The Black Swan* that Laird had a titanic tantrum.[11] Rouben Mamoulian, during *Rings on Her Fingers*, had predicted that if Laird continued "fuming," he'd be, within a year, "impossible" to handle. On *The Black Swan*, Laird answered a call to the set in full Sir Henry Morgan regalia—wearing the long hot wig, corseted into the 50-pound costume, sweltering under the Technicolor lights. There were delays on the set, as there often are, and he sat idle for most of the day. The next day, same wig, same corset, same costume ... and a similar delay.

Laird exploded. In his fury, he demanded Fox cancel his contract. For a man usually so sweet and charming, it was a frightening spectacle to see. At any rate, director Henry King weathered the storm and the studio, fortunately, ignored Laird's demands for a terminated contract.

The shooting of *The Black Swan* would go a-rollicking into July. Meanwhile:

Saturday, May 2: Columnist Erskine Johnson reported in the *Los Angeles Daily News* that Laird would star in George S. Kaufman's new play about a Nazi officer, *That Terrible Man*. No such play ever opened in New York.

Friday, May 8: Erskine Johnson wrote that Laird was trying to sell Fox on remaking 1929's *Seven Faces*. In the '29 movie, Paul Muni (promoted by Fox back then, *à la* Lon Chaney, as "the man with a thousand faces") played Papa Chibou, an old porter in a wax museum who believes seven waxworks come alive and speak with him. Salka Viertel played Catherine the Great, and Muni the Great, in elaborate makeup, played the other half-dozen figures: Don Juan, Napoleon, Franz Schubert, a Cockney "pearlie" named Willie Smith, a satanic, long-fingered creature named Diablero, and black prizefighter Joe Gans. Come the climax, Muni's Chibou went mad, stole the wax Napoleon and was chased through the streets.

Laird as Napoleon, Schubert, Smith and Diablero? Maybe. As Don Juan? Unlikely. As black boxer Gans? No way. As Catherine the Great? Only at a Hollywood party.

At any rate, the *Seven Faces* remake didn't happen, and Johnson wisecracked, "A more appropriate title with Cregar in the role would be *Seven Chins.*"

Wednesday, May 13: This Gun for Hire opened at the Paramount Theatre on Broadway, with a stage show boasting the Woody Herman Orchestra, the Ink Spots and comic Wally Brown. "Boxoffice Dynamite!"[12] boasted Paramount in *Variety*. Alan Ladd was a sensation as Raven, and *Look* magazine opined that Laird "gives the best performance of many good ones in the picture."

Tuesday, May 26: Ten Gentlemen from West Point had a special pre-release preview at West Point.

Friday, May 29: John Barrymore died this night. He was an epically dissipated 60 years old. His end-of-life atrocities had included urinating in public and trying to get his daughter Diana to go to bed with him.[13] Laird, learning of the death, must have had complex emotions; Barrymore had been his boyhood idol, and his praise had meant the world to Laird; however, the traumas of the dinner party and Barrymore's profanity had left a significant scar.

Sunday, May 31: Laird was set to guest star on radio's *Chase and Sanborn Show*, starring Edgar Bergen and Charlie McCarthy, as well as Abbott and Costello and Ray Noble and His Orchestra. He was to split the $750 fee with Fox.[14] However, for reasons unknown, Laird cancelled. His replacement, ironically: John Carradine, who, that weekend, was flamboyantly bereaving Barrymore. The surviving script[15] shows Carradine boasting of his screen villainy, delivering lines originally written for Laird as he shared this badinage with Charlie:

> CARRADINE: So, you're not afraid of me, eh?
> CHARLIE: No, I'm not!
> CARRADINE: Why, you little woodcarver's nightmare—I'm the meanest man since Fagin.

This segues into an *Oliver Twist* skit, conceived as a showcase for Laird: Carradine as Fagin, Charlie as Oliver, Bergen (in falsetto) as Nancy. Carradine's Fagin says, "Nancy, go out do a little stealing—and bring me back the booty, me beauty."

Tuesday, June 2: John Barrymore's invitation-only funeral took place at Calvary Cemetery in East Los Angeles. Writer-producer Nunnally Johnson, who attended the funeral, remembered, "The first thing I saw when I walked in was old John Carradine sitting there, rocking back and forth and keening so you could hear him all over the church."[16]

Laird was not among the invited.

* * *

Betsey's time with Uncle Sam remained joyous. She showed an early interest in acting, and Laird, of course, was thrilled to think she might follow his footsteps. More and more, he thought of her as his own daughter. She had become, perhaps even more so than his mother, the steadying influence in his life. One day, while Betsey was outside playing with their dog Paddy, her Uncle Sam decided it was time she learned one of his favorite talents:

> Uncle Sam's cartwheels! Once, behind the house on Palm Drive, Uncle Sam was trying to show me what a cartwheel was, and I couldn't get it—I kept falling on my rear end. And he said, "Now go over there and sit down, and I'll show you." At that time he had to weigh close to 300 pounds—he was huge! And he was wearing a white summer suit, as I remember, and that man did a cartwheel ... he was like a giant snowball! But he was so graceful! He was like an acrobat! He was just wonderful! And he turned around and said, "See? That's all you have to do!"
> Uncle Sam could do almost anything, in my opinion!

Thursday, June 25: Ten Gentlemen from West Point opened at Grauman's Chinese and Loew's State. The same date, *This Gun for Hire* opened at the Paramount Hollywood and Downtown Theatres.

Betsey attended a premiere of one of her Uncle Sam's films. She thought it took place at Grauman's Chinese, but wasn't sure, nor did she remember what film it was. What she did remember, vividly, was the thrill she felt that night:

> Uncle Sam was going to take me to a premiere of one of his movies, and he said, "You need a special dress." So, we went to the costume department at 20th Century–Fox and we were looking through all these dresses. He was asking, "Do you like this one? Do you like this one?" Well, we

came across one that was beautiful—it was blue satin, but it was kind of revealing on the top, like a strapless gown.

So I said, "Oh, Uncle Sam, I like that one!" [Laughs] And he said, "Well.... Okay, let me see what I can do." So he talked to the costumer, and she said, "I can put a little lace or something up over that top.... Sure, I'll have it for you in about a week." So she made this dress for me.

Well, I'll tell you ... at the premiere, my grandmother and aunt had already been seated ... and I felt like an absolute queen walking down that aisle with my Uncle Sam! It was ... [Laughing emotionally] It takes my breath away every time I think of it, because everybody was watching, and applauding, and ... it was just wonderful! It was really one of those fairy tale nights that I'll never forget!

17

The Hideaway and a Sad Farewell

The longer I stick around, the more convinced I am that Hollywood was never, never made for big boys. Somewhere in this town there must be fellows who are six foot three and weigh 300 pounds. Somewhere there must be girls who go with them, and clothing stores to serve them, and places where they can go and get whatever they want as easily as other people.
The only things I can buy ready-made are a bag of peanuts and a handkerchief.[1]
—Laird Cregar, 1942

Sunday, July 26, 1942: Tyrone and Annabella Power hosted a fundraiser at their Brentwood estate for the Free French Relief Committee, of which *Joan of Paris'* Michele Morgan was honorary president.[2] The goal: raise money to buy and equip an ambulance for Free French in Africa.

Power and Ingrid Bergman sold autographed photos, Charles Boyer offered his own engraved cigarette case, and Joan Crawford promised to auction her favorite negligee. Among the stars present: Lana Turner, Gene Tierney, Linda Darnell, Merle Oberon and husband Sir Alexander Korda, the Jack Bennys, the Henry Fondas, the Don Ameches and the Edward G. Robinsons. Laird attended with actress Jan Sterling.

Tuesday, July 28: Laird celebrated his twenty-ninth birthday. He knew what he wanted for a present: To adopt Betsey.

The decision said a lot about the man and his priorities. For a year he'd had great joy in spoiling Betsey, giving her everything she could want, taking her along to Fox, delighting in her discoveries at the studio:

My Uncle Sam wasn't involved in this production, but it was, I think, *Springtime in the Rockies*, with Cesar Romero and Carmen Miranda. Uncle Sam was friendly with them, and they said, "Well, bring her over!" So he did, and I was absolutely fascinated by Carmen Miranda. In those days, the stars had dressing rooms, but also, off the set, they had little tables with mirrors, so instead of running back and forth to your dressing room, you could fix whatever you had to fix right there. So [laughs], Carmen Miranda was there, and she got her hat on with all the fruit and everything, and I'm looking down at her hands ... just staring at her hands.
  And she said, "What's the matter?"
  And I said, "You have green nail polish!"
  And she said, "Yes, I do!"[3]

If Laird adopted a daughter, in the social reality of 1942, he'd surely have to alter his private homosexual identity. Nevertheless, he made a definitive decision: Laird called Betsey's mother, imploring her to agree to the adoption.

Uncle Sam really wanted me to stay. He tried to talk my mother into letting me stay. But my mother said, "No, she's my daughter, I can't leave her there. Maybe she can come back to visit another year, but no, you can't keep her." Unless you're a really strange woman, who can give up her child? So Uncle Sam said, "Well, okay. I guess I understand."

Laird was heartbroken. Betsey stayed until late summer, when her mother came to retrieve her. In the next months, he'd make life changes of considerable significance.

Friday, August 14: Harrison Carroll had often name-dropped Laird in his column, so Laird was pleased to "pinch hit" for Carroll that August. The "guest column" show-cased his humor and exasperation at his bulk and screen reputation:

I'm the guy who has to walk in a specially dug ditch on the set so as to stay in camera range with the five-foot-two leading lady.

I'm the one who has to have special lights to kill my shadow ... because it looks like a crowd's following me....

It's gotten so that I feel alone in the world. I've yet to meet anyone in Hollywood who is as tall as I am and simultaneously weighs my figure. The few tall people I know are usually skinny. But even so they feel as I do—Hollywood simply isn't for big fellows. Not as big as Laird Cregar, anyhow.

I've fallen through scaffolding tested by three heavy men.... And when there's mayhem afoot, Cregar's a cinch to be on the receiving end. I don't know why it's particularly funny for a big man to get hit, doused, kicked or get his hair combed with an electric mixer....

Somewhere there must be fellows like me, with problems like mine. But I've given up trying to find them. I don't want to stop being an actor. I want to stay in the theatrical profession. I think I know a way to make a couple of my dreams come true. I'm going to join a circus. I'm going to be a midget. I'm going to be the biggest midget in the world.[4]

Five days later, Harrison Carroll referred to Laird's guest column and wrote that Laird had leased a new home, enlarging the shower and making other changes to "accommodate his bulk."

"On top of that" wrote Carroll, "he crashed through the porch floor and had to have all the planking reinforced."

Cregar's new address was 9510 Cherokee Lane, a redwood cottage, high in pastoral Coldwater Canyon. The house, flanked by tall oak trees and sycamores, sat above a stream, and one crossed a bridge to enter it. As Laird described the cottage: "I have a small home ... back in a lemon grove and it is so tiny that one must enter it with a shoe horn. I cook my own meals, dust and make the beds—and have a cleaning woman in once a week. I have 22 acres, but the house has only five rooms. My rent is $50 a month, and I've signed a five-year lease."[5]

Adjustments were made in late summer. The L-shaped living room, with yellow upholstery and a green rug, had a fireplace flanked by bookshelves, an original painting by Polish-born French artist Moise Kisling (1891–1953) which Laird called his "prize possession," and a piano, where Laird enjoyed composing.[6] The dining room, also in yellow and green, held Laird's selection of old silver and a china service. There was a kitchen and a simply furnished bedroom that offered a view of the estate. He eventually added a guest bedroom.

Laird raised a Victory garden: corn, beans, tomatoes, lettuce and squash. His orchard, beside lemons, produced apples, apricots, limes, pears and walnuts. The wildlife included foxes, coyotes and rattlesnakes.

A short distance north in Coldwater Canyon, at 2320 Bowmont Drive, was the

Mexican farmhouse of Boris Karloff. The horror king was then starring in Los Angeles in the national company of Broadway's super-hit *Arsenic and Old Lace*, in which Karloff had created the role of mad Jonathan Brewster.

Laird moved his mother and Aunt Nean into a Beverly Hills apartment, and Paddy the dog came to live with Laird. Laird planned a farewell party for Betsey to take place on Cherokee Lane. Meanwhile, Betsey's mother Marie made the trip by train to Los Angeles to fetch her daughter.

> Uncle Sam talked to my mom on the phone and said, "When you come out here, bring a formal dress for the party." So Mom brought the dress she thought would be the most appropriate—it was white, long but very plain, nothing fancy. And I must say, at the party, I looked at her and as an eight-year-old thought, "My mother looks just as good as these movie stars!" And she did! She really looked lovely.

The party guests played "Indications" and Betsey saw her Uncle Sam in action. She also noticed how calf-eyed he was, as usual, around Linda Darnell. Betsey would miss several people as she went home:

> As much as I was going to miss my Uncle Sam, he was the entertainer ... he was the one who entertained me, and saw that I was having a wonderful time. My grandmother was the one who showed me off: "Oh, this is Sam's niece." Wherever I went, there were elegant tea parties or elegant lunches, and she would always introduce me that way.
> But the one person I really missed when I left was my Aunt Nean. She was the one who used to take care of me, do my laundry, feed me, dress me.... If my grandmother said, "We're going down to Beverly Hills, so make sure she looks okay, Nean," Aunt Nean would dress me. She was like a second mom. She was always that way, she was used to that role, because she had raised the six boys, essentially. A great woman.
> And there was our maid, a black maid named Freddie. She also took care of me, and she was a dear, and ... oh, I loved that woman. She was so sweet.

There was an emotional farewell. Once again Betsey's Uncle Sam picked her up over his head, kissing her goodbye, waving as the train pulled away with the woman he'd wanted to marry taking away the daughter he wished was his own. As noted, he'd managed his time with her to be joyful, and Betsey recalled she never saw Laird's tempestuous side, at times on display elsewhere: "I never saw him really angry. I saw him upset at home if something wasn't going right, or maybe something at the studio bugged him, but I truly never saw him angry. I'm sure he got angry once in a while, but I never saw it. Which I think was considerate ... he wasn't going to show me that side."

She headed home to a stepfather, a new baby sister and a modest home life far different from what she'd known for the past 15 months. As for her arrival:

> I was thrilled to be going home, and Mom was telling me all about my new sister. So we got into Philadelphia, and the train pulled up, and I was talking to Mom, and you know there's a little space between the exit where you get down on the steps from the train and where the landing is. So, I'm talking, not looking where I'm going ... and I fell right through the space! I was all the way down there, with just my hand hanging up! And my mother's hanging onto me with one hand! Finally, a couple of gentlemen came over and picked me up, and Mom said, "Boy, I'm glad you're home.... I don't have to worry about this any more!"

Betsey didn't realize it, but she might have died in a way frighteningly similar to the way William F. Cregar had died at Holmesburg Junction in 1890.

The family moved to Brewster, New York. In Los Angeles, Elizabeth Cregar and Nean settled into their apartment at 135 South Camden Drive in Beverly Hills. Laird drove nightly up to his new canyon home amidst the foxes and coyotes, alone. He was suddenly very lonely. And, as always, he had the taunting sensation he hadn't long to live.

No time... No time...

PART IV

"We Want You Just As You Are, Mr. Cregar."

When I began my career in films, I found it rather frustrating not to be cast in romantic parts, since it seemed to me that I was just as handsome, dashing and heroic as any of my contemporaries. But I soon became adjusted to the idea that I would always be cast as the villain...

I made a much better adjustment to this sort of thing than did our poor late-lamented Laird Cregar, an actor of great talent, who was virtually assassinated by Hollywood.

Since Laird's physique was rather too robust, his eyes rather curiously slanted and his features inconsistent with the general mold of the fashionable leading man, he was invariably cast as a fiend. In the preamble of every script there is a description of the leading characters.

In the case of Laird's roles, the description would always be that of a subhuman monster. Time and time again, after reading the preamble in the script of a picture he was about to do, Laird would go into the makeup department and ask the chief makeup man what fantastic distortions of his face would be required for the part.

The makeup man would invariably answer, "We want you just as you are, Mr. Cregar."—George Sanders, *Memoirs of a Professional Cad*, 1960

18

Who Was Who in the Zoo

I have not yet played a lover, but I intend to do so. A fat man, I believe, can be believable in love. I may have to play the frustrated lover, or the psychopathic lover, the Cyrano de Bergerac touch. But, as I have said, the dark places of the heart intrigue me. The pain of love is more compelling than the pleasure.[1]
—Laird Cregar, 1942

In the sex sagas of Hollywood, the story goes that John Barrymore, in his legendary trysts, actually had a secret weapon: a "banshee screech." Upon reaching climax, he'd unleash this unearthly scream, contrived to fulfill three purposes: (1) convince his lover that he was indeed in sensual Nirvana, (2) compliment his bed partner for taking him to such heights of ecstasy, and (3) startle the woman so harrowingly that she forgot she hadn't climaxed herself.[2]

Was the Great Profile a sexual sham? Not according to his idolater John Carradine. "He had a *wang* that was a *world-beater!*"[3] Carradine proclaimed of Barrymore, a testimony he'd offer time and again—and loudly—during the 46 years he'd survive his hero.

What of the famous sex sagas and scandals of Hollywood? In 1921, did Fatty Arbuckle really rape Virginia Rappe with a Coke bottle? In 1932, did Paul Bern actually kill himself after attempting coitus with bride Jean Harlow while wearing a dildo? In 1940, did Lionel Atwill truly host a Yuletide orgy while dressed as Santa Claus?

Often, the truth is in the eye of the beholder and the agenda of the writer. When in doubt, historians often do a *Man Who Shot Liberty Valance*: They print the legend ... and the legend often morphs to suit the time.

In the legend and lore of Laird Cregar, such as it is, a significant part of his 2017 fame comes as a champion in the limited but growing canon of Gay Hollywood history. These accounts claim he lived proudly and openly with a male lover, and was a pioneer in fighting for homosexual-lesbian rights. This is at odds with an equally distorted 1940s notoriety, which cast Laird as a sexual "deviant" mama's boy, presiding, *à la* Nero, over homosexual soirees at his Coldwater Canyon cottage, an in-your-face "poof." As such, the absurd revisionist history of today has clashed headlong into the senselessly vicious gossip of over 70 years ago. Both extremes are ridiculous, and make a valid analysis of Laird's private life a challenge.

The truth about Laird Cregar's sexuality is complex, and quite tragic. Covering it fairly requires a look at the moral climate in World War II Hollywood. First, it must be noted that, as far as the Cregar family was concerned, Laird Cregar was not a homosexual. In 2012, Betsey Cregar Hayman went on record with me:

> I have re-researched some articles about my uncle online and can't believe that some of them hinted (more than hinted!) that he was gay. I think because he was a sensitive man, and took into consideration all people and their feelings, that was the assumption. He was also so taken with making himself the best actor he could be, he was not interested in dating steadily or getting married. But he was not gay. As I said, having been around him for more than a year, even at seven and eight years old, I could have recognized that! He was shy around women, and his talent for acting much surpassed his talent with being around women that he admired. He was much more comfortable around his fellow male actors.[4]

Laird and his mother, Elizabeth Bloomfield Smith Cregar.

What to make of this claim? As Peggy Stewart noted, a pre-fame Laird was candidly open about his homosexuality with her and her mother during the 1939 production of the play *The Great American Family*. And with all respect to Betsey, who died in 2015, it's doubtful that a seven- or eight-year-old child in 1941–42 would have recognized a homosexual nature in an uncle she adored, especially at a time when such a topic was never openly discussed.

Yet Laird had a serious relationship with Betsey's mother Marie prior to her marriage to his brother William; he more or less steadily dated Peggy Stack; he dated various other women. Were Peggy and all the others no more than "beards"? Was Laird perhaps bisexual?

Debating whether or not a subject was homosexual may strike some readers as instantly homophobic. Others may take the attitude, "Who cares, and what did it matter in Hollywood?" This misses the cold reality that the film colony, in its hypocrisy, was in some ways as violently prejudiced against gays as anywhere else in 1942 America.

The truth was that Hollywood welcomed and protected those who engaged in heterosexuality, homosexuality or bestiality, as long as the collaboration was *profitable*.

Consider, for example, Charles Laughton, who arrived at Paramount Studios in 1932.[5] Although he was wed to Elsa Lanchester, he was overtly homosexual. The ultimate pre–Code actor, Laughton won the Academy Award for Alexander Korda's British-made *The Private Life of Henry VIII* (1933) and became a major star ... so much so that, when he left Paramount and signed with MGM in 1934, he had such clout that he eliminated the traditional morals clause in his contract.[6] It was a stipulation that Metro producer Irving Thalberg willingly accepted.

On the other side of the coin, there was James Whale, who elegantly directed the Universal horror hits *Frankenstein, The Old Dark House, The Invisible Man* and *Bride of Frankenstein*; he also was at the helm of the 1936 version of the musical *Show Boat*. Whale was as frank about his sexuality as he'd been in the London theater, living openly in Hollywood with producer David Lewis. The Universal regime of Carl Laemmle, Jr., protected him. However, once new management gobbled up the studio and Whale's *The Road Back* (1937) was a flop, his homosexuality became another nail to drive into his professional coffin. He soon had little choice but to retire. In 1957, ill and suffering from fear of insanity, he drowned himself in his pool.[7]

Also, homosexuality was acceptable as long as the gay person's predilections stayed known *within* the filmland boundaries. It was one thing for Hollywoodites to prattle at a party about Marlene Dietrich sleeping with women, or Van Johnson sleeping with men. It was another thing for a 1942 small-town movie fan to visit her beauty parlor of choice, pick up *Photoplay* and read about what she'd shockingly perceive as Hollywood "perverts." It was as unthinkable as seeing a story in which "King of the Movies" Clark Gable talked about his dentures[8] or "Oomph Girl" Ann Sheridan chatted about her falsies.[9]

The truth: For all its supposed open-minded sophistication, 1940s Hollywood was a bitch-fest, and could be as cruel and basically intolerant as any Bible-belt small town.

In the cold, hard case of Laird Cregar, for example, consider the Canterbury Tale allegedly tattled by Louise Allbritton. Allbritton was a tall, blonde actress, under contract to Universal; in early 1943, she donned a black wig and played the female vampire in *Son of Dracula* with Lon Chaney, Jr. Louise had a reputation as a Hollywood playgirl. With women's stockings at a premium during the War, the actress reputedly made a bet with one of her girlfriends that she could seduce Laird Cregar, and "bring out the man" in him. If she did, she got to keep the new desirable stockings. If her siren act failed, her gal pal got the pair.

The saga became a slapstick sex farce: the alluring Louise vamping the wide-eyed Laird, luring him to her lair, accidentally intruding on Laird as he was removing his girdle, and from there, everything went south. Louise's girlfriend got the stockings.[10]

Although there's no proof this actually ever happened, the story circulated, embellishments surely added. True or false, *l'affaire Allbritton* became a cruel standby for gossips and homophobes, and Cregar was a large, easy, bull's-eye target.

Then there were the rumors about Laird's new home. The cottage on Cherokee Lane, high up in the lemon grove, was so secluded that rumors claimed Laird had selected the site for secrecy, a salon for gay parties, picnics ... and orgies. Faye Marlowe, who turned 16 in 1942 and destined to co-star with him in *Hangover Square*, lived in Coldwater Canyon, where her parents owned extensive property. "Laird lived just a short distance up Coldwater Canyon from where I lived," Marlowe told me. "He had a house sort of tucked away, hidden in some shrubbery. He was gay, and I later heard that's where he entertained his little retinue of young men."[11]

Maybe. After Betsey went back east, and with his mother and Aunt Nean now living in their apartment Laird, lonely, had the freedom to entertain. However, Laird also used the house and property for other occasions, such as a dance he generously hosted for the WAACs (Women's Army Auxiliary Corps) in the fall of 1942. He provided an orchestra, an open-air dance floor, and invited Tyrone Power, Cesar Romero and John Payne to be dance partners for the wide-eyed WAACs.[12]

Hollywood history has been quick to "out" Laird as a homosexual. Charles Higham, who wrote best-sellers about such stars as Errol Flynn (whom Higham claimed was not only bisexual, but also a Nazi spy), wrote about Laird in his 1983 biography of Merle Oberon, *Princess Merle* (co-authored with Roy Moseley):

> Cregar, for all his extroverted rash flamboyance on the screen, was bitter, murky and private. He was tormented by his sexual needs and was frustrated in fulfilling them because he was grossly overweight and therefore ruled out from the fiercely competitive, body-oriented, and maniacally sensual world of homosexuality. His only recourse was to buy the sexual favors of men, which left him more frustrated than before.[13]

Higham and Mosely gave no source for their information about Laird buying "sexual favors of men." As for their description of him as "bitter, murky and private"—well, maybe on a bad day, but the adjectives hardly jibe with the "St. Bernard" impression Laird made on most others who actually knew him.

Such stories spread. Even a pulpy magazine entitled *Afternoon TV Showcase Exclusive: Hollywood Tragedies*, published in 1985 and devoted to such legends as Marilyn Monroe, James Dean and Natalie Wood, made room for Laird:

> There was some studio worry.... Laird was known to have some slightly neurotic friends, since effeminate men of the time were considered to be in that vein.... There had been many stories making the rounds about Cregar's behavior at that time. It was said he indulged in sexual activities deemed a mite kinky for the average person. But, studio publicity people were paid to batten a hatch of such rumors.[14]

The reality? It appears to be a complex mix. Betsey was right; Laird was a very sensitive man, shy around women, rather in awe of them. Higham and Moseley were right; Laird was "frustrated" in the "maniacally sensual world of homosexuality," and not at ease there either. Even *Afternoon TV Showcase Exclusive* was right about "stories making the rounds about Cregar's behavior."

Louise Allbritton, Universal starlet and Hollywood playgirl.

The best evidence shows that Laird was sexually conflicted, and in actuality, it was almost a moot point: The true torment was his weight, and the sad fact that he felt unattractive to anybody, male or female. That a 29-year-old, 340-pound man could have a vigorous sex life certainly wasn't out of the question—there were always possibilities—but it was reportedly problematic, especially considering Laird's deep sensitivity and his lifelong hang-ups about his appearance. Handsome men and beautiful women were stars; he was, in his own words, "an oddity." Additionally, most 29-year-old single men were in the Armed Forces.

He was not a champion for gay rights ... nobody was in 1942. For one thing, it would have violated the morals clause of his Fox contract. For another thing, he was hardly "hedonistic." As soon as he'd achieved some degree of fame and fortune, he'd brought his family to Los Angeles, set up his mother and aunt in his house, and eventually tried to adopt his niece. He was by nature defiant, but not stupid, hardly about to risk his fame by any showboating, not about to embarrass and shame his beloved Mom, Aunt Nean and his family over what most people, homosexual or heterosexual, perceived in those days as a totally private matter.

Nevertheless, the tattling continued. It actually festered, and near the end of his life, as will be noted, the rumors became almost horrifically sordid. The gossip hurt Laird deeply. Increasingly and tragically, it became, for him, an obsession.

*   *   *

"Swashbuckling becomes genuinely swashy, and certainly is not a bit
swishy, on the screen at Loew's State and Grauman's Chinese theatres...."
—Edwin Schallert, review of *The Black Swan*,
Los Angeles Times, November 14, 1942

Friday, August 28: Harrison Carroll reported that Laird had been at the Hollywood Tropics with starlet Gayle Lord (aka Teddi Sherman, the daughter of *Hopalong Cassidy* producer Harry Sherman).

Thursday, September 3: The transport vessel USS *Wakefield*, formerly the SS *Manhattan*, on which Laird had served in the Merchant Marine in 1934, burned in the Atlantic Ocean. The Navy saved all 1600 passengers as well as the crew of 600 to 700. The blackened hull was towed to port and a Naval spokesman said there was suspicion of sabotage.[15]

Saturday, September 26: Beverly Hills' City Hall hosted "Salute to Our Heroes Day," which sold $1,000,000 worth of war bonds. Laird was one of the masters of ceremonies, along with Dennis O'Keefe, Nigel Bruce and Evelyn Ankers, Universal's "Scream Queen" of such horrors as *The Wolf Man*.[16]

Saturday, October 3: This night saw the gala dedication of the Hollywood Canteen. Laird served as a busboy. Among the other stars on hand were Marlene Dietrich, Bette Davis, Abbott and Costello, Rosalind Russell, John Garfield and Kay Kyser.[17]

Wednesday, October 7: 20th Century–Fox announced that Laird would play Javert in the studio's remake of Victor Hugo's *Les Miserables* (Charles Laughton had played the part in the 1935 version). Mary Anderson was to play Cosette; the heroic role of Jean Valjean (played by Fredric March in the 1935 film) was still open.[18]

Monday, November 2: Fox began shooting the Technicolor musical *Hello Frisco, Hello*, starring Alice Faye, John Payne, Jack Oakie and June Havoc, and directed by H. Bruce Humberstone. Laird landed the featured role of Sam Weaver, a bearded "wild man" prospector. Oakie's character, asked if he ever met Sam, replies, "No, but I've been bitten by him." Sam crashes in here and there to beg honky tonk impresario Johnny Cornell (Payne) for a grubstake: "Johnny! I got a new bonanza! An El Dorado! A Comstock! And no one knows about it but me! … Oh, Johnny, you'll never regret it, boy! Why, one of these days, we'll be pitchin' gold watches down Market Street, just to see how far we can throw 'em! Why, we'll be ridin' in carriages…. So long Johnny! I'll be seein' ya! God bless ya, my boy! God bless ya!"

Late in the show, Laird's Sam comes back at a midway on the beach, throwing gold watches. He's struck it rich! … or *has* he? The answer sets the stage for the happy finale of this $1,660,000 musical, with Payne and Faye singing "You'll Never Know."

Thursday, November 12: The Black Swan opened in Los Angeles at Grauman's Chinese Theatre and Loew's State Theatre. Dorothy Manners wrote in the *Examiner*, "Laird Cregar is both amusing and menacing as Capt. Henry Morgan and looks cute in his wigs after reformation sets in." The film was an immediate smash hit and *Photoplay* hailed the Technicolor romp as "a gorgeous riot."

Tuesday, December 22: The Film Daily announced its "Filmdom's Famous Fives," for movies released from late 1941 to late 1942, the honorees voted by reviewers across the country.[19] The Five Top Supporting Actors: (1) Donald Crisp, *How Green Was My Valley*; (2) Frank Morgan, *Tortilla Flat*; (3) Van Heflin, *Johnny Eager*; (4) William Bendix, *Wake Island*; and, in a tie for the fifth spot, Cregar for *I Wake Up Screaming* and Alan Ladd for *This Gun for Hire*.

A tie for fifth failed to do Laird justice, especially since Ladd (who also scored as one of the "Finds" of the year) had *This Gun for Hire*'s starring role. Nevertheless, it was an honor, and more than the Academy had provided Laird since he'd achieved prominence.

Wednesday, December 23: The Black Swan had its New York City opening, the Christmas show at the Roxy Theatre, with Carmen Miranda live on the stage. It shattered the Roxy record with an amazing $110,000 its first week.[20] The film became Fox's biggest box office attraction to that date: worldwide rentals of $5.7 million, and a profit of $2.3 million.

Also on December 23: Harrison Carroll wrote, "On doctor's orders, Laird Cregar, oversized film star, will enter a sanitarium soon to lose one-fourth of his weight. The giant actor must

Laird serves as a busboy at the Hollywood Canteen.

drop 75 of his 300 pounds, he revealed today, before undergoing a needed abdominal operation."

In fact, Laird now weighed about 335 pounds, but 300 was an acceptable round figure. Note that the amount of weight he had to lose had risen from 50 pounds to 75 pounds. Later, there would be other reasons for the weight loss, but at this time, Laird was adamant that the diet was only temporary. "Immediately I enter upon the post-operative phase," he said, "I shall return to my normal habits."[21]

The year 1942 ended memorably for Laird: On December 29, Harrison Carroll reported that Laird had been at Ciro's, dancing with Judy Garland.

*   *   *

"It is not true that at the annual visit of the circus to Hollywood,
Joan Blondell's young son tried to feed peanuts all through the performance to
Laird Cregar in the delusion the actor was an elephant. Laird says the
little boy only thought so at first until he discovered the actor
had no trunk."—Cal York, *Photoplay*, January, 1943

As the New Year of 1943 began, Laird made plans for his epic diet. He entered Good Samaritan Hospital, actually living there, leaving each morning for work and

Laird and Marlene Dietrich boost morale at the Hollywood Canteen.

returning every night, so to avoid any midnight binging. His calorie intake reduced from his usual 5,000 to a mere 800. Doctors monitored his progress as he ate hospital-prepared meals, taking a diet lunch with him to the studio. Annabella daily visited Laird's cottage to feed his dog Paddy. To stay occupied in the hospital, Laird began editing *Make Me a Child Again*, his mother's manuscript about turn-of-the-century Philadelphia.

Monday, January 25, 1943: Laird reprised his quivering Willard Gates in *This Gun for Hire* on Cecil B. DeMille's *Lux Radio Theatre.* Alan Ladd was again Raven and Joan Blondell played Veronica Lake's role.

Monday, February 8: He was back on *Lux Radio Theatre* in *The Maltese Falcon*, happily cast in Sydney Greenstreet's role of the Fat Man. Edward G. Robinson took on Bogart's Sam Spade and Gail Patrick played Mary Astor's Brigid O'Shaughnessy.

Thursday, February 11: George E. Phair in his *Variety* "Retakes" column wrote, "Laird Cregar diets off 14 pounds and nobody notices the change but the press agent and the Fairbanks Scales Co. If John Carradine lost 14 ounces, that would be something."

Monday, March 1: The New York Times reported that Fox was preparing *The Lodger*. Laird, set to play Jack the Ripper, his first starring role, was overjoyed.

Meanwhile, another striking performance was about to come.

* * *

"I am practically unprepared...."
—Greer Garson's opening remarks
in her Oscar acceptance speech for *Mrs. Miniver*, 1943

Thursday night, March 4: The Academy Awards banquet took place at the Coconut Grove of the Ambassador Hotel. It began at 8:30. It was still going on well after midnight.

The Grove was so crowded, many of the 1200 people present had trouble standing as Jeanette MacDonald sang two verses of "The Star-Spangled Banner." Marine Private Tyrone Power and Army Private Alan Ladd had problems of their own, trying to unfurl the American flag as MacDonald sang.[22] The ensuing pace was agonizing.

"[T]he dull and inept Academy Awards banquet Thursday night was a humiliating fiasco of political preening and tedious back-scratching,"[23] lamented an aghast W.R. Wilkerson, editor of *The Hollywood Reporter*, who'd devote no less than three days of editorials to attacking the ceremony. Mary Pickford was so appalled she actually resigned from the Academy, claiming "No one person could arrange anything so boring."[24]

Laird was present, on leave from the hospital, having grown a beard, and having failed again this year to rate an Academy nomination. He was excited about his casting as *The Lodger*, and watched this train wreck of a ceremony with wry amusement.

Best Picture, *Mrs. Miniver.* Best Supporting Actor, Van Heflin (in Air Force lieutenant uniform), *Johnny Eager.* Best Supporting Actress: a sobbing Teresa Wright for *Mrs. Miniver.* Best Actor, James Cagney, *Yankee Doodle Dandy.* The climactic honor, for Best Actress: Greer Garson, *Mrs. Miniver.*

Her red hair lustrous, Garson took to the stage, and in her Queen of MGM style began, "I am practically unprepared...." Legend would claim she spoke for 45 minutes, but the *Guinness Book of World Records* clocks it at six minutes, still a hell of a long speech. Meanwhile, the hour had reached 1:00 a.m. It was a self-indulgent finale to an interminable evening.

That weekend, with the Oscar fiasco the talk of Hollywood, Danny Kaye hosted a party with his wife, Sylvia Fine. "Parties in Hollywood are a dime a dozen," wrote columnist Edith Gwynn in *The Hollywood Reporter* on March 9, "but the one at the Danny Kayes the other night was one for the book." Among the 100-plus guests were Claudette Colbert, Judy Garland, Mickey Rooney, Van Johnson, Keenan Wynn, Harold Arlen, June Havoc and Joe Pasternak. The pre-buffet entertainment: an off-color version of *The Mikado*, written by Kaye, which he performed with John Garfield and Groucho Marx.

"[R]eally something!" wrote Gwynn.

Then, after supper, the Kayes presented a wildly irreverent "mock version" of the Academy dinner. The big winner: Laird Cregar, for "Best Female Impersonator of the Year for *The Black Swan*." Of course, in *The Black Swan*, Laird, as Capt. Henry Morgan, had worn the long curly black wig, but as all the guests knew, the award carried a *double entendre* significance. The bearded honoree strode up to accept his prize. "I am practically unprepared...," began Laird.

The guests roared, and Laird went on, and on ... always a brilliant mimic, hilariously lampooning Garson's diva act, with all her posing and English accent intonations, peppering the parody with ribald asides, going on with his acceptance speech, according to Mason Riley and Damien Bona in their book *Inside Oscar*, "dragging it out to a ludicrous length."[25]

Hello Frisco, Hello: **Laird as Sam Weaver, prospector.**

"In no time," wrote Riley and Bona, "Hollywoodites started 'remembering' that Garson bored everyone for over an hour and her speech became a Hollywood legend." Indeed, when the two authors interviewed Garson for their book, she asked a favor: "Please clear up this myth. It was funny for two weeks, but now I'm quite tired of it."

If the party speech had an impact on Garson, it also boomeranged on Cregar, at least in Hollywood. His outlandish Garson take-off was so funny, and inspired so much gossip, that the "Best Female Impersonator" prize and his epically flouncy response came off as an out-of-the-closet performance and admittance.

It had been Oscar Wilde as Mrs. Miniver. And on March 8, amidst all of the gossip about the mock Oscars, Fox announced that Laird would play a role for which Greer Garson likely thought him well-suited: the Devil.[26]

19

Three in 1943

As Henry Van Cleve's soul passed over the Great Divide, he realized that it was extremely unlikely that his next stop could be Heaven. And, so, philosophically, he presented himself where innumerable people had so often told him to go.
—opening to *Heaven Can Wait*, 1943

It's Hell in Technicolor Art Deco, glistening with the "Lubitsch touch." A door opens and a man with a cane—Don Ameche, in old-age makeup—makes his way down the stairs to a towering figure he calls "Your Excellency."

Sporting a Van Dyke beard, a widow's peak and a most charming manner, "His Excellency," aka Satan, is only vaguely sinister, and that's due to the fact that playing him is Laird Cregar. He's instantly impressive; the weight loss is obvious, the cutaway coat flattering, the manner soothing.

"I presume your funeral was satisfactory?" asks Laird.

"Well," says Ameche, "there was a lot of crying, so I believe everybody had a good time."

Ameche's Van Cleve assumes he belongs in Hell, and he gets a point in his favor when an old flame, Edna Craig (played by frumpy Florence Bates, who'd acted with Laird at the Pasadena Playhouse), demands an audience. "Really, I don't want to seem rude, but I don't think I belong here!" says Edna, who recognizes Van Cleve. When he recalls Edna having had beautiful legs, she slowly raises her dress to show them to him. Laird's His Excellency pushes a button—and Edna falls screaming through a trap door as flames and smoke billow from below. Laird places a comforting hand on Ameche's arm. "Those things are better left to memory," he says.

Laird's Lucifer was a wonderful creation. Ernst Lubitsch directed this fantasy, which also starred Gene Tierney and Charles Coburn, with the same flair he'd handled *Trouble in Paradise* (1932) and *Ninotchka* (1939). Laird appeared only in the opening and the finale, but the impression was vivid—especially come the finale. Ameche despairs that if he tries to enter Heaven, "The doorman might not even let me in." Laird's Lucifer responds, with great charm:

> Well, you never can tell. It's worth trying. Sometimes they have a small room vacant in the annex. Not exactly on the sunny side, and not so very comfortable. The bed may be hard, and you might have to wait a few hundred years until they move you into the main building.
>
> Well, it doesn't hurt to try. After all, they may inquire about you among the residents in the main building. I think you'll find a lot of people will give you a good reference. That always helps. For instance [smiling and stroking his beard], there were several young ladies ... some of them

145

might be there. And from what I can see, you've made them very happy. I'm sure they'd like to see you happy too...

And if all else fails, there's still someone else.... And she will plead for you.... You know she will....

The "she" that His Excellency refers to is Henry's wife Martha (Tierney), the love of his life, who has predeceased him. The Devil escorts Henry Van Cleve to the elevator.

"Down?" asks the elevator attendant as Ameche boards it.

"No," smiles Laird's His Excellency, pointing heavenward. "Up."

Heaven Can Wait completed shooting April 10, 1943. The film, released that summer, earned giant rentals of $3,963,600, made a profit of $1,286,200, and won three Academy nominations: Best Picture, Best Director, Best Technicolor Cinematography (Edward Cronjager). Laird deserved a Best Supporting Actor nomination for his satanic His Excellency. He didn't get it.

*   *   *

Laird as "His Excellency," aka Lucifer, in *Heaven Can Wait* (courtesy John Antosiewicz).

Don Ameche and Laird in *Heaven Can Wait*.

Laird's three-month hospital stay had resulted in his losing almost 70 pounds. Back at Cherokee Lane, he had an unhappy surprise: Burglars had made off with all his silver flatware, six pairs of shoes, three suits ("enough to relieve wool shortage," quipped Harrison Carroll) and an electric alarm clock. The switchboard ladies on the Fox lot took the place of the stolen alarm clock by telephoning him for his morning call.[1]

As 1943 continued at 20th Century–Fox, Laird faced the return of a rival: Vincent Price. After a year on Broadway starring in *Angel Street*, Price came back to Los Angeles on December 12, 1942, on a new pact with Fox.[2] He landed one of the year's plum character roles: *The Song of Bernadette*'s Vital Dutour, the prosecutor who tries to commit Jennifer Jones' Bernadette to an asylum. Late in the film, Dutour, a dying man, goes to Bernadette's shrine, kneels and movingly pleads, "Pray for me, Bernadette." It might have seemed an ideal role for Laird, but Price played it superbly.

Price was precisely what Laird wanted to be: a tall, slender, handsome man with the versatility to play villain and hero. He was also an accomplished Broadway leading man, which Laird aspired to.

Meanwhile, Linda Darnell, Laird's long-time crush, landed an unbilled cameo in *The Song of Bernadette* as the Blessed Virgin vision, who beatifically appears to Bernadette.

Other events had impacted Laird, professionally and personally.

Thursday, March 18, 1943: Hello Frisco, Hello had opened in Los Angeles at Grauman's Chinese, Loew's State and the Ritz Theatres. The Los Angeles *Evening Herald Express* review found Laird "more or less at loose ends" in his small role as the gold prospector, but audiences loved Alice Faye, the tunes and the Technicolor. Worldwide rentals would soar to $4.3 million; the profit, $1.2 million

Tuesday, March 30: Laird's pal Van Johnson, then starring with Spencer Tracy and Irene Dunne in MGM's *A Guy Named Joe,* had almost died in a car accident that nearly severed his scalp. The saga goes that the first rescue workers to reach the accident site couldn't help because the wreckage was 50 yards over the county line where they had jurisdiction; Johnson allegedly slapped his scalp back on and crawled the 50 yards for care. Doctors placed a metal plate in Johnson's head, his forehead carried a scar for the rest of his life, and Spencer Tracy ordered *A Guy Named Joe* be shut down until Johnson recovered.[3]

Also "shaken up" in the accident was Keenan Wynn, son of Ed Wynn. At age 27, Keenan had recently begun his character actor career at MGM. Johnson recovered that spring at the Wynn home, tended to by Keenan and his wife Evie. Laird became good friends with Keenan as well and, throughout the rest of his life, often joined the parties hosted by the convivial Wynns. Keenan's son Ned Wynn (born April 27, 1941) wrote in his excellent 1990 book *We Will Always Live in Beverly Hills* about how, as a child, he told a fan magazine reporter visiting his Brentwood home about all the celebrities he knew:

> I tell her about Cesar Romero who's handsome and lives up the street and Mickey Rooney who's funny and short and Gene Kelly who teaches me to sword fight at Metro and Peter Lawford who's English and wears loafers with tassels and Laird Cregar who's very fat and plays with me in my sandbox. And Marlene who brings me meatballs with colored toothpicks and kisses my neck.[4]

Monty Woolley, Laird and Gracie Fields in *Holy Matrimony*.

The Van Johnson–Keenan Wynn friendship later morphed into classic Hollywood gossip: Keenan's wife Evie divorced him in 1947, married Van four hours after her divorce was final, and they had a daughter. After their 1968 divorce (Johnson allegedly had left Edie for his male tennis instructor), Evie eventually claimed the marriage had been a set-up arranged by Louis B. Mayer. The mogul, desperate to squelch the rumors of Johnson's homosexuality, said he'd improve Keenan's Metro contract if Evie ditched him and married Van. It was, promised Mayer, "a win-win" scenario for everybody involved. Evie in her later years told Ned that Laird Cregar had warned her years before that Van (who didn't remarry) was homosexual, but she hadn't believed him. Evie died in 2004; Van Johnson in 2008, at age 92.

Meanwhile, the whispering had continued in Hollywood that Laird Cregar and Van Johnson were lovers. In 2014, I asked Ned Wynn about the rumors. "Not too far-fetched," he replied.[5]

* * *

> For my opinion, sir, you are a thorough-going, double-dyed, triple-plated rogue and scoundrel—and I wouldn't lift one finger to save you from frying in Perdition for the remainder of eternity. Good day, sir!
> —Monty Woolley to Laird Cregar, *Holy Matrimony*

Meanwhile, Laird was fuming again.

On Monday, April 5, while Vincent Price enjoyed his showcase role in *The Song of Bernadette*, Fox had started shooting the comedy *Holy Matrimony*. Monty Woolley played a misanthropic painter, hiding on a South Seas island, invited back to London to receive knighthood. Once in the city, however, he panics. When his valet (Eric Blore) dies suddenly, Woolley assumes his identity while the valet is buried with pomp at Westminster Abbey. Trouble ensues when Woolley marries Gracie Fields who, thinking her spouse an amateur artist, sells some of his paintings.

Laird played Clive Oxford, an art dealer who suspects Woolley's true identity and wants to make a killing with his canvases. Laird later confessed he'd balked at accepting the assignment:

> I think the average actor goes overboard when allowed to pick and choose, and when it comes to casting, we're all average, I'm afraid.
> I disliked the part of Mr. Oxford in *Holy Matrimony* more than most of the things given me. He was stuffy, unimportant and his lines sprang from a ponderous mentality. But I made up my mind to do the best I could with scant material. To my surprise when I saw it on the screen, I thought it was one of the best pieces of work I've done. It was a lesson to me. It taught me that we must always try to be superb in the smallest parts.[6]

Once again, Laird made the role "effete." When his secretary crosses her legs and reveals a glimpse of stocking, he shoots her an if-looks-could-kill glance. Directed by John Stahl, *Holy Matrimony* was a festival of character players: Alan Mowbray, Una O'Connor, George Zucco, Franklin Pangborn and Fritz Feld. "Laird Cregar was a wonderful man," said Feld. "We would play chess. He and his mother were very friendly.... He was always telling stories, always very jolly, always very happy."[7]

Laird looked great, attired, as in *Heaven Can Wait*, in cutaway coat and a jowl-hiding goatee. He'd shed more weight, and with the period fashion, he looked almost slender in certain shots, much to his delight. Released in August, *Holy Matrimony* proved popular: $1.57 million in worldwide rentals and a profit of $267,400.

It's fun to see the two *Man Who Came to Dinner* men in the same picture, as elegant adversaries. Woolley was openly homosexual, and one story goes that during World War II, on a trip to New York City, he visited one of his favorite haunts, a gay bar, making an elaborate entrance. "Stand up, faggots!" shrieked Woolley. "Your mother's here!"[8]

Thursday, April 8: Harrison Carroll reported that Laird, intent on losing more weight and enlisting in the Marines, had "a hospital reservation for August 8" for his abdominal operation.

Monday, April 12: Laird made a third guest visit to *Lux Radio Theatre*, this time for "Once Upon a Honeymoon," co-starring with Claudette Colbert, Brian Aherne and Albert Dekker. Laird played the big shot Nazi that Walter Slezak had portrayed in the RKO film. During rehearsals, Laird reminded Colbert of the time in the late 1930s that he'd sneaked her past the crowds into the Paramount Theatre. To his delight, she remembered the incident, or at least was sweet enough to claim she did.

Monday, April 26: Sidney Skolsky reported that Laird was dating Claire Trevor, the blonde-haired star popular due to her excellent performances in *Dead End* (1937) and *Stagecoach* (1939).

The big gossip about Laird, however, was his new crush on Dorothy McGuire, a 27-year-old, angel-faced actress who'd triumphed on Broadway in *Claudia*. When 20th Century–Fox began shooting the film version on April 29, Dorothy reprised her part as the title role child bride, defeating contenders Joan Fontaine, Katharine Hepburn and Jennifer Jones.

Head over heels about Dorothy, Laird appeared virtually obsessed. The press was fascinated, since many reporters believed Laird was gay. As Cal York would write in *Photoplay*, "Even Laird Cregar confessed to old Cal that Dorothy was the one girl he'd gone overboard for. And what a splash it made! Laird won't mind us telling his secret now that he has at last wangled a date. But, boy oh boy, what competition he has among the males at 20th Century–Fox!"[9]

Laird reportedly serenaded Dorothy with "boxes of lilies and pails of fruit," and one wonders what effect Laird's McGuire fixation had on Claire Trevor, Peggy Stack (his on-again, off-again lady friend of the past two years) and his gay companion.

His personal life, as always, remained complicated.

* * *

Laird sent letters to Betsey, whom he missed very much. One of them at this time read:

My Dearest Betsey:
  Your very sweet letter arrived this morning, for which many thanks. It was so nice to hear from you and to learn that you are doing good work in school. Always remember that the harder you work on your lessons when you are young, the more substantial your education becomes; and consequently, the easier your studies will be as you grow older.
  I left the hospital two months ago after having lost sixty-six pounds and have since finished two pictures, *Heaven Can Wait*, with Gene Tierney (who always remembers you kindly), and *Holy Matrimony*, with Monty Woolley and Gracie Fields. I wore my own beard in the picture, which I grew in the hospital. Now, however, it is shaven off, as it became quite long and bothersome. I also went off the diet while making the picture because they had to alter my clothes every few days to keep up with my reduction; but I'm fasting again now and feeling much better.
  I have started to take piano lessons and singing lessons and am quite interested and pleased with them. Of course I have to study and practice very hard. So you see, we're never too old to learn.
  Everyone here loves you very much and misses you mightily—mostly,
  Your loving Uncle,
  Sam[10]

Thursday, June 10: Fox reported it had bought the rights to Vera Caspary's mystery novel *Laura*.[11] George Sanders was set to play the detective who falls in love with a murdered woman after studying her portrait, and Laird was assigned the plum role of Waldo Lydecker, the waspy columnist climactically revealed to be the killer. The rogues' gallery of roles Fox had lined up for Laird was impressive: Jack the Ripper, Javert, and Waldo Lydecker; he'd already done Lucifer.

Tuesday, June 15: Columnist Sheilah Graham wrote that Fox would produce a film version of the Broadway musical *By Jupiter*, with Laird in a change-of-pace role: "[I]t will be interesting to see how he tackles the assignment as a rather effeminate creature in submission to Amazon females. Martha Raye is also in the film, as are Laurel and Hardy, and the whole thing sounds too, too funny."[12] It did, but it was never produced.

Friday, July 2: Variety reported that Fox was "readying" *The Lodger*, a "genuine horror picture about Jack the Ripper." Robert Bassler would produce, and the film, as *Variety* wrote, "will carry higher-than-average budget."

Tuesday, July 6: Darryl Zanuck returned to Fox after adventures in the U.S Army Signal Corps. William Goetz, husband of Louis B. Mayer's daughter Edie, had been in charge since Zanuck's departure. As Scott Eyman wrote in his biography of Mayer, *Lion of Hollywood*:

> Darryl Zanuck returned to Fox after his service in the war, and found that Goetz, who had been running things in his absence, had redecorated his office, the swimming pool, barbershop and steam room. Zanuck's boudoir, a room off his office where he bedded starlets, had been turned into a filing room. More important Bill Goetz had inveigled some of the creative heavyweights around the lot (Nunnally Johnson, Joe Mankiewicz) to write letters to the board of directors saying that they had never been happier than under his own leadership, implying that they had been miserable peons under Zanuck.
>   The attempt at undercutting Zanuck failed, and he wouldn't walk onto the lot until Goetz left....[13]

Monday, July 12: Barré Lyndon completed the first draft script for *The Lodger*. Lyndon, who'd written the popular play *The Amazing Dr. Clitterhouse*, had changed the Ripper's inspiration from prostitutes to actresses, notably a music hall entertainer named Kitty Langley.

Tuesday, July 13: Variety reported that John Brahm would direct *The Lodger*. Brahm, who had directed the 1942 Fox horror film *The Undying Monster*, took pride in his independent streak. In fact, Fox had bounced him off the Sonja Henie vehicle *Wintertime* and replaced him with Archie Mayo. Things had been looking very bad for Brahm in Hollywood. "I was a fallen angel, a black sheep," said Brahm. "Then Zanuck came back, and remembering *The Undying Monster*, gave me *The Lodger* to do."[14]

Thursday, July 15: Joseph I. Breen, having reviewed the script for *The Lodger*, sent his concerns, mainly: "Page 39: Here and elsewhere, we assume that the costumes of Kitty and the girls will be adequate, and that there will be no offensive or suggestive movement in Kitty's dance...."[15]

Tuesday, July 20: Merle Oberon was set to star as Kitty in *The Lodger*.[16] Best remembered for her death scene in Goldwyn's *Wuthering Heights* (1939), Oberon was now Lady Alexander Korda, having wed the British filmmaker in 1939. As she was set to accompany her husband back to England later in the fall, Zanuck obliged Oberon by moving up the starting date for *The Lodger*. He also promised her top billing.

Saturday, July 24: "Laird Cregar is carrying the torch for Dorothy McGuire and plenty," wrote Louella Parsons. Her quote was dated six days *after* McGuire secretly married John Swope, a photographer with whom she eventually had two children and stayed married until his death in 1979. McGuire went on to enjoy a long career, perhaps best-remembered as the mother in Disney's *Old Yeller* (1957). She died in 2001.

As for the broken-hearted Laird, he, according to fan magazine writer Barbara Berch, "gave vent to his grief in a mashed-potato binge."[17]

Sunday, July 25: Laird appeared on radio's *This Is Our Cause*, a patriotic variety show. Laird played King Louis XI, "gloating" over Francois Villon going to the guillotine.

Tuesday, July 27: On the eve of his thirtieth birthday, Laird guest-starred on *Suspense!* in "The Last Letter of Dr. Bronson." As the title doctor, Laird, fascinated with death and murder, wonders, "Why do men behave as they do? ... Why don't they kill one another, as animals do?" Bronson believes there are "five basic checks" that discourage murder, and selects five guinea pigs to test his theory. The fifth, unknown to the doctor, is a madman (played by ace heavy George Coulouris), who enjoys going out late at night and slaying dogs ... and who, come midnight, kills Dr. Bronson.

In introducing the show, *Suspense's* "The Man in Black" told the audience, "Heading our starring Hollywood cast tonight is Mr. Laird Cregar, who will be seen shortly in the 20th Century–Fox production of one of the great suspense stories of all time, *The Lodger.*"

In fact, *The Lodger* hadn't even started shooting yet, but like a child before Christmas, Laird could hardly wait.

20

Horror

A Double Dose of Devastation! Mighty Monsters in Mortal Conflict!
GORILLA GIRL! ... Flesh of rapturous beauty.... Fury of an untamed beast!
—Publicity for Universal's double bill
Frankenstein Meets the Wolf Man and *Captive Wild Woman*, 1943

On the night that Laird Cregar guested on *Suspense!*, July 27, 1943, the Paramount Hollywood and Downtown Theatres in Los Angeles were packing the houses with a Universal horror double feature, *Frankenstein Meets the Wolf Man* and *Captive Wild Woman.*

The former's full moon climax saw Lon Chaney, Jr.'s werewolf acrobatically battling Bela Lugosi's Frankenstein Monster in a wreckage of a laboratory, the bounteous blonde Ilona Massey as the prize. As for *Captive Wild Woman*, mad doctor John Carradine transformed a gorilla into hubba-hubba starlet Acquanetta, who became an ape woman when sexually jealous.

The spectacle of the voluptuous Massey, screaming in her braids and negligee, and Acquanetta's gorilla girl, cavorting in a skimpy circus costume and high heels, proved a crowd-pleaser. Surely part of the duo's calculated appeal: the sex element.

It had been over a decade since *Film Daily*, in 1931, had hailed Lugosi as having created "one of the most unique and powerful roles of the screen" in *Dracula*,[1] since *Variety* had praised Karloff for his "fascinating acting bit of mesmerism" in *Frankenstein*.[2] There had been acclaimed horror films—RKO's 1933 *King Kong* and Universal's 1935 *Bride of Frankenstein* among them—but the genre had quickly become Hollywood's carnival sideshow. Great Britain had created the "H" certificate in 1937, prohibiting younger audiences from seeing horror films. Universal's 1939 *Son of Frankenstein*, an all-star horror epic boasting Basil Rathbone, Boris Karloff, Bela Lugosi and Lionel Atwill, had revived the genre, and there were shockers a-plenty during World War II.

Still, Horror was Hollywood's most disreputable arena, sold as much with sex as with monsters.

Mark Robson, of the Val (*Cat People*) Lewton unit at RKO, sniped that Universal's "prevailing idea of horror was a werewolf chasing a girl in a nightgown up a tree."[3] However, the Lewton films had their own quirks. Robson had just made his directorial debut with Lewton's *The Seventh Victim* (1943), scripted by DeWitt Bodeen (Laird's pal from Pasadena Playhouse, who'd also scripted *Cat People*) and, interestingly enough, Charles "Blackie" O'Neal (Laird's adversary producer from *Oscar Wilde*).[4] The star character:

Jacqueline (Jean Brooks), a former Greenwich Village devil worshipper who, in her Cleopatra wig, looks like a gay bar diva and who, in flagrant defiance of the Production Code, hangs herself. At least five characters in the film are implied lesbians.

Sex naturally prevailed in horror propaganda. MGM's *Hitler's Madman* (1943) starred John Carradine as Reichsprotektor Reinhard Heydrich, whose assassination inspired the Nazis' barbaric massacre of the village of Lidice. Carradine, wearing a false nose that evoked a vulture, slapped a priest, wiped his boots on sacred cloth and, as this real-life monster, likely caused World War II moviegoers more nightmares than Universal's goblins and *The Seventh Victim*'s devil-worshipping floozy did—combined. As for the sex: Metro, buying the independently produced film, added a racy episode in which Carradine leered at Czech girls he planned to send to the Russian Front as prostitutes. (One of the actresses was a pre-stardom Ava Gardner.) The scene ran afoul of the Breen Office, almost costing *Hitler's Madman* its release certificate.[5]

Even the Poverty Row horrors had their fetishes: Monogram's *The Ape Man*, for example, climaxed with Louise Currie lashing Bela Lugosi's hairy menace with a long black whip.

In addition to the sex, horror films, for mass audience appeal, needed a powerful star performance. Few mainstream actors would dare accept a horror role; very few succeeded in playing one. Charles Laughton had triumphed in *The Hunchback of Notre Dame* (RKO, 1939), but that was more medieval epic than horror film. Spencer Tracy had starred in *Dr. Jekyll and Mr. Hyde* (MGM, 1941), flanked by Ingrid Bergman and Lana Turner, playing Hyde as a sex sadist. The worldwide receipts hit a walloping $2,351,000, but Tracy received wildly mixed reviews (he personally thought he was awful) and the infamous performance haunted him.

Of course, Universal was starring Lon Chaney, Jr., who by now had played the studio's Wolf Man, Frankenstein Monster, Mummy and Count Dracula, but Chaney's was a kitschy stardom, impressive only in his own "B" environs. In fact, although Universal had promised Chaney the title role in their 1943 remake of *Phantom of the Opera*, providing the chance to play one of his father's legendary parts, the studio reneged and cast Claude Rains ... much to Chaney's bitterness. Universal clearly felt that Rains[6] had more "legitimacy" as a star, and would be more at home in the $1,600,000 Technicolor production. At any rate, *Phantom of the Opera* was more spectacle than horror film, with Nelson Eddy and Susanna Foster billed above Rains, whose Phantom was decidedly sympathetic (and even hinted to be the father of the heroine).

Laughton claimed he couldn't believe he looked as horrible as he had as Quasimodo; Tracy abhorred himself as Hyde; Rains fought with Universal makeup man Jack P. Pierce to use as non-horrific a makeup as possible as the Phantom.

Curiously, although Fox had such players as John Carradine, Lionel Atwill, Peter Lorre and Vincent Price under contract at various times, Zanuck basically eschewed horror movies. The closest thing to one was 1939's *The Hound of the Baskervilles*, the first film in which Basil Rathbone and Nigel Bruce played Sherlock Holmes and Dr. Watson. Carradine and Atwill were on hand, but as red herrings; the true horror was the dog.

Then, in the summer of '42 Fox did something that was a corporate anomaly: It produced a pair of horror films.

On July 6, *Dr. Renault's Secret* began shooting, starring J. Carrol Naish as a pitiful ape man and George Zucco as the ruthless mad doctor who'd created him. The director was former post–Impressionist painter Harry Lachman. On August 3, Fox started the aforementioned *The Undying Monster*, a werewolf saga, directed by John Brahm. The latter film followed a studio melodrama of its own: George Sanders had refused to play one of the leading roles, and Fox suspended him. Sanders had declared he was over-worked and needed a rest, but *Variety* made a joke of his suspension: "Mebbe He Was Scairt," headlined the trade paper.[7]

James Ellison inherited the Sanders role, and Bramwell Fletcher[8] moved into Elli-son's. Playing the werewolf was John Howard, glimpsed only briefly in lycanthrope makeup. Both *Dr. Renault's Secret* and *The Undying Monster* were slick thrillers, released in the fall of 1942 as a double bill, and *The Undying Monster* had a special vignette, bril-liantly captured by director Brahm and cameraman Lucien Ballard: The camera *became* the werewolf, lunging and jerking along a seaside cliff as it pounced on a female vic-tim.

Brahm and Ballard were significant talents. Brahm, 49, was a German émigré who'd fled the Nazis in 1934. Bald, exacting, evoking a benign Otto Preminger, he was known for meticulously preparing blueprints for camera angles and set-ups. Ballard, 38, had worked his way up from loading trucks at Paramount to become a superb cinematog-rapher who, with director Josef von Sternberg, shared the 1935 Venice Film Festival Best Cinematography Award for Paramount's *The Devil Is a Woman.*

The rentals on the two Fox horrors hardly had been impressive: *Dr. Renault's Secret* lost $11,600, and *The Undying Monster* squeezed out a profit of $1600.

Now come mid-summer 1943, Brahm and Ballard would be working with Laird on *The Lodger.* Fox had learned from the competition how to produce a full-blooded horror film. *The Lodger* would definitely play up the sex. And Laird Cregar had absolutely no reservations about how far he wanted to go in playing Jack the Ripper.

21

"Don't Let Him Catch Ya, Dearie!"

I love the confused mentality of the man. The Ripper is a religious fanatic, a man obsessed with the idea all beautiful women are too dangerous to live, a man with a vengeance obsession. Good and Evil are constantly battling in his murderous mind. It's a role any actor would go for![1]—Laird Cregar

First, of course, there was the sex element.

When Donald Rumbelow, renowned "Ripperologist," gives his popular Jack the Ripper tour through Whitechapel, he notes early in the evening that the victims were not the alluring sexpots usually seen screaming deliriously in Ripper cinema.[2] Mary Ann Nichols, "Dark Annie" Chapman, "Long Liz" Stride, Catherine Eddowes and "Black Mary" Kelly, all slaughtered by the Ripper between August 31 and November 9, 1888, were poor, filthy prostitutes. Disease was so rampant among the Whitechapel whores that many wore false noses, their own eaten away by rot and sickness.

Merle Oberon, star of *The Lodger*, had her own nose; however, she'd had extensive plastic surgery, to repair scars from a 1937 car accident and cosmetic poisoning.[3] As Kitty, she'd mouth slightly risqué songs (Lorraine Elliott would dub her[4]); Joe Breen demanded to see the lyrics to "The Parisian Trot."

Oberon would do most of her own dancing, and Breen demanded to see pictures of her can-can costumes. On August 6, three days before shooting began, the studio sent Breen a shot of Oberon, showing her lacy panties and dark stockings. Breen approved, but warned, "Of course, camera angles and exercises like kicking in the 'Parisian Trot' chorus costume would, if flesh is shown above the stockings, prove to be unacceptable...."[5]

Then there was the "scream" gimmick. As Zanuck enthusiastically wrote in a studio memo:

> This is an essential point: in all the killings, we must get over the fact that when these women find themselves face-to-face with the Ripper, and know that they are to be murdered, their great fear of what is about to happen paralyzes their vocal cords, so although they try desperately to scream, they can't do it. Then we'll have a great situation at the end with Kitty, when we see her open her mouth to scream, but no sound comes out. Finally she manages to cry "John!" but there should be a great moment of suspense before she does so, when we believe that she, too, may meet the fate of the other victims of the Ripper.[6]

Oberon had top billing, and George Sanders had second as John Warwick, the Scotland Yard inspector. It was the third-billed actor, playing the Ripper, who was the powerhouse, and his bravura interpretation was both daring and intensely personal.

*   *   *

> "Mr. Cregar ... has become a fixture in the Hollywood firmament,
> a symbol of velvety, sardonic evil ... he seems to ooze malevolence
> from every pore, and he has the torpid wickedness of a gorged python."[7]
> —Donald Kirkley, *The Baltimore Sun,* August 15, 1943

Murder Number One.

Blonde, British Helena Pickard is the wife of Sir Cedric Hardwicke, hence Lady Hardwicke, although most of her friends call her "Pixie."[8] She's claimed the role of *The Lodger*'s Annie Rowley, once a music hall star, now a raggedy doxy ... and a Ripper victim. "Pixie" has won the part over Helga Moray, Doris Lloyd and the Bride of Frankenstein herself, Elsa Lanchester.[9] She had an ace in her casting: husband Hardwicke is playing Robert Burton, the Lodger's landlord.

She acts her death scene on the Whitechapel set, located on the northeast hill of Fox's back lot, on what used to be a golf course. Pickard plays drunk, dancing and singing in the cobbled street, her fellow revelers cavorting with her. Drunken, cackling laughter.

Laird Cregar doing a makeup test for *The Lodger.*

"Watch out for Jack the Ripper!" teasingly cries a woman.

"Don't let him catch ya, dearie!" bellows a man.

The song is "What Cheer 'Ria," and Joseph Breen, reviewing the lyrics, has objected to a spoken section regarding an old man with a wooden leg, referred to as "Half a Man and Half a Tree." Breen axes the line. "This is in order," he writes, "to avoid offending members of the audience with similar physical afflictions."[10]

As John Brahm has directed, Helena Pickard[11] ventures down the dark street alone, waving a liquor bottle, still singing: "What cheer 'Ria? 'Ria's on the job...."

She weaves past a mounted policeman, through man-made fog so virulent and oppressive that the company takes breaks between takes, hurrying to the parking area for fresh air. Annie moves around a corner. The audience can see neither her, nor Jack the Ripper. Annie starts to scream, but, as directed, she can't.

As *not* scripted, the Ripper screams instead.

In 1975, Joel Greenberg wrote that "Cregar found in the role of the Ripper an almost therapeutic alleviation of his private Angst, the misogyny of a tormented homosexual."[12] The cultural climate has changed since 1975; some would object to the words "Angst" and "tormented" in regards to Laird's homosexuality. As far as "misogyny," there was little evidence of that, aside, perhaps, from Greer Garson. Nevertheless, as Jack the Ripper, slaughtering women so terrified they can't scream, Cregar appeared to be playing a horrific parody of his gay self.

His "Mr. Slade" was an effete poseur, a hater of actresses because one destroyed

Merle Oberon doing a costume test for *The Lodger*.

his beloved brother. The peculiarity is there from his first entrance, when Slade appears through a fog that's so eerie in its black-and-white cinematography that it seems a miasma produced by the Ripper himself.

"I've lived in London," said producer Robert Bassler to cameraman Lucien Ballard after seeing the rushes, "and fog doesn't look like that!"

"You may have *lived* in London," replied Ballard, "and fog *doesn't* look like that— but that's how it *should* look!"[13]

Brahm directed *The Lodger* with a Germanic, Expressionistic flourish, planning many of his shots, as was his habit, via elaborate storyboards. He could be egotistical and demanding, but he also had a sense of humor. He and Laird collaborated closely and amiably.

"He admired Laird Cregar and had great sympathy for him," Brahm's daughter Sumishta Brahm recalled. "He was so sorry for him. He knew he was homosexual, and that was a bad time to be publicly so inclined."[14]

Perhaps partly due to this sympathy, Brahm let Laird loose, admiring the unbridled passion of Laird's Ripper portrayal. The director found that Laird "couldn't wait to get to work each day"[15]: They'd join in lengthy consultations with Ballard, about possibilities with the camera; and most of all, he seemingly delighted in peppering the performance with all variety of "depravity." In one of *The Lodger*'s best scenes, Slade shows his land-

John Brahm, Merle Oberon and Laird on the set of *The Lodger*.

lady, Ellen Burton (played by Sara All-good), a cameo picture of his dead brother:

> I can show you something more beautiful than a beautiful woman—something much more beautiful. I had a brother and he was a genius, and I loved him very dearly. Here is a portrait he painted of himself. Isn't that a wonderful face? Look at that remarkable brow, lofty. See the life in those eyes, they're fine and clear. There's a sensitivity about his lips. You're looking at the work of a genius! It's as real as though he were alive! I can almost hear his voice again as I look at this. Isn't that a marvelous piece of work to come from the hands of a man ... a *young* man?

He looks lovingly at the cameo, whipping up the scene into barely suppressed hysteria, and then ends with a pitiful whimper: "He need not have died," he says ... having injected not only a homosexual flavor to the scene but, considering the dead man was his brother, an incestuous one as well.

Always, almost as perversely, there's a strange, personal sympathy at

Laird Cregar as the Lodger.

play, as when "Slade" speaks to Kitty about his love of the Thames at night: "Have you ever held your face close to the water ... and let it wash against your hands as you look down into it? Deep water is dark, and restful ... and full of peace...." Indeed, one of *The Lodger*'s most haunting shots is the brief image of Laird's Ripper, after one of his horrific murders, silently bowed in a boat, washing his bloody hands in the Thames.

"Laird Cregar," remembered Brahm later in his life, "said the Ripper would do this as a religious ceremony, to ease his conscience.... Laird was magic to direct in this, to say the least."[16]

On September 3, *Variety* reported that a black widow spider had crept onto the set of *The Lodger* the previous day and bitten Ballard, who was "removed immediately to hospital for serum treatment."[17] It seemed to suit the atmosphere, where Laird was creating one of the most fascinating monsters in Hollywood history.

*　　*　　*

Murder Number Two.

Doris Lloyd, a contender for the part of Annie Rowley, won instead the role of Jennie, a Whitechapel hag who, in her rosy youth, had also been a music hall dancer ... and who will be a Ripper victim.

A beauty in her day, Lloyd had played Nancy in Monogram's 1933 *Oliver Twist* and had become a busy character actress; horror fans remember her in such Universal

Laird and Sara Allgood in *The Lodger.*

shockers as *The Wolf Man*. Jennie is a showy role; she imitates Kitty Langley in a pub, dancing and thrusting out her derriere, *à la* Oberon. Years later, her friend, actor David Frankham, will teasingly encourage her to reprise her thrust from *The Lodger* at her home in Santa Monica. Ms. Lloyd always laughs and obliges.[18]

Doris Lloyd is amused that her Jack the Ripper is her dear friend "Sammy" Cregar, although the audience will never see him in the death scene. Replacing him is Lucien Ballard's camera, following this script direction:

> She is rigid from horror, and staring. We know that Jack the Ripper has come into the room, although we cannot see him. Jennie realizes who he is, and she knows why he is there. She starts slowly to back away.... We see the dread in her eyes, and hear her gasping voice as she pleads in terror.... She's so afraid that she cannot find her voice. She is looking into our eyes as she looks into the eyes of Jack the Ripper.[19]

Doris Lloyd nails it in one unforgettable take. Years later, she'll laugh about fan mail she received from an admirer who claims he saw *The Lodger* 13 times because her death scene "gave him a tingle."[20]

* * *

As *The Lodger* continued shooting, it was an interesting time at Fox. Alfred Hitchcock was shooting *Lifeboat*; Laird and "Hitch" had a bet as to who could diet off weight faster. Laird enjoyed gossip and games in the commissary with *Lifeboat*'s star, Tallulah Bankhead. Betty Grable was starring in *Pin-Up Girl*. William Wellman was directing

Joel McCrea and Maureen O'Hara in *Buffalo Bill*, and Laird got a kick out of the sight of his adored Linda Darnell, also in *Buffalo Bill*, made up as an Indian called Dawn Starlight.

It was a busy time for Hollywood horror. August 20: Columbia began shooting *The Return of the Vampire*, starring Bela Lugosi, complete with a werewolf henchman (Matt Willis). August 23: Universal started *The Mummy's Ghost*, starring Lon Chaney as the 3,000-year-old Mummy and John Carradine as his Egyptian high priest. August 26: RKO began *The Curse of the Cat People*, in which producer Val Lewton, forced to make a film to suit the title, outfoxed the front office by crafting a beautiful study of a lonely child (Ann Carter), befriended by the beatific ghost of Simone Simon's Cat Woman.

Doris Lloyd as Jennie, too terrified to scream, in *The Lodger*.

For production value, *The Lodger* left all these horrors in the dust. Indeed, its final negative cost of $869,300, which would include retakes and Hugo Friedhofer's thrilling musical score, would be approximately double the cost of the three aforementioned films combined. Fred Othman, a reporter in Hollywood, visited the set and filed this August 23, 1943, report, writing that he'd met Jack the Ripper on Fox's Stage 3:

> It was our shuddery pleasure this morning to watch this fiend in gray silk gloves and a bottle-green cape hide behind the screen in the dressing room of a beautiful can-can dancer, wait until she started to undo her garters, then pounce on her. It was quite a pounce.
>
> This Ripper is six feet three ... and has yellow hair (the studio bleached it that way). His name, of course, is Laird Cregar. Gives you the shivers to shake his hand. We don't suppose there ever was a more dastardly villain to stalk innocent beauties across the silver sheet...
>
> The picture is titled *The Lodger*.... The studio thinks it will be the horror film to end horror films.[21]

*   *   *

Murder Number Three ... almost.

Merle Oberon has found *The Lodger* a chore: "I wouldn't choose that part, you know," she'll say decades later.[22] Nevertheless, Zanuck and John Brahm have pampered her, as promised, and Lucien Ballard has photographed her with exquisite care, designing a special light he calls an "Obie" to hide her facial scars. (She's so grateful that following her divorce from Korda, she will marry Ballard in 1945.)

Yet from the beginning, Oberon realizes that Laird Cregar totally upstages her.[23]

She competes with him with a peacock performance of high-spirited sexuality, throwing herself with abandon into what one Manhattan critic will call "a remarkable front-view can-can," posing for a surprising number of stills showing her lacy panties and seamed stockings. Still, with the vocal dubbing, the wigs and the special lighting, a vain artificiality results; one starts wondering what she'd look like after taking the Ice Bucket Challenge.

Come *The Lodger*'s climax, Oberon is at the mercy of Laird, figuratively and literally. She's performed her "Parisian Trot," Laird's Ripper watching in anguish from the audience, so agonized that, when Oberon climaxes the spectacle with a thrust of her derriere in panties, it seems almost sadistic. Now they are in her dressing room, she in his gloved clutches:

> CREGAR: You are so exquisite ... more wonderful than anything I've ever known.... You corrupt and destroy men, as my brother was destroyed. But, when the evil is cut out of a beautiful thing, then only the beauty remains...
> [*He draws his knife.*]
> OBERON: ... But, isn't it the life in the thing that makes it beautiful? If you take the life away, then...
> CREGAR: Then it becomes still. Then it is even more beautiful....

In his sly delivery of these lines, Laird has topped all previous Hollywood bogeymen in his daring. His Ripper is a necrophile, who wants to tear Kitty apart with his knife,

Merle Oberon and Laird Cregar in *The Lodger*.

but somehow make love to her mutilated corpse. He proclaims, "I have never known such beauty as yours ... nor such evil in such beauty. Men will not look at you again as they did tonight!" His face starts to twitch, to quiver, as if he's about to explode. Oberon agonizingly tries to scream; if she actually felt terror, nobody would be surprised. Sanders' Scotland Yardsman bursts into the room to her rescue. He shoots, striking the Ripper on the left side of his neck, and the climax of *The Lodger* is on fire, Cregar's rampaging Ripper running madly amok up and down the Victorian theater, a caped, wild-eyed, gasping, bleeding monster, lurching up into the catwalks, the Hugo Friedhofer score exhorting his madness.

The Ripper lunges across the catwalk, toward the camera ... the light below the grillwork rippling over him, creating the bizarre Expressionistic effect of a rampaging were-zebra...

A final attempt to kill Kitty—cutting sandbags that fall, rather like the *Phantom of the Opera*'s chandelier—fails. Sanders shoots him again and again, Laird's Ripper taking more bullets, to quote the *New York Times* review, "than even Frankenstein's Monster was ever asked to absorb,"[24] seemingly possessed by Satan himself. Scotland Yard corners the Ripper high in the theater. He's gasping heavily, seemingly no longer human, a beast, his eyes wide and monstrously bright, reflecting the ultraviolet lights that Brahm and Ballard aim at them.[25] As the *New York World-Telegram* would write of Laird after *The Lodger*'s Broadway opening: "Without the aid of any fantastic makeup, he conveys intensity of evil fascination to his audience. None of his crimes need to be seen. His presence is sufficiently malign and revolting to make it almost painful to wait for his demise."[26]

There's one final wild-eyed close-up, one of the most haunting images in 1940s Hollywood. The demise finally comes with a burst of music, a crash of glass ... and the Ripper throws himself through a window, falling into the "dark and restful" waters of the Thames.

* * *

Laird Cregar has committed his second on-screen suicide. A performance that might have started as a "therapeutic alleviation" of homosexuality had become a raging exorcism.

It was bizarre that, as Laird made *The Lodger* a parable of a homosexual, agonizingly kicking and screaming against the lures of heterosexuality, Louella Parsons described Peggy Stack as the lady "who gossips say will wed Laird Cregar,"[27] reporting later, "Peggy Stack no longer denies that she is romantically interested in Laird Cregar."[28]

More oddly ironic was that, as Laird was playing Jack the Ripper, a close friend of his died of a brutal stab wound. Like the Ripper, the killer was never apprehended. And the ensuing scandal, including homosexuality, a male brothel and a marriage of a homosexual and a lesbian, threatened to wreck Laird Cregar's career ... just as he was about to achieve full stardom.

22

"Gloomy Sunday"

"David G.G. Bacon, 28, died as he acted—in a whodunit...."
—*Variety,* September 14, 1943

Sunday, September 12, 1943.

About 5:00 p.m., a maroon, low-slung, British-made car known as an Austin, heading away from the beach, began "to weave a crazy path," jumped a curb and drove into a bean field at Washington Boulevard and Thatcher Street. A 12-year-old eyewitness named Lorraine Smith saw the car from her home. Warned by her mother that it was probably a drunk driver, she fetched a telescope to watch what happened.

She saw a man, clad only in denim swim trunks, "stagger" from the car, "lunge" into the field, and "slump" into the dry bean stalks. "Help me! Help me!" he cried, and then he died.[1]

The dead man: actor David Bacon. The cause of death: a six-inch-deep stab wound of the left lung by a stiletto-style knife, causing an internal hemorrhage.[2] *Variety* erred in reporting his age—he was actually 29 years, five months and 11 days—and was the socialite son of former Massachusetts Lt. Governor Gaspar G. Bacon. He was also the grandson of Robert Bacon, Secretary of State to Theodore Roosevelt and Ambassador to France under William Howard Taft; an alumnus of Harvard; the husband of Austrian opera singer and chanteuse Greta Keller; and a close friend of Laird Cregar.

Bacon had appeared in six Hollywood productions. The first had been 20th Century–Fox's *Ten Gentlemen from West Point*, with Laird; the last had been the Republic serial *The Masked Marvel*, in which he played the title role.[3] It had been shot that summer and not yet released at the time of Bacon's murder. The *Boston Globe* claimed that, during the shooting of a fight scene, all the actors involved but Bacon had been injured, and that Bacon had joked, "I'll probably get hurt going home in the car." It was prophetic: His murder date was 25 days after the serial wrapped up, and his killer inflicted the fatal wound while Bacon was in the Austin.

Investigators estimated that Bacon had been stabbed 15 to 20 minutes before he died. Robbery wasn't a motive, as Bacon was wearing two valuable rings and had $13 in his wallet. Part of the mystery was why Bacon had been driving, instead of immediately seeking medical help. And one witness claimed to have seen Bacon shortly before his murder, driving with "a black-haired man of dark complexion."

It all became a morbid holiday for the press.

The David Bacon house, known as Castle Hill, sat at 8444 Magnolia Drive, high on Lookout Mountain above Laurel Canyon; it came complete with an upstairs swimming pool and ten showers. His Vienna-born, 40-year-old brunette wife Greta, 11 years his senior, was sleekly attractive, evoking a brunette Marlene Dietrich. She was five months pregnant at the time of the tragedy.

Greta, learning the news, collapsed. A *Los Angeles Examiner* photographer got into Castle Hill and snapped a picture of her in bed. The prostrate widow would be unusually candid in her remarks to police, stating that she and David had quarreled that Sunday morning because he wanted to make love and she wasn't "in the mood." She claimed he'd left the house about 2:00 p.m., saying he was driving to the ocean for a swim. "But he didn't take the dogs with him," said Greta. "He always took our three cocker spaniels with him when he was actually going swimming."

The investigation quickly uncovered that Bacon had a police record. On September 9, 1939, he'd answered the door of the house at which he was living at the time (located very near where he died, ironically), clad only in his pajama tops, when teenage newsboy Curtis Larsen of Venice came to collect money. Bacon invited him upstairs to see his paintings, claiming he was an artist for MGM. When Larsen came upstairs, Bacon made a sexual advance. Larsen fled and told police. Bacon received a suspended sentence for contributing to the delinquency of a minor, and had to leave California for three years.

However, Bacon only went so far as Santa Barbara. A short time later, he'd returned to Hollywood, a "discovery" of Howard Hughes, and had tested for the role of Billy the Kid in Hughes' infamous *The Outlaw*. Jack Buetel won the part, co-starring with Jane Russell (who wore the cantilevered brassiere Hughes supposedly personally designed for her). Bacon reportedly went through three agents, Zeppo Marx, the William Morris Agency and Sue Carol. After his murder, all claimed to have known him only "very slightly."

In a comprehensive account of the David Bacon murder published in the *New York Sunday News* (May 21, 1944), Peter Levins noted that Bacon had appeared in *Ten Gentlemen from West Point*, in which "Laird Cregar, gigantic friend of the New Englander, played a sadistic role as the commandant of the academy." Meanwhile, Greta Keller, in her open European way, feigned no surprise when investigators shared their discovery about Bacon's delinquency of a minor charge. "David liked tall blond boys best," she said.

Laird immediately rushed to Magnolia Drive to help Greta Keller[4] in whatever way he could. Bacon's family superseded him. Lt. Ben R. Toland, Bacon's cousin, a Marine stationed at Camp Pendleton, Oregon, flew to Los Angeles and "took over affairs at the house." Bacon's brother, Dr. William Benjamin Bacon, obstetrician at the Boston Lying-in Hospital, also came to Los Angeles and ordered Greta to report to Hollywood Hospital. Both men clearly were upset with Greta for all she was telling, and Dr. Bacon refused to allow police to question her further. This was after Greta had turned over to police a page from a ledger, written by David in code, mysteriously referring to addresses in Santa Barbara, San Francisco, Boston and Washington, D.C.

The Cunningham and O'Connor Mortuary at Rosedale Cemetery in Los Angeles cremated David Bacon, the ashes to be sent to the Church of the Messiah Cemetery, Woods Hole, Massachusetts. Also, Bacon's attorney revealed that his will, dated June 14, 1943, left his $100,000 estate to Greta. The fact that Bacon had written the will on a single piece of paper caused the *Boston Globe* to speculate, "What strange urge early last June prompted David G.G. Bacon, Jr., Hollywood actor and scion of a prominent Massachusetts family, to make out his will and leave it all to his wife? Did young Bacon, who was mysteriously slain last Sunday, have a weird premonition that his own end was near?"

Meanwhile, police revealed a clue: a navy blue sweater, found in the Austin, believed to have belonged to the killer. The sweater supposedly checked with "the kind issued to letter-winning athletes at a beach high school five years ago."

Then tragedy struck again. "Son of Murdered 'Masked Marvel' Is Born Dead," headlined the *Long Beach Independent* on page one of its September 24, 1943, edition:

> Hollywood, Sept. 23—The slayer who fatally stabbed David Gaspar G. Bacon, star of the *Masked Marvel* movie serial, was revealed today as having been the cause of a second death.
> Dr. William Bendow Thompson disclosed that the child expected by the actor's wife, Mrs. Greta Keller Bacon, former concert singer, was born dead last Monday night.
> The physician said that the stillborn birth was directly attributable to Mrs. Bacon's shock and grief over her husband's death. Mrs. Bacon collapsed when told that her husband had been slain and has been under hospital treatment ever since.

There appeared to be no mercy or privacy for the widow. Dr. Bacon revealed that the baby "had been conceived outside the uterus, and that it never had a chance to be born normally."

Increasingly, the rumors of Bacon's homosexuality (and Greta's) spread.[5] In the aforementioned *Sunday News* feature, the paper ran a large picture of Bacon painting his fingernails and toenails as "Mrs. Hoopencliffe" in the Harvard Hasty Pudding Club's production of *The Lid's Off*. The gossip presented Bacon as a gay blueblood, Greta as a cradle-robbing lesbian, and their marriage one of convenience that had produced a stillborn baby.

It grew worse. The macabre story circulated that Greta loved singing "Gloomy Sunday," aka "The Hungarian Suicide Song," so melancholy that it was reputed to have inspired at least 19 suicides.[6] The composer was Rezso Seress, the lyrics by Laszlo Javor. The report claimed that her obsession with warbling that morbid piece (which Billie Holiday had recorded in 1941, and which the BBC had banned during World War II as detrimental to morale) had caused her divorce from her first husband, American dancer Joe Sargent. It also reputedly had led to the termination of her engagement to Austrian Count Theodore Zichy.

Bacon, of course, had died on a Sunday.

Eventually, Dr. Bacon went back to Boston, and Ben R. Toland returned to the Marines. Police, after investigating the Austin, had asked Toland to come and get the car. Toland protested, asking who was going to clean up the gore. "It makes me ill to see blood," said the Marine.

As noted, Hollywood tolerated homosexuality, as long as it remained a secret. The unsolved murder was anything but a secret, and Greta Keller was a pariah. She'd inherited a nest egg, but if anyone needed a friend in Hollywood in the fall of 1943, it was Greta, who'd so heartbreakingly lost her husband and her baby.

She had a friend: Laird Cregar.

One can imagine how 20th Century–Fox demanded he stay clear of this brewing disaster, considering Laird himself was already the topic of gossip. He told them to go to hell. Indeed, after her hospitalization, Laird brought Greta to live with him at his Coldwater Canyon cottage during the later stretch of the exhaustive shooting of *The Lodger*. It must have been strange to come home after a day as Jack the Ripper to an ill, bereaved woman whose husband had been knifed to death. Nevertheless, Laird was faithful to Greta, and helped nurse her back to health. As Hedda Hopper wrote in her column November 3, 1943: "Mrs. David Bacon, since the mysterious death of her husband and her operation, has been living at the home of Laird Cregar. She'll go to Florida any day now...."

Presumably, Greta did go to Florida, but by the spring of 1944, she'd be back in Hollywood. In the *Sunday News* coverage of the murder, Peter Levins offered this information:

> During the investigation late in the winter a curious sort of call house was unearthed in Venice. Instead of girls being sent out, as is the usual order, this house sent good-looking young men. They all gathered around a bath house half way between Venice and Santa Monica.
>   The stabbing could have taken place at that spot, the police said.

The male brothel, however, offered no conclusive clues. The David Bacon case was never solved.

Greta Keller, who recovered in no small way thanks to Laird Cregar, continued as a singer for over 30 years, long after her husband's death, and Laird's. She became rather an international living legend. In *Cabaret* (1972), her voice is heard on a record singing the song "Heirat" ("Married")—another irony, considering her marriage to David Bacon. She made many recordings, appeared in films and on television, and performed late into her life, wearing slinky gowns as she sang such favorites as "September Song." Keller died in her native Vienna in November of 1977, at the age of 74.

Peter Levins closed his exhaustive 1944 coverage of the Bacon murder in the *New York Sunday News* with this final sentence: "Laird Cregar, the ponderous actor who was such a good friend of [Keller's] husband, had remained a good friend to her, too." A compliment to Laird's kindness, it was also a harpoon, insinuating in its wording of "such a good friend" that Laird and Bacon were likely lovers.

In retrospect, one wonders how Bacon's murder might have affected Laird's portrayal of *The Lodger*. One can't claim the tragedy was responsible for the acting choices Laird made as the Ripper—he'd been playing the role for a month before Bacon's death. Nevertheless, the murder by knife of a close friend, the insinuations of "perversion," the coming home nightly to the dead friend's grief-stricken widow ... it likely created an eerie bond between real-life tragedy and on-screen performance. Refusing to avoid such discomfort, not caving under studio pressure, and never shirking what he saw as his responsibility to a devoted friend, he did what he needed to do.

For Laird Cregar, it was one of his most macabre but finest hours.

23

The Ripper in Person

Lots of people get a great kick out of evil efficiently wrought, and they write in and pat me on the back. Then, too, there are the righteous people who think I'm actually the kind of person I portray on the screen, and who enumerate the various ways in which they would like to eliminate me. The ones I really like are the letters from the few kind souls who realize that I'm only an actor trying to make a living.[1]—Laird Cregar, January 1944

Yuletide approached.

Laird, in boyish high spirits, took a train to New York City, almost a month before *The Lodger*'s scheduled January 19, 1944, premiere at Broadway's Roxy Theatre, to give interviews, guest-star on radio, visit the night clubs, and anticipate what promised to be his greatest triumph. He had another reason to be in New York: He and his pal Keenan Wynn had put together a comedy act, and he was awaiting a State Department permit to go overseas to entertain the soldiers.

There'd been some gnawing distractions. Laird had campaigned for the part of Pvt. Francis Marion, the whimsical, poetry-reciting soldier of Maxwell Anderson's *The Eve of St. Mark,* which had begun shooting at Fox September 13, while *The Lodger* was still in production. "I was told I was too tall and too big, which made me appear too mature," said Laird.[2] Winning the part of Pvt. Marion: Vincent Price, who was one inch taller and two years older than Laird. Price later claimed it was his favorite role.[3]

Also, MGM was preparing a lavish production of Oscar Wilde's *The Picture of Dorian Gray*, with Albert Lewin set as producer and director. Up for grabs: the role of Lord Henry, a Faustian incarnation of Wilde himself, who purrs some of the Great Man's best epigrams, including the always popular: "The only way to get rid of a temptation is to yield to it." Obviously, Laird was ideal for Lord Henry, having originally won his fame as Oscar Wilde on the Hollywood stage in 1940. It would require a loan-out from Fox and, of course, the blessing of Lewin.

"They tested everyone in sight for the Oscar Wilde part!" Laird ranted. "Do you think they even asked me to test for it? No!"[4]

MGM might not have tested Laird, but he was under consideration for Lord Henry. The studio had narrowed the part to three candidates: George Sanders (who had played the Gauguin-like painter in Lewin's 1942 *The Moon and Sixpence*), Basil Rathbone and Laird. Rathbone appeared to be the frontrunner, since he was under contract to Metro at the time, and both Sanders and Laird would require farming out by Fox.

170

On Christmas Eve, 1943, *The Hollywood Reporter* announced the winner: George Sanders.

Still, since completing *The Lodger*, Laird had approached the acclaim he'd always desired. For example, on Sunday, October 17, he'd headlined the War Chest Drive for the Hollywood Victory Committee at a mass meeting in San Francisco.[5] He was dieting again, and had now lost over 80 pounds, weighing 252. He wanted to lose more weight before undergoing the delayed hernia operation. Also, Fox was now considering switching him from villain Javert to hero Jean Valjean in the upcoming *Les Miserables.*

The Broadway opening of *The Lodger* promised to be his big moment in time. As if he still had a strange, lingering premonition that his life would be short, he wanted to make every moment count.

Laird took up quarters at the Sherry-Netherland Hotel, celebrated Christmas and threw himself into a series of radio appearances and interviews.

New Year's Eve, 1943: An interview with Laird by Irene Thirer appeared in the *New York Post.* She tried to corner him on the topic of matrimony, and Laird did a nice sidestep: "I've got to be absolutely sure she's right before I take the step. I've seen too much phony marriage around me. I'd hate to take a bride, split up after a year or so and find myself giving some unworthy person half of my very, very hard-earned goods."[6]

Friday, January 7, 1944: Laird was the guest star on radio's *The Kate Smith Show.* Appropriately, his showcase was "Yours Truly, Jack the Ripper," based on the Robert Bloch story published in the July 1943 issue of *Weird Tales.*

Saturday, January 8: Laird appeared in the *Inner Sanctum* episode "The Death Laugh."

Sunday, January 9: An interview with Laird by Otis L. Guernsey, Jr., conducted in the Oak Room of the Plaza Hotel, appeared in the *New York Herald-Tribune.* Laird spoke of his screen notoriety:

> The other night I went to a Broadway night club with some friends. We were standing next to the cigarette girl when she glanced upward and looked at me. She gasped a quick "Oh!" and fled. Later on in the evening she came up to the table and apologized, explaining that she had never entirely recovered from seeing the thriller *I Wake Up Screaming.* I had given her quite a shock until she managed to disassociate my person from that part in the picture![7]

Claiming "everything I've been has been a little sadistic," Laird spoke of *The Lodger* ("the most sadistic picture of all"), and said he'd love to appear on the Broadway stage ("but that probably won't be for some time yet"). "And I may be doing something non-villainous for the motion pictures one of these days," said an upbeat Laird. "I have a feeling the studio is almost beginning to consider me an actor now, instead of a type."

Guernsey noted that, at the interview's conclusion, a woman came up to Laird, asking him to turn around: "I'd like to see what you look like off the screen." According to Guernsey, Laird smiled, and then "beat a hasty retreat."

"It's too bad," the woman said. "In spite of everything, he's really rather handsome."

Also on Sunday, January 9: Laird guest-starred on *Philco Radio Hall of Fame,* in a drama entitled "Moonlight."

Monday, January 10: Ed Sullivan interviewed Laird on his radio show.

Tuesday, January 11: Laird attended the New York premiere of Hitchcock's *Lifeboat* at the Astor Theatre, interviewing, for WQXR radio, the celebrities who made an appearance.

Monday, January 17: At noon, Times Square became the rally site for the Fourth War Loan Drive. Appearing before the 5,000 spectators were Laird, Jeanette MacDonald, Brian Donlevy, Laraine Day, Lloyd Nolan, Tommy and Jimmy Dorsey, Kathryn Grayson, Bill Robinson, June Allyson, Rags Ragland, Albert Dekker and Helen Walker.

Meanwhile, there was, as columnist Radie Harris reported, an "avalanche"[8] of stars in the Big Apple: Greta Garbo, Marlene Dietrich, James Cagney, Jean Arthur, Mary Pickford, Annabella, Wendy Barrie, Nancy Kelly, Diana Barrymore, Brian Aherne and his wife Joan Fontaine. The bobbysoxers were having a field day, chasing the celebrities for autographs. Laird found himself constantly being pursued.

Indeed, Broadway was booming as America entered its third year of fighting World War II. The Great White Way offered everything from Sonja Henie's annual ice skating spectacular at Madison Square Garden, to a new edition of *The Ziegfeld Follies*, to Paul Robeson and Jose Ferrer in a supercharged *Othello*. The movies big in the Big Apple

Laird Cregar, heading east in December 1943 for the Broadway opening of *The Lodger*.

were *A Guy Named Joe* at the Capitol, starring Spencer Tracy, Irene Dunne and Van Johnson, and *Madame Curie* at Radio City Music Hall, starring Greer Garson.

Tuesday, January 18: Laird was guest star on *Molle Mystery Theatre*, starring in an adaptation of "The Most Dangerous Game" as Rainsford, hunted down as an animal by a madman on a forsaken island.

The next morning was the big day.

*   *   *

Men will not look at you again as they did tonight!
—Laird Cregar as Jack the Ripper in *The Lodger* (1944)

Wednesday, January 19: Broadway's 5,886-seat Roxy Theatre, nicknamed "The Cathedral of the American Motion Picture," hosted a decidedly unholy attraction: *The Lodger.*[9] The Roxy presented *The Lodger* with a festive stage show, including the Gae Foster Roxyettes and "the Voice of Over 10,000,000 records," Helen Forrest.[10] Tucked down in the corner of the *Times*' opening day ad was an easy-to-miss notice:

In Person!
LAIRD CREGAR
TODAY ONLY!
All Performances!

The Lodger already had opened in some cities. *Variety* reported it was "Fat" in Baltimore and a "Smash" in Detroit. Two weeks previously, reviewing a preview of *The Lodger* in Los Angeles, *Variety* had written, "Cregar manages every shading and every sickly manifestation of a distorted creature, every cunning trick and lure, with finest artistry to justify his new rating of stardom."[11]

Now, the "distorted creature" himself sat in the Roxy's first balcony, with the critics. He was jittery, for the key gauge of success rested in New York City. As Thomas M. Pryor reported the next morning in his review of *The Lodger* in the *New York Times*:

> [Laird] had seen *The Lodger* three times previously, but obviously was not prepared for the ripples of laughter which greeted his more ominous movements on the screen. "Interesting reaction," he mumbled at least three times. There were several times when this spectator wanted to laugh right out, too, but suppressed the desire, for we suspect that *The Lodger* was not rigged for laughs. Perhaps if Mr. Cregar weren't quite so big and hadn't happened to occupy the next seat, we wouldn't have been so timid.[12]

Pryor had missed the point: The laughter was a nervous response. Kate Cameron in the *New York Daily News* would accurately report that "squeals of fright and sudden laughs from released tension sweep over the audience at intervals,"[13] while Irene Thirer of the *New York Post* wrote that the Roxy audience "took it with hysterical shrieks and, on occasion, with the kind of petrified silence during which you could hear the proverbial pin drop."[14]

The laughter the *Times* cited had not been disrespectful; it had been an understandable reaction to one of the most fascinating, disturbing, and truly brilliant performances of 1940s cinema. As Thirer reported the next day in the *Post*:

> This department simply must report that, while Scotland Yard's finest were feverishly scouting the on-screen theater for the Ripper, the affable Mr. Cregar was seated in the press section, calmly

enjoying the picture. A little while later, the popular actor made a personal appearance on stage—and took a five-minute ovation before he finally made his exit.[15]

Laird Cregar had triumphed. Magnificently. Exhilarated by the opening day response, he guest-starred at 10:30 that night on radio's *Star for a Night*, broadcast from Broadway's Ritz Theatre. Paul Douglas was host, and the weekly show presented a drama or comedy in which three amateur contestants appeared with a name star. The contestant who gave the "most entertaining or amusing" performance won $1001. This night's show: *Dr. Jekyll and Mr. Hyde*. The first part of the broadcast survives, garishly revealing how Fox already was full-bloodedly promoting Laird as a horror star.

"Monster, I mean *Mister*, Laird Cregar!" says Douglas in his introduction, and Laird enters in a burst of gunshots, screams and his own diabolic laughter.[16] He reminisces about his childhood, claiming he used to serenade the butcher daily, singing, "Oh, Give Me Something to *Dis*member You By." The jokes are pretty lame, although this exchange got a big laugh from the audience:

> LAIRD: For instance, there was my twelfth birthday. How well I remember. I spent the whole day looking over bodies.
> DOUGLAS: Oh, how horrible!
> LAIRD: Oh, they had some pretty good burlesque shows in those days!

He name-drops Karloff, Lugosi and Lorre, eventually proceeding into a spoof version of *Dr. Jekyll and Mr. Hyde*.

Thursday, January 20: The New York newspapers carried the reviews of *The Lodger*. Most were raves; G.E. Blackford of the *Journal-American* was almost rapturous:

> [I]n *The Lodger*—story of London and Jack the Ripper—Mr. Cregar has gone to town as never before. Which is by way of saying that in his newest film, Mr. Cregar is scarcely, if at all, short of being terrific.
> This psychological story of the maniacal killer who terrorized London and baffled Scotland Yard was made to order for Cregar. It is a high-voltage chiller and dispenses its thrills with a perfect hand. It just goes to show what Hollywood can do with a whodunit when it really wants to.
> And what Mr. Cregar can do, given half a chance.[17]

Howard Barnes of the *Herald Tribune* praised the film for its "blood-and-thunder terror," hailed John Brahm for creating "a crescendo of excitement," and saluted Laird for his "frightening job."[18] Kate Cameron of the *Daily News* wrote that Laird's stage appearance, in which he reenacted a scene from *The Lodger*, had managed to "send the audience into further spasms of vicarious horror."[19] Alton Cook of the *World-Telegram* wrote, "That the suspense is so gripping is largely due to the performance of Laird Cregar as the Ripper," and significantly noted, "This is a horror picture that will reach 'way beyond the specialized audience that follows the claptrap to which Hollywood has reduced this style. *The Lodger* is a magnificent example of its type and a magnificent picture as well."[20]

The *Times'* critique, of course, was a slam: "It might have been different, and a good deal more interesting, if Mr. Cregar's character were less that of a posturer and if he didn't continually go around trying to scare the daylights out of everyone." The public clearly disagreed, and *Variety* headlined on January 26: "B'Way Boffo; *Lodger*-Stager Wow 104G."[21]

The first week of *The Lodger* at the Roxy took in $104,480,[22] which *The Hollywood Reporter* called "sensational" and *Variety* "terrific." Among Broadway film attractions that week, it was second only to MGM's *Madame Curie*, which, in its sixth week at Radio City Music Hall drew $108,000.[23]

Laird was thrilled and amused: He and Greer Garson were Broadway's biggest movie house attractions.

The question arises: How many people caught on to Laird's subversive shadings as Jack the Ripper? Ironically, the one surviving response to Laird's performance that perceived the homosexual interpretation was from his pal Tyrone Power, then in the Marines. In his book *Tyrone Power: The Last Idol*, Fred Lawrence Guiles cites a letter Power had written to his close friend J. Watson Webb, Jr., who'd edited *The Lodger*, expressing that he'd been "thrilled" to have seen Webb's name on the credits:

> Then he went on to criticize Cregar's performance as being "very naughty" in some scenes and he wished the director had "tamed down Laird a bit." He was referring to Cregar's obvious projection of the killer as a homosexual, an interpretation Cregar knew well how to play since he was quite open in his sexual preference around the studio.[24]

*   *   *

> One way to keep a kid off the streets in the wintry evenings of old, and to send him running to the safety of the family fireside, was to mention Jack the Rip-

Laird at the Stork Club with Nancy Walker.

per.... Now comes *The Lodger*.... If Jack the Ripper walked the village street tonight he would be mobbed by kids demanding his autograph.
—George E. Phair, "Retakes," *Variety*, January 28, 1944

Laird continued his radio guest spots: January 22, *Inner Sanctum*, in "Song of Doom"; January 28, a return gig on *The Kate Smith Show*, playing in a dramatic skit titled "Concrete Evidence." Meanwhile, *The Lodger* had a big second week at the Roxy— $93,000[25]—and as it started its third week on Wednesday, February 2, Laird replaced Helen Forrest as the stage show headliner. On Friday, February 4, E.C. de Lavigne sent this Western Union telegram to E.P. Kilroe of 20th Century–Fox:

> Mr. Schreiber informs us that he has granted Laird Cregar permission to play one week at Roxy Theatre in New York commencing Wednesday February Second. Deal was set through Cregar's local representative Nat Goldstone. Understanding is that for this one week's services Cregar is to be paid twenty-five hundred dollars for his services and we are to be paid an additional twelve hundred fifty dollars by the Roxy Theatre in consideration of our granting consent for his appearance....[26]

Meanwhile, on January 26, Fox's *The Song of Bernadette* had opened at Broadway's Rivoli, to almost reverential acclaim and big box office. Once again, there was irony: Two of New York City's biggest draws were Jennifer Jones as Bernadette and Laird Cregar as Jack the Ripper.

Saturday night, February 5: Laird enjoyed a special radio role that not only boosted his horror star status, but won him splashy publicity. *Inner Sanctum* presented "Dealer in Death," the saga of infamous early 1800s grave robber Will Hare, of Burke and Hare fame (Burke not appearing in the show). Laird played Hare, an innkeeper whose wife Helen (Ruth Matteson) threatens to leave him unless he can make more money for her to spend on herself. Will, learning from a lodger (George Karger) that Dr. Knox (Ernest Cossart) buys cadavers for dissection, kills the lodger and sells the body to Knox for £10.

Will Hare, we learn, eventually murders 24 victims. Helen's actress sister Mary (Virginia Gilmore, whom Laird had dated in 1942) comes for a visit, and Will dopes her and smothers her. Helen finds Mary's clothes hidden in a chest, realizes her husband is the killer, and runs from the inn. "Murderer!" she screams.

Will runs ahead of the police to Dr. Knox and demands, "You must destroy [Mary's corpse] at once!" However, in a truly creepy touch, Knox declines, saying that Mary's cadaver is "too pretty to look at." Will stabs the implied necrophile. When Helen shows up with the police, Will stabs her too. "I did it all so I could give fine things to you," says Will to the dying Helen, and then he surrenders his knife and himself to the police.

This episode of *Inner Sanctum* received a two-page, 11-picture "pictorial enactment" in *Life* magazine (February 7, 1944).[27] George Karger, who played the lodger whom Will murdered, was also a *Life* photographer, and took the cast to the antique shop of Gimbels department store in Manhattan. They wore full 19th-century costumes, posed on well-dressed sets, and treated *Life* readers to some chillingly atmospheric photos, including three of Virginia Gilmore as a corpse.

"Leading role in the show, as in these pictures," wrote *Life*, "is Laird Cregar, the satiny-voiced Hollywood bogeyman."

* * *

The Lodger ended its Roxy run with a third-week take of $72,500 ("very big," as *Variety* expressed it[28]). For a time, Laird stayed in New York.

Friday, February 11: Laird was the guest star on radio's *Stage Door Canteen.*

Tuesday, February 15: He guested on *Duffy's Tavern.* On that same date, Radie Harris reported in *Variety* that Laird had been ringside at the sold-out Copa to watch Jimmy Durante. When Laird dropped a napkin and bent over to retrieve it, Phil Baker wisecracked, "Better hurry, or the waiter will put a table cloth over you and six chairs around you!"[29]

Friday, February 18: There came a blow-up. Laird was set to star in a radio adaptation of *The Lodger* on *The Philip Morris Playhouse.* Wendy Barrie was his co-star. As *The Billboard* reported:

> Cregar took one look at the script, flung it down, and loudly proclaimed: "This isn't *The Lodger*! I won't go on the air with this. Where's the scripter?" Milton Geiger, the said scripter, was nowhere to be found.
>
> Whereupon Cregar, together with several others, began to "rewrite" the show. While the actors waited around, a few of them were written out of the story. For hours Cregar raged, while the issue remained in doubt, and then at long last, a satisfactory script emerged.
>
> Except for a few minor changes, *The Lodger* was still the same. And the show went on. Everyone was happy, [and] even those who had been called and subsequently written out were paid for waiting.[30]

Saturday, February 19: Laird was a guest on radio's *What's New?* with Jim Ameche, Ed Gardner and Perry Como.

Meanwhile, the permission for Laird to travel abroad and entertain soldiers never came through. Laird planned to return to Los Angeles, proud of the success of *The Lodger*, refusing to be humbled by the critical minority who attacked his performance: "Now I don't try to be modest about that picture at all. I think it's a wonderful picture, no matter how I am.... As for underacting, I don't believe in it. I've never yet seen an actor who underacted who could hold his audience. Maybe you've noticed that when I find a climax in a picture I make the most of it."[31]

Meanwhile, he was still ill, suffering from his ventral hernia and trying to schedule time in his very busy schedule to have the operation he'd needed for over two years. On March 2, Hedda Hopper bitched in her column, "Aren't you getting just a little fed up with Laird Cregar and his operation? I am."

Tuesday, March 7: The Lodger opened in Los Angeles at three theaters: the Egyptian, the Los Angeles and the Ritz. It played with a supporting feature, *Calling Dr. Death*, the first of Universal's *Inner Sanctum* series, starring Lon Chaney, Jr., and Patricia Morison. The duo did, in *Variety's* word, "Sockeroo" business.

The Lodger reaped a terrific worldwide rental of $2,295,500, earning Fox an excellent profit of $657,700. The shocker had scored with all the proper (or improper) spices: sex (rarely did a 1940s film so lovingly showcase legs in stockings), a clever gimmick (the female victims too terrified to scream) and, of course, Laird's deliriously perverse take on Jack the Ripper. John Brahm's direction was superb, Lucien Ballard's cinematography glistening, Hugo Friedhofer's score spine-tingling, and the entire cast superb; but it was Laird who'd haunt the nightmares of those who'd feared *The Lodger.* "The Ripper," said Laird, "is the kind of plum part which keeps an actor in fear that what he does next will in no way live up to it. I'm hoping!"[32]

Meanwhile, Betsey Cregar, who was now living in Brewster, New York, had turned ten. She and some of her girlfriends managed to see *The Lodger*, and her Uncle Sam had her friends covering their eyes and hiding behind their seats. "But he's not really like that *at all!*"[33] Betsey kept repeating.

* * *

The Lodger was a triumph, but one that carried a potentially looming curse for the actor who'd played it with so personal and palpable a passion. In his *New York World-Telegram* review of *The Lodger*, Alton Cook had written that "Laird Cregar is so full of sinister menace that he may find himself confined to such roles as a specialty from now on."[34]

It was a prophecy that had thrown a chill into Laird Cregar himself.

PART V

"A Beautiful Man"

Why so pale and wan, fond lover,
Prythee, why so pale?
Will, if looking well can't move her,
Looking ill prevail?
Prythee, why so pale?

—poem by Sir John Suckling,
used by Patrick Hamilton as introduction
to his novel *Hangover Square*

24

Hangover Square's First Draft, and the Debacle of *Laura*

Do you know the music a man would hear ... if he could stand upon a cloud and listen? ... He'd hear the stars singing and the planets spinning.... If a man could ... stand upon a cloud ... and listen....
—George Harvey Bone's dying words, in Barré Lyndon's first draft script for *Hangover Square*, February 12, 1944

Returning to Hollywood, Laird Cregar had three properties awaiting him: *Les Miserables*, in which he'd play either Jean Valjean or Javert; *Laura*, in which he'd play waspy Waldo Lydecker; and the vehicle Fox had bought especially for him: *Hangover Square*, a novel by Patrick Hamilton, in which he'd play a pitiful schizophrenic named George Harvey Bone.

He, of course, had no idea of the debacles awaiting him regarding each of these films.

While Laird was in New York in early 1944, *Angel Street*, the play he'd planned to top-line on Broadway in 1941, was in its third year and still going strong.[1] MGM had completed a film version, starring Charles Boyer and Ingrid Bergman (who'd win an Oscar for her terrified Mrs. Manningham), set for May release under the title of *Gaslight*.

Despite the boon of *Angel Street*, Patrick Hamilton was hardly a happy man. Slender, bespectacled, chain-smoking, he was an alcoholic from an early age; in the mid–1930s, a car went out of control, drove up onto a sidewalk, struck him and left him facially scarred.[2] The scars were far worse in his mind than in reality; nevertheless, if Laird Cregar had considered himself a "grotesque" because of his size, the hypersensitive Hamilton considered himself a "grotesque" due to his scars.

For all the success of *Angel Street*, many believed Hamilton's masterwork was his novel *Hangover Square*, published in 1941, when Hamilton was 37. The tale told the tragedy of George Harvey Bone, whose description might have fit Laird after a hard night:

> He was 34, and had a tall, strong, beefy, ungainly figure. He had a fresh, red complexion and a small moustache. His eyes were big and blue and sad and slightly bloodshot with beer and smoke. He looked as though he had been to an inferior public school and would be pleased to sell you a second hand car.[3]

The novel opens on Christmas Day 1938 as Bone walks the cliffs, suffering one of his "dead moods," realizing: "He had to kill Netta Longdon." Netta is a cheap, vulgar would-be-actress who humiliated Bone time and again. Finally, in a "dead" mood, he murders her. The book has a violent sexuality, and in his excellent biography of Patrick Hamilton, *Through a Glass Darkly*, Nigel Jones reveals why: Hamilton himself was almost homicidally obsessed with an actress, Geraldine Fitzgerald.

Of course, Ms. Fitzgerald was by no means cheap or vulgar; nevertheless, without trying, she'd bewitched the unfortunate Hamilton. Fitzgerald sensed Hamilton was a genius, but also a mystery. He had concealed from her that he was married; once Hamilton learned Fitzgerald was in love with another man, he suffered "a kind of breakdown." His behavior became "disturbing and vaguely menacing," as Jones wrote:

> She became aware that meetings with her fiancé in her London flat were sometimes observed by Patrick, who would ring to ask if the man was still with her. At other times the phone would ring, and the person on the end of the phone would not speak when Geraldine answered. Though she had no proof that the mystery caller was Patrick, she strongly suspected it was him. On other occasions she would observe Patrick standing alone in the street opposite her apartment, watching the windows.[4]

"Disturbed and frightened," as Jones expressed it, Fitzgerald sought the advice of Bill O'Brien, a theatrical agent who knew Hamilton. O'Brien's opinion: Hamilton "could be capable of doing her physical violence and might even go so far as to kill her." Fitzgerald moved to a houseboat moored on the Thames, living there with her family, careful that Hamilton not discover her new locale. Later, when the actress went to Hollywood for 1939's *Wuthering Heights* and *Dark Victory*, Hamilton followed, found her and offered her *Angel Street*, at extremely generous terms, as her own Broadway vehicle.

She declined the offer. And in her relations with Hamilton, Fitzgerald made another unnerving discovery: He was "absolutely obsessed with prostitutes."[5]

In *Hangover Square*, Hamilton's prose betrays his infatuation with the real-life "Netta," as Bone fantasizes about her:

> ... Netta. The tangled net of her hair—the dark net—the brunette. The net in which he was caught—netted. Nettles. The wicked poison-nettles from which had been brewed the potion which was in his blood. Stinging nettles. She stung and wounded him with words from her red mouth. Nets. Fishing-nets. Mermaid's nets. Bewitchment. Sirens— the unearthly beauty of the sea. Nets. Nest. To nestle. To nestle against her. Rest. Breast. In her net. Netta....[6]

Climactically, George Harvey Bone kills Netta Longdon, as she reclines in her bathtub:

> He saw her staring at him, first in surprise, then in terror; he saw that she was trying to speak, but that nothing would come from her throat; he saw that she was trying to scream, but that nothing would come out.

Geraldine Fitzgerald, the inspiration for Netta in Patrick Hamilton's novel *Hangover Square*.

"Don't bother!" he said. "It's all right. Don't be frightened! Don't bother! Don't bother!"

He seized hold of her ankles firmly and hauled them up in the air with his great strength....

Then he grasped both her legs in one arm, and with the other held her, unstruggling, under the water.[7]

The pitiful Bone then kills Netta's paramour by smashing his skull with a no. 7 golf club, and gasses himself. He leaves a suicide note that concludes with "Please remember my cat."

The novel was a great success in London. James Agate in the *Daily Express* called it "the best study of a trull since Shakespeare's Cressida."[8] Geraldine Fitzgerald, inspiration for the "trull," read it too, and was shocked to see how Hamilton had exorcised his obsession over her.

Hangover Square was a success in the U.S. as well. Louella Parsons reported on March 17, 1942, that Laird had been negotiating with Random House for the rights, hoping to produce it as first a play and later a movie. Fox optioned the property for him.

Strangely, from the beginning, trouble loomed over what eventually seemed a cursed production, beginning with Barré Lyndon's curious response to the novel. Lyndon (who'd scripted *The Lodger*) had met Hamilton in London, where he'd cordially traded Hamilton a copy of his (Lyndon's) play *The Amazing Dr. Clitterhouse* for a copy of Hamilton's play *Angel Street*. As Lyndon told Joel Greenberg in *Focus on Film*: "So when I saw that he'd written *Hangover Square*, I bought a copy, or got one sent over here. I read about half of it and thought, 'This is a weird one, I can't understand it at all,' and gave it to the guy at the garage to read."[9]

When Lyndon checked back onto the Fox lot late in 1943, Robert Bassler, who'd produced *The Lodger*, offered him three properties to script. Lyndon found *Hangover Square* the least bad of the trio and left the conference with the book, but rather than begin re-reading it, went to the story department and read a three-page synopsis. He "suddenly saw the way to do it":

You see, this fellow is supposed to suddenly go off his head, and it just "happened." What triggered me was the thought, "Now if there were a noise, or something we could see—either hear or see—something big, something noisy, like a truck spilling a load of piping"—and if you've ever heard that you won't forget it! And then—oh boy!—I went straight back and sold this to Bassler. "Oh yes," he said, "of course!" ... I heard Patrick Hamilton was rather annoyed with the way it was treated, but then I treated it for motion pictures, not for realism at all. I took the basic idea and went on from there....

To say Hamilton was "rather annoyed" with the treatment is an understatement. More on that later.

Saturday, February 12, 1944: Lyndon completed the first draft of *Hangover Square*.[10] The work was startlingly different from both the novel and the ultimately released film.

It begins on the corner of Hangover Square and Church Street, the Bank Holiday, 1937. A banjo player and Cockney are performing the ragtime song "Grizzly Bear." When two of the banjo player's strings break, George Harvey Bone, a brilliant young composer (as opposed to the jobless loser of the novel), steps up from the crowd and continues playing the song on the broken banjo.

"That's George Bone," says a potman. "He can get music out of anything!"

Bone suffers dead moods, brought on by sudden jarring sounds; afterwards, he can't remember where he was or what he did. The previous night, he never came home … and had stolen a Venetian dagger from a pawnbroker's shop.

We meet Middleton, an old detective who never solved a murder; Barbara Leigh, a "dark, slim, soignee" psychoanalyst who admires Bone's musical genius and is aware of his dead moods; Christopher Wyndham, a 12-year-old who idolizes Bone and hopes to be a fine pianist to whom George will give lessons; and Sir Henry Chapman, a famed composer. Barbara has brought Bone's Concerto in "A" Major to the attention of Chapman, who encourages Bone to complete it; if he does, Chapman will conduct it and George will be at the piano.

Enter Netta Longdon—appearing in "a very fetching negligee" as she paints her toenails. Netta, George's neighbor, has given him a Siamese cat which, as Barbara notes, is "strangely like her, somehow." An ambitious chanteuse, Netta flirts with George, distracting him from his concerto, charming him into writing music to accompany the insipid lyrics her crony Mickey writes for her:

> I'm not civilized…. I've a jungle urge…
> Oh-h-h…
> I'm a bad little girlie, but I don't give a damn….

The disturbed Bone finds his way one night to St. Saviour's Church, sits alone in the balcony, hears celestial music in his mind, and finds the inspiration to resume work on his concerto. However, the wicked Netta saps his creativity, seducing him into writing songs for her show, *Gay Love.* Eventually he learns she's cheating on him and, in one of his trances, he strangles her while she sits at her mirror. There followed the original script's big horror centerpiece: Bone drives Netta's corpse to an excavation site, where a theater is under construction, throws the cadaver into the hole and pours a ton of concrete on top of it.

George is warned that, if his mental illness worsens, he'll remember the crimes he might have committed and suffer a fatal physical and mental collapse. Of course, he has the breakdown the night he triumphantly plays his concerto. Old Middleton has unraveled the case, and the police, who have exhumed Netta's body from her concrete grave, arrive at the theater. Bone escapes into a snow-covered London and, accompanied by little Christopher, who attended the concert, goes to a park. They sit by a moonlit pond, Christopher saying, "I want to be good enough to play your music" and pleading for Bone to coach him, Bone concealing from the hero-worshipping boy that he's dying:

> GEORGE (*after a moment*): I'll always be by you, when you're playing … (*glancing*) Now I'll put you in a taxi, and send you home…
> CHRISTOPHER (*surprised*): Aren't you coming…?
> GEORGE (*slowly*): No…. There's somewhere else that I want to go….

George goes alone to St. Saviour's Church, sits in the balcony, hears the theme that he heard before, and looks out the window at "the snowy roofs, moonlit, and the clouds in the sky." An organ plays the theme "caressingly," the music becomes a lullaby, the twilight music from the concerto. George looks toward the "mellow-lit and beautiful" altar, softly saying, "Play my music, Christopher…. Play my music…." The light from the altar is on his face, and he closes his eyes. "[H]is hand drops slowly back and becomes still…. The sweet organ music swells." The film fades out and ends.

It was an unwieldy script, almost insultingly different from Patrick Hamilton's novel. Still, Lyndon had done wondrous things with the George Harvey Bone role, at least as far as Laird was concerned: a sad, pitiful musical genius, with a magnificent death scene. Fox executives boosted Laird's enthusiasm by promising he could play his own musical compositions in the film. He believed them.

* * *

> You'd better watch out, McPherson, or you'll end up in a psychiatric ward.
> I don't think they've ever had a patient who fell in love with a corpse.
> —Waldo Lydecker in *Laura*

The Fox front office placed *Hangover Square* on hold. Zanuck had reservations about Lyndon's script, but was too personally involved with his dream project, *Wilson*, the saga of America's 28th president. Alexander Knox played Wilson, Henry King directed, and the huge supporting cast included Vincent Price as William Gibbs McAdoo.

Zanuck was also preoccupied with *Laura*.

The perils of *Laura* were many.[11] The producer was Otto Preminger, whom Zanuck had fired years before while Preminger was directing *Kidnapped* (1938), banishing him with the promise that Preminger would never again direct a Fox film. William Goetz, in charge at Fox while Zanuck was in the Army, engaged Preminger as a producer-director; Zanuck, back at the studio, summoned Preminger to his beach house. Refusing to look at him, Zanuck told Preminger he could still produce at Fox but, once again, he'd never direct. Set to direct *Laura* was Rouben Mamoulian, who'd directed Laird in *Blood and Sand* and *Rings on Her Fingers*, and who'd returned to Hollywood after staging the sensational Broadway success, Rodgers and Hammerstein's *Oklahoma!*

As noted, *Laura* had been on Fox's slate since June 1943, originally announced for Laird Cregar as killer Waldo Lydecker and George Sanders as detective McPherson. (Some who recall Dana Andrews' tough guy interpretation of the detective might wonder how Sanders would have fit the bill; however, in the original concept, McPherson was an erudite Ellery Queen type.) At any rate, Sanders' scheduled loan-out to MGM for *The Picture of Dorian Gray* removed him from *Laura*.

Thursday, February 24: Variety announced Gene Tierney would star in the title role.

Monday, March 6: Clifton Webb, Broadway star and musical performer with minimal film credits, opened in the touring company of *Blithe Spirit* at the Biltmore Theatre in Los Angeles, winning excellent reviews.

Thursday, March 16: Laird guest-starred on *Suspense!* The episode was "Narrative About Clarence," with Laird as the sinister title character, a mad hypnotist who returns from Calcutta wearing a cat's eye ring … and who plans to kill his half-sister and her daughter. When his brother-in-law (Hans Conried) demands to know why, Laird replies:

> Because … my mother meant more to me than anything in the world! She died in giving birth to this silly, shallow person you call your wife! I have hated her since the day she was born! And I hate the child, because having no right to life, she commits the sacrilege of inheriting my mother's beauty! They must both be destroyed … the murderer and the imposter!

One wonders if the show disturbed Laird, considering his own feelings for his mother and his niece Betsey.

Friday, March 17: Variety reported that Jennifer Jones, who on March 2 (her 25th birthday) had won the Best Actress Oscar for *The Song of Bernadette*, would portray Laura.

Preminger, meanwhile, was adamant: He did *not* want Cregar in *Laura*. He argued that Laird's familiarity as a heavy would instantly tip off the audience that Lydecker was the murderer. Lydecker had killed a woman (thinking in the dark it was Laura) by shooting her in the face with a shotgun; it sounded like a deed worthy of Hollywood's Jack the Ripper. Preminger had another actor in mind: Clifton Webb, whom he'd just seen in *Blithe Spirit*.

On one hand, Preminger was right: Laird was a very obvious heavy. On the other, Laird was absolutely ideal for Lydecker; indeed, in the novel, Vera Caspary had described Waldo as fat, and Laird would have been superb tossing off such Lydecker lines as, "Laura, dear, I cannot stand these morons any longer. If you don't come with me this instant, I shall run amok."

Debate ensued. Zanuck scoffed at Preminger's suggestion of Webb, replying, "He flies!"—a reference to Webb's rather open homosexuality, and the fact that Webb lived with his mother Mabel. Of course, Laird also allegedly "flew" and, for a while in Hollywood, had lived with *his* mother, so that argument rather cancelled itself out. In yet another irony, Zanuck now toyed with casting Monty Woolley as Waldo ... which put three homosexuals in the running.

At length, Preminger paved the way for Webb to make a screen test for Waldo Lydecker; Webb refused to test, but offered to perform his favorite monologue from *Blithe Spirit*. Zanuck vetoed such a test; Preminger shot it anyway, on the sly, with cinematographer Joseph La Shelle.

Monday, March 20: After Webb had completed his two-week L.A. run of *Blithe Spirit*, and had departed to play in Oakland, Zanuck wrote to Preminger, copying Mamoulian and Samuel Hoffenstein (whom Mamoulian had engaged to rewrite the script):

> Waldo should be able to say the most insulting things but at the same time know where to draw the line to preserve his own skull. We will decide in the next day or two what actor is to play this role, and of course this will influence the writing. If we decide to use Laird Cregar, you should again look at those scenes in *Blood and Sand* in which he was so magnificent as the sardonic super-critic. And a great deal of Waldo's dialogue can have the biting flavor of *The Man Who Came to Dinner*....[12]

Of course, just as Laird had triumphed in a Hollywood theater production of *The Man Who Came to Dinner* in 1941, Webb had also scored in the play, having headlined the national company. In Oakland, Webb recalled receiving a wire reading, "Decision cannot be made about your playing the part until tomorrow." Webb gathered that Mamoulian was "very anxious that Laird Cregar play the part," and composed a telegram about it, to the tune of *Oh, What a Beautiful Morning*:

> Oh, what a beautiful morning,
> Oh, what a beautiful day.
> Baby's right back where he started,
> Mamoulian wants Cregar they say.[13]

Webb went with *Blithe Spirit* to Portland, where he received another wire: "Mamoulian, after seeing other tests, entirely in your favor ... decision now rests with Darryl Zanuck." Eventually Zanuck agreed, and Webb learned the news as he continued his tour in Seattle. "Webb in *Laura* Spot," headlined *Variety*, March 31, 1944.

Laird was mortified and frightened. He'd always dreaded typecasting, and now his notoriety as a villain had cost him what many saw as the plum film role of the year. Additionally, Vincent Price would win a flashy role in *Laura* as Shelby Carpenter, the gigolo whom Lydecker refers to as "a male beauty in distress."

It would be just the beginning of turmoil for *Laura*. On *Laura's* first proposed day of shooting, April 24, Jennifer Jones refused to report for work. Fox threated to sue and Gene Tierney went back into the role. Preminger and Mamoulian fought so bitterly that Mamoulian barred Preminger from the set. Ultimately, on May 15, following more than two tumultuous weeks of shooting, Preminger would take over the direction after Mamoulian resigned or was fired (sources differ). Even the famed musical theme was born amidst misery: David Raksin composed it one weekend after receiving a letter from his wife, saying she was leaving him.

It was shaping up as a bad spring for Laird Cregar. Summer and fall would be considerably worse.

25

A Failed Romance, a Revised Script, Abbott and Costello Meet Laird Cregar, a Female Stalker, and the Tragedy of *Henry VIII*

I would not be a queen / For all the world.
—Henry in Shakespeare's *Henry VIII*, Act I, scene ii

Tuesday, April 4, 1944: Universal began shooting *House of Frankenstein*.[1] In this "monster rally," mad doctor Boris Karloff, aided by hunchback J. Carrol Naish, unleashed the Wolf Man (Lon Chaney, Jr.), Frankenstein's Monster (Glenn Strange) and Count Dracula (John Carradine).

For Carradine, once Laird Cregar's rival at Fox, it had been a trap-door plunge into horror star infamy. On October 24, 1943, "John Carradine and his Shakespeare Players" had opened in *Hamlet* at San Francisco's Geary Theatre. The actor was producer-director-star-sole owner of the company, having largely financed it via horror films for Universal and Monogram. Carradine toured the West Coast to acclaim as Hamlet, Shylock and Othello, and opened his troupe at Los Angeles' Biltmore Theatre on December 6. However, no booking agent would take on Carradine's company, and his dream of opening on Broadway on April 23, 1944, Shakespeare's 380th birthday, went up in a blast of fire and brimstone.

In the wake of the troupe's failure, Carradine had left his wife and sons, taking up residence at Hollywood's Garden of Allah with his Ophelia-Portia-Desdemona, blonde Sonia Sorel. Her behavior, then and later, led some to consider her insane.[2] *House of Frankenstein* was the latest indignity: For $3,500 a week on a two-week guarantee, John Carradine took on Dracula's top hat and cape, selling his soul to Hollywood horror.[3]

Laird Cregar observed it all with concern. Based on recent crises in his career, could the curse of horror typecasting fall upon him?

Wednesday, April 5: Laird was the guest star on *The Eddie Cantor Show*, broadcast from the Torney General Hospital in Palm Springs, which treated Army Air Force patients. In a comedy skit, he claimed he was writing a mystery play, with Cantor as a detective and Laird as "Mr. X":

187

CANTOR: What can you tell me about the murderer?
LAIRD: Well, he moved into the 13 Palms Hotel on the 13th of the month, and checked into Room
    1313.
CANTOR: Are you sure?
LAIRD (*lisping*): Thertainly!

Laird's fee: $1500. Fox let him keep the entire amount "for his own use and benefit."[4]

Monday, April 10: Columnist Erskine Johnson ran this item:

KARLOFF VS. CREGAR
    Sight of the Week: Boris Karloff and Laird Cregar in opposite booths of the Brown Derby
mugging horrific glares at each other. A waiter, caught in the crossfire, squirmed like an impaled
moth.[5]

Saturday, April 15: Laird was guest star on the Groucho Marx radio show. The
broadcast doesn't appear to have survived, but a record of Laird's fee does: $1000, which
Fox, again, let him keep "for his own use and benefit."[6]

Monday, April 17: Louella Parson reported, "The Laird Cregar–Peggy Stack
romance has gone pfft."

The one-liner carried a punch. Peggy Stack had been dating Laird on and off for
over two and a half years; there had been recent rumors they were engaged. Nobody
went on record as to why things went "pfft," but the story made the rounds that Peggy,
patient for too long, had demanded proof of Laird's commitment to her ... including
his physical commitment.

Considering all the gossip about Laird's homosexuality, it seems impossible Peggy
wouldn't have heard at least some of the prattle. Conflicted about his sexuality, Laird
had come to an impasse. He tried to salvage the relationship.

Friday, May 12: "20th Preps *Valjean* for July 1 Start," headlined *Variety*:

Jean Valjean, after nearly two years preparation ... has been given starting date of July 1 at 20th-
Fox under production reins of William Perlberg. Victor Hugo classic will be directed by John
Brahm, and Laird Cregar will portray the French detective, Javert, nemesis of Valjean, the escaped
convict.

Thursday, May 18: Laird was the guest star on *The Abbott and Costello Show*. On
the broadcast, Costello was supposedly having trouble sleeping, and agreed to go to
Laird's house for a midnight séance, so Laird could examine his subconscious
mind.[7]

"I tell ya, Abbott," protested Costello, "I don't want to go to this Laird Cregar's
house. He's a dangerous man—a regular Jack the Ripper!"

Of course, the séance takes place, and Laird concludes:

LAIRD: Well, I think I can finally give you a diagnosis. You are suffering from an adhesion of the
    telencephalon, which in conjunction with the opacity of the perilax, causes your cerebellum to
    press on your medulla oblongata!
COSTELLO: CREGAR, WATCH YOUR LANGUAGE! I got my mother's picture in my pocket!

Laird's fee for the evening: $1250.[8]

Friday, May 26: "20th Shelves *Valjean*, Lacks Name Player," *Variety* headlined. The
article noted that "Production of *Jean Valjean*, on William Perlberg's slate, has been
indefinitely postponed at 20th-Fox because important name player for title role is not

available. Gregory Peck was in line for Valjean, with Laird Cregar as Javert, but Peck is committed to other pictures."

Fox, still considering casting Laird as Valjean (but clearly favoring him as Javert), decided to move up *Hangover Square*, which Barré Lyndon had revised for the second time, slating the show as Cregar's next film.

Saturday, June 3: Laird was set to return as the guest star on Groucho Marx's *Blue Ribbon Town* radio show, but cancelled.[9] Marx's producers, seeking a last-minute replacement, signed Boris Karloff, which gives indication of Laird's cinema notoriety at the time.

Thursday, June 15: Louella Parsons: "Peggy Stack's long romance with Laird Cregar is no more. She leaves for Mexico City Saturday."

Laird was traumatized. Based on later evidence, he returned to his male lover. Meanwhile, he despaired about winning back Peggy.

The professional and personal troubles mounted.

Friday, June 23: Barré Lyndon finished his third complete script for *Hangover Square,* still following the basic premise and characterizations of his first draft.[10]

Monday, June 26: Darryl Zanuck detailed his problems with the scenario:

> The story should be laid in London in 1910. It is essential that we put it back to 1910 in order to get the flavor of mystery that goes with that period. Today when you think of crime you think of the F.B.I. and scientific filing systems, etc., and all the mystery has gone out of it.
>
> The story is entirely overwritten from the standpoint of sets, and it will have to be radically confined to a budget of $850,000. This means finding ways and means of avoiding expensive sets. I see no reason why we cannot use all of the streets and sets as they are from *The Lodger.*[11]

In his nine-page memo, Zanuck continued to dictate changes, calling for an opening murder ("It should be frightening and exciting and very brief"); he also ordered that the character of Middleton, the old Scotland Yard investigator who'd never caught a killer, morph into a "romantic" character and "a good role for George Sanders." Zanuck decreed that Netta's body be consumed by fire, and that Bone die by fire as well while playing his final musical composition. The producer noted in the same memo: "We must get a very sexy woman, possibly a foreigner, for Netta. She should have the same lure that Marlene Dietrich had in *The Blue Angel....*"

Also, Zanuck suggested that, for the climactic fire in Sir Henry's house, the studio use the White House East Room set from the recently completed *Wilson.* "It will be fascinating to us to watch," wrote Zanuck, "how this Jekyll-and-Hyde development conquers him."

Monday, July 10: Laird, unaware of Zanuck's revamping of *Hangover Square,* starred in summer stock at the Strand Theatre in Stamford, Connecticut, reviving his acerbic Sheridan Whiteside in *The Man Who Came to Dinner.* The engagement was partly a personal favor to his friend Gus Schirmer, Jr., whom Laird had met at the Pasadena Playhouse. Laird also coaxed Tallulah Bankhead to play *Private Lives* at the Strand. After the "straw hat" appearance, both Laird and Tallulah were set to report to 20th Century–Fox ... he for *Hangover Square,* she for *The Czarina* (released as *A Royal Scandal*).

Featured in the Stamford *Man Who Came to Dinner* was a vainglorious ghost from Laird's past: Carol Goodner, who reprised her vampy Lorraine Sheldon, which she'd created in the original Broadway production. Five years previously, Goodner had starred in the ill-fated West Coast try-out of *The Great American Family*, in which she'd tried to get Laird fired. It must have been a strange reunion.

Yet Laird behaved himself. Appearing at the Strand in the play was a young actor named Roger Kinzel, who remembered that Laird performed smoothly with the cast, pulled no "big star" act, and had "beautiful manners."[12] Kinzel also recalled his nightly post-performance service: providing Laird a milkshake.

July 10: On the same day that Laird opened in *The Man Who Came to Dinner* in Stamford, the *New York Times* reported: "It's now up to 20th Century–Fox, which has Laird Cregar under contract, whether the actor can get away from Hollywood long enough to make it worthwhile for Billy Rose to engage him for the title role in *Henry VIII*...."[13]

Indeed, it appeared that Laird's engagement in Stamford had brought him east for a major confab with two theatrical dynamos: producer Billy Rose and director Margaret Webster.

Rose, 44 years old and 4'11", was a force of nature in the American theater. A producer-director-composer-lyricist-writer and theater owner, he'd written the lyrics to such songs as "Me and My Shadow"; produced the 1939 New York World's Fair Aquacade, starring his Olympic swimmer wife Eleanor Holm[14]; and produced the George Bizet–Oscar Hammerstein II musical *Carmen Jones*, then playing SRO on Broadway. He was a show business legend, as was his night club, Billy Rose's Diamond Horseshoe, which the impresario had established in Times Square's Paramount Hotel in 1938.

Margaret Webster, 39, was the daughter of actress Dame May Whitty and the lover of actress Eva Le Gallienne.[15] She'd directed Maurice Evans in his Broadway *Hamlet* of 1938 and had achieved her ultimate triumph at New York's Shubert Theatre on the night of October 19, 1943, as director of the legendary *Othello*, starring Paul Robeson as the Moor and Jose Ferrer as Iago. Webster's *Othello* (in which she played Emilia) had just closed July 1, 1944, after 296 performances, one of the most vibrantly overpowering Shakespearean productions in theater history.

Now, Webster wanted to direct Shakespeare's *Henry VIII*. Rose saw it as a classical spectacle. And for the title role, both Webster and Rose wanted, as third choice, Laird Cregar.

*   *   *

One might fancifully argue that Shakespeare's *Henry VIII* carried a curse. On June 29, 1613, during a performance of the play at the Globe Theatre, a cannon, fired for effect, set the Globe's thatched roof ablaze and the theater fell in flames. The play, politically correct in the Elizabethan era, skirted the event most audiences were eager to see, namely, the beheading of Anne Boleyn. Also, the text was generous toward Cardinal Wolsey, the play's villain. Indeed, when Sir Henry Irving staged *Henry VIII* in 1888, he preferred to forsake the title role and play Wolsey.[16]

Nevertheless, Cregar as King Henry VIII would be top Broadway showmanship. As previously stated, he wasn't the first choice of Rose and Webster—their dream cast was Charles Laughton (an Academy Award winner for 1933's *The Private Life of Henry*

VIII) and Basil Rathbone as Wolsey.[17] Both men, however, were lucratively settled in the film colony. So was the subsequent choice, the corpulent Edward Arnold.

Laird was thrilled. He'd make his Broadway debut as Henry VIII, in a spectacular production supervised by America's most prodigal showman and staged by the American classical theater's most acclaimed director. It promised to be a sensational success, making him a New York stage star and a noted Shakespearean actor ... in one swoop! Laird believed this could possibly change the way Hollywood saw him, and maybe the way he saw himself, profoundly.

Everything rested, however, on Zanuck agreeing to release Laird for the play.

Wednesday, July 12: As Laird took bows in Connecticut, and Billy Rose blueprinted *Henry VIII*, Barré Lyndon completed his fourth version of the *Hangover Square* script.[18] He'd basically followed Zanuck's directives:

1. The era was now 1903.
2. The script opened with a "frightening," "exciting" and "very brief" murder: Bone knifing an old antiques dealer to death, and setting the shop afire.
3. Middleton was no longer an aged and seasoned inspector; he was George Sanders.
4. Barbara Leigh shed her profession, becoming Sir Henry Chapman's daughter and George's demure girlfriend.
5. Little Christopher Wyndham, whom the dying George had asked, "Play my music," disappeared entirely.
6. The disposal of Netta's corpse by dumping her in an excavation pit and pouring concrete atop her, gave way to her cremation atop a Guy Fawkes bonfire.

Lyndon later explained the Guy Fawkes concept:

Well, I'd got a body and I didn't know what to do with it, you see, because it was 1903. And at first I had the idea of sinking it into the foundations of a building beneath falling cement and limestone. But I have a feeling that Zanuck didn't like the idea, so I had to think of something else, and suddenly I thought of Guy Fawkes Day, November 5. I don't know if kids do it now in England, but they used to go around collecting pennies with "Guys" in a perambulator. Also organizations like breweries used to have a yard and they often did have a big bonfire in it for their employees, who'd go and drink beer in the yard.[19]

Finally, as Zanuck had requested, Bone now met his death, *à la* Frankenstein's Monster, in a fire.

Meanwhile, back in Connecticut, the stock engagement of *The Man Who Came to Dinner* provided Laird a stalker, who was a female teenager to boot. "Love For Film Idol Nets Runaway a Broken Leg," headlined the *New York Daily News*,[20] which reported:

Some like 'em hot, some like 'em cold. Others like 'em short, dumpy and old. But 15-year-old Judith Marston, from swanky Roslyn Estates, Nassau, likes 'em tough, thick-lipped, snarly.... In short, she loves that scoundrel of the screen, Laird Cregar.

Yesterday, Judy found that the course of true love leads to a hospital bed. Furthermore, she learned that before it gets you to the hospital, it takes you to the police station in Stamford, Conn., and, lastly, she discovered it makes you run away from home, lie to your pappy about where you're going and, finally, jump out of windows.

The story went that Judy, who hero-worshipped Laird, learned of his appearance in Stamford, "disappeared" from her uncle's home at 20 The Maples in Roslyn Estates, sent her father, actor-playwright John Marston, a letter claiming to be heading to Mexico as companion to an elderly lady, and checked into the Roger Smith Hotel in Stamford under the name Hester Worsley from Hollywood.

Once settled in, Judy, aka Hester, described by the *Daily News* as having "mannish bobbed brown hair, blue eyes and a chipped middle tooth," set upon stalking Laird Cregar.

Meanwhile, John Marston, learning that Laird was in Stamford, suspected the true story and alerted police to search for his missing daughter. Detective Frank Raymond found her at the Strand after a performance and took her to the police station. As the *Daily News* continued the saga:

> For a brief, hopeless period Judy maintained that she indeed was Hester Worsley of Hollywood. Then she smiled sheepishly and gave up. Raymond smiled, told her that her dad was coming up for her and stepped into the next room to phone.
>   Then Judy did it. She dashed across the room and dived out the window. She hit the sidewalk, one story down. The cops found her there, her right leg broken. They took her to the hospital.

The Daily News was rather incredulous that Laird had inspired such passionate female devotion. John Marston told reporters, "She is very young and, like the very young, she is impressionable. Cregar doesn't have to be handsome; she admires him for his style of acting and, I suppose, his forcefulness of strength. You know how youngsters are." He added that Judy was fanatically stage-struck.

"She's good, too," said Marston. "She'll be a good actress one day."

Monday, July 17: Darryl Zanuck's office responded to Barré Lyndon's latest *Hangover Square* script:

> Mr. Zanuck thinks this is a tremendous improvement over the previous script. We now have a story which is not only psychologically interesting, but physically interesting as well. All the changes which were discussed and decided upon at the last conference have worked out splendidly. The Guy Fawkes Day thing is great; so is the first killing.[21]

The seven-page memo largely concerned itself with beefing up Sanders' role of Middleton. In fact, Zanuck was right: Hamilton's novel had more depth, but Lyndon's new script offered far more cinematic potential than had the book, and the earlier script drafts.

Tuesday, July 18: Variety reported:

> CAPSULE CRITICISM: Laird Cregar shoulda stood in Hollywood for all the good his 3000-mile trip to Stamford, Conn., for one week's appearance in *The Man Who Came to Dinner* did him. Unlike Tallulah, Gloria Swanson and Connie Bennett, his "in person" draw proved vastly disappointing. Opening night found 1600-seat house half-filled, with business the rest of week way off....[22]

The failure of the play wounded Laird—perhaps he wasn't the attraction that his recent fan mail has made him believe himself to be?

Tuesday, July 25: The New York Times reported:

> Booked to open at the Alvin the week of October 30 is *Henry VIII*, Billy Rose's venture into the Shakespearean field. By tomorrow, the producer expects to know whether Laird Cregar can get sufficient time off from Hollywood to act the title role. Because the production is on the massive

side, there will be no pre–Broadway tour. Consequently, the opening will be preceded by several previews.[23]

Also on July 25: The Hollywood Reporter wrote that Marlene Dietrich was "within 48 hours" of signing with Fox to star in *Hangover Square*. She, of course, was precisely the star Zanuck had mentioned in his June 26 memo.

Dietrich and Laird Cregar, co-starring in a melodrama, packed with sex, fire and murder ... it had dizzying potential. However, it was only now, as Laird returned to Hollywood to plead his case for a leave of absence to do *Henry VIII,* that he fully learned about the revised *Hangover Square* script.

What he discovered shocked him. How he responded shocked Hollywood.

26

"The Bette Davis of the 20th Century–Fox Lot"

Guy, Guy, Guy,
Stick him up on high,
Hang him to a lamppost
And let him die!
—traditional chant from Guy Fawkes Bonfire
celebration in England, used in *Hangover Square*

London after midnight, November 5, 1605.

Investigators, warned by an anonymous tipster, searched the cellars below Parliament ... and found 36 barrels of dynamite. A group of Catholic Restorationists had plotted to blow up Parliament, King James I, his family, the Protestant aristocracy and even part of the Catholic aristocracy, to strike a vengeful blow against violent prejudice toward English Catholics.

History heralded it as "The Gunpowder Plot of 1605." In charge of planting and detonating the dynamite: Guy Fawkes.[1]

On the night of November 5, after Fawkes' arrest and the foiling of the plot, Londoners lit bonfires to celebrate James' safety. Meanwhile, Fawkes faced gruesome torture at the Tower of London, and on January 31, 1606, went with other conspirators to Old Palace Yard in Westminster to be hanged, drawn and quartered. The process: The executioners would drag the victim on a hurdle to the gibbet, hang him until *almost* dead, castrate and disembowel him, burn the genitalia and intestines before the victim's eyes, behead the victim and cut the body into quarters. Then all five parts—the head and four sections of the body—received a "gibbeting," that is, a public display in various locales of London.

Guy Fawkes, however, triumphed ... sort of. After the other conspirators were executed, and before his persecutors could hack off his testicles, tear out his intestines and roast it all before his eyes, Fawkes either fell or leaped off the gallows and broke his neck—a grim last laugh, but one surely not without its satisfactions. November 5 became part of British Isles folklore, known as Guy Fawkes Day, and on Guy Fawkes Night, young Londoners burned "Guys," horrific dummies, on bonfires.

Very little of this history could make it into the film *Hangover Square*—censorship and political-religious diplomacy would never have allowed it. But the bonfire did. Indeed, it became the high Gothic *tour de force* of this brilliant, fiery, doom-laden film. While Laird Cregar didn't play Guy Fawkes, he shared a concern with him. In forcing him into a refashioned *Hangover Square* that he saw as a rip-off of *The Lodger,* Zanuck and 20th Century–Fox, artistically, were figuratively cutting off Laird's balls.

He was ready to jump off the gibbet, if necessary.

After Laird came back from Connecticut, and saw what had happened to his new vehicle, all hell broke loose at 20th Century–Fox: He absolutely rejected *Hangover Square.* A domino effect resulted; Marlene Dietrich, learning of Laird's defiance, possibly informed personally by him of the script's revamping, never signed her contract to play Netta.

Zanuck had a film set to start shooting in two weeks, with no leading man or leading lady.

It was a bombshell in Hollywood: Laird had persuaded Fox to buy a property especially for him, it was to be his first starring role ... and now he refused to do it! Zanuck, outraged, had no time for this defiance. On the night of August 1, 1944, *Wilson* would have its world premiere at the Roxy Theatre in New York City. Zanuck's pride and joy, the Technicolor epic had cost $2,997,900 with an additional $1.8 million set for advertising—Fox's most expensive production to date. He saw it as both mass entertainment and a political message to nations that might soon be ending World War II. Consumed with *Wilson's* success, Zanuck had no patience with Laird's tantrum.

Even in more placid times, Zanuck was never a man to cross. Richard Widmark, whose tenure at Fox began via his giggling psycho gangster Tommy Udo in *Kiss of Death* (1947), remembered rejecting a role in *O. Henry's Full House* (1952) because it was Udo-esque. The actor recalled that Zanuck called him in, promising the part would give Widmark's career "a whole new facet!"

> The next morning, I called my agent and said that I still didn't want to do it. He had Zanuck on the other line and held the phone up to my receiver. Zanuck is saying, "I'll ruin the s.o.b.—professionally, socially, morally!" He was screaming like an insane man. So, I did it....[2]

Thursday, July 27: Zanuck left Los Angeles via the Streamliner to New York for the *Wilson* premiere. Before departing, he shot down Laird's request to do *Henry VIII* on Broadway ... and slapped him with an eight-week suspension.

"First thing you know," said Laird, "I'll be known as the Bette Davis of 20th Century–Fox."[3]

The quip had several layers. Bette Davis had made her mark playing neurotic roles, so there was that comparison. More significantly, Davis had waged many battles with Jack L. Warner and had taken a well-publicized suspension in 1936. Perhaps most interestingly, Laird had compared himself to a woman ... and one whom many in Hollywood regarded as a diva.

Laird holed up in Coldwater Canyon, seething, defiant. Meanwhile, *Wilson* opened in New York to a predominately excellent press and enormous box office. The film appeared, at this point, to be a major triumph for Zanuck. It was all very ill-timed: Laird's option had come up at Fox. Perhaps Laird believed that if he rebelled sufficiently, Fox would refuse to lift his option, cut him loose, and he'd be free to head to New York and sign for *Henry VIII.*

The story circulated that George Sanders would play George Harvey Bone; another, that Fox would cast Glenn Langan, from Fox's "Victory Players" little theatre group in Santa Monica, in the star part; and yet another, that Langan would play Sanders' original role.

Tuesday, August 8: Louella Parsons wrote in her column:

> Laird Cregar is sulking, and even if he has thinned down you must admit there's plenty of Laird to sulk. He's turned down the lead in *Hangover Square* at 20th and has been rewarded with an eight weeks salary layoff—eight weeks being the time it would take to make the picture. Meanwhile the studio may interest George Sanders in the part. Looks as if the Hangover part of the title should be changed to *Headache Square.*[4]

Laird was trapped. He was off salary. He was legally unable to do *Henry VIII.* His defiance had tossed him into career limbo.

Thursday, August 10: Wilson had its gala invitational Los Angeles premiere at the Carthay Circle Theatre. Zanuck was back in town for the big night.

Friday, August 11: Louella Parsons noted that Geraldine Fitzgerald, under contract to Warners, was enjoying a personal triumph in Fox's *Wilson* as Edith Galt, Wilson's second wife. (Fitzgerald made the cover of the August 7 *Life* magazine.) The columnist reported that Jack L. Warner would loan Fitzgerald to Zanuck again: "Jack, who is as pleased over [Fitzgerald's] success as if he had made *Wilson,* has loaned her for the femme lead in *Hangover Square.* This is the picture over which Laird Cregar battled and went on an eight weeks' suspension. But that won't keep the film from going before the cameras shortly with another actor in Cregar's spot."[5]

It was another bombshell, although very few realized it: Geraldine Fitzgerald, as previously noted, was the very actress who'd inspired Patrick Hamilton to create the evil Netta in *Hangover Square!* The irony of this casting, and the harrowing memories of Hamilton stalking her, probably creeped out Fitzgerald, but she could hardly make public her reservations.

Saturday, August 12: The New York Times wrote:

> 20th Century–Fox reports that Laird Cregar has been removed from contract suspension on his agreement to go into the cast of *Hangover Square*.... Glenn Langan, who was named for the part after Cregar's withdrawal, is now out of the cast. It is also understood that Fox is trying to obtain the services of Geraldine Fitzgerald from Warners for the feminine lead.[6]

Also on August 12: Apparently *Henry VIII* was still in discussion. *The New York Times,* referring to Billy Rose as "the mighty mite,"[7] reported that he "is trying to stave off tantrums waiting for some definite word from Laird Cregar relative to that role in *Henry VIII.* Casting, though, goes forward, and Arnold Moss and Charles Hanson now are in the line-up...."

Thursday, August 17: The *New York Times* wrote:

> Tied up with Hollywood matters, Laird Cregar can't break away to act the title role in *Henry VIII* for Billy Rose. That much was regretfully admitted the other day by the producer. Not in the least discouraged, Mr. Rose is still aiming to put the ambitious revival into rehearsal Sept. 20. Among those mentioned for the part are Monty Woolley, but he will not be available until January, and John Alexander. When things look darkest for the bantam producer, he generally emerges with an inspiration....[8]

Laird compares legs and hosiery with actress Iris Adrian at the wedding reception of his pal Tom Neal and actress Vicky Lane. The picture is stamped July 1944.

The article noted a time pressure: The Alvin Theatre was waiting for *Henry VIII* and if it wasn't ready by the last week of October, Rose would have to make "certain financial arrangements" with the theater's management.

Friday, August 18: Hedda Hopper wrote in her column:

> Geraldine Fitzgerald has turned down the part in *Hangover Square* in favor of doing one for her boss, Jack Warner. She'll probably do *Nobody Lives Forever* with John Garfield, and if she does, it will be one of the best parts she's had. Linda Darnell does the role Geraldine was considering in *Hangover Square*, which will be the best part she's had on her home lot. She got this on the strength of *Summer Storm*, which she did on loan-out to Seymour Nebenzal.[9]

It's hardly surprising that Fitzgerald bailed out (and she did do *Nobody Lives Forever*, shot in the fall of 1944 and released in 1946). It's significant that the new Netta was Darnell, Laird's special "crush" on the Fox lot. As Hopper continued:

> Too bad Darryl Zanuck couldn't see his way to release Laird Cregar to do *Henry VIII* on Broadway, where Laird would have had the benefit of Margaret Webster's direction. He'd have returned a star. But his option has just been lifted for another year, the script troubles straightened out on *Hangover* so that Laird is now happy about the whole thing. Also, George Sanders stays in the picture for another important role....

It was PR puffery; Laird, of course, was by no means "happy about the whole thing." However, there was more contributing to his misery than losing out on *Henry VIII* and being bullied into doing *Hangover Square*. His personal life, too, was approaching a crisis.

*   *   *

In 2014, David Frankham remembered:

> In 1944, I saw *The Lodger* at the Gaumont Cinema, in Rochester, Kent, on the River Medway. I had just turned 18, was about to be drafted, was reluctantly studying architecture at my parents' insistence, and had just played Falstaff in a school production. It was my first kick of adrenalin at not being myself, at being somebody else. *The Lodger* opened on a Sunday, played through the following Saturday—and I went every night. After six nights of watching it, I was just besotted by Laird Cregar's talent. And I knew, I absolutely knew, that I had to do what he was doing, somehow, someday.[10]

Frankham happily achieved his dream as a prolific, versatile actor. In fact, in one of his best-remembered TV roles, Larry Marvick in "Is There in Truth No Beauty?" on the original *Star Trek* series (October 18, 1968), he emulated his favorite star: "I was wreaking havoc everywhere," laughed Frankham, "breaking up the set, determined to blow up the *Enterprise*.... Well, I was channeling Laird Cregar ... the whole thing was the end of *The Lodger* for me!"

When Frankham came to Hollywood in the mid–1950s, he played in "Pride and Prejudice" on TV's *Matinee Theatre* (broadcast live October 1, 1956), with British character actress Doris Lloyd, whom Laird's Ripper had slaughtered in *The Lodger*. "On the first day," remembered Frankham, "we met at a rehearsal hall at NBC for a read-through of the script, and through the door came Doris Lloyd! [*Laughs*] I shot out of my chair (I must have scared her to death!) and said, 'Miss Lloyd! I enjoyed your work so much in *The Lodger*!' I'm sure Doris was thinking, 'Who is this *nut*?'"

Frankham became close friends with Lloyd, often visiting her at her hacienda-style home at 935 Chautauqua Boulevard in Pacific Palisades, where she lived with her sister Milba, a sculptor. To Frankham's delight, he learned that Lloyd had been very close to Laird Cregar, and he asked her for stories:

> Doris said Laird was a very emotional man. Great fun, always witty and jolly. He was a regular at what Doris called her "soirees" ... close friends in for dinner or lunch, and he was full of jokes and happy and fulfilled. But quite emotional...
>
> Laird always came to Doris' house with the same friend.... Doris referred to this man as his "companion." And at one of these evenings or lunches, there was some kind of tension between them, and at one point this man said to Laird, "Oh, you fat pig! If you don't lose weight, I'm going to leave you!"
>
> Well.... Doris remembered that Laird really became very disturbed and upset. He said to Doris, "I'm so sorry. This is no concern of yours, I apologize," and they left shortly afterwards.

Who was the companion? Was it the same man who'd been Laird's "little boyfriend" since his early days and nights of celebrity? As Frankham observes, Doris Lloyd never mentioned his name, and it was strange that she even told the story: "Doris was never a gossip. She must have had wonderful anecdotes about her career, but she never, ever talked about it. She was gentle, sweet and generous." Clearly, the "fat pig" story had disturbed her considerably.

Most of all, the "fat pig" insult haunted Laird Cregar. In fact, it shows again that the mystery as to whether he was homosexual or heterosexual was a moot point. The true torment was his weight, and the fact that he felt unattractive in his lover's eyes, and in his own.

It was almost cruelly funny; having lost 80 pounds, he was still fat. He wanted to lose more weight before his hernia operation. Much more.

* * *

Laird was frightened. Of being typecast. Of being fat, unattractive, alone. The approaching tempest of *Hangover Square* had intensified his feelings that he was doomed to be a horror star. Arrogant, hypersensitive, always neurotic about his looks and sexuality, heartbroken by Peggy Stack having left him and by his male lover's threat to leave him, the trauma of *Hangover Square* had pushed him over the brink.

He crashed ... and in that state, he formed a plan.

George Sanders noted that "a tragic resolve was born in Laird's mind to make himself over into a beautiful man who would never again be cast as a fiend."[11] Sanders, as Laird's friend, realized there was more than the fear of horror typecasting, although he wasn't comfortable alluding to it in his 1960 memoir. Charles Higham wrote that Laird "became convinced he could turn from the gloomy restricted life of the homosexual to the more optimistic world of the heterosexual and perhaps could attract a woman and find fulfillment with her."[12] Joel Greenberg wrote, "Impelled by vanity and the prospect of consolidating his first heterosexual relationship, [Cregar] embarked on a crash diet, the effects of which prematurely killed him."[13]

It was DeWitt Bodeen, Laird's friend since their time together at the Pasadena Playhouse, who put it most succinctly: "It was not only his desire to play heroic roles that made him diet, but the hope that he would attract a young lover through his own beauty. He never did, and he was too innately shy to be aggressive."[14]

Yes, he'd become a "beautiful man." It would be *Dr. Jekyll and Mr. Hyde*, in reverse. His magic elixir would be a 500-calories a day diet, powerful amphetamines, thyroid shots[15] and plastic surgery. It was a plan that, in 1944 Hollywood, was defiantly heroic, freakishly unnatural, and ultimately destructive.

It would be Laird Cregar and his demons, starring in *Hangover Square*.

27

Blowing Up

A Woman ... desirable! Half-devil!
A Man ... tortured! Half-mad!
A Murder ... shocking beyond belief!
—Publicity for *Hangover Square*

Seventy-three years after its anguished shooting, *Hangover Square* plays as a horror tragedy of remarkably morbid ironies.

There was Linda Darnell as Netta, music hall vamp, spectacularly cremated as her masked corpse burns on the Guy Fawkes bonfire. Darnell died as a result of a 1965 fire that ravaged over 90 percent of her body.[1]

George Sanders portrayed Dr. Middleton, Scotland Yard crime specialist, purring his lines with defiant boredom. Sanders' 1972 suicide note read "Dear World: I am leaving because I am bored....."[2]

And, of course, Laird Cregar played George Harvey Bone, musical genius, burning alive as he pounds Bernard Herrmann's "Concerto Macabre" at the piano, disappearing mystically in the smoke-and-flames fade-out.

Hangover Square would be released two months after Laird's death.

* * *

In its "Hollywood Inside" column of August 21, 1944, *Variety* reported that

Hangover Square, which is slated to get underway today at 20th-Fox, finally rolls after jumble of casting which had everyone at studio guessing as to exactly who would be in it. Originally intended as co-starrer for Laird Cregar and George Sanders, studio dropped Cregar and substituted Sanders for his role, casting Glenn Langan then in Sanders' spot. Geraldine Fitzgerald was named as leading femme character. Linda Darnell now has just been cast in top femme part. Miss Fitzgerald is not to appear in picture.... Laird Cregar resumes his original role and Sanders goes back to his....

It was a real-life Hollywood melodrama, with explosions of temperament, a near-fatal fire and, although nobody realized it at the time, a dying-before-your-eyes star.

Hangover Square began its first week's shooting based at Fox's Western Avenue lot, in the heart of Hollywood, and during a heat wave. George Sanders remembered that Laird promptly sought him out, bitterly pouring out his "beautiful man" strategy: "He confessed this to me on the first day of shooting. He told me he was going to have an operation on his eyes and make various other changes. And that above all he was going to reduce until he became as slender as a sapling."[3]

It had to be a secret. For 1944 moviegoers, a half-century away from Meg Ryan and Mickey Rourke, plastic surgery—even the relatively modest type, which Laird was planning—was creepy. It belonged in horror movies and gangster sagas. The giant stage hit of the war years, *Arsenic and Old Lace*, saw Boris Karloff as Jonathan Brewster, a murderous fiend transformed by a drunken plastic surgeon so he resembled ... Boris Karloff. On September 1, Warners would release the film version of *Arsenic and Old Lace*, in which Peter Lorre, as the soused surgeon, had done the Karloff number on Raymond Massey, as the horrific Jonathan, complete with scars *à la* Frankenstein's Monster. The idea of plastic surgery to make one more handsome or beautiful was even creepier ... unless performed on war heroes disfigured in battle.

Laird was ill. Everyone sensed it. It was frightening to see. The 500-calories a day starvation diet and the rumored amphetamines[4] were quickly taking a toll. John Brahm forced Laird to wear his hair in bangs for most of *Hangover Square*, calling it "a hangover haircut."[5] Jimmy Starr joked that Laird looked "cute!" in his bangs, but they made Laird evoke a sissy fat boy at a British boarding school ... maybe Winchester College, which Laird claimed to have attended.

"[A]ll through the film he behaved so badly," Brahm would recall of Laird, "like a naughty little boy, whereas he'd been charming when I directed him in *The Lodger.*... Actually, his confused and confusing off-screen personality coincided a good deal with his last screen characterization...."[6] Laird seethed, sick, frustrated, temperamental, arrogant, resentful over the loss of *Henry VIII*, hating the idea that he was now a new Karloff. The *Hangover Square* crew came to dislike him ... quickly.

"And I wish I could tell you Laird Cregar's nickname," wrote columnist Sidney Skolsky. "Oh, the things you learn on a movie set."[7]

While the nickname is lost to the ages, it was probably no less flattering than the words his lover had said to him: *You fat pig.*

Early in *Hangover Square*, Laird played a scene with 17-year-old starlet Faye Marlowe, as Barbara, and 41-year-old Alan Napier, as her father, Sir Henry Chapman. Sir Henry was offering George Harvey Bone the chance to play his concerto at a "musical soiree" at the maestro's home. A reporter filed this story:

> Over at 20th Century–Fox, the thermometer on Stage 14 registered 104, and Laird Cregar, who, in spite of his dieting, is still a mighty fat boy, was blaming the heat for his repeated blow-ups. Usually Mr. Cregar is letter perfect in his lines.... The star has only four words to say ... "I am enormously complimented" ... But he still can't get them out.

Laird as George Harvey Bone in *Hangover Square*.

The script dialogue went this way:

GEORGE: And you'd be conducting, Sir Henry?
SIR HENRY: Yes.
GEORGE: I am enormously complimented.

Those last four words confounded him. Laird sweated, stuttered ... went blank. The morning moved along and the heat rose. Brahm, good-humored and, at this early stage, still having hopes for a happy set, went for take 11.

GEORGE: And you'd be conducting, Sir Henry?
SIR HENRY: Yes.
GEORGE: I am enormously complicated.

Complicated for *complimented*. "Oh well—who isn't?" wrote Edith Gwynn, relating the blooper in her "Rambling Reporter" column in *The Hollywood Reporter,* noting that Brahm and the crew "had to pick themselves off the floor" after Laird blew the line.[8] It was probably Fox's Freudian slip of 1944, but Laird's trouble reciting a four-word line wasn't funny. Robert Bassler called lunch half an hour early so Laird could recover.

"Fat Laird Cregar Suffers and Blows Up," read one headline. It was the kind of story, and verbiage, publicity departments were masters at squelching. Yet Fox made no effort to do so. The studio evidently was putting Laird in his place for his defiance, humiliating him. It was war now between studio and actor. It was soon to become vicious.

There was always a chance that, with luck, *Hangover Square* would wrap up early, and Zanuck would reverse his decision about *Henry VIII*. Brahm cast the roles of Mickey (Netta's pimp) and Eddie Carstairs (an impresario who becomes engaged to Netta, and whom Bone almost strangles to death) with actors he knew and trusted from Fox's Victory Players—respectively, Michael Dyne and Glenn Langan.[9] The latter had been mentioned previously as a possible replacement for Laird or Sanders during Laird's suspension period.

Having greenlighted Laird's flourishes on *The Lodger*, Brahm now proved to be a formidable adversary. He was probably remembering his battle scars from *Hangover Square* when, in late 1945, he told *Motion Picture* magazine:

> I have been called many things by many people—stubborn, difficult, temperamental, over-exacting. Maybe they are all true. I know I will do a scene 100 times if necessary to get what I want on the screen. I know I cannot have my actors dominate me or my judgment, lest my bird's eye view of the picture as a whole be distorted by so much as one false note. An artist painting a portrait knows just where the highlights must be. The subject cannot have the same perspective.
>
> I know, too, that I must make myself independent of dictation or interference of any kind. I will not compromise with what I know to be right.[10]

Faye Marlowe also had acted for Brahm in the Victory Players' *There's Always Juliet.* As she began *Hangover Square,* she knew almost nothing about Laird, other than gossip she'd heard about the "retinue of young men" who partied at his Coldwater Canyon cottage: "I do know he was dieting, very strenuously, and I think may have dieted too quickly, and maybe had a heart problem he wasn't aware of. He was rather a 'grand dame,' but in a nice way ... just a very nice chap."[11]

Faye, then a protégée of John Brahm, admitted over 60 years later how she landed the role of Barbara:

"Unhousebroken sex": Linda Darnell as *Hangover Square*'s vampy (and ill-fated) Netta.

John sort of had a "thing" for me. I wasn't his mistress or anything, I was too young—I was 17! But I think he cared for me, and that was why he cast me in *Hangover Square.*

John lived at Malibu, high on a cliff, overlooking the Pacific Coast Highway, and he used to go swimming every single day, winter and summer, in the ocean. He was amazing ... he was 50 when we did *Hangover Square*, and sometimes I went down and spent a day at the beach, and we'd go swimming. He had the body of a man in his 30s, because he was so fit from swimming. In the coldest winter he'd go into the ocean for a half an hour ... a very hardy fella!

Brahm was in his glory on *Hangover Square*, directing with Germanic Expressionistic flair, exulting in offbeat angles, brilliant use of lighting, and bravura set-ups. The director subtly but definitely uses an excavation fissure in the Square as a macabre metaphor for both Bone's cracked, schizophrenic mind and Netta's vagina; significantly, at one point, Bone falls into the fissure. Brahm also does cleverly suggestive things with witchy Netta's Siamese cat, which seems to be both her "familiar" and her feline *doppelganger.* At one point, the cat enjoys an "Aren't I Gorgeous?" close-up, while snuggling on George's lap.

Full of vigor and jokes, Brahm and his machismo intimidated his highly strung star. However, perhaps the most vivid personality on *Hangover Square*, and not in any positive way, was George Sanders. For Faye Marlowe, making his acquaintance was rather a shock:

I'd always had a tremendous crush on George Sanders. Oh! The curled lip, and the snarl ... very appealing to a 17-year-old girl! So when I learned I was going to be playing opposite him, I thought it was so exciting.

George Sanders and Faye Marlowe in *Hangover Square.*

Well ... he was such a *boring* man! He was just very cold, and I think particularly, he looked down on me—"Who is this little nothing I'm supposed to be playing opposite?" In between takes, he spent his time stretched out snoozing on a sofa, or playing mournful Russian tunes on the piano. He was pleased with his Russian ancestry, but apparently it was a very gloomy one. He was interesting in that way, but he was far from the seductive screen personality that had appealed to me.

Alan Napier, Sanders' pal, landed his role of Sir Henry thanks to Sanders. Nevertheless, Napier would be totally forthcoming about the havoc his friend created on this film, with Sanders at "his best/worst":

A day on *Hangover Square* might begin as follows. I would receive a royal summons—would I go to Mr. Sanders' dressing room. There George would be lying on the day-bed, half-dressed. The dialogue director would be trying to hear his lines. These he had not even looked at, so he declared them unspeakable.

"Nape," George would say, "write me something. I can't possibly say this crap." Since the script was by my good friend Barré Lyndon, I usually persuaded him to accept minimal changes.[12]

As Laird was already in a rebellious mood, Sanders encouraged his defiance. Indeed, Sanders might have been misbehaving so extravagantly on this film because he knew how very unhappy Laird was, and intended to amuse himself as he and Laird both aggravated Zanuck and the studio in every way possible.

Hangover Square: **Laird looks up from the piano toward the soundstage catwalks between scenes.**

However, Sanders also was concerned: Laird was genuinely ill. The ventral hernia continued to cause high fever, severe abdominal pain, bowel blockage, nausea and vomiting; there was also the inability to urinate, defecate or even pass gas. Laird's stomach was ripping itself up as he dieted, which could have caused more complications, such as halitosis. According to DeWitt Bodeen, stories circulated that Laird was consuming diet amphetamines, and these clouded his clarity.

A "beautiful man," indeed. Undoubtedly, Laird fretted about how he'd look, feel and smell when it came time to play love scenes with his longtime crush, Linda Darnell. "Netta. The tangled net of her hair.... Stinging nettles ... her red mouth. Nets. Fishingnets...." And fishnet stockings. Darnell, resplendently alluring in her Toulouse-Lautrec–inspired costumes, played the wicked Netta as sleekly feline as the vixen's Siamese cat. The Breen Office warned Fox repeatedly, "The costume of Netta described here and elsewhere must not be objectionably revealing,"[13] but Darnell went on a-prancing in her snug panties and fishnets. *Time*'s *Hangover Square* review bestowed on her this elegant honor: "Hollywood's most rousing portrayer of unhousebroken sex."[14]

"And I taught her how to kiss," Brahm would boast, "with her mouth open."[15]

It was a rather audacious quote for 1944; at any rate, Brahm worked smoothly with Darnell, his ease and banter with her causing Laird jealousy, adding to his overall unhappiness. Undeen Hunter, Darnell's loving and devoted sister, and who always referred to Linda as "Tweedles," remembered that Linda soon became aware of Laird's various torments on *Hangover Square*. "Tweedles felt terribly sorry for him," said Undeen.[16]

Day by day, he was losing control. As Alan Napier would observe, Laird was

> ... a great acting talent, but sexually disorientated and neurotic. Some actors who are homosexual are quite content, and have become shining stars. Cregar was not content—he wanted to be Clark Gable. So he was never real in private life; only when he was acting....
>
> He was fundamentally shy and insecure as a human being, behind a front of talent and success. Sadly, on *Hangover Square*, he was playing, offstage, "the great Laird Cregar"—but, tragically, he didn't really believe in it.

The *Hangover Square* company reported its second week to the 20th Century–Fox lot in Westwood, where the Old Chicago Street from *In Old Chicago* and Whitechapel Street from *The Lodger* served as exteriors. Fox added to the set two new "permanent streets," each two blocks long with a cross street, especially built for *Hangover Square*.

"Thoroughfares represent Whitechapel district in London in 1903 period," wrote *Variety*, "complete with theaters, pubs, restaurants and shops. Sets will be utilized later for other productions."[17]

Friday, September 8: A bombshell, as reported by Sam Zolotow in *The New York Times*:

> Stymied by the scarcity of actors capable of shouldering the central role in *Henry VIII*, Billy Rose finally decided yesterday to postpone the Shakespearean spectacle for which Robert Edmond Jones had designed 14 sets. Mr. Rose had counted on bringing the revival to the Alvin early in November. His announcement pointed out that the show would be "ready for rehearsal along about January." By that time, it is expected, Laird Cregar, whose film commitments prevented him from accepting the assignment earlier, will be available. The producer and director Margaret Webster searched everywhere for the right player, but to no avail....[18]

Among the actors Rose had considered was Sidney Blackmer,[19] but Rose realized Cregar was his man. Suddenly, Laird was smack back in the machinations of *Henry*

VIII. As *Hangover Square* continued shooting, he begged, cajoled and demanded that Fox give him his release. Brahm would remember Laird as "a nervous wreck,"[20] desperately hoping Zanuck would grant him a temporary absence, or cancel his contract altogether.

Tuesday, September 12: Hedda Hopper announced, "Ian Keith will do *Henry VIII* on Broadway for Billy Rose this fall...."[21] Keith was a classical actor and film character player whom Universal originally announced for *Dracula* in 1930 before Bela Lugosi claimed the title role. The announcement meant little; Rose was using Keith's name the same way he'd used Blackmer's ... for publicity.

Laird sweated it out, hoping that Zanuck would see the advantages of the release. *Henry VIII,* as with all Billy Rose productions, would receive lavish publicity; *Les Miserables,* his next scheduled Fox film, had been on the studio's schedule since 1942, and been delayed time and again; why couldn't it be delayed again now?

Sunday, September 17: The final decision from Zanuck had come to pass, and Hedda Hopper reported it succinctly: "20th Century will not grant Laird Cregar his release. Laird is mighty unhappy because he can't play *Henry VIII* for Billy Rose. I hear Rose will cancel the play. To date he can't round up a cast...."[22]

It appeared final. Laird fumed bitterly. Reminding him daily of this heartbreaking lost opportunity was the new Technicolor Betty Grable musical now filming at Fox. Its title: *Billy Rose's Diamond Horseshoe.*

*   *   *

In worldwide perspective, it seemed absurd. Many men who were Laird's age were in the war. The Nazis and Japanese were shooting at them. These men would have thought they'd died and gone to Heaven if they found themselves starring in a Hollywood movie, earning $1,500 a week, and making out with Linda Darnell ... with her mouth open.

For Laird Cregar, however, this was all he had. Being an actor had been his lifelong dream, his deepest passion. Zanuck had scuttled what Laird saw as the greatest chance of his life, Broadway's *Henry VIII,*

Laird, sporting his *Hangover Square* hairdo, signs an autograph in a picture dated September 15, 1944.

forcing him into what the actor despised as a rip-off of *The Lodger,* cast yet again as a sexually deranged madman.

Still, the diet continued. So did the tantrums. Yet the performance was remarkable ... sad, sensitive, startling. The merciless close-ups of Laird's George Harvey Bone suffering his fits are still chillingly disturbing today. Eyes bulging, face contorted—it's as if he's suffering a seizure or an electrical shock. Bone's pet devils ravage him in *Hangover Square* just as Laird Cregar's were seething in Hollywood. Indeed, perhaps part of Laird's animosity toward the film was his identification with its pitiful, self-destructing hero.

Bone was fated to fall in flames, and soon. So, sensed Laird, was he. And now, as if he didn't have enough problems with *Hangover Square*, he and Greer Garson attended the same party. Hedda Hopper reported that Laird congratulated Greer on her performance in MGM's recently released *Mrs. Parkington*. "I hope you won't use it for another imitation of me, as you did my speech at the Academy dinner," said Garson.

Laird was gallant, but made no apology. "Your speech was comic—your performance, excellent," he replied.[23]

Meanwhile, there was much more of *Hangover Square* to go, including several fires ... one of which came close to killing two of the stars.

28

Fox Infernos

I hate Hollywood.[1]—Laird Cregar, 1944

Monday, September 25, 1944: Erskine Johnson, writing about Hollywood typecasting in his syndicated column, was clearly perturbed about the subject:

> Sometimes we get a little weary listening to the wails of people in Hollywood about being typed. In fact, the lah-de-dah glamour girls who gush about playing "Camille" and the nervous comics who buttonhole you on the sidewalk to tell you about a test they made as bloody Jack the Ripper give us a pain in the neck.
> Why can't they be happy with their thousand dollars and up a week and leave us alone? If there were no movies, they probably would be repairing loose manhole covers.

Johnson, however, made an exception in regard to Laird Cregar:

> The other day we were talking to Laird Cregar, who has become typed with homicidal maniac roles. He was moaning:
> "I hate Hollywood. I'm typed in morbid, morose roles. I'm unhappy. I want to be funny—and they cast me as a killer. I never want to see Hollywood again when I complete my contract."

Johnson rallied to Laird's defense: "Laird is a very fine actor and would never have to repair loose manhole covers. In his case, we don't blame him for being bitter. He deserves better things."

Also on Monday, September 25: The *Hangover Square* company was scheduled to start shooting the Concerto.[2] The composer of the "Concerto Macabre" was the formidable Bernard Herrmann, legendary for his temperament, as well as for his scores for *Citizen Kane* and *The Devil and Daniel Webster*, the latter an Academy Award winner. Later celebrated for his Alfred Hitchcock scores, Maestro Herrmann had already added to *Hangover Square*'s many tensions.

"He came out, a typical New Yorker, who didn't think anything of pictures," remembered Barré Lyndon, who met Herrmann during production. "[T]wo minutes spent with him was enough, if you know what I mean."[3]

The Concerto was brilliantly chilling, a thunderous symphony with which Lucifer might have serenaded himself on Halloween night. Although Ignace Hilsberg actually would play the pre-recorded music, Laird had to rehearse to coordinate credibly his hands at the keyboard. It was yet another agony for him. "It's awful," he said. "You can't imagine how difficult it is to try and get your hands and fingers in the right places at the right time so the camera and recording will click. But it's got to be done!"[4]

The *Hangover Square* schedule provided nine shooting days for this Wagner Gone Crazy climax, shot on Stage 3 at Fox's Western Avenue annex.[5] Most of these days required the presence of Laird, Sanders, Faye Marlowe, Alan Napier, various featured players, 30 musicians, 75 extras, four stunt doubles and 20 "Ad Lib Bits," as well as the special effects of fire, smoke and snow. As Middleton and his Scotland Yard men arrived, all of George Harvey Bone's crimes came back to him, his breakdown wildly exhorted by the mad music. The authorities take him to a side room as Marlowe's devoted Barbara takes over playing the concerto. But Bone, desperate to hear his music, escapes, starts a fire and runs to the balcony as the concerto climaxes.

In a movingly tragic touch, Laird gently wipes a tear on a balcony curtain.

The guests scream, fleeing the fire with the musicians. Sanders saves Marlowe as Laird again takes his place at the piano, playing the final chords as Joseph La Shelle's camera retreats up the chandelier, itself afire. George Harvey Bone perishes ... and Laird Cregar commits his third on-screen suicide.

It was a very complex and thrilling scene; as Brahm would boast, "I defy anyone to tell me that the photographed music, expressing the musician's thoughts, is not equally as engrossing as any of the romantic sequences; as truly exciting as a chase!"[6]

A candid shot of *Hangover Square*'s bonfire set.

It was also a dangerous one—the whole set (previously used as a White House interior in *Wilson*) would burn. Faye Marlowe remembers:

> Yes, the day we shot that scene, the whole set was burned down. John, of course, was a meticulous planner.... In his home he had this huge, enormous table in his living room, where he plotted all the scenes and set up everything on his own. He couldn't do retakes, this had to be it.
>
> And he said to us all, "Now, this all has to be perfectly timéd, because there will be no more set when we finish!"[7]

Brahm instructed Faye and Sanders that, during the fire, they'd run through a "safe exit" to get out away from the flames. He gave the extras their instructions and coordinated the scene with firemen stationed on the set. Laird took his place at the piano stool. The crew ignited the fire. Marlowe recalls:

> I'm trying to get Laird off the piano stool, and then George breaks down the door and comes rushing in and pulls me away ... and as we started toward our "safe exit," suddenly it was covered with flames! And we didn't know where to go, because we were surrounded by flames! I had this very flammable dress on, and as we went off camera, I pulled it around me—I didn't know what to do.
>
> And George ... it was the first time he seemed to lose a bit of his cool. He pulled me into this one little corner, which seemed to be safe. We were both frightened—and all I remember thinking was, "This is the end!"
>
> Someone came from the camera crew and threw blankets over us to protect us. Then they hosed everything down, and the shot was taken. Well, John looked just absolutely ashen, and the cameraman, Joseph La Shelle—he later told me, "You know, I thought you and George were both goners, I just couldn't stay there and watch you both burn to death"—and he'd fled the building! He'd run out of the soundstage!

It took time for everyone to calm down, and afterwards, Brahm discovered he needed a pre-fire close-up of Sanders against a bookcase. Fortunately, it hadn't burned in the fire. Marlowe recalls that Sanders took his place and removed a book from the shelf. "I always make a point," said Sanders, "of reading a few verses of the Bible before doing a scene like this one!"

He also removed what Marlowe remembers as his "elegant cigarette case" from his inside breast pocket, taking out a cigarette. "I say," purred Sanders, "has anybody got a fire?"

As for Laird, he had to be the final player amidst the flames, which appear to consume him. This required a special effects method, as he had to be able, of course, to escape the inferno surrounding him in the last shot. A Fox publicity release explained how this was done:

> For each take, tiny gas jets, carefully concealed in the woodwork, emit flames which ignite strips of wood which have been soaked in coal oil. Surrounding wood has been fireproofed. Drapes, also fireproofed, are wet with alcohol in spots; this produces a quick flashy flame. After every shot, the gas jets are turned off, firemen rush in with hoses, and the set is prepared all over again.[8]

The story, which reported that the fire scene was shot over ten days, appeared in the *Baltimore Sun* more than two months later and at an eerily ironic time: Sunday, December 10, the morning after Laird's death. The title: CREGAR'S PYRE 10-DAY BLAZE.

*   *   *

"Cregar, whose very few remaining friends call him Sammy, became the Man Who Went on a Diet and now his barbed ire is strictly from hunger. Cregar is bringing all his weight to bear in his struggle against humanity...."[9]
                    —Barbara Berch, *Screenland* Magazine, January 1945

As *Hangover Square* continued, miserably, Laird's goal remained to lose at least four pounds a week.

And now, as if things weren't bad enough, a writer named Barbara Berch of *Screenland* magazine came to Fox to interview Laird, for a hatchet-job feature eventually titled "Bold, Bad (Bluffing) Cregar." Fired up by Laird, who wasn't behaving nicely, and obviously fed information by studio personnel in on the kill, Ms. Berch prepared a story that was basically a bitch-slap. Among the alleged atrocities:

- That Laird had "upstaged" a syndicated columnist who'd visited the *Hangover Square* set because the columnist had ignored him when visiting a set two years before, when Laird was only a "featured" player.
- That, once reprimanded for drinking an extra cup of coffee (during coffee rationing) in the Fox commissary, Laird bitterly responded by spitefully dumping the coffee, and proceeded to "surge past three weeping, head-shaking waitresses, one hysterical hostess, and the irate manager-in-chief, and eat at the Beverly Brown Derby regularly until the commissary manager made a formal apology."
- That he now replied to autograph requests by roaring "No!" but then changed his mind, "scrawled" his signature, and, as Ms. Berch concluded her account, hoped "the kids aren't trading three Laird Cregars for one Frank Sinatra!"

The surprise wasn't that Laird had behaved this badly—his temperament was indeed raging. It was that Fox, which carefully monitored fan magazine coverage of its stars, gave its blessing for Barbara Berch to harpoon Laird so gleefully. The loophole of the story was that Laird was "bluffing," but it was still a mercilessly unflattering profile. *Screenland* scheduled it for its Christmas issue.

*   *   *

Too Much Killing, Cregar Quits.
—*The Winnipeg Tribune*, Manitoba, Canada, October 4, 1944

Adding to Laird's woes, a newspaper article appeared and claimed that "Laird Cregar has asked for his release from 20th Century–Fox and will receive it after finishing *Hangover Square*. Cregar and the studio don't see eye-to-eye over the horror killing business."

The article went on, detailing Laird's villainy in *The Lodger* and *Hangover Square*, reporting that he "wants to be a comedian" and writing that "it is likely he will find his chance to be funny on some other lot." As later events prove, Fox did not give him his release after *Hangover Square* was completed, and did announce other projects for him.

However, as the article shows, he was still battling for his release and Fox was apparently at least seriously considering giving him the heave-ho.

Meanwhile, Laird protested, long and loud, that he'd refuse to play the scene showing him strangling Linda Darnell. He also told Sanders, surely with mischief on his mind, that Sanders should refuse to say the final line of the film, although it was shot out of sequence, because theatrical superstition claimed it was bad luck. Sanders wasn't one for superstition, but he championed anything that might cause havoc at 20th Century–Fox.

Which takes us to Monday night, October 9, 1944.

The *Hangover Square* schedule called for the shooting of the final scene, the burning of the exterior of Sir Henry Chapman's house, after Bone goes mad at the piano. The special effects crew decorated the house and streets with prop snow. The fire engines were on standby.

Alan Napier would remember it as the night of "The Great Refusal":

> The last scene in *Hangover Square* was the fire scene.... It was night shooting on the back lot, and very expensive, as half a street had to go up in flames. The dialogue over the scene concerned me, my daughter [Faye Marlowe] and George. We came together, through the snow. I said something, and George was supposed to reply.

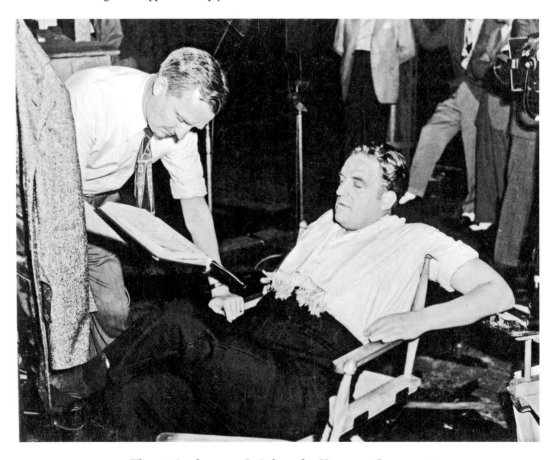

The strain shows on Laird on the *Hangover Square* set.

Well, at the first rehearsal run-through, George told John Brahm, the director, that it was a bloody awful line and that he did not intend to say it. Brahm was much too concerned with the mechanics of the complicated scene to pay any attention.

We came to the final rehearsal before the fires are set for the take. Brahm checks with the camera; everyone was on their marks.

"Sound? I didn't hear Mr. Sanders' line."

"I told you I'm not going to say that bloody stupid line," says George.

Brahm looks at him with a mixture of cajolery and apprehension. "Now George, you wouldn't...." He turns to the sound man. "He'll be all right in the take."

He wasn't.

The fire was lit—the street in flames. On our cues, the actors move into position. I say my line. From George, silence.

I don't remember how many times (and thousands of dollars) later it was before Brahm gave up and sent for the producer, Robert Bassler. It was all rather embarrassing and I did not wish to be associated with Sanders. We waited about in the cold. I sat in a studio chair, wondering what would happen.

Then I heard the rustle of a stiff, Mackintosh raincoat. It was little Bobbie Bassler, hurrying to enforce authority. I'm sure he'd had two or three quick Scotches to nerve him for battle...

Bassler started interrogating Sanders, who remained relaxed and silent, lying back in his studio chair until Bassler shouted at him, "How dare you, you arrogant son of a bitch!" Bassler was leaning right over him. So George, who was powerfully built, had no difficulty in knocking poor little Bassler out from a seated position with one well-placed punch.

Fox arranged for all the parties to have lunch together the next day and, after Bassler had apologized to George for throwing aspersions on his mother, a happy compromise was reached over the offending line....[10]

Naturally, Fox tried to keep it all quiet, but the news leaked. "Actor Punches Producer in Film Jinx Row," headlined the *Los Angeles Times* on October 11. *The Los Angeles Examiner* also covered the donnybrook: "Hollywood had a new contender for the duration one-punch championship of the film colony" and publishing Bassler's "post battle communique": "I'm sorry the news broke out because we shook hands and straightened the whole thing out.... I'm not carrying any scars."[11]

Meanwhile, the damn scene still had to be shot. Also on October 11, Bassler, doing his best to be positive during what must have been acute humiliation, sent this memo to Brahm:

Here is the revision on the last scene in *Hangover Square*. I really feel good about it. Middleton's line has more significance, is less dry in its implications, and can be read, I believe, with considerable feeling, because it signifies that no matter whether or not Bone escapes the fire, his fate is nevertheless sealed—either he will be hanged for murder or committed for life to the asylum for the criminally insane at Broadmoor.... [I]t is important that the lines be read with sadness and resignation and weltschmerz.[12]

And so, as Alan Napier put it, "the street went up in flames just once more." The building burned, Napier, Sanders and Marlowe ran from the fire, and the final dialogue went this way:

NAPIER: Listen ... [*hearing the concerto*] Why didn't he try to get out?
SANDERS: It's better this way, sir.

As fate had it, October 11, 1944, was significant in yet another way: *Laura* opened at Broadway's Roxy Theatre. "[T]he surprise hit of the year," proclaimed the *New York Journal-American*, praising Clifton Webb for his "loathsome but superlatively amusing variant of the *Man Who Came to Dinner* character he played on the road."[13] *Laura* became a smash, greatly boosting the stock of Laird's friend Gene Tierney in the title role, as well as his Fox rival Vincent Price as the gigolo. As for Webb, he became an overnight movie star.

Laird had missed out on 1944's top sleeper. Clifton Webb became the talk of Hollywood at Laird's expense. And *Hangover Square* went on ... and on.

* * *

> "Boys at 20th are asking whose body will be hanging in *Hangover Square*
> when that picture winds up.... Whole thing has been a case of gripe
> and double-gripe, I'm told. Because of this, it will be good."
> —Hedda Hopper, *The Los Angeles Times*, October 14, 1944

The fire that *Hangover Square* fans remember most vividly is the Guy Fawkes Bonfire: George Harvey Bone, having strangled Netta, dresses her corpse as a "Guy" for the bonfire, puts a mask over her face and carries her cadaver through the singing, chanting crowd at night: "Guy, Guy, Guy, Stick him up on high...."

As Bernard Herrmann's piccolos shrilly serve as a screeching, demonic dirge for Netta, Laird carries the body up a ladder, placing her atop the yet-unlit bonfire; as he climbs, the mask partly slides away, and we see Netta's fully rouged mouth. Laird descends, the revelers attack the pyre with their torches, the flames rise, the crowd sings, forms a circle and dances, Laird is caught in the Hell on Guy Fawkes night spectacle, his face a mask of horror as he watches the flames cremate the lover he's killed.

For this masterpiece episode, alive with demonic theatricality, the Fox call sheet listed Laird, Linda Darnell, 140 extras, one bit player, two doubles, two musicians, the special effects of fog and smoke and, of course, the 40-foot-tall bonfire.[14] The site was the old golf course on Fox's back lot. The studio's fire department was on call, as were other local stations. Laird was almost burned in the scene as he climbed down the ladder and nearly came too close to a reveler's torch. "Boy, you sure like your ham well smoked!" he reportedly said to Brahm.

Throughout all these miseries and misadventures, there was a payoff: Laird's George Harvey Bone was a brilliant performance. There's no rash bravado, which marked his Jack the Ripper and other key portrayals in the Cregar canon. Instead, shyness, sensitivity and sadness dominate. No one can tell how much of this bled in from his personal turmoil, or how much from his genius and professionalism; but Laird brought Bone to tragic life, playing with a haunting, heartbreaking credibility.

Still, the attacks came. On October 19, Jimmie Fidler, aware of Laird's behavior on *Hangover Square*, wrote this zinger: "Nominated for the most actorish actor award: Laird Cregar."[15]

Friday, October 20: Louella Parsons wrote:

> Laird Cregar, who wasn't happy about playing a "heavy" in *Hangover Square*, can perk up. He reverts to a hero in his next, *The Spider*, the old Fulton Oursler-Lowell Brentano play. He'll play a mind reader who is suspected of murdering a man in a crowded theater when he is giving a performance. In fact, the entire action takes place in the theater. Lest I leave a wrong impression, I

Laird and Linda Darnell in *Hangover Square*. Evidence of his extreme weight loss is obvious in this still.

understand Cregar is now very happy about *Hangover Square* and sorry he kicked up his heels in the beginning.

The report was yet another insult, calculated by Fox and thrown into Laird's face. *The Spider* (a remake of Fox's 1931 *The Spider*, which had starred Edmund Lowe as the mind reader) was, from its inception, a lowly "B," and Laird had never played in anything but "A" films since joining Fox. Enacting a character called "The Great Garonne" would have struck him as hopelessly hokey, especially in a potboiler with so tacky a title. Clearly the studio's purpose was to embarrass and humiliate Laird with such drivel, make him worry about his future at Fox, and warn him that Zanuck had the power to toss Laird Cregar into the "B" unit underbelly.[16]

The Spider would start shooting in June 1945. The 62-minute potboiler ended up starring Richard Conte as a detective, *Hangover Square*'s Faye Marlowe as the leading lady and Kurt Krueger as "The Great Garonne." It was slated for the bottom half of double bills.[17]

As for Parsons' claim that Laird was "very happy" about *Hangover Square*, it was balderdash.

On October 24, in the *Salt Lake Tribune*, Hopper wrote, "Well, well! John Brahm, who's battled Laird Cregar over every foot of *Hangover Square*, will direct him in *Jean*

Valjean, with Faye Marlowe." Actually, Brahm had been set to direct *Jean Valjean* for some time; the surprise was that Fox kept Brahm on the production, considering how bitterly he and Laird had been fighting on *Hangover Square*. And Fox had decided Laird would play Javert, not Jean Valjean.

A heavy he was, and a heavy he'd stay, as *Hangover Square* went on ... Fox seemingly delighting in persecuting its defiant star.

29

The Last Act

Now twilight lets her curtain down
And pins it with a star.
—McDonald Clarke, "The Mad Poet of Broadway" (1798–1842)

Of all the torments for Laird Cregar on *Hangover Square*, the worst of all were the almost ghoulish tales regarding his homosexuality.

For decades, a vicious story circulated in Hollywood that, during the film's tempestuous shoot, Laird, half-mad due to dieting, amphetamines and sexual frustration, went on the prowl at night to Long Beach and other dock areas, soliciting sailors, paying them to ejaculate into a vial. He then took the vials home to Coldwater Canyon, safe from being caught *in flagrante delicto* with a sailor, and drank the contents, performing a solitary, by-proxy fellatio. The habit, according to tellers of this singularly sordid tale, made him ill and brought on his death.[1]

It was a creepily outrageous slander, even by *Hollywood Babylon* standards, clearly calculated to humiliate Laird and threaten his career and reputation. Was Zanuck to blame? Had Fox started this repulsive whisper campaign? If not, who did?

It's impossible to prove, but it appears at least possible that Fox was trying to destroy Laird as punishment for his defiance. The accumulation of evidence—the "Fat Laird Cregar Suffers and Blows Up" report, the Barbara Berch *Screenland* story, the pitting of Brahm vs. Cregar in *Jean Valjean* despite their animosity on *Hangover Square*, the announcement of *The Spider*, and the spiteful, continued refusal to grant him a leave of absence for *Henry VIII*—all combined with the sudden rush of sex sagas—indicate the studio was sabotaging him. In a way, it made no sense; Zanuck had masterfully built Laird into a star, and it would be foolish to destroy his investment.

Or would it, considering it would teach a lesson to other recalcitrant actors, that the studio was considering dumping Laird anyway, and the fact that Fox had Vincent Price ready to jump into the breach?

Hangover Square had finally entered its last days and nights of shooting. Brahm filmed the opening episode—Bone's fiery murder-by-dagger of the old antiques dealer (Francis Ford, John Ford's grizzled brother). Always handsome despite his size, Laird now appeared a drawn, goggle-eyed hybrid of "beautiful man" and horror star. Brahm noticed that Laird, previously impeccably tailored, looked sloppy in his street clothes, which hung on him.[2]

Laird's infatuation for Linda Darnell continued throughout the picture. The stran-

One of the final stills ever taken of Laird Cregar (with unidentified extras), as *Hangover Square* neared the end of shooting on Fox's back lot, late October, 1944.

gling scene had been shot at Brahm's insistence and, very late in the shooting, Laird and Darnell played the scene in which he carried the corpse of Linda's Netta out of her flat. Undeen Hunter, Darnell's sister, remembered this saga from *Hangover Square*:

> Tweedles told me when they shot that scene, Laird carried her out, and banged her head—accidentally, of course—against a door frame! And he hit her head so hard that she actually passed out!
>
> Tweedles said when she came to, she was in a chair off the set, and Laird was kneeling beside her, apologizing over and over, terrified he'd hurt her. She kept saying she was fine, he kept saying he was sorry, and he was so upset, Tweedles said, she finally couldn't help it—she started to laugh. And Laird started to cry![3]

Very upset, he brought flowers to his leading lady in atonement.

Hangover Square finished shooting Wednesday, October 25, 1944.[4] The schedule called for process shots of Laird, more hypersensitive than ever and ravaged by his diet, with the exterior bonfire, interior music room and night; also, montage work with Laird, Darnell, Glenn Langan and 40 extras.[5] Brahm shot these final scenes on the Western Avenue lot.

The tantrum had been building for a long time; finally, it exploded.

"Well, I think we've worked together long enough," said Laird, lambasting Brahm in front of the company, "to know that we never want to work together again!"[6]

These 18 words were all that *The Hollywood Reporter* quoted from his tirade. It became well-circulated gossip, and was also a mistake: Brahm was very popular with his crew. And did this mean that, if Brahm remained director of *Jean Valjean*, that Laird would refuse to do the film?

Thursday, October 26: "Laird Cregar has dropped a total of 102 pounds," reported Edith Gwynn in her *Hollywood Reporter* column, "but the end isn't in sight."[7] He'd lost the weight since starting his diet in early 1943, although folklore soon claimed he'd shed the 100-plus pounds during the two months of filming *Hangover Square*. His current weight: 235 pounds.

Friday, October 27: Edith Gwynn wrote: "If a canvas were made among the principals and extras of the *Hangover Square* company, we don't think John Brahm would win any personal popularity poll. Not from the remarks that have poured into our shell-pink ears! Cregar is off to Del Monte for three weeks' rest before having that long-delayed operation...."[8]

The column outraged the crew of *Hangover Square*, fiercely loyal to Brahm. They suspected (probably correctly) that it was Laird who'd been prattling to Gwynn. This made him all the more unpopular with this unit of the Fox lot. George Sanders, by now, was considered detestable.

Then, for Laird, the unthinkable happened: Darryl Zanuck, displeased with the rough cut of *Hangover Square*, ordered the film back into production. Barré Lyndon recalled:

> I remember that he called everybody in to see the rough cut. We saw that in his private projection room near his office, and he had everybody in there, the writer, the producer, the wardrobe people—everybody who'd had anything to do with making the picture was there. He ran it reel by reel and at the end of each reel he'd stop it and make his remarks and ask his questions—and you'd better have some answers too! He'd consider shooting new scenes or cutting others out. He went right through it, and we were there till past 3:30 in the morning and back again at nine next day.[9]

Laird had taken off to Del Monte up the coast, but Fox ordered him back: *Hangover Square* was going again before the cameras. Brahm directed the first new scene—the dance hall episode, with Darnell flaunting her fishnets as she mouthed the playback to "Have You Seen Joe?" (Kay St. Germain Wells dubbed her singing.)

Wednesday, November 1: The *Hollywood Reporter*'s Edith Gwynn ran this notice: "Whatever John Brahm's troubles with the cast in *Hangover Square* may have been, the crew is for him 100% and just sent us a signed petition saying so."[10]

*   *   *

> *How oft when men are at the point of death*
> *Have they been merry! Which their keepers call*
> *A lightning before death...*
>   —*Romeo and Juliet*, Act V, scene iii

Hangover Square continued. Several times the trade papers announced it had wrapped, only for it to resume perversely, an apparently cursed production, seemingly doomed never to end. Rumor claimed that Zanuck was toyingly keeping the film in production to punish Laird and George Sanders for their defiance. Perhaps he was; the only added sequence in the final film was the "Have You Seen Joe?" song; the rest were capricious, Zanuck-ordered retakes. The mogul would also make significant cuts in Sanders' role, pruning Middleton's romantic scenes with Barbara. This was surely due to revenge on Sanders rather than improving pace: *Hangover Square* would run only 77 minutes, a very spare length for an "A" feature.

Brahm, probably expecting fireworks to resume (especially due to Laird's now-scuttled Del Monte sojourn), was surprised: Laird, with his hernia operation on the horizon, behaved. On the set, he was hardly jolly, but a least he was stoical ... almost eerily so, as Brahm remembered:

> For all his obstinacy and childishness, he attended to every necessary detail—such as retakes, dubbing, stills—before going to the hospital, even though I suggested that many matters could be left for his return, since the release date was far off. He insisted on finishing up, and then—he

Laird proudly reveals his weight loss.

made a will, carefully disposing of all his personal belongings. No doubt, he had a premonition that he would not return.[11]

It sounded like Hollywood fiction, but it was true: Laird contacted Irving G. Bishop, attorney and counselor, and prepared his Last Will and Testament. The four-page will did not, as Brahm said, carefully dispose of personal belongings; it mentioned none, and addressed only the Cregar family:

> I give, devise and bequeath all of my estate, of every kind and character and whatsoever situate, to my mother, ELIZABETH BLOOMFIELD CREGAR of 135 South Camden Drive, Beverly Hills, California, and to my aunt, EUGENIA FRANCIS SMITH of 135 South Camden Drive, Beverly Hills, California, if they shall both be alive at the time of my demise, in the shares set opposite their respective names:
> ELIZABETH BLOOMFIELD CREGAR—Sixty percent.
> EUGENIA FRANCIS SMTH—Forty percent.[12]

The will went on, impersonally directing how his estate should be distributed in the event of his mother's death or Aunt Eugenia's. It further directed its distribution in the case of the deaths of the secondary heirs, i.e., his four brothers and his niece Betsey. He appointed brothers Edward and John, both of whom now lived in Los Angeles, as his executors. The document was intriguing, for it not only revealed Laird's sense of impending death as he faced his operation: It had a sense of the Cregar Family Against the World.

And, for all the gossip about the man or woman who "inspired" Laird's self-destruction, the will named no "significant other" in his life, male or female.

* * *

As *Hangover Square* shot retakes and Laird prepared for his operation, a new controversy arose: *Dragonwyck*.

Fox has purchased Anya Seton's bestseller about Nicholas Van Ryn, a Byronic patroon who rules a Hudson River estate (Dragonwyck) and descends into drug addiction and madness, as witnessed by his young bride Miranda. Zanuck, producer-director Ernst Lubitsch and writer Joseph Mankiewicz had lured red-hot star Gregory Peck to play the role. Gene Tierney was set for Miranda, and production scheduled to begin early in 1945.

Trouble intervened. "Gregory Peck won't do *Dragonwyck*," reported Hedda Hopper in her November 22, 1944, column, "which leaves Gene Tierney without a male partner...." Peck had bailed out, possibly because Lubitsch became ill and Mankiewicz took over as director, perhaps because Peck opted to star in David O. Selznick's *Duel in the Sun* ... or maybe for both reasons. The original idea had been that a romantic star would play a heavy, rather than a heavy playing a romantic. However, Zanuck now eyed *Dragonwyck* to star one of the lot's two major villains: Laird Cregar or Vincent Price, the latter fresh from *Laura*.

The project probably appealed to Laird; Van Ryn was a villain, but a glamorous one. Laird was set for *Jean Valjean*, but that production could be shelved again. And as a leading lady, he'd have his pal Gene Tierney. Meanwhile, Price, then acting at Fox in *A Royal Scandal* with Tallulah Bankhead, campaigned for the Van Ryn part. Mankiewicz, *Dragonwyck*'s writer-director, wasn't encouraging; he'd produced Fox's

Keys of the Kingdom (1944) in which Price (who had a tendency to gain weight) had played a role the actor later referred to as "that fat priest."[13] In the original opinion of Mankiewicz, who was still pining for Peck, Price was hardly suited to the role.

Zanuck scheduled a screen test for Price, who began dieting. Both Fox heavies were counting calories as Laird allowed himself for consideration.

Perhaps his premonition was that he'd never live to play *Dragonwyck* anyway.

* * *

"My last glimpse of [Cregar] was when he was on his way to a kid party Lana Turner gave. He was done up as Buster Brown in a blond wig and knee breeches and I'll never forget the twinkle in his eyes as he called out hello. "Why, he's just a big kid after all," I said to my friends as we drove by. I little dreamed I'd never see him again."[14]—Hedda Hopper

Maureen O'Hara, on the audio commentary for *The Black Swan*, told film historian Rudy Behlmer that she had dinner with Laird the night before he entered the hospital for his operation, which would have been Wednesday, November 29:

I went to dinner with him and there was somebody else, I can't really remember who it was. We went to dinner at a restaurant on the corner of Sunset Boulevard called Ciro's. And of course, with Laird, you chit-chat and gossip and you laugh and you have a wonderful time. I was very proud—I'd saved enough money to buy a mink coat.... There I was in my mink coat, and rather than have it in my lap or sit on it, or damage it, I took it and folded it up and on the seat beside me. And with the laughter and the chit-chat I wasn't paying attention ... and my coat wasn't there! And I thought, "My God, I didn't see anyone touch it. Where is it? Where is it?"

And I looked, and sitting next to me was a lady who was known as the Countess Di Frasso. And she had my mink coat wrapped around her puny little dog! I was absolutely livid! On the seat—he was on the seat! And I took that mink coat, and I pulled it up in the air, and that dog went flying.... I got my coat back, and Laird laughed his head off, and I was ready to kill him![15]

Note that Ms. O'Hara didn't remember the other diner, or professed not to. Perhaps he was Laird's "companion," who, wherever he was that night, was likely pleased with Laird's weight loss.

Also on November 29, an article in the *Harrisburg* (Illinois) *Daily Register* had Laird claiming that he had lost 105 pounds, as well as ten inches off his waistline, five sizes off his shirts and three sizes off his shoes.[16]

Meanwhile, as the date of the surgery approached, Laird coped with his haunting sense of an early death. He made a call to his lawyer, who later claimed Laird told him: "If anything happens, I don't want any grieving. I've done the two things I wanted most. I've been on the stage and I've been on the screen."[17]

Thursday, November 30: Laird entered Good Samaritan Hospital in Los Angeles. Doctors had scheduled the operation for Monday, December 4.

Saturday, December 2: His Last Will and Testament was ready for his signature, and Laird signed the document, presumably at Good Samaritan.

Monday, December 4: "This is cutting-up day for Laird Cregar," wrote Hedda Hopper in her column.[18] Edith Gwynn noted that day in *The Hollywood Reporter*, "Laird Cregar called before going into Good Samaritan for that big operation, and said he'll

Laird exercising at his Coldwater Canyon house, fall, 1944.

have only a local anesthetic and will watch the entire proceedings. Well, that's one way of being entertained!"[19]

Tuesday, December 5: Variety announced that Vincent Price had won the lead in *Dragonwyck*. It was a giant break for Price, who now had the potential to match or surpass Laird as Fox's top screen scoundrel.[20]

Wednesday, December 6: Variety reported that John Brahm and producer William Perlberg were "huddling on possible early start for *Jean Valjean* at 20th-Fox."[21] There'd been no news in the trade papers about Laird's condition following his operation.

Friday, December 8: A mysterious item appeared in *The Hollywood Reporter*: "With the possibility that *Jean Valjean*, his announced next assignment, will be pushed back on the 20th-Fox schedule, director John Brahm is reading several other scripts, one of which he may do as his next picture."[22]

Although Cregar wasn't mentioned in this article, the impact on his career was huge. With *Jean Valjean* "pushed back" yet again, and with Vincent Price winning *Dragonwyck*, Laird had no immediate film project.

Of course, nobody can say with certainty today what Laird's private thoughts were on Friday night, December 8. Yes, he'd lost over 100 pounds, and perhaps the plastic surgery he'd planned would be his personal Christmas gift.

His Hollywood fame had been a virtual miracle, perhaps coming earlier and more surprisingly than it should have; he'd hardly had the time to process it. He was still very young and, for all his intelligence, lacked the years and experiences that might have helped him cope with the inevitable highs and lows of so incredibly mercurial a profession. For a time, he'd reveled in his celebrity, masterfully built up by a studio devoted to showcasing his undeniable genius.

Yet how 1944 had exploded in his face since his triumph in *The Lodger*! The loss of *Laura*. The doomed battle to do *Henry VIII*. The break-up of his engagement to Peggy Stack. The "fat pig" ultimatum from his male lover. The horrors of *Hangover Square*. His gone-sour relationship with Zanuck, Brahm and many Fox co-workers. Now, just this week ... even after allowing his consideration to stay typecast in *Dragonwyck*, he'd seen the studio bypass him. And *Jean Valjean* was on a back burner again.

He'd spent much of the year personally and professionally seething, anguished by relationships, wracked by dieting. He had been fighting his demons in aggressive ways, defiantly, maybe even heroically, but with dangerously consuming obsession. The bitter battle had severely taken its toll.

On Saturday morning, December 9, at about 4:00 a.m., Laird suffered a heart attack.

The Good Samaritan doctors began a desperate fight to save his life. Dr. Charles T. Sturgeon[23] placed him in an oxygen tent, and by late morning, he appeared to be rallying. Then, at midday, there came a second heart attack. He couldn't survive two attacks only eight hours apart.

A death watch began.

Throughout the cloudy, overcast day,[24] Elizabeth Cregar was at the bedside, along with brothers Edward and John. A brave woman, she had already lost her son William, and now she watched her youngest one critically failing. His passion and brilliance had taken her from the world she'd known and cherished in Philadelphia, where he'd made faces for the neighbors, to a more exciting and defining one she'd enjoyed in Los Angeles, where he'd made some of the same faces for a worldwide audience. She was proud of his achievement and his ongoing devotion to her.

Alerted of the situation, 20th Century–Fox dealt with the press. Late in the day they reported Laird's condition as "grave," explaining that he "had dieted away 100 of his original 300 pounds in preparation for the surgery." The Fox spokespeople, as *The Washington Post* would print, "admitted that may have contributed to the heart attack."[25]

At 4:52 p.m., as night neared in Los Angeles, Samuel Laird Cregar died. He was 31 years old. The death certificate would read, "Acute

"A Beautiful Man": A glamour portrait of Laird, after his weight loss and shortly before his death.

myocardial failure," due to "Operation," due to "Post-Operative Ventral Hernia," which dated to his appendix operation three years previously.[26]

Forest Lawn took the body that night to its mortuary. The mourning Elizabeth Cregar had people to call. One was her ten-year-old granddaughter Betsey, home in Brewster, New York. "Oh, my, I was destroyed," Betsey remembered.[27]

The sad news spread throughout the film colony. Ironically, at the Pasadena Playhouse, where Laird had first acted in California, John Carradine, his former "rival" at Fox, was starring this night in *My Dear Children*, the comedy John Barrymore had played on Broadway in 1940. Carradine did his riotous Barrymore impression, and Sonia Sorel, who would marry Carradine in March 1945, co-starred with him.[28]

The corporate powers of 20th Century–Fox addressed the tragedy with all due formality. An inter-office correspondence memo from Lew Schreiber to George Wasson, both men in Fox's legal department, would put it all very succinctly:

> Dear George:
> The LAIRD CREGAR contract is to be officially closed as of the night of December 9th.[29]

PART VI

Denouement

When the gods wish to punish us they answer our prayers.—Oscar Wilde

30

What I Wanted for Christmas

"Dear Santa:

"As one large man to another—surely you know what I mean when I say the only thing I want out of your pack is a new kind of screen role. Okay, I am not exactly a small guy. Neither are you. But do I have to be a mysterious and sinister oversized guy, year after year?

"I know. You're typed, too. But nobody hates a jolly fat man, especially when he's so free and easy with the presents. But my kind! Little kids whimper when they pass me in the streets.

"You've probably forgotten, Santa, but I used to be a comedian. Then somebody found out I had a pretty nasty leer in stock. I should have kept it a secret. I'm trapped now. Nothing can save me but a miracle, or a word from you, dear Santa, to the headman at my studio.

"Put in a word for me, friend, and I won't even ask you for those extra red ration points I really need to keep up my strength."[1]

—Laird Cregar, Yuletide 1944 issue of *Photoplay*

It would be a private funeral.

Sunday, December 10, 1944: The day after Laird's death, rain fell intermittently as the family visited Forest Lawn, Glendale, to make arrangements for the funeral and burial. The paperwork survives with the breakdown of costs[2]:

- Interment Space 2, Lot 37, Eventide: $300
- Mortuary Service: $485
- Ground Vase: $0.85
- Concrete Box: $12
- Interment and Recording Charge: $35.50
- Minister's Honorarium: $25
- Sales Tax: $6.38

Total cost: $864.73.

Incidentally and ironically, as Laird's family planned his burial, Darryl F. Zanuck was in New York City where, that Sunday evening, he was the guest at the American Nobel Anniversary Dinner, honored for *Wilson*, which the Nobel Committee called a "vital contribution to the cause of world peace."[3] The producer gave a speech, broadcast over the radio, and the night was a triumph for him. There was one consolation in all this: As Zanuck would be in New York this week, there was no chance he'd demand a pass to Laird's private rites.

Elizabeth Cregar selected Forest Lawn's Church of the Recessional as the site for

Laird Cregar's funeral took place at the Church of the Recessional, Forest Lawn, Glendale, California, on December 13, 1944 (author's photograph, 2016).

the funeral. Built in 1941, it sits high on a north hill of the cemetery, and is a reproduction of the St. Margaret Parish Church, Rottingdean, Sussex, England. The original had been the church Rudyard Kipling attended; the replica is named after his poem "Recessional." Carole Lombard's funeral had taken place there in 1942.

Then there was the selection of the six pallbearers,[4] all friends of Laird and involved in theater, movies or music: Keenan Wynn, Laird's pal who'd planned to accompany him overseas to entertain troops; Tom Neal, a close friend since Laird's arrival in Hollywood, and whose wedding to sultry starlet Vicky Lane was attended by Laird that summer; Richard Whorf, dark, mustachioed Broadway actor, who'd appeared in Warners' *Yankee Doodle Dandy*, played in Deanna Durbin's *Christmas Holiday* (1944), and had recently directed MGM's *Blonde Fever* (1944); Johnny Green, 36-year-old composer and musical director, who'd go on to win five Oscars for Best Music Scoring, starting with MGM's *Easter Parade* (1948), and wed six-foot MGM "Glamazon" swimmer-actress Bunny Waters; and the songwriting team of 30-year-old Bob Wright and 29-year-old Chet Forrest.

Perhaps most significant, and surprising, was Elizabeth Cregar's choice to deliver the eulogy: Vincent Price. There was apparently no resentment in the Cregar family about *Dragonwyck*. Almost half a century later, Price sounded surprised himself about the honor as he told David Del Valle in a *Video Watchdog* (May/June 1992) interview:

> Laird was an extraordinary man. He was an *enormous* man. He was a giant, you know, and all his family were giants. I happened to know his mother and his brothers.... I read the eulogy at his funeral, strangely enough, though I didn't know him that well. His mother wanted me to do it because I'd been with him in his first picture [*Hudson's Bay*]. He was a wonderful actor, Laird, and he died much too young.[5]

Again, there was sadness here: a eulogist who didn't know Laird "that well," who was actually a potentially eclipsing rival, selected for the rather distant reason that he happened to work with the deceased in his first notable film appearance.

Wednesday, December 13: The Laird Cregar funeral began on this windy, partly cloudy day[6] at 2:30 p.m. at the Church of the Recessional. The Reverend Smith of All Saints Episcopal Church in Beverly Hills officiated.[7] Forest Lawn, likely assisted by 20th Century–Fox, provided security, strictly heeding Elizabeth Cregar's insistence on a private funeral. Edward and John were there, Marshall came from Alaska, and, of course, Aunt Nean was present. *The Hollywood Citizen-News* reported on the day of the funeral that "Hollywood's motion picture colony and friends outside the industry who knew Laird Cregar"[8] would be in attendance, but no detailed descriptions of the funeral, list of celebrity mourners, or photographs subsequently appeared in the newspapers.

Meanwhile, there was an ostracizing. As Doris Lloyd remembered, the Cregar family bitterly blamed Laird's never-identified companion for the fanatical fatal dieting.[9] While it wasn't entirely his fault, it was an understandable response. The family had markedly excluded him from the pallbearers. Whether he was allowed to attend the funeral isn't known.

The gravesite was near the road in the upper area of Eventide. Night comes soon in December, and it fell over the freshly covered grave. Eventually the family added a flat headstone marker which mysteriously errs in the year of birth, giving it as 1914.

Thursday, December 14: The day after Laird's funeral, Hollywood had a new tragedy: Lupe Velez committed suicide by overdosing on Seconal tablets.[10] The press coverage was far more aggressive, reporting that Lupe was pregnant and her lover, Harald Ramond, was the father. Photographers snapped pictures of Lupe's mother and sisters grieving at the bier, as well as one of Ramond standing by the body to pay his last respects.

Still, rumors circulated sinuously about Laird Cregar's death, due to his youth, the suddenness of his demise, and probably the private nature of his funeral. After all, this was a town where Jean Harlow's 1937 passing at age 26 (actually due to kidney failure) was attributed to everything from syphilis of the eyes to bestiality with a gorilla.

Maureen O'Hara, in her aforementioned commentary on *The Black Swan*, dismissed Rudy Behlmer's remark about Laird's fatal dieting with asperity. "Who told you that?" she snapped. Ms. O'Hara claimed Laird's death had "nothing to do with weight" and that the Cregar family had told her it was simply due to a post-operation blood clot that had gone to his heart. It makes sense that the family took this stand, as it was far less traumatic than saying he'd basically dieted himself to death due to personal and professional anxiety. It's also possible that he had a heart condition similar to the one that killed his brother William, and his doctors had misdiagnosed it.

At any rate, the family certainly was aware of the actual factors, or at least most of them, that had contributed to Laird's death. Betsey Cregar had been told and always believed that her beloved uncle had fatally overdone his diet in a desperate attempt to change his screen type.

Meanwhile, posthumous stories circulated about Laird Cregar. *Screenland* magazine published Barbara Berch's "Bold, Bad (Bluffing) Cregar," in its January 1945 issue, available in December. It was too late to recall the highly unflattering story; its timing was grievously unfortunate.

Also, Laird had accepted an invitation from *Photoplay* magazine to contribute to its "What I Want for Christmas" feature for the January 1945 issue, also on newsstands in December. He'd joined Shirley Temple, Pat O'Brien, Margaret O'Brien, his friend Van Johnson and his non-friend Greer Garson in what the magazine called "some candid tinsel talk by six stars with standout ideas."

Laird's letter, citing his typecasting and weight troubles and quoted at the opening of this chapter was, in retrospect, heartbreaking.

*   *   *

Monday, December 18: Laird Cregar's will was filed for probate, his estate temporarily valued at over $10,000.[11]

Meanwhile, his legacy also included a film that, remarkably, was *still* in production. It wasn't until Saturday night, December 23, two weeks after Laird's death, that John Brahm completed supervising the dubbing on *Hangover Square*. The film's final cost would be $1,154,400, over $300,000 more than Zanuck had originally planned to invest in it.

It was, inevitably, a freak attraction, a sex-horror film cursed by the stigma of a leading man who was now dead. Jean Harlow had died during MGM's *Saratoga* (1937), and the studio finished the film with a body double and a voice double. On July 22, 1937, 45 days after Harlow's death, *Saratoga* had opened at New York's Capitol Theatre and had been a box office sensation.[12]

Of course, Cregar wasn't in Harlow's pantheon of stardom, but the fact that he'd died before the release of *Hangover Square* surely set up the film for a strange, macabre reception. On January 11, 1945, 33 days after Laird's demise, Fox previewed it in New York. *Variety's* review expressed it very well: "This is a picture more notable for the omniscience of a single player than any other factor."[13]

Wednesday, February 7, 1945: *Hangover Square* opened at the Roxy Theatre on Broadway. One year previously, Laird had appeared at the Roxy for *The Lodger*. Now his pal Milton Berle headlined the stage show that also featured Connie Russell, Ben Yost's Vikings, the Slayman Ali Troupe, the Three Rockets, the Gae Foster Roxyettes, and Paul Ash and the Roxy Theatre Orchestra. "Let Yourself Go! *Broadway's Biggest Show!*" promised the *New York Times* advertisement.

"The late Laird Cregar," wrote *Time* magazine (February 12, 1945), "brilliant and touching in his embodiment of the hero's anguished, innocent, dangerous confusion, will have cinemaddicts pondering sadly on the major roles he might have played."[14] The Manhattan critics had a mixed response, but *Hangover Square* and Milton Berle proved to be a powerhouse attraction. *Variety* reported the first week's take a "socko $103,000."[15] The only film doing bigger business on Broadway that week was Columbia's *A Song to Remember,* reaping $123,000[16] in its third week at Radio City Music Hall. The film was the story of Chopin (played by Cornel Wilde) and boasted two former Cregar co-stars, Merle Oberon as George Sand (French novelist) and Paul Muni as Prof. Joseph Elsner (Chopin's teacher and friend).

Meanwhile, John Brahm was in New York for the premieres of both *Hangover Square* and *Guest in the House*, a United Artists thriller which he'd also directed and which opened February 15 at the Capitol. In its second week at the Roxy, *Hangover Square* did a big $84,000, tying that sum in its third and final week.[17] As a Broadway attraction, the film performed very well.

Yet for any fan, friend or admirer of Laird Cregar, *Hangover Square* was, and is, a trauma. From the opening episode, presenting George Harvey Bone and his knife murder of the antiques dealer, the film's akin to paying respects at a funeral parlor. We see a frazzled Laird, walking like a zombie on the exterior set at night, almost gaunt from the angle we observe him, wearing his funereal black hat, both a pathetic Bone and a tormented Cregar, carrying his figurative cross through this remarkably troubled Calvary of a movie ... maybe sensing it was the final film of his life.

Then he turns, looks back at the fire his character started, and the camera focuses for a haunting, mercilessly intense close-up. His eyes are large, his face anguished in the glow of the fire, and his personal misery seems to peer through the character he's playing. Brahm later said that the "beautiful man" dream had "devastated" Cregar, physically and emotionally,[18] and we know now that as he played this scene, he had so little time to live.

Why had he destroyed himself this way? For a man? A woman? A career? It was a tragic, terrible waste, and one recalls again the Sir John Suckling poem Patrick Hamilton used to introduce his novel, *Hangover Square*:

> Why so pale and wan, fond lover,
> Prythee, why so pale?
> Will, if looking well can't move her,
> Looking ill prevail?
> Prythee, why so pale?

31

Legacy

The time's too short for all I want to do.[1]—Laird Cregar

In her "Good News" column in the March 1945 edition of *Modern Screen* magazine, Louella Parsons wrote:

> Two deaths rocked Hollywood within a week of one another. The first was Laird Cregar. The second, Lupe Velez.
>
> In many ways, perhaps Laird's was the more tragic of the two—because, in spite of the mental torment that brought on Lupe's death, she had lived and lived fully. She had been a bright flame that attracted much happiness and laughter, fame and fortune to herself as well as the dross and heartache that unfortunately overshadowed everything else at the time of her death.
>
> But I remember her best as a laughing girl. A modern pagan who had loved life greatly even though she sought her own death.
>
> But Laird was different.
>
> He had never really lived at all.
>
> At 28 [*sic*] years of age, Laird was a young giant who had never known life or love or marriage or home or mental peace and happiness.
>
> He joked about his great weight and size, but it made him unhappy. That's why he dieted so strenuously to lose 100 pounds.
>
> He once told me, "No matter how nice people are to me, I'm still something of an oddity to them. And being an oddity—isn't fun."[2]

Few people in Hollywood ever admitted respect for Parsons' insights—John Barrymore had referred to her as "a quaint old udder"[3]—and her eulogy might appear a conventional 1945 woman's distortion of a gay man's life. After all, Laird had achieved a spectacular success, and had delighted for a time in all it meant and made possible.

Yet, Louella had hit a near-bullseye; Laird's weight, and to a lesser degree his sexuality, had self-sentenced him to life as an "oddity," costing him his "mental peace"; and for all the fame and fortune, it ultimately wasn't "fun." In his brief life, he'd missed having a father, had endured an adventurous youth at least as much as he enjoyed it, and had desperately wanted what he'd lost as a boy—a happy family life. It had been why the first thing he did after achieving fame was to move his family west with him. It was why he'd been so eager to adopt Betsey. It was why he'd embarked on his fatal diet to attract a lifelong companion.

It's wildly politically incorrect to assume that Cregar's homosexuality was a torment; it perhaps seems trite to write that his ultimate epiphany was "There's no place like home," or, "Be careful what you wish for, it might come true." Yet it would also be relatively and tragically accurate. In the social reality of 1944, real men in their late 20s and early 30s went off to fight in World War II; meanwhile, an obese "deviant" stayed in Hollywood, playing Jack the Ripper as a priss. It was what he had been born to do, destined to do, what he'd been a genius at doing ... but at only 31 years old, he hadn't come to terms with that reality. Hence Laird's fervent wish to get permission to go overseas and perform for the soldiers. And the fighting men all dreamed of coming home happily-ever-after to their wives and sweethearts—not to someone who threw out epithets such as "you fat pig."

Elaine Barrie, the fourth divorced wife of John Barrymore, the man whom Laird had hero-worshipped, the man who'd broken his heart, once said of Barrymore, "You couldn't hate him, because he was such an abomination to himself."[4] Laird, on the other hand, dying at only 31, caught in a four-and-a-half-year whirlwind of celebrity, never had the years or the sabbatical he needed to make peace with himself. Coming to Hollywood as a "grotesque," he'd become, in his own eyes, an abomination.

To destroy the abomination, he'd raged desperately, bitterly ... and finally fatally.

March 30, 1945: Hangover Square opened at four Los Angeles theaters: Grauman's Chinese, Loew's State, the Uptown and the Carthay Circle. The support feature: Columbia's *Swing in the Saddle,* starring Jane Frazee, Guinn "Big Boy" Williams and a bevy of cowboy musical performers. Playing at the Egyptian Theatre, across Hollywood Boulevard from Grauman's Chinese, was MGM's *The Picture of Dorian Gray,* starring Hurd Hatfield in the title part and George Sanders in the Lord Henry role Laird had so coveted. It also was playing at the Los Angeles and the Ritz theatres.

"Cregar did a swan song that will long be remembered by his followers," reported the *Los Angeles Examiner* review.[5]

In London, the release of *Hangover Square* caused a virtual scandal, due to the liberty Fox and Barré Lyndon had taken with Patrick Hamilton's well-praised novel. "A masterpiece turned into rubbish," wrote James Agate, adding, "[T]his is the worst betrayal of a first class novel that I ever remember...."[6] In *Through a Glass Darkly: The Life of Patrick Hamilton,* Nigel Jones wrote, "Fox's treatment of the novel was not so

Billboard for the Los Angeles opening of *Hangover Square* in March 1945, over three months after Laird's death.

much a mutilation as a mass murder—and indeed, a mass murderer was what they made poor George Harvey Bone out to be."[7]

Meanwhile, while Fox insisted that *Hangover Square* was breaking records in London, it did poorly in some U.S hinterlands. The manager of the Liberty Theatre in Columbia, Kansas griped in *Motion Picture Herald*: "If every exhibitor had seen this previewed first, it would have gone into the ashcan.... Dark scenes in London streets and a skulking murderer striking in the gloom. Nothing pleasant about this, and the box office was idle both nights. Not the type for small towns especially."[8]

Yet the film had many admirers. At some point, Stephen Sondheim, 15 years old in 1945, saw *Hangover Square.* The film and Bernard Herrmann's "Concerto Macabre" eventually inspired Sondheim to compose the Tony Award–winning music and lyrics for the demonic 1979 Broadway musical *Sweeney Todd.*

Hangover Square earned worldwide rentals of $1,798,500. The modest profit: $27,700. At least it ended up in the black; Zanuck's "baby" *Wilson*, despite critical acclaim and solid box office, couldn't recoup its gigantic cost, losing over $2.2 million.

Laird's final film, and the only one in which he had top billing, long suffered the reputation as an inferior rip-off of *The Lodger.* It would be decades before critics awarded *Hangover Square* the reappraisal it deserved. Indeed, along with RKO's *The Body Snatcher* (1945), which starred Boris Karloff in the title role, it's arguably one of the two finest horror films of the 1940s ... and Laird's George Harvey Bone is one of the great lost souls of dark cinema.

* * *

Vincent Price assumed Laird's place at Fox. *Dragonwyck* opened at Broadway's Roxy Theatre in April 1946, taking in a huge $109,000 in its first week and a remarkable $116,000 in its second.[9] (The worldwide rentals of $3,897,400 surpassed those of *The Lodger* and *Hangover Square.*) Curiously, Price also inherited three Cregar roles on radio's *Hollywood Star Time*: Bone in "Hangover Square" (with Linda Darnell, April 7, 1946); the title role in "The Lodger" (with Cathy Lewis in Merle Oberon's role, May 19, 1946); and Ed Cornell in "Hot Spot" (aka "I Wake Up Screaming," with Brian Donlevy in Victor Mature's role, July 27, 1946). He left Fox in 1947, eventually becoming a horror superstar via Warner Bros.' 3-D *House of Wax* (1953). Price made his most memorable mark in the Roger Corman American International Pictures' Poe homages of the early 1960s such as *House of Usher* and *Pit and the Pendulum.*

Many conjecture that Price inherited the career that Laird Cregar would have had. Ironically, one of Price's late-in-life triumphs was his one-man show *Oscar Wilde in Diversions and Delights*, in which he toured to acclaim in the late 1970s, and appeared briefly on Broadway in 1978.[10] A beloved presence, Price enjoyed a career that spanned almost 60 years. He died in Los Angeles October 25, 1993, at the age of 82.

"My father talked about Laird Cregar all the time," Price's daughter Victoria told me in 2015.[11]

20th Century–Fox announced that it would honor Laird Cregar by establishing a scholarship in his name at the Pasadena Playhouse.[12] It never happened.

* * *

Ward Bond, who'd played in two of Laird's films (*Ten Gentlemen from West Point* and *Hello Frisco, Hello*), moved into Laird's cottage at 9510 Cherokee Lane in Coldwater Canyon, living there the rest of his life. He died in Dallas on November 5, 1960. A member of John Ford's stock company, Bond had achieved stardom in TV's *Wagon Train.*

*   *   *

Shakespeare's *Henry VIII* eventually made it to Broadway, opening at the International Theatre on November 6, 1946. Billy Rose didn't produce (the American Repertory Theatre did), but Margaret Webster directed it, and Victor Jory played the title role.[13] It ran in repertory with James M. Barrie's *What Every Woman Knows*, Henrik Ibsen's *John Gabriel Borkman*, Sean O'Casey's *A Pound on Demand* and George Bernard Shaw's *Androcles and the Lion* (the last two performed the same nights). *Henry VIII* played 40 performances.

*   *   *

20th Century–Fox finally produced *Les Miserables*, released in 1952. Michael Rennie, who'd just starred as Klaatu in Fox's *The Day the Earth Stood Still* (1951), played Jean Valjean; Robert Newton, best-remembered as Long John Silver in Disney's *Treasure Island* (1950), was Javert. Lewis Milestone directed. It's a workmanlike version, with Newton, like the film itself, curiously restrained.

*   *   *

Fox produced two 1953 remakes of Laird's significant hits: *I Wake Up Screaming* became *Vicki*, and *The Lodger* became *Man in the Attic*. Richard Boone played Ed Cornell, and Jack Palance played the Ripper. See the appendix for more information on these films.

Sydney Greenstreet, Laird's competition as the villainous fat man of the movies, outlived him by nearly a decade, wonderfully detestable in such films as *The Hucksters* (MGM, 1947). At 10:50 p.m. on January 18, 1954, Greenstreet died at his home, 1531 Selma Drive in Hollywood, from Bright's disease, due to diabetes. (Greenstreet's death certificate noted that he'd suffered from "Obesity" for 50 years.[14]) Seventy-four years old, he was survived by his wife Dorothy and son John. On January 22, 1954, Greenstreet was cremated at Forest Lawn, Glendale, where his ashes were interred in the Great Mausoleum.

*   *   *

In October 1945, 20th Century–Fox had sent out this curious press release:

> It looks as though the late Laird Cregar's ambition will be realized, and that his favorite actor, Sydney Greenstreet, will star in the one mystery yarn the gifted Cregar authored before he died last December 9th.
>
> Laird's mother, Mrs. Elizabeth Cregar, sent the manuscript of her son's who-dunnit, *A Night of Terror*, to Greenstreet, with a note about her son's admiration for him and his hope that the story would be worthy of Greenstreet's great talents.
>
> The famed fat man read it, and was so intrigued with the subtly sinister tale of the mad surgeon who transferred the brains of brilliant patients to the skulls of idiotic ones, that he's asked his studio to read it with a view to starring him in the Cregar horror opus.

Greenstreet's studio was Warner Bros., and if Greenstreet actually submitted Laird's story to his bosses, it was never produced.

*　*　*

Laird's mother Elizabeth Cregar and her sister Eugenia stayed on in Los Angeles after Laird's death, in their 135 South Camden Drive apartment. Bess remained her queenly self, and Nean was with her to offer the reliable support and companionship she'd provided since their earliest days in Philadelphia. On October 17, 1945, *Variety* reported that MGM had optioned Elizabeth's book *Make Me a Child Again,* and that Macmillan would publish her first novel, *She, in Armor Clad.*[15] However, the film was never made and neither book was ever published. One of the ways Elizabeth passed the time: playing cards with Theda Bara, the legendary, long-retired vamp of the Silent Screen.

Eugenia died February 23, 1958, in her seventy-sixth year. She was buried at Forest Lawn in Eventide, the same section as her nephew. Elizabeth, staying on at Camden Drive, soon became ill with cancer of the bowel. Shortly before her grandmother's death, Betsey Hayman, then 25, called her grandmother with the happy news: she'd given birth to a son, William Cregar Hayman, named after Betsey's father, who'd died in 1938.[16]

Elizabeth Cregar, 78, died March 17, 1959, at Good Samaritan Hospital, where Laird had died over 14 years previously. She was also buried at Forest Lawn.[17] There was presumably no room for her to be buried near her son or her sister; thus, her grave is in Ascension, above Eventide. The marker reads:

> ELIZABETH B. CREGAR
> 1880–1959
> OUR BELOVED MOTHER

*　*　*

Laird's mother and aunt had lived to see the stardom of Raymond Burr, who, ironically, had idolized Laird Cregar. Born in British Columbia, Burr had been working at the Pasadena Playhouse during the World War II years and eventually made his mark as a "heavy heavy" in such films as Hitchcock's *Rear Window* (as the wife killer, 1954). He was also impressive as the sexually deranged loser who kidnaps Natalie Wood in *A Cry in the Night* (1956). His life and career took a new direction when he won the role of TV's *Perry Mason,* for which, reminiscent of Laird, he lost 100 pounds. Burr played the lawyer from 1957 to 1966, twice winning an Emmy, and had a second successful TV series as the wheelchair-bound detective *Ironside* (1967–1975).

Elizabeth "Betsey" Cregar Hayman in her later years.

Burr was an enigma. He claimed he'd had two wives (and even a son) who'd died. The suspicion was that he was fabricating this past to conceal his homosexuality.[18] He was a remarkably interesting and generous man who made many trips to visit servicemen in Vietnam (at his own expense), owned an island in Fiji and a winery at his Dry Creek Valley Ranch in California, and donated to many charities. Burr died September 12, 1993, and left an estate of $32,000,000. At the end of his life, he was reportedly writing an autobiography, battling the tabloids that had claimed his marriages were tall tales and that he'd had a homosexual relationship with his companion of over 30 years, Robert Benevides.[19]

*   *   *

After playing Shakespearean roles at the Old Globe Theatre in San Diego and various TV appearances, Victor Buono shot to prominence in *What Ever Happened to Baby Jane?* (1962) as Edwin Flagg, the obese pianist who joins Bette Davis' crazed Baby Jane in her comeback dream.[20] When the film was released, Buono was only 24. *Variety's* Army Archerd wrote, "Buono blasts thru the screen as an explosive new addition to the Biz ... in the class of early Orson Welles, Sydney Greenstreet and Laird Cregar." Buono received Oscar and Golden Globe nominations for Best Supporting Actor.

The Cregar comparison continued as Buono starred in *The Strangler* (1964) as a mama-obsessed maniac killing young women. He was immense in every way as King Tut on television's *Batman* (a guest villain Laird might have reveled in!); recorded a comedy album titled *Heavy!*; and was a popular TV guest star, including an episode of *Taxi* ("Going Home," December 17, 1980), as the father of Jim Ignatowski, played by Christopher Lloyd (who was only eight months younger than Buono). Reportedly gay but closeted, Buono was 43 when he died January 1, 1982, in Apple Valley, California, of a massive heart attack. He was buried with his mother, Myrtle Belle Buono, at Greenwood Memorial Park in San Diego. At last report, only her name appears on the crypt.

Like Laird Cregar, Buono supposedly had a sense he'd die young.

*   *   *

In 1997, a biopic simply titled *Wilde* premiered, starring British actor Stephen Fry in the title role, with Jude Law as a very unsympathetic Lord Alfred Douglas. The acclaimed film included Wilde's trial and imprisonment. Fry, standing over 6'4", bears a striking, almost uncanny resemblance to Laird Cregar; in his flair and audacity as an actor, a fanciful historian might even call him a "reincarnation."

The world has changed significantly in its tolerance since the 1940s. On January 17, 2015, Fry married his lover, Elliott G. Spencer. Fry was 57, Spencer, 27. Fry has boasted about using cocaine in Buckingham Palace, claims the honor of having said the word "fuck" on a live broadcast more than any other actor, and enjoys an open life and thriving career.

Yet Fry is bipolar, and has spoken and written openly about his two suicide attempts.[21] Social acceptance evolves, taboos vanish, but private demons remain. Always, they provide the deepest anguish.

By the time Stephen Fry starred in *Wilde*, Laird Cregar had been dead for 53 years.

* * *

In 2007, Constantine Nasr of New Wave Entertainment produced the special features for a three-DVD set entitled *Fox Horror Classics: A Terrifying Trilogy of Terror*. The films were *The Undying Monster, The Lodger* and *Hangover Square*, all directed by John Brahm. Among the bonus features was *The Tragic Mask: The Laird Cregar Story*, a worthy documentary produced by Nasr with the cooperation of 20th Century–Fox. I was privileged to have been one of the "talking heads" on the documentary.

* * *

Elizabeth Francis Cregar Hayman, Laird's beloved Betsey, died on March 29, 2015, at the Hospice of the Foothills Compassionate Care facility in Grass Valley, California, after a battle with cancer. Her husband Ron, a psychiatrist and medical director, had died November 24, 2014; they'd been married 57 years. She's survived by her son William, daughter Valerie, a granddaughter and a sister.

Betsey worked as a nurse, but her uncle's impact on her was strong and lasting: Wherever she lived, she'd become involved in local theater as a producer, director, actress and writer. Betsey had cherished a special memento from her time with her Uncle Sam so many years ago: the giant spoon he'd use to amuse his guests at the house on Palm Drive. In 2016, Kino-Lorber released a Blu-Ray of *The Lodger*, for which I provided a new audio commentary. (This was in addition to the 2007 one by Alain Silver and James Ursini.)

* * *

As for Laird Cregar's final resting place at Forest Lawn...

The grave on Laird's right hand side is sold, but there's no marker and the grave possibly not yet occupied. Eventide has been sold out for many years; as noted, neither Laird's Aunt Nean nor his mother are buried beside him, which leads one to believe that someone purchased the gravesite as long ago as 1958, or longer.[22]

Forest Lawn, of course, will not divulge who owns the gravesite. If the person is still alive, it might be someone who was significant in Laird's life; if so, that person would be very old in 2017. It might be a fan. Or perhaps it is—or was—someone who simply selected the plot for its view and near-the-road location.

After 73 years, it's yet another mystery in the tragically brief, "enormously complicated" life of Samuel Laird Cregar.

32

A Final Tribute

As noted in the beginning of this book, this biography concludes with a Laird Cregar story that the reader may accept or reject, but which I present in all honesty, and with no embellishment.

December 1981. My first book, *It's Alive! The Classic Cinema Saga of Frankenstein*, had been published that summer. My wife Barbara and I got away for a week from our Pennsylvania home and flew to Los Angeles, where I wanted to place the book in the hands of several people who'd given me colorful interviews, including Elsa Lanchester and Elena Verdugo.

It was an exciting, wonderful week, coinciding with December 9, 1981 ... the 37th anniversary of the death of Laird Cregar.

It had occurred to me some months before that, when in Los Angeles, I should visit Forest Lawn and pay tribute to Laird, considering our "history." This was decades before the Internet and "Find a Grave"; the only way to learn precisely where a celebrity was buried was to write to the cemetery. Aware from previous experience that it was not Forest Lawn's policy to disclose such information—its first priority, as the management expressed it, was serving the families—I inquired nonetheless.

I noted that Samuel Laird Cregar had been dead for 37 years and (as far as I knew) his immediate family was long gone as well. "Mr. Cregar is interred in the Eventide section, Lot 37, Space 2," kindly responded a Forest Lawn vice-president. He even enclosed a map with the area circled. (Forest Lawn is far stricter now in its policies than it was in 1981. If you visit there to see celebrity graves, expect no cooperation.)

I brought the information along, just in case we had time to visit Forest Lawn. It wasn't in our original, very busy itinerary. And then began the bizarre December 9, 1981, coincidences:

- Barbara and I had plans to interview Susanna Foster, star of 1943's *Phantom of the Opera*, that afternoon. Ms. Foster asked to change plans to the next evening. This left the afternoon free.
- Although reluctant to visit Laird's grave on this anniversary, as there was a slight chance we might intrude on an old acquaintance who'd come to pay respects, we decided to go anyway.
- Staying in Brentwood, we headed east toward Glendale on Sunset Boulevard. Sunset runs east and west. It's hard to get lost on it. We got lost.
- Eventually we got back on Sunset and found Glendale Boulevard. It runs north and south. It's hard to get lost on it. We got lost ... again.

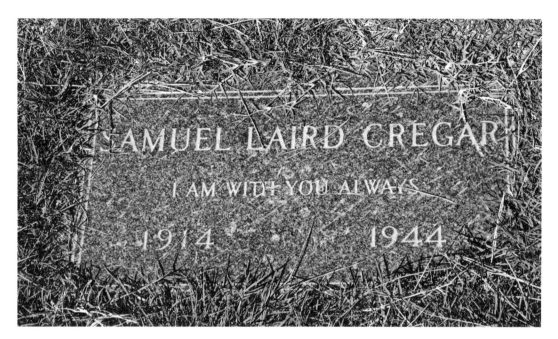

Laird Cregar's grave marker at Forest Lawn: "I Am with You Always" (author's photograph, 2016).

The afternoon, overcast and gloomy, was growing later and darker as we finally saw the giant iron gates of Forest Lawn, Glendale. We drove up to the information booth, the swan lake to the left, the mortuary to the right. I showed the woman at the booth my letter from the Forest Lawn VP and she pleasantly directed us to Eventide. Up we drove, past the towering steeple of the Great Mausoleum, which houses the crypts of Jean Harlow, Lon Chaney, Clark Gable, Carole Lombard and many others. Eventually we found Eventide, a sprawling colony of graves with flat, modest headstones, overlooking the City of Angels.

We got out of the car in the fading light. As we began to look for the grave, the sprinkling system came on ... with a vengeance.

For a time we kept looking, young, defiant and increasingly soaked. We regrouped in the car, waiting for the sprinklers to stop. They didn't. Finally, we headed back to the gate and told the lady in the booth. She was entirely sympathetic and promised to send a worker to turn off the water.

Back up to Eventide. Promptly a driver in a truck came hurrying to our rescue. He jumped out of the truck, trotted up to a tree, stuck his hand inside the trunk and shut off the water. (Forest Lawn clearly took pains to prevent mechanical apparatus from effacing the ambience. It was rather endearing.) As it was getting darker and time was limited, we told him the site we were seeking: "Lot 37, Space 2," I said.

"Oh, you're far off," he replied. "Follow me."

We did, still dripping, walking over the darkening ridge of Eventide, a Laird Cregar zealot and his very patient wife, intent on seeing through this apparently cursed pilgrimage.

"Now," asked the worker, "you said Lot 2, Space 37, right?"

"No," I said. "Lot 37, Space 2."

"Oh," said the worker sheepishly. "You were in the right area the first time."

And so we made our way back, high on the ridge in the twilight. Down in the city, lights were on and we seemed very far away from it all, lost in this Southern California necropolis that had inspired Evelyn Waugh's *The Loved One.* The worker got in his truck and rode away, leaving Barbara and me alone in the gathering gloom, surrounded by graves.

"Laird Cregar is watching us, and laughing his celestial ass off," I said to Barbara.

"Let's keep looking," she said.

We did, although by now the markers were increasingly hard to read in the near-darkness. I was ready to give up, and then...

"Greg! I found it!"

I hurried up the hill. Yes, there was the name: Samuel Laird Cregar.

I saw the dates 1914–1944, surprised that Cregar's birth date was off by a year.

Then it happened. I'm not a person inclined to claim psychic-paranormal activity, but I swear I heard a soft voice, saying, "Look at your watch." I did. It was 4:52 p.m.

Laird Cregar died on December 9, 1944, at 4:52 p.m.

It was then that I noticed the words under the name, and I knelt down to read them: "I Am with You Always."

They are, of course, words from Matthew's Gospel, 28:20, but considering the delays that caused us to stand at the grave at this precise moment, and my history with Laird Cregar's presence in my life, I felt a tremendous chill.

"He knows who I am!" I exclaimed. "He knows I'm here! That's why there were delays! Why we got lost! Why the sprinklers were running! We were *supposed* to get here at 4:52! I heard a voice!"

On I blathered. And it wasn't over yet.

* * *

Leaving Forest Lawn, we headed for Antonio's, a Mexican restaurant on Melrose Avenue. We needed margaritas, at least.

It was a good distance away and we got lost again. We also got stuck in traffic and for a long time, we sat next to a large building. Barbara was driving and I eventually decided to try to see what the building was.

It was Good Samaritan Hospital—where Laird Cregar had died.

* * *

Over the years we've made other visits to Laird Cregar's grave, although always in bright daylight.

I still have the *Hangover Square* poster, displayed upstairs in my den, so I see Laird Cregar's likeness every day. The beat goes on.

Is he with me always?

I like to think so.

Filmography

Granny Get Your Gun

Studio: Warner Bros.; *Executive Producer:* Jack L. Warner; *Executive Producer:* Hal Wallis; *Associate Producer:* Bryan Foy; *Director:* George Amy; *Screenplay:* Kenneth Gamet (based on Erle Stanley Gardner's *The Case of the Dangerous Dowager*); *Dialogue Director:* Ted Thomas; *Photographer:* L. William O'Connell; *Editor:* Jack Killifer; *Art Director:* Hugh Reticker; *Gowns:* Milo Anderson; *Sound:* C. A. Riggs; *Music:* Howard Jackson; *Assistant Director:* Lester D. Guthrie; *Running Time:* 56 minutes; *Production Dates:* October 11–25, 1939; *Negative Cost:* $98,000; *Release Date:* February 10, 1940; *Worldwide Rentals:* $256,000; *Profit:* $14,000

Cast: May Robson (Minerva Hatton), Harry Davenport (Nate), Margot Stevenson (Julie Westcott), Hardie Albright (Phil Westcott), Clem Bevans (Smokey), Clay Clement (Riff Daggett), William Davidson (Fitzgerald), Arthur Aylesworth (Sheriff Quinn), Granville Bates (Tom Redding), Ann Todd (Charlotte), Vera Lewis (Carrie), Max Hoffman, Jr. (Frayne), Archie Twitchell (Joe), Walter Wilson (Judge), Nat Carr (Wadsworth), Edith Conrad (Prison Matron), Laird Cregar (Court Clerk), John Deering, Creighton Hale (Reporters), Earl Dwire (Jake—Checkers Player), Jimmie Fox (Shorty), Eddie Graham (Fitzgerald's Assistant), Jack Mower (Bailiff), George Ovey (Cass), Harry Semels (Juror), Garland Smith (Mechanic), Dave Willock (Timid Driver), George DeNormand, Sol Gorss, Chuck Hamilton (Stunts)

Synopsis: Gold City, Nevada. After Julie Westcott is accused of killing her wastrel husband Phil, her gutsy grandma Minerva Hatton gets herself sworn in as sheriff, appoints her old swain Nate as deputy, rides wildly in an open car, (non-fatally) shoots the real murderer Riff Daggett, and tells Nate that, had he proposed when she was 18 years old, she'd have married him!

Production Notes: May Robson, 81 years old at the time of *Granny Get Your Gun*, had been Oscar-nominated for *Lady for a Day* (1933), and was a beloved supporting player in such films as *A Star Is Born* (1937) and *Bringing Up Baby* (1938). Warner Bros. publicity insisted that Robson did her own stunt work in the film's climactic car chase scene (and that her car, a vintage Ford, was so damaged in the fray that it had to be junked!). At any rate, the venerable (and durable) Robson went on to appear in another half-dozen films, including *Joan of Paris*, which also featured Laird Cregar.

Prolific character actor Harry Davenport, 73, at the time, had directed silent movies during the World War I years; in 1939, the year he starred in *Granny Get Your Gun*, he appeared in 13 releases, including Selznick's *Gone with the Wind* (as Dr. Meade) and RKO's *The Hunchback of Notre Dame* (as King Louis XI). A founder of Actors Equity and the brother-in-law of Lionel Barrymore, Davenport chalked up over 160 film appearances. He died in Los Angeles on August 9, 1949. He was busy to the end, and his final three films were released posthumously: *Tell It to the Judge* (1949), *That Forsyte Woman* (1949) and *Riding High* (1950).

Margot Stevenson (1912–2011) played the ingénue lead in the original Broadway production of *You Can't Take It with You* (1936); she had a brief sojourn at Warners, and later appeared as Lady Macduff on the November 28, 1954, telecast of *Macbeth* with Maurice Evans and Judith Anderson.

Director George Amy (1903–1986) was an ace Warner Bros. editor on such product as *Doctor X* (1932), *Mystery of the Wax Museum* (1933), *Captain Blood* (1935), *The Charge of the Light Brigade* (1936) and *Dodge City* (1939). After he directed a few films, he returned to editing, winning a Best Editor Academy Award for Warners' *Air Force* (1943). He was also nominated for *Yankee Doodle Dandy* (1942) and *Objective, Burma!* (1945).

Cinematographer L. William O'Connell (1890–1985) was cameraman on 180 films, including *The Bells* (1926, starring Lionel Barrymore, with Boris Karloff as a sinister hypnotist), the Paul Muni gangster classic *Scarface* (UA, 1932), the Karloff Warner Bros. melodramas *West of Shanghai* (1937) and *The Invisible Menace* (1938), and the Bela Lugosi starrer *The Return of the Vampire* (Columbia, 1944). His final credit: the Hugh Herbert short *The Gink in the Sink* (1952).

According to the American Film Institute notes, Warners originally set Humphrey Bogart for the role of Riff Daggett (played by Clay Clement) and Jane Bryan for the part of Julie Westcott (played by Margot Stevenson). There's no report why neither appeared in the film; in Bogart's case, he probably raised hell at being assigned to such a potboiler. Also, Vincent Sherman was originally announced as director.

The film goes down easy, sparked by Robson's high-spirited trouping and the usual Warner production values. Cregar received no on-screen billing. He's heard in the film briefly before he's seen, and his sudden bit part appearance as the court clerk (a bit past the film's 31-minute mark) might come as a shock to anyone unaware of his pre-fame efforts to break into the movies.

Review: "Warners has adorned May Robson with a stellar crown for *Granny Get Your Gun,* as nifty a piece of entertainment as has emerged from the Bryan Foy division of Burbank lot in many a moon.... [E]xcellent fare for family trade." (*Variety,* January 2, 1940)

Oh, Johnny, How You Can Love!

Studio: Universal; *Associate Producer:* Ken Goldsmith; *Director:* Charles Lamont; *Screenplay:* Arthur T. Horman (based on Edwin Rutt's story "Road to Romance"); *Photographer:* Milton Krasner; *Art Director:* Jack Otterson; *Associate Art Director:* Ralph M. DeLacy; *Editor:* Philip Cahn; *Set Decorator:* Russell Gausman; *Gowns:* Vera West; *Musical Director:* Charles Previn; *Songs:* "Oh! Johnny!" (written by Abe Olman and Ed Ross); "Swing, Chariot, Swing" and "Maybe I Like What You Like" (written by Frank Skinner and Paul Girard Smith); "The Blue Danube Waltz" (by Johann Strauss); "Bring Back My Bonnie"; "Swing Low, Sweet Chariot" (by Wal-

lis Willis); "Oh Susanna" (by Stephen Foster); *Sound Supervisor:* Bernard B. Brown; *Sound Technician:* William Hedgcock; *Running Time:* 63 minutes; *Production Dates:* November 24–December 9, 1939; *Negative Cost:* $100,000; *Release Date:* January 1, 1940

Cast: Tom Brown (Johnny Sandham), Peggy Moran ("Kelly" Archer), Allen Jenkins (Weasel), Donald Meek (Adelbert Thistlebottom), Isabel Jewell (Gertie), Juanita Quigley ("Junior"), Joseph Downing ("Doc" Kedrick), Horace McMahon ("Lefty" Hodges), Matt McHugh (Charlie), Jack Arnold ("The Chaser," i.e., Motorist trying to pick up Kelly), Betty Jane Rhodes (Singer of "Oh! Johnny!"), John Hamilton (Jonathan Archer), Thomas E. Jackson (Chief of Police), Eddie Acuff (Motorcycle Cop), Bill Burt (Specialty Dancer), Renie Riano (Junior's Mother), Laird Cregar (Sam—Thistlebottom's Mechanic), Harris Berger (Newsboy), Kernan Cripps (Policeman), Hugh McArthur (Gas Station Attendant)

Synopsis: Salesman Johnny Sandham serenades himself with "Swing, Chariot, Swing" as he drives his truck, a "traveling catalogue," through the countryside. Trouble ensues when he nearly runs into the roadster of runaway heiress Carol Ann "Kelly" Archer. Soon they are duetting "Maybe I Like What You Like" and meet up with "Ed, the Weasel," an escaping bank robber, who takes over the truck and orders Johnny to drive him to Canada.

When the truck's brakes fail, the trio end up at the Super Motor Court of Adelbert Thistlebottom, who wears a cowboy suit and names his push-button cabins after female movie stars. (The cabin where Johnny, Kelly and Ed stay: "Claudette.") During the Saturday Night Dance and Community Sing, a toothy young lady sings "Oh, Johnny, How You Can Love" while Johnny and Kelly smooch in the woods and a huge mechanic named Sam fixes Johnny's truck's brakes.

The plot thickens as the Weasel's cohorts, "Doc" and "Lefty," show up at the auto court. The climax sees literal fireworks as the push-button room goes out of control, police rout the Weasel and his robbers, and Johnny and Kelly find true love.

Production Notes: The film's original title was *The Road to Romance.* However, Bonnie Baker had recorded a version of the song "Oh, Johnny, How You Can Love" (which dates to 1917) on August 20, 1939, with Orrin Tucker and his Orchestra. The record sold 1.5 million copies in 1940. The Andrews Sisters recorded their version on November 9, 1939, 15 days before this movie began shooting. Before the film was finished, Universal had retitled it *Oh, Johnny, How You Can Love*.

Tom Brown (1913–1990) began as a child model and actor, played the title role in *Tom Brown of Culver* (Universal, 1932) and was one of the O'Leary brothers in *In Old Chicago* (20th Century–Fox, 1938). He played a title role again in the serial *The Adventures of Smilin' Jack* (Universal, 1943). Brown was a paratrooper in World War II and a lieutenant colonel in Korea. He was a regular on TV's *Mr. Lucky* (1959–1960) and a semi-regular on *Gunsmoke* (1968–1974).

Peggy Moran (Marie Jeanette Moran, 1918–2002), the daughter of pinup artist Earl Moran and dancer Louise Moran, won attention as one of the sexy cigarette girls in MGM's Garbo classic *Ninotchka* (1939). The lovely, charmingly ski-nosed actress became one of Universal's most versatile ingénues, appearing with Deanna Durbin, Abbott and Costello, the Andrews Sisters and, perhaps most memorably, with Tom Tyler's Mummy in *The Mummy's Hand* (1940). ("I was really kind of afraid of him, you know?" Moran told me in 1993. "He gave me an eerie feeling!") In 1942, Peggy married director Henry Koster (1936's *Three Smart Girls*, 1950's *Harvey*, 1953's *The Robe*, etc.) and retired from acting. ("I don't want all the electricians pinching you on the set!" Koster told her.) They had two sons. Koster died in 1983 and Peggy attended various nostalgia conventions, including Fanex 12 in 1998, where I had the privilege of presenting her a Fanex award. Peggy Moran died in Camarillo, California, on October 24, 2002.

Allen Jenkins (Alfred McGonegal, 1900–1974) played not-too-bright tough guys and stooges in many Warner Bros. films of the 1930s; he was especially fine as "Hunk," sidekick of Humphrey Bogart's doomed "Baby Face Martin," in *Dead End* (UA, 1937). Jenkins later won attention as the voice of Officer Dribble on TV's Hanna-Barbera cartoon series *Top Cat* (1961–1962).

Donald Meek (1878–1946), bald, 5'4", Scottish-born player, began his acting career at age eight with the legendary Sir Henry Irving. Meek's adventures included being a high-wire acrobat (several falls forced him to quit) and fighting in the Spanish-American War (where he was wounded and lost his hair to yellow fever). In 1939, he gave his most famous performance: Mr. Peacock, the milquetoast whiskey drummer who takes an Indian arrow in the chest in John Ford's *Stagecoach* ... and survives!

Betty Jane Rhodes (1921–2011), who sang the title song in the film, later scored her biggest hit with "I Don't Want to Walk Without You" in the film *Sweater Girl* (Paramount, 1942).

Isabel Jewell, who played Gertie, the blonde waitress, had an exciting 1939: She'd played Curley's wife in the West Coast production of *Of Mice and Men*, co-starring Wallace Ford and Lon Chaney, Jr., which had opened at Hollywood's El Capitan Theatre in April; and she'd portrayed Emmy Slattery, the "white trash" vixen in *Gone with the Wind*. A superb character actress, Jewell was 62 when she died on April 5, 1972, at her home, 6130 Franklin Avenue in Hollywood. The investigation ruled the death a suicide.

Juanita Quigley (born 1931), who played "Junior" with the ear-splitting laugh, had been known as "Baby Jane" when she played in such films as *Imitation of Life* and *The Man Who Reclaimed His Head*, both 1934 releases from Universal. At MGM, Quigley appeared in *Riffraff* (1935), starring Jean Harlow, and in *The Devil-Doll* (1936), directed by Tod Browning; she later showed up in Republic's *The Lady and the Monster* (1944). Her most famous credit, perhaps, was as Malvolia Brown in MGM's *National Velvet* (1944). Quigley later became a nun in the Daughters of Mary and Joseph, decided she'd made a mistake, left the order, married an ex-priest and had two children. In 1983, she made a "comeback" of sorts as an uncredited woman at a rally in the R-rated *Porky's II: The Next Day*. For this gig, she used her previous stage name of "Baby Jane."

Renie Riano (1899–1971), who played Junior's mother, was Laird's alleged "romance" when she played Miss Preen to his Sheridan Whiteside in a 1941 Hollywood stage production of *The Man Who Came to Dinner*. She'd played housekeeper Effie Schneider in Warner Bros.' *Nancy Drew: Detective* (1938), *Nancy Drew ... Reporter* (1939) and *Nancy Drew ... Troubleshooter* (1939), and landed uncredited roles such as "Ugly Saleswoman" in MGM's *The Women* (1939) and "Homely Woman" in Warners' *The Smiling Ghost* (1941). Riano did win a stardom of her own as the shrewish Maggie Jiggs (of the *Bringing Up Father* comic strip) in Monogram's *Bringing Up Father* (1946), *Jiggs and Maggie in Society* (1947), *Jiggs and Maggie in Court* (1948), *Jiggs and Maggie in Jackpot Jitters* (1949) and *Jiggs and Maggie Out West* (1950). She also turned up on various TV episodes, including *Green Acres* and *Mayberry R.F.D.*

Laird Cregar's bit as Sam the mechanic would be his only film for Universal, but qualified him as a member of "The Universal City Club." On Tuesday, April 22, 1941, Laird attended the Club's fifth annual dinner dance at the Palladium. Abbott and Costello were the masters of ceremonies, and the performers included Rudy Vallee, the Andrews Sisters (whose song "Boogie-Woogie Bugle Boy" had proved a sensation in Abbott and Costello's *Buck Privates*), the Merry Macs, Anne Gwynne, Dick Foran and Anne Nagel, all under contract to Universal. There was also a chorus of "16 femme beauties," Richard Himber's orchestra ... and Laird Cregar. It's not known what "act" Laird performed, but columnist Jimmy Starr called it "a real rip-roaring evening" ("Daily Diary," *Evening Herald Express*, April 24, 1941).

Review: "Throughout the first half of the Forties, Universal tacked the title of a popular song onto a programmer and called it a musical. A really half-witted effort, *Oh, Johnny, How You Can Love*, exemplified the pitfalls of this approach." (Clive Hirschhorn, *The Universal Story*, 1983)

Hudson's Bay

Studio: 20th Century–Fox; *Producer:* Darryl F. Zanuck; *Associate Producer:* Kenneth Macgowan; *Director:* Irving Pichel (and Rouben Mamoulian, uncredited); *Screenplay:* Lamar Trotti ("Based on incidents from the Life of Pierre Esprit Radisson; Technical Advisor, Clifford Wilson, Historian, Hudson's Bay Co.") (Art Arthur, Richard Collins, uncredited); *Music:* Alfred Newman (and David Buttolph, Cyril J. Mockridge, uncredited); *Photographers:* Peverell Marley, George Barnes; *Art Directors:* Richard Day, Wiard Ihnen; *Set Decorator:* Thomas Little; *Editor:* Robert Simpson; *Costume Designer:* Travis Banton; *Sound:* Alfred Bruzlin, Roger Heman, Sr.; *Wardrobe Supervisor:* Sam Benson; *Assistant Director:* Aaron Rosenberg; *Orchestrators:* Alfred Newman, Edward B. Powell, Conrad Salinger, Walter Scharf, Herbert W. Spencer; *Technical Advisors:* James Curtis Havens, C. Bland Jamison, Harold Lloyd Morris; *Running Time:* 95 minutes; *Shooting Dates:* August 21 to October 2, 1940; added scenes, October to November 1940; *Negative Cost:* $869,600; *Opening Date:* Roxy Theatre, New York City, January 9, 1941; Grauman's Chinese Theatre and Loew's State Theatre, Los Angeles, January 15, 1941; *Worldwide Rentals:* $1,395,300; *Profit:* $88,500

Cast: Paul Muni (Pierre Esprit Radisson), Gene Tierney (Barbara Hall), Laird Cregar (Gooseberry), John Sutton (Lord Edward Crewe), Virginia Field (Nell Gwynn), Vincent Price (King Charles II), Nigel Bruce (Prince Rupert), Morton Lowry (Gerald Hall), Robert Greig (Sir Robert), Chief Thundercloud (Orimha), Frederick Worlock (English Governor), Florence Bates (Duchess; scenes deleted), Montagu Love (Governor D'Argenson), Ian Wolfe (Mayor), Chief John Big Tree (Chief), Jody Gilbert (Germaine), Denis Green (John Randall), Lumsden Hare (Capt. Alan MacKinnon), Lionel Pape (Groom of the Chamber), Jean Del Val (Captain), Lilyan Irene (Maid), Keith Hitchcock (Footman), Dorothy Dearing (Girl), John Rogers (Sailor), Reginald Sheffield (Clerk), Robert Cory (Orderly), Eugene Borden, Constant Franke (Sentries), Dennis d'Auburn, David Cavendish, Eric Wilton (Councilors), Sonny Chorre, Boone Hazlett, Bob Lugo, Joe Molina, Andrew Pena, Jay Silverheels, Jimmy Spencer, Tony Urchel (Indians).

Synopsis: In 1667, a pair of rogues, Pierre Esprit Radisson and the giant Gooseberry, dream of riches as fur trappers in the beautiful wilderness of Canada, under the French flag. Thrown into jail by the English governor of Albany, they escape with a fellow adventurer, Lord Edward Crewe. All three set off for the northern wilderness, befriending the Indians as they build a fortune in pelts. When the French governor of the region, D'Argenson, seizes the pelts, the heroes steal his ship, reclaim some of the furs and head to England, where Edward is in love with Lady Barbara Hall.

They meet King Charles II and his mistress, Nell Gwynn, and soon win the king's secret charter to return to Canada and acquire a fortune of furs for him. Accompanying them is Barbara's wastrel brother Gerald. While Radisson and his men are away from Fort Charles, Gerald trades brandy to Indians for pelts that the Indians steal from the French. A drunken band of Indians kills a band of friendly Indians, and to avoid a full-scale Indian war, Radisson orders the execution of the man responsible: Gerald.

They return to England. A shocked Lady Barbara renounces Edward when he defends Radisson's decision to kill Gerald. Radisson, Gooseberry, and Edward face execution. However, Radisson tells King Charles that, if he is killed, the Indians in Canada will side with the French ... and there will be no more fortune in pelts heading to England. King Charles waives the execution, Edward and Lady Barbara reconcile, and Radisson and Gooseberry, with a fur empire awaiting them back in Canada, dance away arm in arm.

Production Notes: The adventures of Pierre Esprit Radisson (1636–1710) and his brother-in-law Medard des Grosseilliers (1618–1696) led to the formation of Hudson's Bay Company. Note that there's no mention of Radisson and Gooseberry being in-laws in the film *Hudson's Bay*; also, note that, while Muni was 18 years older than Cregar, Gooseberry, in real life, was 18 years older than Pierre.

Neither man came to a happy end. Radisson lived his last days in England on a Hudson's Bay Company (HBC) pension that was reportedly "irregularly paid"; 19 years after his death, HBC donated ten pounds to his widow, as she was "ill and in great want." Gooseberry became so exasperated with the politics associated with his explorations that he "retired in disgust" to a Trois-Rivieres and a small seigneury.

Both David O. Selznick and Cecil B. DeMille had proposed films on Hudson's Bay Company. DeMille planned to star Fred MacMurray and shoot on location in Canada. Fox persevered; on February 8, 1939, *The Hollywood Reporter* wrote that Tyrone Power was set for Radisson, but the project had been shelved due to poor box office prospects.

Muni received a reported $100,000 for *Hudson's Bay*. Based on personal tastes, his scenery-gnashing performance is either praiseworthy or dismal. His temperament eventually capsized his film career. In *A Song to Remember* (Columbia, 1945), the Technicolor box office smash starring Merle Oberon as George Sand and Cornel Wilde as Chopin, Muni played Prof. Joseph Elsner; Wilde recalled Muni's behavior on the set as "insufferable" and "atrocious." He gradually faded away, but on April 21, 1955, he came back, big, in Broadway's *Inherit the Wind*, written by Jerome Lawrence and Robert E. Lee, based on the Scopes Monkey Trial. For his portrayal of Henry Drummond, inspired by Clarence Darrow, Muni won a Tony. Late that summer, he had to leave the play, losing an eye to a tumor; however, after recovery, Muni triumphantly returned.

One of the more colorful Muni sagas involves his starring in *At the Grand*, a musical stage version of *Grand Hotel* which opened at the Los Angeles Philharmonic on July 7, 1958. Muni played Kringelein, the dying clerk portrayed by Lionel Barrymore in MGM's 1932 all-star classic. Joan Diener (later Aldonza in the original cast of Broadway's *Man of La Mancha*) was the leading lady, and her husband Albert Marre (who'd direct *Man of La Mancha*) was director. Singing and dancing on-stage, Muni

Hudson's Bay: **Laird Cregar as Gooseberry.**

threw fits off-stage, fighting all attempts to juice up the sagging show, demanding it not become risqué. He decided to bow out after the show moved to San Francisco, and it failed to get a green light to Broadway. On the final night of the run, the now out-of-work cast had its revenge on Muni: The chorus girls, knowing he was half-blind and disoriented in the wings during the blackouts, pulled down the bodices of their costumes, shoving their breasts into the old grump's face. Come the curtain call, Joan Diener took her bow in a mink coat, turned to acknowledge Muni, opened her mink and, stark naked under it, vindictively flashed him.

Muni made one more film, *The Last Angry Man* (1959), starring as a crusty inner-city doctor, winning a Best Actor Oscar nomination, losing to Charlton Heston of *Ben-Hur*. Muni died on August 25, 1967, of congestive heart failure at his home, 1069 Hill Road in Montecito, California. He was 71 and left an estate valued at $1,200,000. His wife Bella died October 1, 1971, and is buried with her husband at Hollywood Forever Cemetery.

Hudson's Bay boasted Gene Tierney (1920–1991) in her film debut, but in fact, she'd already co-starred with Henry Fonda in Fox's *The Return of Frank James* (1940). Tierney would star in two more films with Cregar, *Rings on Her Fingers* and *Heaven Can Wait*.

The *Albuquerque Journal* critic wrote that Tierney, based on her appearance in *Hudson's Bay*, "should sue the cameraman." Actually, the two cameramen were world-class: Peverell Marley (1901–1964) had been Oscar-nominated for Fox's *Suez* (1938), would receive a second nomination for *Life with Father* (1947), and would be cinematographer on the 3-D *House of Wax* (1953). Marley's third and last wife was Linda Darnell, whom he wed in 1943; they divorced in 1951. George Barnes (1892–1953) won the 1940 Oscar for his cinematography on *Rebecca*; he racked up a total of seven additional nominations, as well as seven wives (one of them Joan Blondell). Marley and Barnes would share a Golden Globe Award for their Technicolor cinematography on Cecil B. DeMille's *The Greatest Show on Earth* (1952).

John Sutton (1908–1963), born in India of British parents, played the hero in Universal's *Tower of London* (1939), foe to Basil Rathbone's Richard III and Boris Karloff's Mord the Executioner. When *Tower of London* opened at San Francisco's Warfield Theatre December 15, 1939, Sutton was in the stage show with Karloff, *Tower of London* leading lady Nan Grey, emcee Mischa Auer and Bela Lugosi, who, although not in the film, came along for the ride. Sutton also starred in Universal's *The Invisible Man Returns* (1940) as the doctor who makes Vincent Price invisible. He'd co-star again with Laird Cregar in *Ten Gentlemen from West Point*, staying at Fox during and beyond the World War II years. He later did lots of TV work, including the recurrent role of Col. Tarleton on the "Swamp Fox" segments of *Walt Disney's Wonderful World of Color* (1959–1960). Two of Sutton's later movies: *Return of the Fly* and *The Bat*, both in 1959, and both with Vincent Price. Sutton died suddenly of a heart attack in Cannes in 1963 at age 54. He'd never married.

Vincent Price (1911–1993) made his ninth film appearance in *Hudson's Bay*. See the text for more information on his life, career and relationship with Cregar.

Blonde, 5'10" Virginia Field (Margaret Cynthia St. John Field, 1917–1992) is alluring as *Hudson's Bay's* Nell Gwynn, King Charles' mistress, but has far too little to do. She'd appeared in Fox's *Lloyd's of London* (1936) and *Lancer Spy* (1937), played Kitty (a presumed prostitute) in MGM's *Waterloo Bridge* (1940), and later had Broadway success in *The Doughgirls* (1942) and *Light Up the Sky* (1948). Her first husband was actor Paul Douglas, her third, actor Willard Parker. Incidentally, a telegram in a Vincent Price Archive auctioned in recent years by Heritage Galleries, sent by Field to Price in 1941, when he was working in stock, before Field wed Douglas and while Price was married to Edith Barrett, insinuates they were lovers ... intriguing, considering their roles in *Hudson's Bay*.

Nigel Bruce (William Nigel Bruce, 1895–1953) plays Prince Rupert minus most of his usual screen mannerisms. By the time of *Hudson's Bay*, he'd already played Watson to Basil Rathbone's Holmes twice, in Fox's *The Hound of the Baskervilles* and *The Adventures of Sherlock Holmes*, both in 1939, and was starring with Rathbone in the radio series. In 1942, he and Rathbone would begin the 12-film Universal *Sherlock Holmes* series.

Morton Lowry (Edward Morton Lowater, 1914–1987), excellent as Gerald, the weakling villain of *Hudson's Bay*, had been the villain in *The Hound of the Baskervilles* (1939). At the time he was wed to heiress Virginia Barnato. Lowry and Laird would both appear in *Charley's Aunt.*

Jay Silverheels (1912–1980), an uncredited Indian in *Hudson's Bay*, later won fame as Tonto on TV's *The Lone Ranger* (1949–1957).

Certainly one of the most interesting figures of *Hudson's Bay* was its director, Irving Pichel (1891–1954), a Harvard alumnus who tallied a fascinating grab bag of offbeat credits as an actor and director. Pichel (pronounced Pitch-ell, like Mitch-ell) was memorable in two 1931 Paramount uber-melodramas, *Murder by the Clock*, as a powerful halfwit, and *The Cheat*, as the sex sadist who brands Tallulah Bankhead. He was Paramount's original choice for the title role in *Dr. Jekyll and Mr. Hyde*, but director Rouben Mamoulian overruled ("Pichel could only play Hyde!") and cast Fredric March, who won an Academy Award for his dual performance. Pichel starred as Fagin in Monogram's *Oliver Twist* (1933) and made his mark most vividly (at least for horror fans) as Sandor, the evil servant to Gloria Holden in *Dracula's Daughter* (Universal, 1936).

Meanwhile, Pichel was also a director: He co-directed (with Ernest B. Schoedsack) the seminal thriller *The Most Dangerous Game* (RKO, 1932) and co-directed (with Lansing C. Holden) the epic fantasy *She* (RKO, 1935). After *Hudson's Bay*, he directed such Fox films as *The Pied Piper* (for which Monty Woolley received a Best Actor Oscar nomination, 1942) and *The Moon Is Down* (based on the John Steinbeck novel, 1943). Among other directorial credits: *A Medal for Benny* (Paramount, 1945, for which J. Carrol Naish received a Best Supporting Actor Oscar nomination), *Mr. Peabody and the Mermaid* (Universal, 1948), and George Pal's *Destination Moon* (1950). Another interesting Pichel credit: He was the adult voice of Huw, played as a child by Roddy McDowall, narrating 20th Century–Fox's Best Picture Oscar Winner of 1941, John Ford's *How Green Was My Valley.*

Review: "Massive Laird Cregar, a newcomer, furnishes a splendid portrayal as Muni's companion, and it is certain that fans and exhibitors will be clamoring to see Cregar in more pictures." (*Film Daily*, December 24, 1940)

Blood and Sand

Studio: 20th Century–Fox; *Producer:* Darryl F. Zanuck; *Associate Producer:* Robert T. Kane; *Director:* Rouben Mamoulian; *Screenplay:* Jo Swerling (based on the novel by Vicente Blasco Ibanez); *Photographers:* Ernest Palmer, Ray Rennahan; *Technicolor Director:* Natalie Kalmus; *Associate Technicolor Director:* Morgan Padelford; *Music:* Alfred Newman (and David Buttolph, uncredited); *Art Director:* Richard Day, Joseph C. Wright; *Set Decorator:* Thomas Little; *Editor:* Robert Bischoff; *Costume Designer:* Travis Banton; *Jewels:* Flato; *Sound:* W.D. Flick, Roger Heman, Sr.; *Production Manager:* William Koenig; *Assistant Directors:* Sid Bowen, Robert D. Webb, Henry Weinberger (all uncredited); *Art Department:* Carlos Ruano Lopis (paintings, uncredited); Ben Wurtzel (construction supervisor, uncredited); *Wardrobe:* Sam Benson (uncredited); Jose Dolores Perez (tailor, toreador costumes, uncredited); *Music Arranger:* Jose Barroso (uncredited); *Music Orchestrator:* Edward B. Powell; *Choreographers:* Budd Boetticher ("El Torero" number, uncredited); Hermes Pan ("Fiesta" number, uncredited); Geneva Sawyer ("El Torero" number, uncredited); *Bullfighting Instructor and Technical Advisor:* Francisco Gomez Delgado (uncredited); *Technical Advisor:* Fortunio Bonanova (uncredited); *Shooting Dates:* location work, Mexico, January 1941; principal photography, Los Angeles, February 3–April 8, 1941; *Running Time:* 125 minutes.; *Negative Cost:* $1,115,200; *Opening Dates:* Roxy Theatre, New York City, May 22, 1941; Grauman's Chinese Theatre and Loew's State Theatre, Los Angeles, May 28, 1941; *Worldwide Rentals:* $2,717,200; *Profit:* $662,500

Cast: Tyrone Power (Juan Gallardo), Linda Darnell (Carmen Espinosa), Rita Hayworth (Dona Sol), Alla Nazimova (Senora Augustias), Anthony Quinn (Manolo de Palma), J. Carrol Naish (Garabato), Lynn Bari (Encarnacion), John Carradine (Nacional), Laird Cregar (Natalio Curro), William Montague (Antonio Lopez), Vicente Gomez (Guitarist), George Reeves (Capt. Pierre Lauren), Pedro de Cordoba (Don Jose Alvarez), Fortunio Bonanova (Pedro Espinosa), Victor Kilian (Priest), Michael Morris (La Pulga), Charles Stevens (Pablo Gomez), Ann Todd (Carmen as a Child), Cora Sue Collins (Encarnacion as a Child), Russell Hicks (Marquis), Maurice Cass (El Milquetoast), Rex Downing (Juan as a Child), John Wallace (Francisco), Jacqueline Dalya (Gachi), Cullen Johnson (Manolo as a Child), Larry Harris (Pablo as a Child), Ted Frye (La Pulga as a Child), Schuyler Standish (Nacional as a Child), Harry Burns (Train Engineer), Kay Linaker (Guest of Dona Sol), Gino Corrado, Fred Malatesta (Waiters), Thornton Edwards (Doctor), Paul Ellis (Ortega), Mariquita Flores (Specialty Dancer), Francis McDonald (Manolo's friend), Francisco Moreno (Train Conductor), Alberto Morin (Bullfight Attendant), Cecilia Callejo, Esther Estrella (Street Gachis), Rosita Granada (Café Singer/Singing Voice of Dona Sol), Anne G. Sterling (Woman Dancing at Party), Armilitas, Francisco Gomez Delgado (Bullring Doubles for Tyrone Power)

Synopsis: A fateful night in Spain. At a festivity celebrating the great bullfighter Garabato, teenage Juan Gallardo hears the great bullfighting critic, Natalio Curro, slander his (Juan's) dead father, who had died in the bullring ... and breaks a bottle of wine over Curro's head.

Ten years later, Gallardo returns home, himself now a rising bullfighter. His quadrilla includes boyhood friends Nacional, who warns Juan of the reactionary nature of bullfighting, and Manolo, who jealously resents Juan's growing fame. Juan hires the now dissolute Garabato as a servant, generously indulges his loving mother Senora Augustias, and marries his lifelong love, the beautiful Carmen Espinosa. Juan's fiery performance in the bullring ignites the crowd, including the now-fawning, hysterically rapturous Curro.

Juan also stirs the passion of Dona Sol, a fickle, red-haired temptress, who seduces him and emasculates him into a besotted wreckage. Carmen leaves him. His cowardice in the ring causes the death of Nacional. Dona Sol takes up with Manolo.

Juan confronts Curro, whom he overhears slandering him, pouring a bottle of wine in his face. As Juan prepares for his final appearance in the ring, Carmen returns to him. He performs magnificently that day, before Dona Sol, Curro and the crowd, but as he acknowledges the cheers, the bull attacks from behind and gores him. Juan lives to profess his love for Carmen—"You're the only *true* one in the world"—and dies as she

kisses him. Meanwhile, the bestial mob shrieks for Manolo, Dona Sol throws him a flower, Curro screams his praises, and Manolo smiles triumphantly in the arena ... close to where we see Juan Gallardo's blood in the sand.

Production Notes: In Paramount's 1922 film version of *Blood and Sand*, directed by Fred Niblo (and an uncredited Dorothy Arzner), Rudolph Valentino played Juan Gallardo, Lila Lee played Carmen and Nita Naldi played Dona Sol. The character of Curro, portrayed by Cregar in the 1941 version, doesn't appear in the 1922 film's cast list.

On May 31, 1937, Power and Loretta Young, in a joint ceremony, had placed their hand prints and footprints in the cement at Grauman's Chinese Theatre. Power wrote in the cement, "To Sid—Following in My Father's Footsteps," a tribute to his father Tyrone Power, Sr., who'd died of a heart attack in his son's arms in 1931. Power was Darryl Zanuck's

Blood and Sand: **J. Carrol Naish and Laird Cregar.**

greatest manufactured star, his box office hits including *In Old Chicago* (1938), *Jesse James* (1939) and *The Mark of Zorro* (1940). At the time of *Blood and Sand*, Power was married to Annabella, with whom he'd co-starred in Fox's *Suez* (1938) and whom he'd wed April 23, 1939. Power and Cregar, good friends, appeared together again in *The Black Swan*.

Linda Darnell (Monetta Eloyse Darnell), only 17 when she made *Blood and Sand*, had added her hand and high heel prints to the Grauman's Chinese Theatre forecourt on March 18, 1940, as promotion for Fox's *Star Dust*. She'd previously co-starred with Power in *Brigham Young* and *The Mark of Zorro*, and would be Laird's leading lady in his final film, *Hangover Square*.

Rita Hayworth (Margarita Carmen Cansino, 1918–1987) would add her prints to Grauman's Chinese Theatre July 24, 1942, along with Henry Fonda, Charles Boyer and Charles Laughton, all stars of Fox's *Tales of Manhattan* (1942). Her inscription: "To Sid Grauman—Thanks." Hayworth hit her apex as *Gilda* (Columbia, 1946). Her five husbands included Orson Welles (1943–1947), Prince Aly Khan (1949–1953) and Dick Haymes (1953–1955); her agonizing downfall and death in 1987 of Alzheimer's led to public awareness of the disease.

Alla Nazimova (Miriam Leventon, 1879–1945) was a legendary stage and screen star, famed for her lush film performances in *Camille* (1921) and *Salome* (1922). The last, which she produced (and for which she was an uncredited director), was too outré even for the Roaring '20s; it cost her a fortune and capsized her career, as did her rumored lifestyle as a lesbian. She had come back in MGM's *Escape* (1940) and made three films after *Blood and Sand*: *The Bridge of San Luis Rey*, *In Our Time* and *Since You Went Away*, all released in 1944. She was aunt to famed horror producer Val Lewton, godmother to Nancy Reagan, and in her day, she owned a mansion at Sunset Boulevard and Crescent Heights, with various villas and a pool shaped like the Black Sea. It later became the fabled Garden of Allah, a hotel where Errol Flynn, Charles Laughton, Elsa Lanchester, John Carradine and many either celebrities lived in the villas and apartments. Late in her life, Nazimova resided in a small apartment at the

Garden, which had once been her sumptuous private home.

Anthony Quinn (Antonio Rodolfo Quinn Oaxaca, 1915–2001) was still struggling to win major recognition in Hollywood and bridling under the pressure of being son-in-law to Cecil B. DeMille. He would appear again with Cregar in *The Black Swan* (1942).

J. Carrol Naish (Joseph Patrick Carrol Naish, 1896–1973), one of the great all-time character actors, received two Best Supporting Actor Academy nominations, for *Sahara* (1943) and *A Medal for Benny* (1945). He won the Golden Globe for *A Medal for Benny*. He also appeared on Broadway (including Arthur Miller's *A View from the Bridge/A Memory of Two Mondays*, 1955–1956), on radio (including starring in *Life with Luigi*, 1948–1953) and on TV (including the series *Life with Luigi*, 1952, *The New Adventures of Charlie Chan*, 1957–1958 and *Guestward Ho!* 1960–1961); and he won distinction in the horror genre, notably for his hunchbacked Daniel in Universal's *House of Frankenstein* (1944). Gladys, Naish's wife of 44 years, died in 1987 and is buried with him at Calvary Cemetery in Los Angeles.

As for John Carradine (Richmond Reed Carradine), *Blood and Sand* was the only film in which he and Cregar appeared together—a shame, as both possessed a similar demonic theatricality. Carradine's performance as Nacional is one of his finest, partly because the role's stylized, mystical nature, a Jesus Christ of the bullring, allows him to play out on the edge, where the actor was at his best. It was a legendary life and career for Carradine, who went on to some of the best films ever made, and, as he often admitted, some of the worst (1966's *Billy the Kid Versus Dracula*, with Carradine as the latter, his personal choice for his bottom-of-the-barrel). He had a 63-year career, four wives, five sons and a demise worthy of his bizarre nature: At a decrepit 82, he'd reportedly climbed the 328 steps of Milan's Duomo Cathedral (the elevator was out of order), collapsed, and died in his son David's arms in a paupers' ward in Milan on November 27, 1988. Due to his stint in the Coast Guard Auxiliary in early World War II, Carradine was buried at sea with military honors.

Rouben Mamoulian (1897–1987) was one

of the great stylistic directors: *Applause* (1929), *Dr. Jekyll and Mr. Hyde* (1931) and *Love Me Tonight* (1932) all are still brilliantly captivating *tour de forces*. Incredibly, he never received an Oscar nomination, although he won the New York Film Critics Circle Award for *The Gay Desperado* (1936). Mamoulian masterfully directed Fox's *The Mark of Zorro*, and directed Cregar again in *Rings on Her Fingers*.

Blood and Sand cinematographers Ernest Palmer (1885–1978) and Ray Rennahan (1896–1980) won the Academy Award for Best Color Cinematography of 1941. Palmer was also nominated for *Street Angel* (1928), *Four Devils* (1928) and *Broken Arrow* (1950). Rennahan had shared an Oscar with Ernest Haller for *Gone with the Wind* (1939), and also received nominations for *Drums Along the Mohawk* (1939), *Down Argentine Way* (1940), *The Blue Bird* (1940), *Louisiana Purchase* (1941), *For Whom the Bell Tolls* (1943) and *Lady in the Dark* (1944).

Lux Radio Theatre, hosted by Cecil B. De-Mille, presented a version of *Blood and Sand* on October 20, 1941, for which Tyrone Power recreated his role of Juan Gallardo. Annabella played Linda Darnell's role of Carmen, Kathleen Fitz had Rita Hayworth's part of Dona Sol, and the supporting cast included Lou Merrill as Curro.

A Spanish-U.S. remake, *Sangre y Arena* (1989), was directed by Javier Elorietta and starred Christopher Rydell as Juan, Ana Torrent as Carmen and Sharon Stone as Dona Sol.

Review: "The better performances come in the lesser roles—Laird Cregar as an effeminate aficionado, J. Carrol Naish as a broken matador, John Carradine as a grumbling member of the quadrilla." (*The New York Times*, May 23, 1941)

Charley's Aunt

Studio: 20th Century–Fox; *Producer:* Darryl F. Zanuck; *Associate Producer:* William Perlberg; *Director:* Archie Mayo; *Screenplay:* George Seaton (based on the play by Brandon Thomas); *Music:* Alfred Newman (and Cyril J. Mockridge, uncredited); *Photographer:* Peverell Marley; *Art Directors:* Richard Day, Nathan Juran; *Set Decorator:* Thomas Little; *Film Editor:* Robert Bischoff; *Costume Designer:* Travis Banton; *Sound:* Joseph E. Aiken, Roger Heman, Sr.; *Visual Effects:* Chesley Bonestell, matte artist (uncredited); *Wardrobe Supervisor:* Sam Benson; *Jeweler:* Eugene Joseff; *Orchestrator:* Conrad Salinger; *Shooting Dates:* May 12–June 25, 1941; *Running Time:* 81 minutes; *Negative Cost:* $889,300; *Premiere:* Grauman's Chinese Theatre, July 31, 1941; *Worldwide Rentals:* $2,278,200; *Profit:* $722,800

Cast: Jack Benny (Babbs), Kay Francis (Donna Lucia), James Ellison (Jack Chesney), Anne Baxter (Amy Spettigue), Edmund Gwenn (Stephen Spettigue), Laird Cregar (Sir Francis Chesney), Reginald Owen (Redcliffe), Arleen Whelan (Kitty Verdun), Richard Haydn (Charley Wykeham), Ernest Cossart (Brassett), Morton Lowry (Harley Stafford), Will Stanton (Messenger), Lionel Pape (Hilary Babberly), Maurice Cass (Octogenarian), C. Montague Shaw (Elderly Man), Claud Allister, William Austin (Cricket Match Spectators), Brandon Hurst (Cricket Match Coach), Stanley Mann (Umpire), Russell Burroughs, John Meredith, Gilchrist Stuart (Teammates), Robert Conway, Bob Cornell, Herbert Gunn, Basil Walker (Students), Vivian Cox (Stand-in for Arlene Whelan)

Synopsis: Lord "Babbs" Babberly faces expulsion from Oxford due to his various escapades. His college cronies Jack Chesney and Charley Wykeham hope to woo away their sweethearts, Kitty and Amy, from the girls' paid guardian, an old skinflint named Spettigue, who will lose his income if the young ladies marry. Planning a visit: Charley's aunt, the beautiful Donna Lucia, a millionairess from Brazil ("where the nuts come from"), and whom Charley has never seen. Jack and Charley plot to engage her as chaperone as they entertain Kitty and Amy at luncheon in their quarters.

Donna Lucia decides to arrive incognito to be sure that Kitty isn't a fortune hunter. Needing a chaperone, Jack and Charley desperately persuade Babbs to masquerade as Donna Lucia (they guess she's a crone, and dress up Babbs in his varsity club show's wig and costume). The bargain: If he plays Donna Lucia, they'll vouch for him to Oxford's Mr. Redcliffe to save him from expulsion.

Among the slapstick complications: Sir Francis Chesney, Jack's father, has come to visit his son, reveals the family's fortune is gone, and—learning of Donna Lucia's wealth—gallantly agrees to propose marriage to her, to replenish the family fortune, and so Jack can marry Kitty. Spettigue, learning of Donna Lucia's money, also pursues her. All the while, Babbs mugs and cavorts in his wig and costume ... lapping wine off a table ... getting his petticoats on behind a wall ... smoking a cigar...

Eventually, the real Donna Lucia discovers Babbs' true identity. So does Sir Francis, who exits roaring with laughter. Babbs secures a letter of consent from Spettigue so Kitty can marry Jack, and Amy can marry Charley. Spettigue, at long last aware of the masquerade, faints. Babbs, from the look of things, also faces matrimony ... with Donna Lucia.

Production Notes: *Charley's Aunt* first played New York on October 2, 1893, starring Etienne Girardot. There were revivals in 1906 and 1925; movie-wise, there was a 1925 Christie Film Company release starring Sydney Chaplin and a 1930 Columbia release starring Charles Ruggles. On October 17, 1940, the play was a hit all over again as Jose Ferrer starred at Broadway's Cort Theatre in a production staged by Joshua Logan. The show ran 233 performances, and Fox paid a reported $125,000 for the rights. Originally mentioned for the cross-dressing star part: Tyrone Power (!), as well as Bob Hope.

Jack Benny (born Benjamin Kubelsky, 1894–1974), was the star of a phenomenally successful radio show when *Charley's Aunt* was produced. He later made a recurrent joke that his films were bombs, but *Charley's Aunt* was a major hit, reported by *Variety* to have been the eighth most popular movie of 1941. As for a later Benny-in-drag performance: Phyllis Diller (who took over the title role in Broadway's *Hello Dolly!* in 1970) claimed that David Merrick had pitched the idea to Benny in the late 1960s to play Dolly, with George Burns as Horace Vandergelder. The mind boggles.

Kay Francis (1905–1968) came to *Charley's Aunt* shortly after professional humiliations at Warner Bros., where the studio had steadily demoted her from one of its major stars into the "B" unit. Francis tallied five husbands and a $1,000,000 estate, some of which she willed to Seeing Eye, Inc., which trained seeing-eye dogs for the blind.

James Ellison (1910–1993) grew up on a Montana ranch, played Johnny Nelson, Hopalong Cassidy's sidekick, in such films as *Bar 20 Rides Again* (1935), and might have achieved major stardom in *The Plainsman* (Paramount, 1936), as Wild Bill Hickok and

co-starring with Gary Cooper and Jean Arthur. However, the film's producer-director Cecil B. DeMille intensely disliked Ellison and his performance, and allegedly tried to blackball the actor. Ellison carried on. His later credits included leads in the horror films *The Undying Monster* (Fox, 1942) and *I Walked with a Zombie* (RKO, 1943). He returned to westerns, later made big money in home construction—Ellison Drive in Beverly Hills is named after him—and died December 23, 1993, in Montecito, California, following a fall in which he'd broken his neck.

Edmund Gwenn (1877–1959), forever Kris Kringle of *Miracle on 34th Street* (Fox, 1947), for which he won a Best Supporting Actor Oscar ("Now I know there is a Santa Claus," he said in his acceptance speech), was superb in many films: *The Walking Dead* (Warner Bros., 1936, as the scientist who brings Boris Karloff back to life); *Mr. 880* (Fox, 1950, for which he received a second Best Supporting Actor Academy nomination as the sweet old counterfeiter); and *Them!* (Warner Bros., 1954, as Dr. Harold Medford, battling the giant ants). Gwenn was star-billed in Hitchcock's *The Trouble with Harry* (1955). He died at the Motion Picture Home on September 6, 1959. Ironically, considering his status as one of the most beloved of Hollywood character actors, Gwenn's unclaimed ashes are held at the Chapel of the Pines, Los Angeles.

Anne Baxter (1923–1985) won a Best Supporting Actress Oscar and a Golden Globe for *The Razor's Edge* (Fox, 1946), but made her most vivid claim to fame in the title role of *All About Eve* (Fox, 1950), receiving a Best Actress Oscar nomination. In 1971, she replaced Lauren Bacall in *Applause*, the Broadway musical version of *All About Eve*, in the star role of Margo Channing. The first of Baxter's three husbands was John Hodiak, from whom she was divorced at the time of his death in 1955. Another memorable Baxter portrayal: her vampy, over-the-top Nefertiri in DeMille's *The Ten Commandments* (Paramount, 1956).

Arleen Whelan (1914–1993) was a red-haired discovery of Fox director Bruce Humberstone, whom she'd provided a manicure in a Hollywood salon. Notable credits: Hannah in *Young Mr. Lincoln* (Fox, 1939, directed by John Ford); one of Broadway's *The Dough-girls* (co-starring with Virginia Field and Doris Nolan, 1942); and *The Sun Shines Bright* (Republic, 1953, also directed by Ford). She married and divorced three times.

Reginald Owen (1887–1972) is best-remembered as Scrooge in *A Christmas Carol* (MGM, 1938), a replacement for wheelchair-confined Lionel Barrymore, who played the role annually on radio. A bit of Owen trivia: After the Ambassador Hotel canceled the Beatles' reservation when they played the Hollywood Bowl in August 1964, the group rented Owen's St. Pierre Road mansion in Bel Air. Also: In the last year of his life, 1972, 84-year old Owen returned to Broadway as Erronius in the musical *A Funny Thing Happened on the Way to the Forum*, starring Phil Silvers.

Richard Haydn (1905–1985) made his Hollywood debut in *Charley's Aunt*, was notable as Linda Darnell's wicked, considerably older husband in *Forever Amber* (Fox, 1947), and found his most famous role as Max Detweiler in the super-hit *The Sound of Music* (1965).

Morton Lowry, glimpsed here briefly as Harley, had appeared in *Hudson's Bay* and found his perhaps best-remembered role as Mr. Jonas, the cruel schoolteacher in John Ford's *How Green Was My Valley* (1941). He played Charles Dickens in Fox's *The Loves of Edgar Allan Poe* (1942), but his career never fully took off. He reportedly died indigent in San Francisco in 1987, many years after his final credited work on the British-produced TV series *The Adventures of Robin Hood* (1959–1960).

Archie Mayo (1891–1968) had directed a bevy of major stars at Warner Brothers— John Barrymore in *Svengali* (1931); James Cagney in *The Mayor of Hell* (1933); Paul Muni in *Bordertown* (1935); and Leslie Howard, Bette Davis and Humphrey Bogart in *The Petrified Forest* (1936). At Fox, he directed such films as *Crash Dive* (1943) with Tyrone Power; his final films were *A Night in Casablanca* (1946), starring the Marx Brothers, and *Angel on My Shoulder* (1946), starring Paul Muni, Anne Baxter and Claude Rains. Always overweight, Mayo reportedly became increasingly obstreperous, which probably contributed to his relatively early retirement. He came back to produce *The*

Beast of Budapest (1958), an anti–Communist film based on 1956 events in Hungary, produced by the Hal Roach Studio, then faded back into retirement. Mayo died December 4, 1968, in Guadalajara, Mexico.

George Seaton (1911–1979), who wrote the *Charley's Aunt* screenplay, later wrote and directed Fox's *Miracle on 34th Street* (1947), which won Seaton a Best Screenplay Oscar.

Fox produced an excellent trailer, titled *Three of a Kind*, for *Charley's Aunt*: Benny dines in the Fox commissary with Tyrone Power (who enthuses about his role in *A Yank in the R.A.F.* and his love scenes with Betty Grable) and Randolph Scott (who's excited about his heroic part in *Belle Starr* and his love scenes with Gene Tierney). Meanwhile, amidst all this machismo, studio aides keep pestering Benny, conferring about the wig, corset, etc., he'll wear in *Charley's Aunt*.

Fox's contract with the play's producers, Carly Wharton and Martin Gabel, promised no alterations would be made in the original scenario. However, Fox made some changes— including a romance for Babbs and Donna Lucia—and on August 26, 1941, only 25 days after the film's release, Wharton and Gabel filed a lawsuit, demanding damages and an injunction to prevent the film being shown. New York Supreme Court Justice O'Brien dismissed the injunction September 23, 1941; the case went to trial, but the decision was never publicized. Presumably, the film still faces legal imbroglios; Turner Classic Movies scheduled the film a few years ago, learned it couldn't get the rights, and instead showed the 1930 version.

On October 11, 1948, a musical version, *Where's Charley?*, opened at Broadway's St. James Theatre, starring Ray Bolger and with a musical score by Frank Loesser, including the hit "Once in Love with Amy." Bolger won a Tony Award and the play ran 792 performances. In 1951, Bolger headlined a 48-performance return engagement; in 1952, Warner Bros. released a film version of *Where's Charley?* with Bolger starring, directed by David Butler. In 1953, Jose Ferrer starred in a *Charley's Aunt* revival; in 1970, Louis Nye starred in a *Charley's Aunt* (it flopped); and in 1974, Raul Julia starred in a *Where's Charley?* revival that lasted 76 performances.

The 1941 *Charley's Aunt* has great pace and offers the spectacle of ace comic performers displaying perfect timing. Laird has one of the best scenes: near the end of the show: Wandering at night in the garden, he sees Benny's Babbs, romantically sharing a bench with Francis' Donna Lucia, his head in her lap ... and his trousers exposed. Laird's Sir Francis begins laughing, goes into the house, "congratulates" Gwenn's Spettigue and, his hilarity rising, finally exits the room and the film roaring with laughter. It's one of the great moments in a very funny movie.

Review: "A gold mine loaded with laughs.... Benny does some of the finest work of his career ... the direction by Archie Mayo is a classic of tempo and timing.... Outstanding are the portrayals of Laird Cregar, Reginald Owen and Edmund Gwenn." ("Hanna," *Independent Exhibitors Film Bulletin*, July 26, 1941)

I Wake Up Screaming

Alternate Title: Hot Spot; *Studio:* 20th Century–Fox; *Producer:* Darryl F. Zanuck; *Associate Producer:* Milton Sperling; *Director:* H. Bruce Humberstone; *Screenplay:* Dwight Taylor (from the novel *I Wake Up Screaming* by Steve Fisher); *Photographer:* Edward Cronjager; *Art Directors:* Richard Day, Nathan Juran; *Set Decorator:* Thomas Little; *Film Editor:* Robert Simpson; *Costume Designer:* Gwen Wakeling; *Makeup Artist:* Guy Pearce; *Sound:* Bernard Freericks, Roger Heman, Sr.; *Musical Director:* Cyril J. Mockridge; *Musical Themes:* "Street Scene" (by Alfred Newman); "Over the Rainbow" (by Harold Arlen); *Songs:* "The Things I Love" (music and lyrics by Harold Barlow and Lewis Harris, based on "Melody," Op. 42, no. 3, by Pyotr Ilyich Tchaikovsky, sung by Carole Landis); "Daddy" (Music and Lyrics by Bobby Troup, sung by Betty Grable; deleted from release print); *Production Manager:* William Koenig; *Orchestrator:* Herbert W. Spencer; *Assistant Director:* Ad Schaumer; *Dialogue Directors:* Arthur Berthelet, George Wright; *Technical Advisor:* Frank L. James; *Running Time:* 82 minutes; *Shooting Dates:* July 21–August 26, 1941; *Negative Cost:* $462,500; *Opening:* Grauman's Chinese Theatre and Loew's State Theatre, Los Angeles, November 12, 1941; Roxy Theatre, New York City, January 16, 1942; *Worldwide Rentals:* $1,491,500; *Profit:* $574,100

Cast: Betty Grable (Jill Lynn), Victor Mature (Frankie Christopher), Carole Landis (Vicky Lynn), Laird Cregar (Ed Cornell), William Gargan (Jerry MacDonald), Alan Mowbray (Robin Ray), Allyn Joslyn (Larry Evans), Elisha Cook, Jr. (Harry Williams), Chick Chandler, Cyril Ring (Reporters), Morris Ankrum (Assistant District Attorney), Charles Lane (Florist), Frank Orth (Cemetery Caretaker), Gregory Gaye (Headwaiter), May Beatty (Mrs. Handel), Harry Strang (Officer Murphy), Pat McKee (Ozinski—Newsman), Stanley Clements, George Hickman (Newsboys), Edward McWade (Old Man at Library), Forbes Murray (Mr. Handel), Harry Seymour (Bartender), Russ Clark (Policeman), Amzie Strickland (Girl at Table), Paul Weigel (Gus—Delicatessen Proprietor), John Breen (Sidewalk Passerby), Heine Conklin (Newspaper Buyer), Cecil Weston (Police Matron), Mike Morelli (Fight Spectator), Sarah Edwards (Customer), Stanley Blystone, Wade Boteler, Eddie Dunn, Ralph Dunn, James Flavin, Philip Morris, Dick Rich, Tim Ryan (Detectives), Jack Gargan, Robert Haines, Albert Pollet (Waiters), Brooks Benedict, Edward Biby, Ralph Brooks, James Conaty, Tom Ferrandini, Stuart Hall, Frank McClure, Howard Miller (Night Club Patrons), Bob Cornell, Basil Walker (Reporters).

Synopsis: When Vicky Lynn is found murdered in her New York apartment, suspicion falls on Frankie Christopher, a promoter who's touted Vicky from a waitress to a glamour girl. Hell-bent on proving Frankie guilty is Ed Cornell, a sadistic detective who takes joy in sending murderers to the electric chair and watching how they behave as they face death.

Assisted by Vicky's sister Jill, Frankie goes on the run, fighting to prove himself innocent. Other suspects include over-the-hill actor Robin Ray and bitchy columnist Larry Evans. The killer proves to be Harry Williams, the creepy switchboard operator at Vicky's apartment house. When Harry tells Frankie that he'd confessed to Cornell that he was the murderer, Cornell had let him go ... preferring to go on hounding Frankie.

Frankie breaks into Cornell's apartment and finds it a morbid shrine to the dead Vicky. Cornell explains that he'd been in love with Vicky ever since peeping at her through the window of the restaurant where she worked as a waitress. He'd dreamed of one day getting the nerve to ask her to marry him, but Frankie's promoting Vicky took her forever out of Cornell's league. The perverse Cornell kills himself with poison, dying before Vicky's picture. Frankie and Jill get married.

Production Notes: Betty Grable (1916–1973) became 20th Century–Fox's hottest star of the World War II years, headlining Technicolor musicals such as *Coney Island*

(1943) and becoming legendary for her peek-aboo over-the-shoulder bathing suit pin-up. On February 15, 1943, Grable placed her leg prints in the fabled concrete at Grauman's Chinese Theatre. An Army sergeant, Navy gunner's mate and Marine sergeant had the honor of holding Grable and lowering her into the wet concrete. The ritual lasted a reported 90 minutes, complicated by the fact that Grable's dress kept riding up as the three men lifted her. At one point, the trio almost dropped her into the goo, and she let out a scream. "I think that girl was a little nervous," observed the gunner's mate.

Victor Mature (1913–1999), Cregar's colleague at the Pasadena Playhouse, won his primary notice in such films as *Samson and Delilah* (Paramount, 1949), *The Robe* (Fox, 1953) and *Demetrius and the Gladiators* (Fox, 1954). He was well known for his modesty ("I'm no actor, and I've got 64 pictures to prove it") and his alleged cowardice (on *Samson and Delilah*, he refused to wrestle a tame lion, much to the disgust of producer-director Cecil B. DeMille). Mature married five times; his last credit was the 1984 TV movie *Samson and Delilah* in which he played Samson's father (and remarked, "If the money's right, I'd play his mother!").

Carole Landis (born Frances Ridste, 1919–1948) became a Hollywood tragedy: five unhappy marriages, nicknames ranging from

I Wake Up Screaming: Alan Mowbray, Victor Mature and Laird Cregar.

"The Ping Girl" to "The Chest," and a Seconal pills suicide, allegedly due to an unhappy affair with Rex Harrison (then married to Lilli Palmer). One individual who didn't remember Landis fondly was Lilli Palmer, who, in her memoir *Change Lobsters and Dance*, confessed that, during Harrison's affair with Landis, she'd been tempted to go visit Landis with a kitchen knife. Landis' memoir *Four Jills in a Jeep*, based on her World War II USO adventures, became a 1944 Fox film, co-starring Landis with Kay Francis, Martha Raye and Mitzi Mayfair (all as themselves).

Alan Mowbray (born Ernest Allen, 1896–1969), a native of London, tallied over 180 film and TV credits, was a founder of the Screen Actors Guild, and a member of "The Bundy Drive Boys," roistering, hard-drinking actors. My personal favorite of Mowbray's performances: the bearded lunatic who resembles Robert Newton's Blackbeard in *Blackbeard the Pirate* (RKO, 1952). Watch Newton and Mowbray together for a lesson in wonderfully over-the-top acting!

Allyn Joslyn (1901–1981) came to *I Wake Up Screaming* direct from Broadway's smash hit *Arsenic and Old Lace*, in which he'd co-starred with Boris Karloff; the play had opened January 10, 1941, and Joslyn had created the role of Mortimer (played in the film version by Cary Grant). He later appeared in such films as *Titanic* (1953), starred in the teleseries *McKeever and the Colonel* (1962–1963), and made several guest appearances on TV's *The Addams Family* (1964–1966).

Elisha Cook, Jr. (1903–1995), morphed in his career from the star juvenile of Eugene O'Neill's Broadway play *Ah! Wilderness* (1933) to one of the cinema's great psychos and heavies. He went into *I Wake Up Screaming* right from *The Maltese Falcon*, in which he played Wilmer, gunsel for Sydney Greenstreet's Fat Man. Before Cook died at age 91, he was *The Maltese Falcon*'s last surviving principal. (He was one of the last *two* surviving principals of *I Wake Up Screaming*: Victor Mature died in 1999.) In an interview with *New West* magazine ("Cook's Tour" by Grover Lewis, June 2, 1980), Cook said, "*They Won't Forget* and *Stranger on the Third Floor* and *I Wake Up Screaming* were all considered 'sleepers' in their day, but I doubt if anybody's seen them in 40 years. They came and they went, and they could be dust by now for all I know."

H. Bruce Humberstone (1901–1984), nicknamed "Lucky," had, strangely enough, co-directed (with Del Lord) a Hal Roach comedy shot titled *Hot Spot* (1932). He worked himself up the ladder at Fox, with some controversy: He directed several Charlie Chan films in the late 1930s, allegedly making sure alcoholic Warner Oland *stayed* drunk to accentuate his stilted Chan delivery. He also took out an ad in the trade papers, claiming he "directed the Fire" in *In Old Chicago*, a boast that the film's director, Henry King, claimed cost him a Best Director Academy nomination. Humberstone went on to direct such Fox hits as *Hello Frisco, Hello* (1943, featuring Cregar).

Edward Cronjager (1904–1960) did a super job of *noir* cinematography on *I Wake Up Screaming*. As Eddie Muller points out in his DVD audio commentary, the effect Cronjager creates with Betty Grable's false eyelashes is alone worth the price of admission. He'd work with Cregar again on *Heaven Can Wait*, for which Cronjager received one of his seven Academy Award nominations.

Fox remade *I Wake Up Screaming* as *Vicki*, released October 5, 1953. Jeanne Crain played Jill, Elliott Reid was *Steve* Christopher, Jean Peters was Vicki and Richard Boone played Ed Cornell. Harry Horner directed. The film lacked the *noir* sexuality of the original and Boone, a fine actor, didn't go for the perversity that Cregar gave the role. Incidentally, playing Harry Williams was Aaron Spelling, who at the time was married to Carolyn Jones. He later became the TV mega-producer of such shows as *Dynasty* (1981–1989) and *Beverly Hills 90210* (1990–2000).

Review: "Laird Cregar steals the picture with his performance of the menace, so sinister that it will immediately bring comparisons with Peter Lorre's memorable portrayal in *M*." (*The Film Daily*, October 17, 1941)

Joan of Paris

Studio: RKO; *Producer:* David Hempstead; *Director:* Robert Stevenson; *Screenplay:* Charles Bennett and Ellis St. Joseph (from a story by Jacques Thery and Georges Kessel); *Music:* Roy Webb; *Musical Director and Composer:* C. Bakaleinikoff (stock music by Bakaleinikoff, Alfred Newman and Max Steiner);

Photographer: Russell Metty; *Art Directors:* Carroll Clark, Albert S. D'Agostino; *Wardrobe:* Edward Stevenson; *Set Decorator:* Darrell Silvera; *Sound Recordist:* John L. Cass; *Film Editor:* Sherman Todd; *Assistant Director:* James A. Anderson; *Makeup Artist:* Mel Berns; *Technical Advisor on French Backgrounds:* Lilo Dammert; *Technical Advisor on German Backgrounds:* William Yetter, Sr.; *Technical Advisor on Religious Scenes:* J.J. Devlin; *Michele Morgan's English Instructor:* Simon R. Mitchneck; *Running Time:* 91 minutes; *Shooting Dates:* September 12–November 11, 1941; Retakes, November 28, 1941; *Negative Cost:* $666,000; *Opening:* Rivoli Theatre, New York City, January 24, 1942; Carthay Circle Theatre, Los Angeles, April 16, 1942; *Worldwide Rentals:* $1,150,000; *Profit:* $105,000

Cast: Michele Morgan (Joan), Paul Henreid (Paul), Thomas Mitchell (Father Antoine), Laird Cregar (Herr Funk), May Robson (Mlle. Rosay), Alexander Granach (Gestapo Agent), Alan Ladd ("Baby"), Jack Briggs (Robin), James Monks (Splinter), Richard Fraser (Geoffrey), Paul Weigel (Janitor), John Abbott (English Spy), Hans Conreid (Second Gestapo Agent), Wilhelm von Brincken (Schultz—Funk's Secretary), Adrienne D'Ambricourt (Dress Shop Proprietress), Fred Farrell (Café Waiter), Bernard Gorcey (Parisian Waiting at Confessional), Payne B. Johnson (French Boy in Schoolroom), Joseph P. Mack (Cab Driver), Paul Michael (German Captain), Benay Parley (Little Girl in Church), Dina Smirnova (Mme. Langlars), René Pedrini (Waiter), Eugenia Rafee (Salesgirl Voice), Otto Reichow (Tough Sergeant), Irene Seidner (Little Old Lady at Confessional), Katherine Wilson (German Woman on Telephone), Marie Windsor (French Girl), Robert R. Stephenson, William Yetter, Sr. (German Sergeants).

Synopsis: Capt. Paul Laville and his fighter pilots from RAF Squadron 701 bail out after fighting Messerschmitts. The five men make their way to Nazi-occupied Paris, where Father Antoine hides them in the sewers as Paul tries to arrange their escape to England. He meets a beautiful young barmaid named Joan, who has a deep devotion to Joan of Arc and prays to her statue in her room ... where she soon is hiding Paul.

Pursuing Paul and the pilots is Herr Funk, a Gestapo chief, whose foppish habit of peeling grapes belies his ruthless fanaticism. He allows Paul to go free, playing cat and mouse, hoping Paul will eventually lead him to the fliers and he'll capture them all. Meanwhile, one of Paul's men, "Baby," dies of his wounds, and Funk eventually traps Joan—who has fallen in love with Paul—forcing her to take him and his soldiers to snare the men.

Joan leads the Gestapo on a wild goose chase through the sewers of Paris, timing her action so that Paul and his men can escape via a waiting speedboat. As Joan exults in her triumph, Funk slaps her face. Joan goes to the firing squad and Paul and the pilots fly off to battle the Nazis.

Production Notes: *Joan of Paris* was the Hollywood debut of both its stars, Michele Morgan (born in France in 1920) and Paul Henreid. Morgan's Hollywood sojourn wasn't a happy one: She disliked *Joan of Paris*, finding co-star Henreid chilly; she lost out to Ingrid Bergman for *Casablanca*; she was expected to sing with Frank Sinatra in *Higher and Higher* (RKO, 1943) and rightly foresaw the movie as a disaster; she co-starred with Humphrey Bogart in *Passage to Marseilles* (Warner Bros., 1944) but found director Michael Curtiz (a "Tartarian-faced Hungarian") the most horrible person she ever worked with, and Bogart was no help. As if this weren't enough, the actress lived in a mansion at 10050 Cielo Drive in Benedict Canyon that seemed to be haunted. Years later, it was the site of the Charles Manson's gang's slaughter of Sharon Tate and others.

Morgan did much better in her native France, winning the Cannes Film Festival Best Actress Award for her portrayal of the blind Gertrude in *Pastoral Symphony* (1946). She played Joan of Arc in the French-Italian production *Daughters of Destiny* (1954). The title of her 1977 memoir: *With Those Eyes*. The actress whom Laird Cregar slapped in *Joan of Paris* died December 20, 2016, in France. She was 96 and the last surviving leading lady with whom Cregar had acted.

Paul Henreid (born Paul Georg Julius Henreid Ritter von Wassel-Waldingau, 1908–1992) followed up *Joan of Paris* with his two best-remembered roles, both for Warner Bros.: Bette Davis' lover Jerry Durance in *Now, Voyager* (1942, in which he lit both her cigarette and his in his mouth), and *Casablanca* (1943, as Nazi fighter Victor Laszlo, flying off with wife Ingrid Bergman in the climax). Later a prolific TV director, he directed Bette Davis in the feature *Dead Ringer* (Warner Bros., 1964).

Thomas Mitchell (1892–1962) won a Best Supporting Actor Academy Award for *Stagecoach* (UA, 1939). The same year, he scored in Columbia's *Only Angels Have Wings* and

Mr. Smith Goes to Washington, RKO's *The Hunchback of Notre Dame* and Selznick's *Gone with the Wind*! He'd appear with Laird again in *The Black Swan*.

May Robson, former star of *Granny Get Your Gun*, made her final screen appearance here as Mlle. Roday, a schoolteacher working for the underground. The venerable actress died in Beverly Hills October 20, 1942, at 84.

Alexander Granach (1893–1945), a Jewish refugee from Hitler's Germany, made a vivid impression as the squat, ubiquitous Gestapo agent who never speaks ... and whom Henreid's hero eventually kills in a steam bath. The actor had studied with Max Reinhardt, appeared as "Knock," the strange real estate agent in F.W. Murnau's *Nosferatu* (1922) and— coming to the U.S.—played in MGM's *Ninotchka* (1939). Among his World War II films: *Hangmen Also Die!* (as a Gestapo inspector, 1943) and *The Hitler Gang* (as Julius Streicher, 1944). Granach was appearing in the play *A Bell for Adano*, which had opened at Broadway's Cort Theatre on December 6, 1944, and starred Fredric March, when he died March 14, 1945.

Alan Ladd (1913–1964) had tallied over 40 screen credits before winning the showy *Joan of Paris* role of "Baby," with a great death scene. Among his pre-stardom roles: a bit as a reporter in *Citizen Kane* (1941), a featured role in Universal's 1941 *The Black Cat*, and— alas, unconfirmed—a gig as one of the beast men in Paramount's *Island of Lost Souls* (1932). Ladd would wrap up *Joan of Paris* and be playing his star-making role in Paramount's *This Gun for Hire* while *Joan of Paris* was still shooting.

Robert Stevenson (1905–1986) had directed the excellent British Boris Karloff mad doctor film *The Man Who Lived Again* (Gainsborough, 1936), co-starring Anna Lee (Stevenson's wife from 1934 to 1944). He later directed a parade of Disney blockbusters, including *Old Yeller* (1957), *The Absent Minded Professor* (1961), *Mary Poppins* (1964, Best Director Oscar nomination) and *The Love Bug* (1968).

Russell Metty (1906–1978), *Joan of Paris's* cinematographer, won an Oscar for his work on *Spartacus* (1960). He was Orson Welles' cameraman on *The Stranger* (1946) and *Touch*

of Evil (1958) and was later active on TV, including shooting 57 episodes of *The Waltons*.

Composer Roy Webb (1888–1992) received an Oscar nomination for Best Scoring of a Dramatic or Comedy picture. The winner: Max Steiner for Warner Bros.' *Now, Voyager*.

Review: "One of the more memorable sequences details the meeting of the RAF squadron leader and the Gestapo head in the latter's ornate offices. Here Stevenson's quiet approach really counts, as an audience is led to believe the Gestapo is being fooled. But wait for the finish! Laird Cregar performs the brains of the secret police with obvious relish, making this mammoth dandy a fascinating menace. It is a great role as Cregar interprets it." (*The Hollywood Reporter*, January 7, 1942)

This Gun for Hire

Studio: Paramount; *Executive Producer:* Buddy G. DeSylva; *Associate Producer:* Richard Blumenthal; *Director:* Frank Tuttle; *Screenplay:* Albert Maltz and W.R Burnett (based on the novel by Graham Greene; Frank Tuttle, uncredited on script); *Photographer:* John Seitz; *Special Photographic Effects:* William L. Pereira, Gordon Jennings, Farciot Edouart; *Musical Score:* David Buttolph; *Songs "Now You See It, Now You Don't" and "I've Got You":* Lyrics by Frank Loesser, Music by Jacques Press; *Art Directors:* Hans Dreier, Robert Usher; *Film Editor:* Archie Marshek; *Miss Lake's Gowns:* Edith Head; *Director of Makeup:* Wally Westmore; *Sound:* Philip Wisdom, John Cope; *Production Designer:* Lynd Ward; *Assistant Director:* George Templeton; *Still Photographer:* Mal Bullock; *Camera Boom Operator:* Buck Walters; *Orchestrators:* George Parrish, Walter Scharf, Leo Shuken; *Technical Advisors on Magic Tricks:* Marian Chavez, Jimmy Grippo, Frank Herman; *Assistant Dance Director:* George King; *Running Time:* 81 minutes; *Shooting Dates:* October 27– December 6, 1941; Retakes, December, 10, 15, 16, 17 and 18, 1941, and January 22, 1942; *Negative Cost:* $512,423.16; *Opening:* Paramount Theatre, New York City, May 13, 1942; Paramount Hollywood and Downtown Theatres, Los Angeles, June 25, 1942; (*Author's note: Rental figures and profits are unavailable for the film.*)

Cast: Veronica Lake (Ellen Graham), Robert Preston (Michael Crane), Laird Cregar (Willard Gates), Alan Ladd (Philip Raven), Tully Marshall (Alvin Brewster), Marc Lawrence (Tommy), Olin Howlin (Blair Fletcher), Roger Imhof (Senator Burnett), Pamela Blake (Annie), Frank Ferguson (Albert Baker), Victor Kilian (Drew), Patricia Farr (Ruby), Harry Shannon (Steve Finnerty), Charles C. Wilson (Police Captain), Mikhail Rasumny (Slukey), Bernadene Hayes (Albert Baker's Secretary), Mary Davenport (Salesgirl), Chester Clute (Rooming House Manager), Charles Arnt (Male Dressmaker), Earle Dewey (Mr. Collins), Clem Bevans (Scissor Grinder), Lynda Grey (Gates' Secretary), Virita Campbell (Little Girl), Emmett Vogan (Police Sgt. Charlie Carlisle), Harry Hayden (Man in Restaurant), Elliott Sullivan (Officer Sullivan), Sarah Padden (Mrs. Mason), Don Barclay (Piano Player), Dick Rush (Lt. Clark), Tim Ryan (Weems—Guard), John Sheehan (Keever), Robert Winkler (Jimmie), Charles Irwin (Old Irishman), Louise La Planche (Dancer), Jack Baxley (Innocent Dupe), George Anderson (Plainclothesman), Ernest Baskett (Porter), Karin Booth (Waitress), Harry Brown, Gordon De Main, John Marston (Superintendents), William Cabanne (Laundry Truck Driver), Eddy Chandler (Demolition Foreman), Jack Cheatham, Chuck Hamilton, George Magrill (Policemen), Kenneth Chryst, Reed Porter (Workmen), Joan Evans (Saleslady's Mother), Jim Farley (Night Watchman), Virginia Farmer (Maid in Dress Shop), Betty Farrington (Woman on Bridge), Sam Harris (Man at Rehearsal), Lora Lee (Girl in Car), Arthur Loft (Man Who Bumps into Raven), Patsy Mace (Young Girl in Reception Room), Charles McMurphy (Detective), Ivan Miller (Doorman), Charles R. Moore (Pullman Waiter), Frances Morris (Receptionist), Pat O'Malley (Conductor), Lee Prather (Gateman), Jack Reitzen (Man at Audition), Cyril Ring (Neptune Club Waiter), Julian Rivero (Man with Monkey), Oscar Smith (Train Porter), Alan Speer (Frog), Edwin Stanley (Police Captain at Train Station), Phil Tead (Machinist), Fred Walburn (Walt—Newsboy), Richard Webb (Young Man), Pat West (Janitor), Gloria Williams (Woman), Yvonne De Carlo (Showgirl at Neptune Club), Martha Mears (Singing Voice for Veronica Lake)

Synopsis: San Francisco, the early days and nights of World War II. Ruthless, diminutive hired killer Philip Raven, who loves cats and has a broken left wrist, kills Albert Baker, a chemist who knows about Nitrochemical Corporation's formula for poison gas. The man who'd hired Raven for the job: Willard Gates, who (unbeknownst to Raven) owns Los Angeles' Neptune Club, is a cowardly Fifth Columnist, and is a cohort of Nitrochemical's wizened, crippled boss, Alvin Brewster, who plans to sell poison gas to the Japanese powers.

After Gates pays Raven in "hot money," he goes to Michael Crane, a Los Angeles detective on vacation in San Francisco, gives him the marked bills' numbers, and claims Raven stole them after killing Nitrochemical's paymaster. Michael's fiancée, Ellen Graham, who (unbeknownst to Michael) is an undercover agent, poses as a showgirl who sings and per-

forms magic tricks, and lands a gig in Gates' Neptune Club.

Raven, aware he's been set up, pursues Gates too. Soon Ellen, Raven, and Gates are on a train bound for Los Angeles. Gates sees them together on the train ... and Ellen helps Raven elude the police.

Now aware of Ellen's danger to him, Gates invites her to his house high in the Hollywood Hills, where Gates' chauffeur, Tommy, plans to drown Ellen in the reservoir. Raven rescues her. Together they flee a manhunt led by Michael. Raven reveals to her his nightmarish past—how his aunt, who raised him, used to beat him, and had smashed his wrist with a red-hot flatiron. Ellen helps Raven escape the manhunt, and Raven promises Ellen he'll get a confession from Gates and Brewster about the poison gas.

Raven, Ellen, and Gates converge in the chambers of Nitrochemical. The ancient Brewster, after signing the confession, tries to shoot Raven with a pen that's actually a gun, but dies of a heart attack. Gates signs too, then hysterically lies that Ellen had tried to betray Raven to the police. Raven shoots and kills him. Michael, still thinking Raven is a danger to Ellen, appears on a scaffolding to rescue her, but Raven, aware that Ellen and Michael are an item, doesn't kill him. Police burst into the chamber and fatally shoot Raven. Michael is now aware of why Ellen had helped Raven, and Raven dies, aware that Ellen had been kind to him and had not betrayed him. Ellen turns to Michael, saying, "Oh, Michael, my darling, hold me."

Production Notes: In 1936, when Paramount first considered producing *This Gun for Hire* (after purchasing the rights to Graham Greene's novel for $12,000), the actor in line to play Raven was Peter Lorre. Fearing a "one-key performance," the studio bailed out on the Lorre idea and the property went through various channels before Albert Maltz began on a new outline in June 1941.

Alan Ladd, 5'6", fresh from his fine death scene in *Joan of Paris*, won the role of Raven largely via the campaigning of agent Sue Carol, whom he wed in March 1942. Always insecure, Ladd was a far better actor than critics admitted, and was unforgettable in *Shane* (Paramount, 1953). In November 1962, he was found unconscious with a bullet wound near the heart; on January 29, 1964, he died of an overdose of sedatives and alcohol. The family claimed the death was accidental.

Veronica Lake (Constance Ockelman, 1922–1973), 4'11", made the famous remark, "I wasn't a sex symbol, I was a sex zombie." The peekaboo bangs and pouty delivery make her one of the stranger screen sirens of the 1940s, and after the smash hit of *This Gun for Hire*, she paired with Alan Ladd in three more films: *The Glass Key* (1942), *The Blue Dahlia* (1946) and *Saigon* (1948). They also had cameos in *Star Spangled Rhythm* (1942), *Duffy's Tavern* (1945) and *Variety Girl* (1947). She married four times (her second husband was director Andre de Toth, 1944–1952); replaced Jean Arthur on the road in the play *Peter Pan* (1951); and had an alcoholic downfall unique in its macabre awfulness. Although her ashes were supposedly spread along the coastline near Miami in 1976, the remains (or some of them) allegedly showed up in Homer and Langley's Mystery Spot antique shop in the Catskills in 2004, where the owner planned an "homage" with "Lake lookalikes."

Robert Preston (1918–1987), a Pasadena Playhouse alumnus, had come to prominence at Paramount in 1939 via Cecil B. DeMille's *Union Pacific* and William A. Wellman's *Beau Geste*. He was originally considered for the Raven role, but he had to wait until 1957 for his career to take off as he starred as Professor Harold Hill in Broadway's *The Music Man*, winning a Tony Award and reprising his role in the 1962 Warner Bros. film version. He won a second Tony in 1967 for *I Do! I Do!*, co-starring with Mary Martin, and was excellent as the aging homosexual in *Victor/Victoria* (1982), receiving a Best Supporting Actor nomination.

Tully Marshall (1864–1943) had a film career that dated back to 1914, with 195 credits and a specialty as evil geezers (example: von Stroheim's 1925 *The Merry Widow*, in which Marshall, as the lascivious Baron Sadoja, dropped dead from lust on his wedding night). Marshall showed up briefly in another Cregar film, *Ten Gentlemen from West Point* (1942); his final film *Hitler's Madman* played theaters several months after Marshall's death.

Director Frank Tuttle (1892–1963) had a career that went back to the early 1920s, most of it spent at Paramount. He was a "namer of names" in the Hollywood witch hunt, admitting to having been a Communist from 1937 to 1947, yet his career continued. When Alan Ladd formed Jaguar Productions, releasing through Warner Bros., he hired Tuttle to direct *Hell on Frisco Bay* (1955) and *A Cry in the Night* (1956).

John F. Seitz (1892–1979), the cinematographer, won seven Oscar nominations in his career. For Ladd's Jaguar Productions, he shot *Hell on Frisco Bay*, *A Cry in the Night* and *The Big Land* (1957).

Albert Maltz (1908–1985) wrote the Academy Award–winning short *The House I Live In* (1945), starring Frank Sinatra, and received Oscar nominations for *Pride of the Marines* (1945) and *Broken Arrow* (1950), for which Maltz, one of the blacklisted Hollywood Ten, used a "front," Michael Blankfort. W.R. (William Riley) Burnett (1899–1982) wrote the novel *Little Caesar* (on which the 1931 film was based), the continuity and dialogue for *Scarface* (1932), the novel and screenplay for *High Sierra* (1941) and the novel *The Asphalt Jungle* (on which the 1950 film is based). He was Oscar-nominated for his work on the screenplay of *Wake Island* (1942).

As *This Gun for Hire* was shooting, Paramount toyed with a new, very grim opening: a sequence entitled "The Dream," on script pages dated November 28, 1941 (just over a month after shooting had started). We were to see Raven stretched out on the bed, as he's introduced in the release version, and via a trucking shot, move into his "Dream World":

> Raven is walking towards us apprehensively through swirling mist. We come close to his face. A voice begins to whisper, "Your father was hanged. Your father was hanged."
> Raven's face dissolves into that of a boy of 14. The boy continues to walk. In a longer shot he approaches a forest of gibbets. He confronts finally a slowly swinging figure, hanging from one of the gibbets. He turns and runs away from it. He weaves away among the gibbets until he finally faces a swing noose which sways too. The Voice now says, "You'll be hanged. You'll be hanged." The boy breaks away and falls. The shadow of the gallows and the noose is upon him as he lies on the ground. He gets to his knees and the camera pans up. Approaching is the vague figure of a woman,

stately—dressed in a timeless garb which blows tight against her. The boy runs to her for protection and throws his arms around her knees. She kicks him away from her. He lands against a rock, his arms spread out. We come to the woman's face. She looks down at him with cold cruelty. From behind her back she produces a heavy object which she slowly raises. The boy recoils in terror. The sinister figure of the woman moves close and brings down the object toward his left arm. We see his wrist. The camera moves up as the object strikes the wrist off scene. The impact is registered by a spray of dust and a deafening crash of the music.

Through the mist Raven's face appears as he lies on the bed. His head jerks up in agony. The camera moves down and we see his right hand grasping his disfigured left wrist....

There was a censorship problem regarding Cregar's *This Gun for Hire* death scene. The Breen Office advised Paramount that Raven couldn't kill Gates for the motive of revenge; hence Laird's Gates starts babbling about Ellen having called the police to trap Raven, and Raven shoots him for what he perceives as a lie.

Paramount produced a remake of *This Gun for Hire* entitled *Short Cut to Hell* (1957), which was the one and only directorial credit of James Cagney. Robert Ivers played Ladd's role, Georgeann Johnson had Lake's, William Bishop had Preston's and Jacques Aubuchon had Cregar's. A 1991 TV movie starred Robert Wagner as Raven; a 1996 *This Gun for Hire* feature had little resemblance to the 1942 original.

Review: "Melodrama, straight and vicious ... that's what this picture is.... Mr. Cregar is a double portion of deceit and cowardice, edging his characterization with a touch of elegance" (Bosley Crowther, *New York Times*, May 14, 1942).

Rings on Her Fingers

Studio: 20th Century–Fox; *Producer:* Darryl F. Zanuck; *Producer:* Milton Sperling; *Director:* Rouben Mamoulian; *Screenplay:* Ken Englund (original story by Robert Pirosh and Joseph Schrank; adaptation by Emeric Pressburger); *Photographer:* George Barnes; *Art Directors:* Richard Day, Albert Hogsett; *Set Decorator:* Thomas Little; *Film Editor:* Barbara McLean; *Costume Designer:* Gwen Wakeling; *Makeup Artist:* Guy Pearce; *Sound:* Joseph E. Aiken, Roger Heman, Sr.; *Musical Director:* Cyril J. Mockridge (Alfred Newman, composer, stock music; Maurice de Packh, Edward B. Powell, Gene Rose, Conrad Salinger, Herbert W. Spencer, orchestra-

tors); *Assistant Director:* Gene Bryant; *Props:* Joe Behm; *Publicity Director:* Harry Brand; *Production Secretary:* Betty Curtis; *Running Time:* 86 minutes; *Negative Cost:* $651,000; *Shooting Dates:* December 3, 1941-January 23, 1942; *Opening Dates:* Roxy Theatre, New York City, April 23, 1942; Grauman's Chinese Theatre and Loew's State Theatre (on a double-bill with 20th Century–Fox's *Moontide*), May 28, 1942; *Worldwide Rentals:* $925,300; *Loss:* $14,100

Cast: Henry Fonda (John Wheeler), Gene Tierney (Susan Miller, aka Linda Worthington), Laird Cregar (Warren), John Shepperd [Shepperd Strudwick] (Tod Fenwick), Spring Byington (Mrs. Maybelle Worthington), Frank Orth (Kellogg), Henry Stephenson (Col. Prentiss), Marjorie Gateson (Mrs. Fenwick), George Lessey (Fenwick, Sr.), Iris Adrian (Peggy), Harry Hayden (Conductor), Gwendolyn Logan (Miss Callahan), Eric Wilton (Butler), Billy Benedict (Newsboy), Sarah Edwards (Mrs. Clancy), Thurston Hall (Mr. Beasley), Clara Blandick (Mrs. Beasley), Charles Wilson (Capt. Hurley), Edgar Norton (Paul the Butler), George Lloyd (Chick), Kathryn Sheldon (Landlady), Frank Sully (Driver), Mel Ruick (Roulette Dealer), Clive Morgan (Charles), Evelyn Mulhall (Mrs. Alderney), Sam Savitsky (Barney), James Adamson (Redcap), Ernie Alexander (Milkman), Herbert Ashely (Policeman), Gertrude Astor (Tall Woman Exiting Ladies Lounge), Hooper Atchley (Onlooker), Brooks Benedict (Craps Dealer), Frank Coghlan, Jr. (Page Boy), G. Pat Collins (Doorman), Mike Lally (Man at Airport), Wilbur Mack (Onlooker at Craps Table), Charles R. Moore (Porter), Russell Huestis, David Newell (Roulette Players), Wedgewood Nowell (Man in Queue), Tom O'Grady (Bystander), Constance Purdy (Party Giver), Edward Biby, James Carlisle, Art Howard, Fred Rapport (Casino Gamblers), Robert Ryan (Attendant), Chet Brandenburg, Phil Tead (Ticket Agents), Herb Vigran (Cab Driver), Poppy Wilde (Mannequin).

Synopsis: Susan Miller, from Brooklyn, sells girdles in a department store. A pair of high-class swindlers, Warren and Maybelle Worthington, discover Susan, dress her up, give her the new name "Linda Worthington" and set her loose as their latest man-bait to seduce and fleece wealthy victims.

At Catalina Island, Susan-Linda goes into action, baiting the hook for John Wheeler. Warren, posing as "Capt. Beasley," sells John a yacht for $15,000. It isn't Warren's yacht, of course, and as it turns out, John isn't rich ... he's a $65-a-week accountant. Warren's scam costs John his life savings.

Susan-Linda falls in love with John and they get engaged, despite Warren and Maybelle's machinations to marry her off to rich Tod Fenwick. True love prevails, Warren and

Maybelle are foiled, and John and Susan escape to California to get married.

Production Notes: As noted in the biography section, Henry Fonda (1905–1982) wasn't happy with many of his films at Fox and *Rings on Her Fingers* was likely one of them—especially as it was a carbon copy of *The Lady Eve*, which Fonda had just played at Paramount opposite Barbara Stanwyck. Much of Fonda's work at Fox was so good— *Jesse James* (1939), *Young Mr. Lincoln* (1939), *Drums Along the Mohawk* (1939), *The Grapes of Wrath* (1940), *The Ox-Bow Incident* (1943)— that it's surreal to see him in *Rings on Her Fingers*, acting goofy as he dances with Tierney, or performing a drunk scene. Among the ironies of Hollywood and indictments against the Oscars is that it took almost to the end of Henry Fonda's life for him to win Academy Awards: an honorary Oscar presented in 1981, and a Best Actor Oscar (for *On Golden Pond*) won in 1982, four months before his August 12, 1982, death.

Spring Byington (1886–1971) received a Best Supporting Actress Academy nomination for Frank Capra's *You Can't Take It with You* (Columbia, 1938) and starred as Lily Ruskin on TV's *December Bride* (1954–1959).

John Shepperd (aka Shepperd Strudwick, 1907–1983) was under contract to Fox and played the title role in the studio's 1942 *The Loves of Edgar Allan Poe.*

Rouben Mamoulian went on to direct Broadway's *Oklahoma!*, the Rodgers and Hammerstein milestone musical that opened March 31, 1943, and ran 2,212 performances. Among the other Broadway shows he directed were Rodgers and Hammerstein's *Carousel*, which opened April 19, 1945, and ran 890 performances. After *Rings on Her Fingers*, and his firing from *Laura* (documented in the text), Mamoulian directed only three films: *The Wild Heart* (1952) and the MGM musicals *Summer Holiday* (1948) and *Silk Stockings* (1957). He was fired from *Porgy and Bess* (1959), replaced (as he'd been on *Laura*) by Otto Preminger; he was also fired from *Cleopatra* (1963), replaced by Joseph L. Mankiewicz. Mamoulian received the Directors Guild Award in 1982 and, at the end of his life, lived in his palatial Beverly Hills mansion, overrun by cats. However, come his death December 4, 1987, he was at the Mo-

tion Picture Home. Mamoulian is buried in the Ascension Garden at Forest Lawn, Glendale.

A bizarre moment in *Rings on Her Fingers*: Henry Stephenson, as Col. Prentiss, who manages Warren's crooked gambling club, greets Laird with the words, "The old walrus himself!" Stephenson was 70 years old—42 years older than Laird!

Review: "Cregar continues to uphold his demonstrated talents as a cunning heavy." (*Variety*, March 11, 1942)

Ten Gentlemen from West Point

Studio: 20th Century–Fox; *Producer:* Darryl F. Zanuck; *Producer:* William Perlberg; *Director:* Henry Hathaway; *Screenplay:* Richard Maibaum (suggested by a story by Malvin Wald; additional dialogue by George Seaton ([Ben Hecht, Talbot Jennings, and Darryl F. Zanuck, uncredited]); *Music and Musical Director:* Alfred Newman (David Buttolph, Cyril J. Mockridge, uncredited; Maurice De Packh, Edward B. Powell, Conrad Salinger, orchestrators); *Photographer:* Leon Shamroy; *Art Directors:* Richard Day, Nathan Juran; *Set Decorator:* Thomas Little; *Film Editor:* James B. Clark; *Costume Designer:* Dolly Tree; *Makeup Artist:* Guy Pearce; *Sound:* E. Clayton Ward, Roger Heman, Sr.; *Special Effects:* Louis J. Witte; *Wardrobe:* Sam Benson; *Second Unit Director:* Robert E. Webb; *Running Time:* 103 minutes; *Shooting Dates:* January 12-March 18, 1942; *Negative Cost:* $1,174,500; *Opening:* Roxy Theatre, New York City, June 4, 1942; Grauman's Chinese Theatre, Los Angeles, June 25, 1942; *Worldwide Rentals:* $1,684,800; *Loss:* $89,000

Cast: George Montgomery (Joe Dawson), Maureen O'Hara (Carolyn Bainbridge), John Sutton (Howard Shelton), Laird Cregar (Major Sam Carter), John Shepperd [Shepperd Strudwick] (Henry Clay), Victor Francen (Florimond Massey), Harry Davenport (Bane), Ward Bond (Scully), Douglass Dumbrille (Gen. William Henry Harrison), Ralph Byrd (Maloney), Joe Brown, Jr. (Benny Havens), David Bacon (Shippen), Esther Dale (Mrs. Thompson), Richard Derr (Chester), Louis Jean Heydt (Jared Danforth), Stanley Andrews (Capt. Sloane), James Flavin (Capt. Luddy), Edna Mae Jones (Letty), Charles Trowbridge (Senate President), Tully Marshall (Grandpa), Edwin Maxwell (Senator John Randolph), Uno the Mule (Old Put), Edward Fielding (William Eustis), Morris Ankrum (Wood), Selmer Jackson (Sersen), Noble Johnson (Tecumseh), Eddie Dunn (O'Toole), Frank Ferguson (Alden Brown), James Seay (Courtney), Jesse Graves (Sam), Chick Collins (Lacrosse Player), Iron Eyes Cody (Indian), Warren Ashe (Orderly), Lane Bradford (Recruit), Olin Howland, Harry Tyler (Carpenters), Payne B. Johnson (Boy in Fort), Eddy

Chandler, Edward Gargan, John Kelly (Bombardiers), Davison Clark, John Dilson, Boyd Irwin, Henry Roquemore, Paul Scardon, Frank Shannon, Carol Stockdale, Harry Stubbs (Senators), Max Cole, Blake Edwards, Eugene Gericke, John Hartley, Dick Hogan, George Holmes, William Kersen, Anthony Marsh, Malcolm "Bud" McTaggart, John Meredith, Tom Neal, Stanley Parlan, Herbert Paterson, Don Peters, Gene Rizzi, John Whitney, Dick Winslow, Gordon Wynn (Cadets), Bess Flowers (Graduation Ceremony Guest), Cap Somers, Ruth Clifford (Graduation Spectators).

Synopsis: Major Sam Carter becomes commander of the politically controversial West Point. A seasoned officer, he hopes to break the young cadets and destroy the school's credibility. Among his cadets are Kentucky frontiersman Joe Dawson and the aristocratic Howard Shelton. Living near West Point, and preparing food for the boys: Carolyn Bainbridge, whose late father had been a champion of the West Point cause. Carolyn is also Howard's fiancée.

When Caroline sends an anonymous letter to Washington, denouncing Carter's brutal tactics, Carter, suspecting one of the cadets is responsible, sadistically punishes the men by ordering them to "ride the cannon," a torture in which two men straddle a cannon barrel while mounted horses drag it over the hills. Ten of the men, realizing Carter's plan to ruin West Point, tolerate the ordeal. Meanwhile, Carolyn is falling in love with Joe.

At news of an Indian outbreak, led by Tecumseh, Carter, his army and cadets report to Fort Harrison in Indiana Territory. The Indians capture Carter and Joe. Howard and the cadets, greatly outnumbered, decide to fight *à la* the Battle of Tours, in which the French had defeated the Saracens by making them think they're surrounded, and "demoralizing" them. The men had learned about this battle in the classroom from teacher Florimond Massey. The cadets and soldiers use trees to catapult flaming leaves into the Indian camp, shouting and whooping, tricking the Indians and achieving victory. Joe rescues Carter, but as they escape, an Indian arrow strikes Joe in the thigh. He survives with a permanently damaged leg. Another cadet, Shippen, dies from wounds in the war, hoping his heroism has redeemed the family from the treachery of his uncle, Benedict Arnold.

Back at Fort Harrison, Carter, now respect-

ing the cadets, offers Joe a commission as an officer. Joe, however, believes the graduating class should be "perfect" and resigns. Caroline arrives and, professing her love, heads back to Kentucky with Joe. Howard and the other seven surviving cadets head back to West Point, where Major Carter proudly presents them their diplomas.

Production Notes: *Ten Gentlemen from West Point* had more than its share of cast changes. According to the American Film Institute notes, the film, originally announced for Tyrone Power, shaped up by the late summer of 1941 with Henry Fonda set as Joe (ultimately played by George Montgomery), John Payne as Howard (played by John Sutton) and Randolph Scott as Major Sam Carter (played by Laird Cregar). Come November, Victor Mature was listed for one of the star roles. Sara Allgood was cast as Mrs. Thompson, then replaced by Esther Dale. Additionally, Fox toyed with the titles *Salute to Heroes* and *School for Soldiers*, and even the location site changed: Plans to shoot in Monterey shifted to Sherwood Forest. The studio kept the set standing for use in *The Loves of Edgar Allan Poe* (1942), starring Shepperd Strudwick (aka John Shepperd, who appeared briefly in *Ten Gentlemen from West Point* as Henry Clay).

George Montgomery (1916–2000), the youngest of 15 children born of Ukrainian immigrants, had been a University of Montana boxing champion (he boxes in *Ten Gentlemen from West Point* with John Sutton, who's beating him soundly via British-style boxing until Montgomery kicks him in the face!). He entered films as a stuntman and made his mark mainly in westerns. He was married to Dinah Shore from 1943 until their divorce in 1963 (two children) and later achieved note as a sculptor, including a bronze bust of his friend Ronald Reagan.

Maureen O'Hara (1920–2015), born Maureen FitzSimons in Ireland, had arrived in Hollywood as Charles Laughton's discovery to star as Esmeralda to his Quasimodo in *The Hunchback of Notre Dame* (RKO, 1939). The actress was now under contract to 20th Century–Fox and had scored as Angharad in John Ford's *How Green Was My Valley*, which won the Oscar as Best Film of 1941 while *Ten Gentlemen from West Point* was shooting.

Among the character actors in the film: Ward Bond (1903–1960), a member of John Ford's stock company and the future star of TV's *Wagon Train* (as well as the man who'd move into Laird's house after his death), as Scully, a lovable buffoon of a sergeant whose big scene was being kicked by a mule in a soldiers-vs.-cadets lacrosse game; Douglass Dumbrille (1889–1974), ace movie villain, in a one-scene appearance as future president Gen. William Henry Harrison; and Noble Johnson (1881–1978), a black actor perhaps best-remembered as the Native Chief in *King Kong*, as Tecumseh.

Henry Hathaway (1898–1985), notorious for his tempestuous style ("To be a good director you've got to be a bastard. I'm a bastard and I know it"), directed such films as *The Lives of a Bengal Lancer* (Paramount, 1935, Best Director Oscar nomination). Among his others: *Brigham Young* (Fox, 1940), *Kiss of Death* (Fox, 1947) and *True Grit* (Paramount, 1969).

Leon Shamroy (1901–1974) received an Academy nomination for Best Black-and-White Cinematography for *Ten Gentlemen from West Point*; he lost to Joseph Ruttenberg for MGM's *Mrs. Miniver*. Shamroy did win the Best Color Cinematography Oscar that year for Fox's *The Black Swan*, which also featured Cregar. Shamroy also won Oscars for *Wilson* (1944), *Leave Her to Heaven* (1945) and *Cleopatra* (1963), and tallied a total of 15 nominations.

Finally, as for Laird's pal Tom Neal, who appeared in *Ten Gentlemen from West Point* as a nameless cadet: He was soon to win attention as the Japanese hero of *Behind the Rising Sun* (RKO, 1943) and, most notably, as Al Roberts, the hapless *noir* anti-hero of Edgar G. Ulmer's *Detour* (PRC, 1945). Neal's scenes with psycho Ann Savage still give chills today, and his killing her—accidentally, with a yanked telephone cord—inevitably conjures up the real-life *noir* elements to come in Neal's own life.

In 1944, Neal wed brunette actress Vicky Lane (Paula the Ape Woman in Universal's *The Jungle Captive*, 1945). They divorced in 1950, and Neal soon achieved his first claim to fame in Hollywood Babylon circles: The time was 2:00 a.m., the date September 14, 1951, the locale the walled courtyard of 1803 Courtney Terrace in Hollywood, outside the apartment of "notorious" blonde actress Barbara Payton. The lady was allegedly engaged to both Neal *and* actor Franchot Tone, and the 37-year-old Neal (a former boxing champ who'd tallied 41 knockouts at Northwestern and Harvard) proceeded to give 46-year-old Tone a broken nose, a smashed cheekbone and a concussion. Payton and Tone (his face never fully recovering) wed two weeks later (they divorced the following year).

Neal's acting career consequently dwindled and he moved to Palm Springs, working as a gardener and landscaper. His aforementioned 1965 killing of his third wife resulted in a conviction (involuntary manslaughter) and he served six years. Neal died at his apartment at 12020 Hoffman Street in Studio City, California, on the morning of August 7, 1972. Cause of death: heart failure. He was 58. "Women in my life brought me nothing but unhappiness," bemoaned Tom Neal late in life.

Ten Gentlemen from West Point, perhaps due to its lack of major male stars, lost $89,000.

Review: "Laird Cregar, as the commandant, all but 'steals' the show." (*The Washington Post*, July 17, 1942)

The Black Swan

Studio: 20th Century–Fox; *Executive Producer:* Darryl F. Zanuck; *Producer:* Robert Bassler; *Director:* Henry King; *Screenplay:* Ben Hecht and Seton I. Miller (adapted by Seton I. Miller, based on the novel by Rafael Sabatini); *Photographer:* Leon Shamroy; *Technicolor Director:* Natalie Kalmus; *Associate Technicolor Director:* Henri Jaffa; *Music:* Alfred Newman; *Art Directors:* Richard Day, James Basevi; *Set Decorator:* Thomas Little; *Film Editor:* Barbara McLean; *Costume Designer:* Earl Luick; *Makeup Artist:* Guy Pearce; *Sound:* George Leverett, Roger Heman, Sr.; *Production Manager:* William Koenig; *Special Photographic Effects:* Fred Sersen; *Wardrobe:* Sam Benson; *Assistant Directors:* Albert R. Broccoli, Henry Weinberger; *Location Director:* Robert D. Webb; *Location Photographers:* John Hamilton, Ray Rennahan, Irving Rosenberg, Al Thayer, Paul Uhl; Assistant Camera, Technicolor, Cliff Shirpster; *Fencing Instructor:* Fred Cavens; *Dialogue Director:* Lionel Bevans; *Production Assistant:* William Gallagher; *Location Manager:* Ray C. Moore; *Technical Advisors:* Harold Godsoe, Harold Lloyd Morris; *Running Time:* 84 minutes; *Negative Cost:* $1,493,800; *Shooting Dates:* April 20–July 22, 1942; *Openings:* Grauman's Chinese Theatre and Loew's State Theatre, November 12, 1942; Roxy Theatre, New York City, December 23, 1942; *Wordwide rentals:* $5,727,000; *Profit:* $2,366,300

Cast: Tyrone Power (Jamie Waring), Maureen O'Hara (Lady Margaret Denby), Laird Cregar (Capt. Henry Morgan), Thomas Mitchell (Tommy Blue), George Sanders (Capt. Billy Leech), Anthony Quinn (Wogan), George Zucco (Lord Denby), Edward Ashley (Roger Ingram), Fortunio Bonanova (Don Miguel), John Burton (Capt. Blane), William Edmunds (Town Crier), Charles Francis (Capt. Higgs), Olaf Hytten (Clerk Reading Proclamation), Cyril McLaglen (Capt. Jones), Charles McNaughton (Mr. Fenner), Clarence Muse (Margaret's Servant), Stuart Robertson (Capt. Graham), Rita Christiani (Dancer), Arthur Shields (The Bishop), Frederick Worlock (Speaker of Assembly), Willie Fung (Chinese Cook), Jody Gilbert (Flossy Lady with Tommy), Keith Hitchcock (Majordomo), Charles Irwin, Frank Leigh, David Thursby (Sea Captains), Arthur Gould-Porter, Boyd Irwin, George Kirby, C. Montague Shaw (Assemblymen), Bonnie Bannon (Lady Waiting in the Courtroom), Helene Costello, Bryn Davis (Women).

Synopsis: Jamie Waring, swashbuckler, is bare-chested and stretched on a rack in a dungeon in Jamaica when pirate king Capt. Henry Morgan arrives in the nick of time, saving "Jamie Boy" (as Morgan calls him) from being split in two. Morgan brings thunderous news: The Crown has given Morgan a king's pardon, appointing him new governor of Jamaica, with the challenge of ridding the sea of the scourge of pirates. "Jamie Boy" is Morgan's choice as his top fighter.

Two firestorms erupt: (a) Jamie romances fiery, red-haired Lady Margaret Denby; and (b) Jamie battles red-bearded Capt. Billy Leech, whom he refers to as "a jabbering ape fit only for the company of baboons." Jamie's boozy second-in-command Tommy Blue stays more or less drunk, Leech's one-eyed second-in-command Wogan leers a lot, and Lady Margaret's father, Lord Denby, engages in political intrigue against Morgan.

Come the climax, an epic battle wages at sea. Jamie drives a sword right through Leech (who lunges away with the sword jutting through him), Lady Margaret (dressed as a pirate wench) bites Jamie and throws herself at him ... and Capt. Morgan decides to forsake being a bewigged governor and return to the joys of piracy.

Production Notes: *The Black Swan*'s climactic swordfight between Tyrone Power and George Sanders grimly prophesied a real-life tragedy. On November 15, 1958, Power, Sanders and Gina Lollobrigida were on location in Spain, starring in *Solomon and Sheba*. The set was cold (puddles on the set were turning to ice), Lollobrigida was raising hell over the discomfort, and 44-year-old Power and 52-year-old Sanders (the latter, as before, extensively doubled) waged a swordfight. Power felt ill, went to his dressing room, was eventually put in Lollobrigida's Mercedes to be rushed to the hospital, and died three minutes into the trip. Cause of death: a massive heart attack. He left a widow, Debbie (carrying his baby son, Tyrone, who was born January 22, 1959). Sanders, deeply affected, gave a tribute at the Air Base in Spain: "I shall always remember Tyrone Power as a bountiful man ... a man who gave more of himself than it was wise for him to give. Until in the end, he gave his life."

Power is buried at Hollywood Forever Cemetery. *Solomon and Sheba* was reshot with Yul Brynner in Power's role. Sanders received his $65,000 salary twice.

Maureen O'Hara is truly gorgeous as Lady Margaret, deservingly winning the soubriquet "The Queen of Technicolor," "The Pirate Queen" and "Big Red" as she starred in such yarns as *The Spanish Main* (1945) and *Against All Flags* (1952). She also was the leading lady of *Miracle on 34th Street* (1947), and was a John Ford favorite in such classics as *The Quiet Man* (1952). Married three times (the first annulled, the second divorced, the third widowed when aviator husband Charles Blair died in a 1978 plane crash), and with one daughter by her second marriage, O'Hara received a special Lifetime Achievement Oscar on November 4, 2014, at the Academy's annual Motion Picture Arts and Sciences Governors' Awards. She died October 24, 2015, at the age of 95.

Thomas Mitchell, in his second of two 1942 releases with Cregar, gets his big scene in *The Black Swan* when he tries to take a wench into a bedroom. Mitchell eventually became the first "Triple Crown" award-winning actor: In addition to his Academy Award, he won a Tony for the Broadway musical *Hazel Flagg* (1953) and an Emmy for Best Television Actor of 1953. Among his other films: *It's a Wonderful Life* (1946), *High Noon* (1952) and his last, *Pocketful of Miracles* (1961). Mitchell died December 17, 1962, at the age of 70. As with Edmund Gwenn, it's odd that the ashes of Mitchell, one of Golden Age Hollywood's greatest character actors, are unclaimed and in vaultage at the Chapel of the Pines, Los Angeles.

George Sanders, at the time of *The Black Swan*, was one of Fox's most recalcitrant stars and most black-hearted villains (e.g., 1941's *Man Hunt*, as the Nazi with monocle who pursues Walter Pidgeon); he also had been appearing as RKO's "The Falcon." As Capt. Billy Leech, in his red wig and red beard, Sanders appears to be having a ball, especially in the scene where he creeps into the cabin Power and O'Hara are sharing, bringing the lady a nightgown he'd pilfered somewhere, lewdly telling Power that after all, they've always "shared" everything—and squeezing O'Hara's thigh through the bedsheet! Sanders would co-star with Cregar in the latter's final two films, *The Lodger* and *Hangover Square*.

Anthony Quinn, as Leech's one-eyed second-in-command, has little to do, but does enjoy one of the film's most suggestive lines: After Power and O'Hara go to their cabin, Quinn leers, "He's got some articles in his cabin what need signin'!" Quinn went on to win Best Supporting Actor Oscars for *Viva Zapata!* (1952) and *Lust for Life* (1956); he also received Best Actor nominations for *Wild Is the Wind* (1957) and *Zorba the Greek* (1964). He wed three times and fathered 12 children, the last born July 5, 1996, when Quinn was 81. He died on June 3, 2001, in Boston, at the age of 86.

George Zucco, as Lord Denby, Lady Margaret's pirate-loathing father, enjoys an impressive role here, at a time he was finding himself increasingly a horror attraction. In fact, he followed *The Black Swan* at Fox in *Dr. Renault's Secret*, as a mad doctor who transforms a gorilla into ape man J. Carrol Naish. Zucco had scored on the London stage in *Journey's End* (1929), directed by James Whale and co-starring with Colin Clive. It was odd that Whale (who'd direct Universal's *Frankenstein*, *The Old Dark House*, *The Invisible Man* and *Bride of Frankenstein*), Clive (who played Henry Frankenstein in *Franken-*

stein and *Bride of Frankenstein*) and Zucco all won notoriety in Hollywood horror. Zucco would appear with Cregar the following year in *Holy Matrimony*.

Henry King (1886–1982) was 20th Century–Fox's top director: *In Old Chicago*, *Alexander's Ragtime Band*, *Jesse James* and *A Yank in the R.A.F.* were all King films. He received Oscar nominations for *The Song of Bernadette* (1943) and *Wilson* (1944), won a Golden Globe for *Bernadette* and received the 1956 Directors Guild Lifetime Achievement Award. "I've had more fun directing pictures than most people have playing games," said King.

Leon Shamroy (1901–1974) won the Best Color Cinematography Oscar for *The Black Swan*. He'd also win Oscars for *Wilson* (1944), *Leave Her to Heaven* (1945) and *Cleopatra* (1963). Among his other films: *Forever Amber* (1947), *The Robe* (1953), *The King and I* (1956), *Snow White and the Three Stooges* (1961) and *Planet of the Apes* (1968).

Fred Cavens (1882–1962) was Hollywood's legendary fencing master, staging the swordplay for *The Mark of Zorro* (1920), *Captain Blood* (1935), *Romeo and Juliet* (1936), *The Adventures of Robin Hood* (1938), *Tower of London* (1939), *The Mark of Zorro* (1940), *The Spanish Main* (1945), *Forever Amber* (1947), *Against All Flags* (1952) and many more. His final work was on the Walt Disney *Zorro* series (1957–1959) and the *Walt Disney's Wonderful World of Color* episode "Zorro: The Postponed Wedding" (1961).

An assistant director on *The Black Swan*, Albert "Cubby" Broccoli (1909–1996) went on to co-produce the spectacularly successful James Bond films.

Review: "It is performed by actors as if to the hokum born.... Laird Cregar, as Morgan, bellows oaths like an irate opera singer...." (*New York Times*, December 24, 1942)

Hello Frisco, Hello

Studio: 20th Century–Fox; *Executive Producer:* William Goetz; *Producer:* Milton Sperling; *Director:* H. Bruce Humberstone; *Screenplay:* Robert Ellis, Helen Logan, and Richard Macaulay (based on a story by Vina Delmar, uncredited); *Lyrics and Music:* "You'll Never Know": Mack Gordon and Harry Warren; *Dance Stager:* Val Raset; *Costume Designer for Musical Sequences:* Helen Rose; *Supervisor of Musical Sequences:* Fanchon; *Photographers:*

Charles Clarke, Allen Davey; *Technicolor Director:* Natalie Kalmus; *Technicolor Associate:* Henri Jaffa; *Art Directors:* James Basevi, Boris Leven; *Set Decorators:* Thomas Little, Paul S. Fox; *Film Editor:* Barbara McLean; *Makeup Artist:* Guy Pearce; *Special Photographic Effects:* Fred Sersen; *Musical Directors:* Charles Henderson, Emil Newman; *Sound:* Joseph E. Aiken, Roger Heman, Sr.; *Wardrobe:* Sam Benson; *Wardrobe Assistant:* Ollie Hughes; *Music Department:* David Buttolph, Charles Henderson, Cyril J. Mockridge, Alfred Newman, composers; Arthur Morton, Walter Scharf, Herbert W. Spencer, orchestrators; *Songs:* "The Streets of Cairo" (aka "The Hootchy-Kootchy Dance"); "Hello, Frisco!" (music by Louis A. Hirsch, lyrics by Gene Buck); "San Francisco" (music by Bronislau Kaper and Walter Jurmann, lyrics by Gus Kahn); "For He's a Jolly Good Fellow" (uncredited, traditional); "Yip-I–Addy-I-A" (music by John H. Flynn, lyrics by Will D. Cobb); "On San Francisco Bay" (music by Gertrude Hoffman, lyrics by Vincent Bryan); "A Bird in a Gilded Cage" (music by Harry Von Tilzer, lyrics by Arthur J. Lamb); "Hello! Ma Baby" (music by Joseph E. Howard, lyrics by Ida Emerson); "By the Watermelon Vine" ("Lindy Lou," by Thomas S. Allen); "Yield Not to Temptation" (music by Horatio R. Palmer); "Little Brown Jug" (music by Joseph Winner); "Ragtime Cowboy Joe" (music by Maurice Abrahams and Lewis F. Muir, lyrics by Grant Clarke); "Sweet Cider Time, When You Were Mine" (music by Percy Wenrich, lyrics by Joseph McCarthy); "The Dance of the Grizzly Bear" (music by George Botsford, lyrics by Irving Berlin); "King Chanticleer" (music by Nay Ayer); "In the Shade of the Old Apple Tree" (music by Egbert Van Alstyne, lyrics by Harry Williams); "Viennese Blood ("Wiener Blut," Op. 354, music by Johann Strauss); "The Emperor Waltz" ("Kaiserwalzer," Op. 437, music by Johann Strauss); "In My Merry Oldsmobile" (music by Gus Edwards); "The Band Played On" (music by Chas. B. Ward); "Sobre las olas" ("Over the Waves," music by Juventino Rosas); "It's Tulip Time in Holland" (music by Richard A. Whiting, lyrics by Dave Radford); "When You Wore a Tulip (and I Wore a Big Red Rose)" (music by Percy Wenrich); "They Always Pick on Me" (music by Harry Von Tilzer, lyrics by Stanley Murphy); "The Sidewalks of New York" (music by Charles Lawlor); "Bedelia" (music by Jean Schwartz, lyrics by William Jerome); "Has Anybody Here Seen Kelly?" (music by C.W. Murphy, lyrics by Will Letters); "By the Light of the Silvery Moon" (music by Gus Edwards, lyrics by Edward Madden); "Gee, But It's Great to Meet a Friend from Your Home Town" (music by James McGavisk, lyrics by William Tracey); "Aloha Oe" (music by Queen Liliuokalani), "Strike Up the Band" ("Here Comes a Sailor," music by Chas. B. Ward, lyrics by Andrew B. Sterling); "I've Got a Gal in Every Port" (music by Charles Henderson, lyrics by Mack Gordon); "The Sailor's Hornpipe"; *Choreographer:* Hermes Pan; *Assistant Directors:* Charles Hall, Aaron Rosenberg; *Technical Advisor:* Sid Grauman; *Director of Publicity:* Harry Brand; *Shooting Dates:* November 2, 1942-February 1, 1943; *Running Time:* 98 minutes; *Negative Cost:* $1,667,200; *Opening:* Grauman's Chinese Theatre, Loew's State Theatre, and the Ritz Theatre, Los Angeles, March 18, 1943; *Worldwide Rentals:* $4,370,500; *Profit:* $1,233,200

Cast: Alice Faye (Trudy Evans), John Payne (Johnny Cornell), Jack Oakie (Dan Daley), Lynn Bari (Bernice Croft), Laird Cregar (Sam Weaver), June Havoc (Beulah Clancy), Ward Bond (Sharkey), Aubrey Mather (Douglas Dawson), George Barbier (Col. Weatherby), John Archer (Ned Clark), Frank Orth (Lou—Bartender at Sharkey's), George Lloyd (Foghorn Ryan—Proprietor), Frank Darien (Missionary), Harry Hayden (Burkham), Eddie Dunn (Foreman of Renovation Crew), Charles Cane (O'Riley—Policeman), Frank M. Thomas (Auctioneer), Kirby Grant (Specialty Singer), Mary Field (Ellie—Cockney Maid), Ted North (Dick Greenwood), Ken Christy (Paul—Headwaiter), Edward Clark (Sam—Stage Doorman), Esther Dale (Aunt Harriet), Edward Mundy (Preacher), James Flavin (Headwaiter), Marie Brown, James Sills (Roller Skating Specialty), Fortunio Bonanova, Gino Corrado, Adia Kuznetzoff (Opera Singers), Kit Guard (Customer at Sharkey's), Theodore Lorch (Barfly at Sharkey's), Fred Brown, Larry Valli (Barkers), Jackie Averill, Jimmy Clemmons, Jr. (Child Dancers), John Sinclair, Jack Stoney (Drunks), Ralph Dunn (Waiter), Edward Earle (Opera House Stage Manager), Lorraine Elliott, Ruth Gillette (Singers), Bud Jamison (Barbershop Quartet Member), Adele Jergens (Chorine), Eric Mayne (Party Guest), Jeffrey Sayre (Chorus Boy in "Grizzly Bear" Number)

Synopsis: The Barbary Coast. The singing-dancing quartet of Johnny Cornell, Trudy Evans, Dan Daley and Beulah Clancy gets fired one night at Sharkey's Colosseum when the act attracts too many customers away from the bar. Johnny, ambitious, goes on to own and manage the "Grizzly Bear," plus other honky-tonks and a roller drome, all the while oblivious that Trudy is in love with him. Instead, he marries a vamp socialite, Bernice Croft, who has lost her Nob Hill fortune and sees Johnny as the answer to her money woes.

As cold-hearted Bernice fleeces Johnny, Trudy becomes a great star in London, coming home in glory to San Francisco. Meanwhile, Sam Weaver, a bellowing prospector, finds the fallen Johnny at a Midway on the beach, a barker for hula dancers. Sam throws gold watches, claiming he's finally struck it rich, and pays Johnny, who has consistently grubstaked him, his share of the fortune.

However, it's all a scam: Sam is *pretending*

he struck it rich, while Trudy and Dan are actually providing Trudy's money so Johnny can rebuild his life. Johnny, realizing the truth, throws Sam out of the Grizzly Bear, joins Trudy on stage, and they duet "You'll Never Know" before the fade-out Technicolor kiss.

Production Notes: Alice Faye (Alice Jean Leppert, 1915–1998) was one of the talismans of 20th Century–Fox, starring in the studio's 1938 mega-hits *In Old Chicago* and *Alexander's Ragtime Band*. However, she walked out after Darryl Zanuck disastrously cut her dramatic role in *Fallen Angel* (1945). She'd been married to Tony Martin (1937–1941); in 1941, she'd married radio star–bandleader Phil Harris; they had two daughters. Faye came back in Fox's *State Fair* (1962) and thereafter worked sporadically, including a tour and very brief Broadway run (16 performances) in the musical *Good News* (1974). Faye's memories of her Fox years were basically happy: "We had so much fun together; we were just like a bunch of kids. We *were* kids!"

John Payne (1912–1989) made his mark at Fox in such films as *Springtime in the Rockies* (1942) with Betty Grable and—his personal favorite—*Miracle on 34th Street* (1947) with Maureen O'Hara. He later starred on the TV western *The Restless Gun* (1957–1959), and come 1974, toured with Alice Faye in *Good News*, but due to lingering physical problems dating to a 1961 accident, when he was hit by a car, didn't star with her in the ill-fated Broadway run. Payne was married three times, and his first two spouses were actresses: Anne Shirley and Gloria De Haven.

Jack Oakie (Lewis Delaney Offield, 1903–1978) managed a long career as a second banana despite the fact he was basically deaf, relying on reading lips and sensing vibrations. His best-remembered role: "Napaloni," a parody on Mussolini, in Charlie Chaplin's *The Great Dictator* (1940), for which Oakie received a Best Supporting Actor Oscar nomination.

Lynn Bari (Margaret Schuyler Fisher, 1913–1989) had a long sojourn at Fox, often as a villainess (she'd played Tyrone Power's selfish sister in *Blood and Sand*) or vamp, eventually winning the nickname "The Woo Woo Girl." She wed and divorced three times. Husband number two, Sid Luft, later wed Judy Garland.

June Havoc (Ellen Evangeline Hovick, 1912–2010) was "Baby June," sister of Gypsy Rose Lee—and so unhappy with the 1957 memoir *Gypsy* and the 1959 Broadway musical of the same name that she never spoke again to her sister until Gypsy was terminally ill with cancer in 1970. A Laird Cregar connection: When Billy Rose was trying to book Broadway's Alvin Theatre for *Henry VIII*, to star Cregar, Havoc opened at the Alvin November 16, 1944, in the title role of the musical *Sadie Thompson*, based, of course, on the saga *Rain*, music by Vernon Duke, lyrics by Howard Deitz, and directed by Rouben Mamoulian. It ran 60 performances.

A "by-the-way" for the horror fans: Appearing briefly as an opera ham is Adia Kuznetzoff, who, only a very short time before *Hello Frisco, Hello* began shooting, played the Festival Singer in Universal's *Frankenstein Meets the Wolf Man* (1943), singing the rousing "Faro-La, Faro-Li" song.

Hello Frisco, Hello won an Academy Award for Best Song, "You'll Never Know" (music by Harry Warren, lyrics by Mack Gordon), and an Academy nomination for Best Color Cinematography (Charles Clarke, Allen Davey).

Lux Radio Theatre presented a version of "Hello Frisco, Hello" on November 15, 1943. Alice Faye reprised her role of Trudy, Robert Young played Johnny, Eddie Marr was Dan, Bea Benaderet was Bernice, Truda Marson was Beulah, and Leo Cleary played Cregar's role of Sam.

Review: "Sets were opulent, costumes stunningly vivid in their Technicolored hues, and there was music everywhere." (W. Franklin Moshier, *The Alice Faye Movie Book*)

Heaven Can Wait

Studio: 20th Century–Fox; *Producer-Director:* Ernst Lubitsch; *Screenplay:* Samson Raphaelson (based on the play by Lazlo Bus-Fekete); *Photographer:* Edward Cronjager; *Technicolor Director:* Natalie Kalmus; *Music:* Alfred Newman (and Cyril J. Mockridge, uncredited); *Art Directors:* James Basevi, Leland Fuller; *Set Decorator:* Thomas Little; *Associate Set Decorator:* Walter M. Scott; *Film Editor:* Dorothy Spencer; *Costumes:* René Hubert; *Special Photographic Effects:* Fred Sersen; *Makeup Artist:* Guy Pearce; *Sound:* Eugene Grossman, Roger Heman, Sr.; *Wardrobe Supervisor:* Sam Benson; *Music Department:* Hugo Friedhofer, music supervisor; Edward B. Powell, orchestrator; *Apprentice Editor:*

Lyman Hallowell; *Diction Instructor:* Georges Jomier; *Shooting Dates:* February 1, 1943–April 10, 1943; *Negative Cost:* $1,115,400; *Running Time:* 112 minutes; *Opening:* Roxy Theatre, New York City, August 11, 1943; Grauman's Chinese Theatre, Loew's State Theatre, Ritz Theatre and Carthay Circle Theatre, Los Angeles, August 5, 1943; *Worldwide Rentals:* $3,963,600; *Profit:* $1,286,200

Cast: Gene Tierney (Martha Strable Van Cleve), Don Ameche (Henry Van Cleve), Charles Coburn (Hugo Van Cleve), Marjorie Main (Mrs. Strable), Laird Cregar (His Excellency), Spring Byington (Bertha Van Cleve), Allyn Joslyn (Albert Van Cleve), Eugene Pallette (E.F. Strable), Signe Hasso (Mademoiselle), Louis Calhern (Randolph Van Cleve), Helene Reynolds (Peggy Nash), Aubrey Mather (James), Michael Ames [Tod Andrews] (Jack Van Cleve), Florence Bates (Mrs. Edna Craig), Clara Blandick (Grandmother Van Cleve), Trudy Marshall (Jane Van Cleve—Jack's Wife), Clarence Muse (Jasper—Butler), Claire Du Brey (Miss Ralston—Jack's Secretary), Alfred Hall (Albert's Father), Grayce Hampton (Alfred's Mother), Scotty Beckett (Henry Van Cleve, age 9), Dickie Jones (Albert Van Cleve, age 15), Marlene Mains (Mary, age 9), Nino Pipotone, Jr. (Jack Van Cleve, as a Child), Michael McLean (Henry Van Cleve, as a Baby), Edwin Maxwell (Doctor), Leonard Carey (Flogdell—Van Cleve's First Butler), Gerald Oliver Smith (Smith—Van Cleve's Second Butler), Anita Sharp-Bolster (Mrs. Cooper-Cooper), Dane Clark (Elevator Operator), Jack Deery, Bess Flowers, Bert Moorhouse, Monty O'Grady (Party Guests), Jay Eaton (Book Store Clerk), James Flavin (Policeman), Anne O'Neal (Day Nurse), Maureen Roden-Ryan (Nurse in Park), Gary Gray (Boy in Park), James Conaty (Man in Park with Top Hat).

Synopsis: Henry Van Cleve, born October 25, 1872, dies at age 70. A roué, believing himself undeserving of Heaven, he visits the grand entranceway to Hell, where he tells his life story to His Excellency, aka Satan. Among the racy memories offered is how, at age 15, he got drunk with a flirtatious French maid called Mademoiselle. Henry's most special memories involve his wife Martha, who had died 20 years before, and is now in Heaven. Henry recalls how he'd fallen in love at first sight with Martha as she tried to buy a book titled *How to Make Your Husband Happy*; how she had been engaged to his stuffy cousin Albert, and Henry had stolen her away from him; how after ten years of marriage, she'd left Henry due to his dalliances and run home to her beef-raising parents, Mr. and Mrs. Strable, in Kansas; how Henry and his high-spirited grandfather Hugo had brought her back home to New York; and how, after 25

years of marriage, she had tried to hide her fatal illness from him, and managed to make their final months together their happiest.

Believing himself unworthy of being with Martha in Heaven (after all, he'd misbehaved the past 20 years, and died after a blonde night nurse had placed a thermometer in his mouth, and his temperature had risen to 110 degrees), Henry is prepared for damnation. However, His Excellency says that several young ladies whom he'd made very happy had spoken in his favor, and that after all, Martha, above, is pleading for him to be with her forever. His Excellency escorts Henry to the elevator. "Down?" asks the elevator operator.

"No," smiles His Excellency. "Up."

Production Notes: Berlin-born Ernst Lubitsch (1892–1947) was famed for his elegantly sophisticated "Lubitsch touch" in such frothy films as *Design for Living* (Paramount, 1933, starring Gary Cooper, Miriam Hopkins and Fredric March), *The Merry Widow* (MGM, 1934, starring Maurice Chevalier and Jeanette MacDonald) and *Ninotchka* (MGM, 1939, starring Greta Garbo and Melvyn Douglas). His film previous to *Heaven Can Wait* had been *To Be or Not to Be* (UA, 1942), starring Carole Lombard and Jack Benny. He received three Oscar nominations for Best Director: *The Patriot* (1928), *The Love Parade* (1929) and *Heaven Can Wait* (losing here to Michael Curtiz for Warners' *Casablanca*). On March 13, 1947, Lubitsch received a special Academy scroll "for his distinguished contributions to the art of the motion picture." Lubitsch, ill at the time, died that November. Mason Riley and Damien Bona wrote in their book *Inside Oscar* that, with Lubitsch's scroll, the Academy instituted the Life Achievement Award, given to "somebody reckoned to be on the brink of death."

Don Ameche (Dominic Felix Amici, 1908–1993) did receive an Oscar, although not for *Heaven Can Wait* (for which he certainly deserved a nomination); his Best Supporting Actor prize came over 40 years later for *Cocoon* (1985), in which Ameche, in his late 70s, break-danced (with considerable aid from a double). Ameche had promised to be 20th Century–Fox's major young male star before Tyrone Power eclipsed him (ironically, Tyrone Power, Jr., acted with Ameche in both

Cocoon and 1988's *Cocoon: The Return*). As it was, Ameche had an impressive career: the title role in *The Story of Alexander Graham Bell* (Fox, 1939); much radio work, including the host of Edgar Bergen and Charlie Mc-Carthy's *Chase and Sanborn Show*, and *The Bickersons* with Frances Langford; much TV, including *Don Ameche's Musical Playhouse* (1950–1951), and leads in such Broadway shows as *Silk Stockings* (1955). Honore, his wife of over 50 years, with whom he had six children, died in 1986, the year he won the Oscar.

Lubitsch was initially very upset over Ameche's casting in *Heaven Can Wait*; head script writer Samson Raphaelson had supposedly blueprinted the part of Henry for Fredric March or Rex Harrison. Lubitsch also toyed with the idea of casting Joseph Cotten. Ameche quickly won his director's favor and in 1946 cited Henry Van Cleve as his favorite role.

Gene Tierney (1920–1991), who'd married Oleg Cassini in 1941, learned she was pregnant during the shooting of *Heaven Can Wait*. Her daughter Antoinette was born October 15, 1943. The child was mentally handicapped, and the cause given that Tierney had caught German measles during her one and only appearance at the Hollywood Canteen. Tierney became a mega–Fox star via *Laura* (1944) and *Leave Her to Heaven* (Best Actress Academy nomination, 1945). She had another daughter, Christina, born November 20, 1948. Tierney suffered from severe depression, and allegedly had affairs with Tyrone Power, John F. Kennedy (while she was starring in *Dragonwyck*) and Prince Aly Khan. Her marriage to Cassini ended in 1952, and on Christmas Day, 1957, she entered the Menninger Clinic after police had talked her down from a building ledge. Shock treatment followed. She eventually recovered, remarried in 1960, worked sporadically, and died of emphysema in Houston, Texas, in 1991.

Charles Coburn (1877–1961), one of the most venerable of Hollywood character actors and nicknamed "The Monocle from Georgia" (he doesn't use the eyepiece in *Heaven Can Wait*), won the 1943 Best Supporting Actor Academy Award for *The More the Merrier*. He was also nominated for *The Devil and Miss Jones* (1941) and *The Green Years*

(1946). His Oscar was auctioned in 2012 by Nate B. Sanders Memorabilia, fetching a winning bid of $170,459.

An interesting behind-the-scenes story: Simone Simon, who'd just made a comeback in RKO's hit horror film *Cat People*, originally won the role of Mademoiselle, who captivates the 15-year-old Henry. The French actress would be returning to Fox, where she'd started her Hollywood career in 1935, and had crashed due to sagas of temperament and a sex scandal. However, once cast as Mademoiselle, Simone reverted to her notorious feline type, demanding the studio enlarge her role and improve her billing. Fox dropped her and borrowed MGM's Signe Hasso, who was excellent in the part.

Glimpsed in the final seconds of the film as the elevator operator: Dane Clark, soon to become a star at Warner Bros.

On April 10, 1943, Harrison Carroll wrote in the Los Angeles *Evening Herald-Express*:

> The Ernst Lubitsch streamlined version of Hell is the set to visit in Hollywood this week.
> As might be expected, the twinkly-eyed director doesn't visualize the hot-place in terms of Dante or illustrator Gustave Doré. Nor is he cramped by the $5000 ceiling on sets. Hell, as shown by Lubitsch in the picture *Heaven Can Wait*, fits very comfortably into one corner of 20th Century–Fox's Stage Eight.
> When I come onto the set, a 75-year-old version of Don Ameche is interviewing his excellence, the Devil, played by Laird Cregar, in a Van Dyke beard, a cutaway coat, dark trousers and with one built-up shoe to simulate a club foot. The 20th Century–Fox research department had a time deciding whether the Devil's club foot was on his right or his left. They finally found an old print showing it to be his left.

As things evolved, we never behold Laird's club foot in the film. Also, Carroll had it backwards: Laird was interviewing Ameche, not the other way around.

On October 10, 1943, *Lux Radio Theatre* presented "Heaven Can Wait" with Ameche reprising his role as Henry Van Cleve and Maureen O'Hara (replacing the originally announced Joan Leslie) as Martha. Laird Cregar's role of His Excellency was played by Arthur Q. Bryan, the voice of Elmer Fudd in Warner Bros. cartoons.

Review: "A superlative feature…. In a palatial underworld office, big enough to be Billy Rose's, Satan, played by Laird Cregar (who else would be so logical for the role?), listens to Henry Van Cleve's story of a long and wayward life.... It is a story told with humor and understanding, with many little sidelights on human nature in the Lubitsch manner, which is irresistible because it assumes intelligence in the observer..." (Marjorie Kelly, *The Washington Post*, August 20, 1943).

Holy Matrimony

Studio: 20th Century–Fox; *Producer:* Nunnally Johnson; *Director:* John M. Stahl; *Screenplay:* Nunnally Johnson (from the novel by Arnold Bennett); *Photographer:* Lucien Ballard; *Art Directors:* James Basevi, Russell Spencer; *Set Decorator:* Thomas Little; *Associate Set Decorator:* Paul S. Fox; *Film Editor:* James B. Clark; *Costumes:* René Hubert; *Makeup Artist:* Guy Pearce; *Sound:* E. Clayton Ward, Roger Heman, Sr.; *Special Photographic Effects:* Fred Sersen; *Music:* Cyril J. Mockridge; *Musical Direction:* Emil Newman (Arthur Morton, Herbert W. Spencer, orchestrators); *Shooting Dates:* April 5–May 20, 1943; *Negative Cost:* $709,000; *Running Time:* 87 minutes; *Opening:* Grauman's Chinese Theatre, Loew's State Theatre and the Fox Ritz Theatre, August 26, 1943; Roxy Theatre, New York City, September 15, 1943; *Worldwide Rentals:* $1,570,700; *Profit:* $267,400

Cast: Monty Woolley (Priam Farll), Gracie Fields (Alice Chalice), Laird Cregar (Clive Oxford), Una O'Connor (Sarah Leek), Alan Mowbray (Mr. Pennington), Melville Cooper (Dr. Caswell), Franklin Pangborn (Duncan Farll), Ethel Griffies (Lady Vale), Eric Blore (Henry Leek), George Zucco (Mr. Crepitude), Fritz Feld, William Austin (Critics), Edwin Maxwell (King Edward VII), Montagu Love (Judge), Ian Wolfe (Strawley), Whit Bissell (Harry Leek), Richard Fraser (John Leek), Geoffrey Steele (Matthew Leek), Alec Craig (Aylmer), Lumsden Hare (Benson—Lady Vale's Footman), Tom Stevenson (Hubert—Postman), Mary Field (Oxford's Secretary), Brooks Benedict (Court Attendant), Colin Hunter (Equerry), Tudor Williams (Canon), Billy Bevan, Yorke Sherwood (Cabbies), Edward Biby (Courtroom Spectator), Matthew Boulton (Sergeant), Colin Campbell (Researcher), Gabriel Canzona (Man with Monkey), Edward Cooper, Keith Hitchcock, Charles Irwin (Constables), Jimmy Aubrey, Cyril Delevanti, Denis Green, Charlie Hall, Marten Lamont (Townsmen), Leslie Denison (Usher), Barbara Denny (Secretary), E. L. Fisher-Smith, Olaf Hytten (Cockneys), Bess Flowers, Wilbur Mack (Mourners), Arthur Gould-Porter (Hat Store Clerk), Leyland Hodgson (Solicitor), Bobbie Hale (News Vendor), Guy Kingsford (Young Policeman), Charles Knight (Organist), Thomas Louden (Court Clerk), William H. O'Brien (Reporter), Milton Parsons (Clerk), John Rogers (Lounger), Eric Wilton (Captain of Waiters), Sam Harris, Stuart Holmes (Jurors), Dorothy Lloyd (Parrot Voice Imitator).

Synopsis: Priam Farll, England's greatest artist in 1905, is a misanthrope—so much so that he'd fled London 25 years before, living in seclusion at various hideaways around the world. He's residing in tropical bliss when a letter arrives, announcing he's to be knighted. Farll reluctantly returns home with his manservant Henry Leek, who falls ill to pneumonia aboard ship. When Leek dies, Farll, eager to avoid recognition, pretends that he's Leek, and that the dead man is Farll.

Complications ensue. Farll is buried in Westminster Abbey, which means Leek is interred there, as Farll watches. Then there's the matter of Alice Chalice, who'd corresponded with Leek via a matrimonial agency ... and soon meets and marries Farll.

When the couple faces money troubles, Farll, who's been painting in his garret, admits to Alice his true identity and suggests he sell some of his recent paintings. She thinks he's delusional, but proceeds, without his knowledge, to sell some of his works. Clive Oxford of the Oxford Galleries recognizes the paintings as genuine Farlls, buys 30 of them for £600 ... and sells them for £60,000. When Lady Vale, purchaser of many of the paintings, discovers they were painted after 1905—the year Priam Farll supposedly died—she threatens Oxford with legal action. Oxford tries to cut a deal with Farll, but he refuses.

It all climaxes in court: Mr. Pennington is lawyer for Lady Vale, Mr. Crepitude counselor for Oxford, and Farll is caught in the middle, refusing to admit if he's Farll *or* Leek. His cousin Duncan testifies that in a childhood fight 45 years before, he discovered that Priam had moles. Alice eventually takes the stand and reveals Farll's moles. The devoted couple escapes notoriety in London by returning to Priam's former tropical paradise.

Production Notes: Arnold Bennett's novel *Buried Alive* had already inspired two films. *The Great Adventure* (1921), produced by Whitman Bennett, starred Lionel Barrymore as Priam, Doris Rankin (Mrs. Barrymore) as Alice and Charles Land as Oxford. Paramount's *His Double Life* (1933) starred Roland Young as Priam, Lillian Gish as Alice and Lumsden Hare as Oxford; in *Holy Matrimony*, the latter had a bit part as a footman.

Nunnally Johnson (1897–1977), writer-producer of *Holy Matrimony*, scripted such

Fox fare as *The Prisoner of Shark Island* (1936), *Jesse James* (1939) and *The Grapes of Wrath* (1940, for which he received a Best Screenplay Oscar nomination); he also received an Academy nomination for his *Holy Matrimony* script. His later scripts included *How to Marry a Millionaire* (which he also produced, 1953), *The Man in the Gray Flannel Suit* (which he also directed, 1956), *The Three Faces of Eve* (he also produced and directed, 1957) and *The Dirty Dozen* (1967).

Monty Woolley (1888–1963), formerly a Yale English professor and dramatics coach, won stardom in Broadway's *The Man Who Came to Dinner*, opening October 16, 1939, creating the role of Sheridan Whiteside. He recreated the role in the Warner Bros.' 1942 film version. He received Best Actor Oscar nominations for *The Pied Piper* (1942) and Best Supporting Actor for *Since You Went Away* (1944). For his *Holy Matrimony* performance, Woolley came in second in the New York Film Critics Circle Awards, tying, probably to his amusement, with Sonny Tufts of *So Proudly We Hail.*

Gracie Fields (born Grace Stansfield, 1898–1979) had ascended from the British music halls to become England's top female star of the 1930s. Fox had sent Victor McLaglen and Brian Donlevy to co-star with her in the studio's British-made *We're Going to Be Rich* (1938); she teamed again with Woolley in Fox's *Molly and Me* (1945). For *Holy Matrimony*, Fields came in third place in the New York Film Critics Circle Awards and won the 1943 Best Actress Award from the National Board of Review. She was awarded the Dame Commander of the Order of the British Empire shortly before her death.

Director John M. Stahl (1886–1950) had a remarkable career as a producer-director. At Universal, he directed such lavish soap operas as *Only Yesterday* (1933) and *Imitation of Life* (1934); he was busy at Fox in the 1940s, including the Technicolor mega-hit *Leave Her to Heaven* (1945).

Una O'Connor (1880–1959), revered by horror fans for her comic eccentricities in *The Invisible Man* (1933) and *Bride of Frankenstein* (1935), has a great showcase in *Holy Matrimony* as Sarah Leek, who shows up with her brawny sons and confronts Woolley as her long-lost husband. Appearing as one of those brawny Leeks: Whit Bissell (1909–1996), prolific character actor who was the mad doctor of *I Was a Teenage Werewolf* (1957) and *I Was a Teenage Frankenstein* (1958).

Holy Matrimony offers quite a few delights for horror fans. George Zucco has a featured role as a lawyer in the climactic courtroom episode. The film's a virtual reunion for several bit players from Universal's *The Wolf Man* (1941): Tom Stevenson (the grave digger killed by Chaney's werewolf in *The Wolf Man*, Hubert the postman here); Olaf Hytten (a villager in *The Wolf Man*, a Cockney here); and Leyland Hodgson (butler to Claude Rains' Sir John in *The Wolf Man*, a solicitor here). Also, Stevenson and Cyril Delevanti (glimpsed in *Holy Matrimony* as a townsman) played the grave robbers in the opening of Universal's *Frankenstein Meets the Wolf Man* (1943). Also for the horror buffs: Dorothy Lloyd, who performed cat sound effects in RKO's *Cat People* (1942), provides the parrot voice in *Holy Matrimony.*

Lucien Ballard, *Holy Matrimony*'s cinematographer, would be cameraman on *The Lodger.*

Holy Matrimony became a Broadway musical starring Vincent Price: *Darling of the Day*, which opened January 27, 1968, at the George Abbott Theatre. Nunnally Johnson wrote the book, Jule Styne (whose Broadway credits included *Gentlemen Prefer Blondes*, *Gypsy* and *Funny Girl*) was the composer, and E.Y. Harburg (whose résumé included writing the lyrics for all of the songs in the film *The Wizard of Oz*) provided the lyrics. Price played Monty Woolley's role of Priam Farll, Patricia Routledge had Gracie Fields' part of Alice Chalice, and Peter Woodthorpe acted Laird Cregar's role of Clive Oxford. Routledge won the 1968 Tony Award for Best Actress, but the trouble-plagued production was a disaster for most others concerned; Johnson had his name removed from the book credit before the New York opening. As for Price, William Goldman wrote in his book *The Season*, "Leonard Harris was, I think, the first critic to use the adjective abysmal about any musical performer's singing voice this season when he accurately summed up the sound of Vincent Price in song." The show ran only 31 performances and lost from $700,000 to $750,000.

Review: "Superb comedy.... Laird Cregar is outstanding in the supporting cast..." (*The Film Daily*, August 24, 1943).

The Lodger

Studio: 20th Century–Fox; *Executive Producer:* Darryl F. Zanuck; *Producer:* Robert Bassler; *Director:* John Brahm; *Screenplay:* Barré Lyndon (from the novel by Marie Belloc-Lowndes); *Photographer:* Lucien Ballard; *Art Directors:* James Basevi, John Ewing; *Set Decorator:* Thomas Little; *Associate Set Decorator:* Walter M. Scott; *Film Editor:* J. Watson Webb, Jr.; *Costumes:* René Hubert; *Makeup Artist:* Guy Pearce; *Music:* Hugo W. Friedhofer; *Musical Director:* Emil Newman; *Sound:* E. Clayton Ward, Roger Heman, Sr.; *Special Photographic Effects:* Fred Sersen; *Dance Director:* Kenny Williams; *First Assistant Director:* San Schneider; *Assistant Director:* George Schaefer, Jr.; *Production Manager:* Max Golden; *Unit Manager:* Sam Wurtzel; *Script Clerk:* Marie Halvey; *Dialogue Director:* Craig Noel; *Camera Operator:* Lloyd Ahearn; *Camera Assistants:* Ray Mala, Vincent Barlotti; *Sound Mixer:* E. Clayton Ward; *Prop Man:* Ed Jones; *Wardrobe Man:* Earl Leas; *Wardrobe Woman:* Louise Knapp; *Hairdresser:* Lilian Meyer; *Grip:* Leo McCreary; *Songs:* "What Cheer 'Ria" (music by Bessie Bellwood, lyrics by Will Herbert); "It's the Syme the Whole World Over" (by John Paul Lock Barton and Bert Massee); "Tink-a-Tin!" (music by John Crook, lyrics by Albert Chevalier); "Yield Not to Temptation" (by Horatio R. Palmer); "The Parisian Trot" (music by Lionel Newman, lyrics by Charles Henderson); *Gaffer:* Eddie Petzoldt; *Best Boy:* Bobby Petzoldt; *Secretary to Mr. Brahm:* Chalmers Traw; *Shooting Dates:* August 9–October 8 or 9, 1943; *Negative Cost:* $869,300; *Running Time:* 84 minutes; *Openings:* Roxy Theatre, New York City, 19 January 1944; Egyptian Theatre, Los Angeles Theatre and Ritz Theatre, Los Angeles, 7 March 1944.; *Worldwide Rentals:* $2,295,500; *Profit:* $657,700

    Cast: Merle Oberon (Kitty Langley), George Sanders (John Warwick), Laird Cregar ("Mr. Slade," The Lodger), Sir Cedric Hardwicke (Robert Burton), Sara Allgood (Ellen Burton), Aubrey Mather (Superintendent Sutherland), Queenie Leonard (Daisy), Doris Lloyd (Jennie), David Clyde (Sgt. Bates), Helena Pickard (Annie Rowley), Frederic Worlock (Sir Edward Willoughby), Lumsden Hare (Dr. Sheridan), Olaf Hytten (Harris—Haberdasher), Colin Campbell (Harris' Assistant), Harold De Becker (Charlie—Stage Guard), Anita Sharp-Bolster (Wiggy), Billy Bevan (Bartender), Forrester Harvey (Cobbler), Charles Hall (Comedian), Skelton Knaggs (Costermonger), Edmond Breon (Manager), Harry Allen (Conductor), Raymond Severn (Bit Boy), Heather Wilde (Mary Bowles—Frightened Witness), Stuart Holmes (Edward, Prince of Wales), Walter Tetley (Call Boy), Boyd Irwin (English Policeman), Herbert Clifton (Conductor), Jimmy Aubrey (Cab Driver), Will Stanton (Newsboy), Ger-

ald Hamer (Milkman), C. Montague Shaw (Stage Manager), Cyril Delevanti (Stage Hand), Connie Leon (Bit Woman), Kenneth Hunter (Mounted Inspector), Donald Stuart (Concertina Player), John Rogers (Down-and-Outer), Alec Hartford (Conductor), Colin Hunter, Yorke Sherwood (Policemen), David Thursby (Sergeant), John Rice (Mounted Policeman), Herbert Evans (Constable), Douglas Gerard (Porter), Ruth Clifford (Hairdresser), Colin Kenny, Clive Morgan, Bob Stephenson, Les Sketchley (Plainclothesmen), Crauford Kent, Frank Elliott (Aides), Wilson Benge, Charles Knight (Vigilantes), Lorraine Elliott (Singing Voice for Merle Oberon).

    Synopsis: A nightmare stalks the streets and alleys of Whitechapel: Jack the Ripper. Meanwhile, in Montague Square, Robert Burton and his wife Ellen accept a lodger who calls himself "Mr. Slade." The lodger is a pathologist, polite, soft-spoken, and pleased to find an old Bible in his garret room: "Mine too are the problems of Life ... and Death," he says. He's unhappy, however, to find framed pictures of actresses on the walls ... in fact, he slams them around backwards.

    "Wherever you went in this room," he tells Ellen, "the eyes of those *women* seemed to follow you about!"

    Also living in the house: showgirl Kitty Langley, niece to Ellen. "Behold, there met him a woman subtle of heart," Slade quotes from the Bible. Kitty soon has Slade hopelessly infatuated. She's also soon infatuates Scotland Yard Inspector John Warwick.

    The Ripper strikes again, slaughtering former music hall attraction Annie Rowley ... and later a doxy named Jennie. After each murder, he bathes his hands in the Thames. Meanwhile, Slade reveals to Ellen that an actress had driven his brother to heartbreak and self-destruction; Slade carries the brother's cameo portrait, which he considers "more beautiful than a beautiful woman."

    Come the night Kitty and her chorus girls perform "The Parisian Trot," Slade is in the theater. Kitty's can-can display of panties and stockings unhinges him, and he confronts her in her dressing room. "You corrupt and destroy men," he says, "as my brother was destroyed ... but when the evil is cut out of a beautiful thing, then only the beauty remains." He reveals his knife to Kitty, but before he can disembowel her, her screams alert Warwick, who breaks in, chasing the Ripper up into the theater eaves, shooting him multiple times. The Ripper rampages until, at last cornered, he throws himself through a window and falls into the Thames.

Production Notes: The first film version of Marie Belloc-Lowndes' novel was Alfred Hitchcock's *The Lodger: A Story of the London Fog* (1927), starring Ivor Novello. Come the first remake, *The Phantom Fiend* (1932), directed by Maurice Elvey, Novello reprised his role. In 1940, the year David Selznick released *Rebecca*, directed by Hitchcock, Selznick and Hitchcock held the rights to *The Lodger*. They sold the property to Fox in 1943 for $25,000.

Merle Oberon (Estelle Merle O'Brien Thompson) was born in India in 1911. Due to her mixed ancestry, she claimed her birthplace as Tasmania. She won notice as Anne Boleyn in *The Private Life of Henry VIII* (1933), produced by Sir Alexander Korda, whom she married in 1939. Oberon won a Best Actress Oscar nomination for *The Dark Angel* (Goldwyn, 1935) and enjoyed her top triumph in Goldwyn's *Wuthering Heights* (1939) as Cathy, opposite Laurence Olivier's Heathcliff.

Laird Cregar lurks in *The Lodger.*

Oberon's final film was *Interval* (1973), an embarrassingly bad vanity project; her leading man was Robert Wolders, her 25-years-younger lover, who in 1975 became her fourth husband. Merle Oberon died on November 23, 1979, at Cedars Sinai Hospital in Los Angeles. Her death certificate gave her age as 62 (she was at least 68) and home address as 23816 West Malibu Road. She was buried at Forest Lawn, Glendale, on November 28, 1979.

Sir Cedric Hardwicke (1893–1964), knighted by King George V in 1934, gave several vividly villainous Hollywood performances, including Frollo in *The Hunchback of Notre Dame* (RKO, 1939) and Mr. Jones in *Victory* (Paramount, 1940). His personal favorite: Mr. Brink, aka Death, in *On Borrowed Time* (MGM, 1939). Tallying 111 film and TV credits, Hardwicke was the heavy in Universal's *The Invisible Man Returns* (1940), a Nazi in Universal's *Invisible Agent* (1942), and joined Universal's Frankenstein family in *The Ghost of Frankenstein* (1942). He narrated *The Picture of Dorian Gray* (MGM, 1945), was Sethi in DeMille's *The Ten Commandments* (Paramount, 1956), and late in his life, guested on *The Twilight Zone* (1963) and *The Outer Limits* (1964). A rare Hardwicke credit: He played hero Sir Dennis Nayland Smith in a 1952 pilot for *The Adventures of Fu Manchu* opposite John Carradine as Fu. Hardwicke's son Edward Hardwicke (1932–2011) was a prolific actor, well-remembered as Dr. Watson in British TV's *The Return of Sherlock Holmes* (1986–1988), *The Case-Book of Sherlock Holmes* (1991–1993) and *The Memoirs of Sherlock Holmes* (1994).

Sara Allgood (1879–1950) had been a member of Ireland's famed Abbey Players, and had received a Best Supporting Actress Oscar nomination for John Ford's *How Green Was My Valley* (1941). Among her other films: *Dr. Jekyll and Mr. Hyde* (MGM, 1941), *The Spiral Staircase* (RKO, 1946), *Mother Wore Tights* (Fox, 1947), *Challenge to Lassie* (MGM, 1949) and *Cheaper by the Dozen* (Fox,

1950). Anna Lee, who acted with Ms. Allgood in *How Green Was My Valley*, remembered the actress as an obstreperous terror to work with, despite her warm maternal image.

Helena Pickard (1900–1959), married to Cedric Hardwicke from 1927 to 1950 (and Edward Hardwicke's mother), ended up, in a sense, with two roles in *The Lodger*. As originally scripted and shot, Pickard's Annie Rowley appeared at the theater, accepted money from Kitty, went on a drinking spree, and wandered down a cobbled street, around the corner, and into the clutches of the Ripper. Darryl Zanuck decided the murder scene was so powerful that he added it to the film's opening. He solved the problem of the dead woman appearing at the theater later in the film by not showing any close-ups of her in the death scene sequence, and by dubbing new dialogue ("Good night, Katy," calls one of her fellow roisterers). In the release version, the audience hears about Annie's death, but doesn't see it; in fact, the audience *had* seen it, but apparently, few *realized* it!

Doris Lloyd (1896–1968), Cregar's close friend and the ill-fated Jennie of *The Lodger*, enjoyed such showy roles as "Limehouse Polly" in Lon Chaney's *The Blackbird* (MGM, 1926, directed by Tod Browning), Kitty the prostitute in *Waterloo Bridge* (Universal, 1931, directed by James Whale) and Nancy in *Oliver Twist* (Monogram, 1933, directed by William J. Cowen). In the early 1940s, she became a regular in Universal horror films: *The Wolf Man* (1941), *The Ghost of Frankenstein* (1942), *Night Monster* (1942), *Frankenstein Meets the Wolf Man* (1943) and *The Invisible Man's Revenge* (1944). She later made appearances on *Alfred Hitchcock Presents* (1958–1962), Boris Karloff's *Thriller* (1961–1962) and *The Alfred Hitchcock Hour* (1963–1965), and late in her life appeared in small roles in two blockbusters: *Mary Poppins* (1964) and *The Sound of Music* (1965). Lloyd was longtime friends with Boris Karloff and James Whale; the latter, who drowned himself in his Pacific Palisades pool in 1957, left the actress $10,000 in his will.

John Brahm (1893–1982) was the son of German director-comedian Ludwig Brahm and the nephew of Otto Brahm, a master of Germanic Expressionism. John spent World War I on the Russian Front, learned his craft on the stages of Berlin, Paris and Vienna, and fled the Nazis in 1934, coming to England, where in 1936 he directed a remake of D.W. Griffith's silent classic *Broken Blossoms*. In 1937, Brahm married the famed German star and fellow refugee Dolly Haas; by the time they divorced in 1941, Brahm had directed such Hollywood melodramas as Columbia's *Penitentiary* (a remake of *The Criminal Code*, starring Walter Connolly, 1938) and Universal's *Rio* (a penal colony saga starring Basil Rathbone, 1939). His first film at Fox: *Wild Geese Calling* (1941) with Henry Fonda, Joan Bennett and Warren William. As noted in the text, Brahm spent time both "in and out" of front office favor at Fox; it was his handling of the studio's *The Undying Monster* (1942) that won him the directing job on *The Lodger*.

Barré Lyndon (born Alfred Edgar, 1896–1972) took his *nom de plume* from William Makepeace Thackeray's 1844 novel *The Luck of Barry Lyndon*, which became a Stanley Kubrick film, *Barry Lyndon*, in 1975. He came to prominence with his melodrama play *The Amazing Dr. Clitterhouse* (Hudson Theatre, March 2, 1937, 80 performances). Sir Cedric Hardwicke played the title role on Broadway, and Edward G. Robinson starred in the Warners 1938 film version.

For the role of Wiggy, played so well by Anita Sharp-Bolster, Fox also considered Una O'Connor and Eily Malyon.

The big success of *The Lodger* surely inspired PRC's *Bluebeard* (1944) starring John Carradine in the title role and directed by Edgar G. Ulmer. The 19th-century story presented Carradine as an artist and puppeteer, who paints a woman beatifically, later learning she's a prostitute. The legend goes that Ulmer completed the film in six days, but the surviving PRC paperwork reveals that *Bluebeard* shot May 31 to June 21, 1944, a total of 19 days; the budget was $108,341.30; the final cost, $167,567.42. (This was over $700,000 less than *The Lodger*!) Carradine (paid $9,333.32 for the film) was superb, and *Bluebeard's* sex element was in key with *The Lodger's*, although the overall film, for all its flourishes, was hardly in its league.

20th Century–Fox released a remake of *The Lodger*, *Man in the Attic*, on December 23, 1953. The director was Hugo Fregonese, Jack Palance had the title role, Constance

Smith was the can-can dancer, Byron Palmer the detective, and Frances Bavier (later Aunt Bee of TV's *The Andy Griffith Show*) and Rhys Williams were the landlords. The remake fell far short of the 1944 film, and Palance, strangely restrained, never approached the flamboyant mania that Laird had given Jack the Ripper.

Among the many other Jack the Ripper movies: the German *Pandora's Box* (1929, directed by G.W. Pabst, which Louise Brooks' Lulu runs afoul of Gustav Diesl's Ripper); *Jack the Ripper* (1960); *A Study in Terror* (pitting Sherlock Holmes vs. the Ripper, 1966), and *Time After Time* (the Ripper, played by David Warner, steals the time machine of H.G. Wells, played by Malcolm McDowell, and travels to contemporary society, 1979). A 2009 version of *The Lodger* found a Ripper copycat butchering prostitutes along Hollywood's Sunset Strip.

Review: *"The Lodger* is undoubtedly the best Jack the Ripper movie ever made. Its casting is bound to satisfy the most discriminating Crime Clubber, both as to villain (Laird Cregar), Scotland Yardsman (George Sanders) and imperiled heroine (Merle Oberon). Its Whitechapel setting is storybook London to the Queen's taste—bowlered bobbies materializing in fog-shrouded byways, glistening cobblestones and clopping cabs, toffs and slatterns slinking in and out of pubs, and finally an Old Vic interior of backdrops, high-spiraling stairways and lofty catwalks for the final closing in." (*New York PM*, January 20, 1944)

Hangover Square

Studio: 20th Century–Fox; *Executive Producer:* Darryl F. Zanuck; *Producer:* Robert Bassler; *Director:* John Brahm; *Screenplay:* Barré Lyndon (based on the novel by Patrick Hamilton); Marian Spitzer and Nate Watt (uncredited); *Music:* Bernard Herrmann ("Concerto Macabre," music for "Gay Love"); *Photographer:* Joseph La Shelle; *Art Directors:* Lyle Wheeler, Maurice Ransford; *Set Decorator:* Thomas Little; *Associate Set Decorator:* Frank E. Hughes; *Film Editor:* Harry Reynolds; *Costumes:* René Hubert, Kay Nelson; *Makeup Artist:* Ben Nye; *Special Photographic Effects:* Fred Sersen; *Sound:* Bernard Freericks, Harry M. Leonard; *Additional Music:* Lionel Newman, composer, and Charles Henderson, lyricist, "Have You Seen Joe?," "Why Do They Wake Me Up So Early in the Morning?," "All for You" and "So Close to Paradise"; Henderson also wrote the lyrics for "Gay Love"); *Transparency Projection Shots:* Edward Snyder, J.O. Taylor; *Sound Mixer:* Eugene Grossman; *Music Mixers:* Murray Spivack, Vinton Vernon; *Production Manager:* Raymond A. Klune; *Dance Coach for Linda Darnell:* Hermes Pan; *Assistant Directors:* F.E. Johnston, Sam Schneider; *Dialogue Director:* Arthur Pierson; *Second Camera:* Lloyd Ahern; *Research Director:* Frances Richardson; *Research Assistant:* Gertrude Kingston; *Shooting Dates:* August 21–October 25, 1944; Retakes: November 1944.; *Negative Cost:* $1,154,400; *Running Time:* 77 minutes; *New York Opening:* Roxy Theatre, New York City, February 7, 1945; Grauman's Chinese Theatre, Loews State Theatre, Uptown Theatre, Carthay Circle Theatre, Los Angeles, March 30, 1945; *Worldwide Rentals:* $1,798,500; *Profit:* $27,700

Cast: Laird Cregar (George Harvey Bone), Linda Darnell (Netta Longdon), George Sanders (Dr. Allan Middleton), Glenn Langan (Eddie Carstairs), Faye Marlowe (Barbara Chapman), Alan Napier (Sir Henry Chapman), Frederic Worlock (Superintendent Clay), J.W. Austin (Detective Inspector King), Leyland Hodgson (Detective Sgt. Lewis), Clifford Brooke (Watchman), John Goldsworthy (William—Chapman's Butler), Michael Dyne (Mickey), Ann Codee (Yvette—Netta's Maid), Francis Ford (Ogilby), Charles Irwin (Manager—King's Head Arms), Frank Benson (Newsman), Connie Leon (Maid), Robert Hale (Costermonger), Leslie Denison (English Policeman), Jimmy Aubrey (Drunk), J. Farrell MacDonald (Street Vendor), John Rogers (Passerby with Baskets), Harry Allen (Pot Man), Thomas Martin (Lamplighter), Constantine Romanoff (Townsman), Leslie Sketchley (Doorman), Frances Spence (Housekeeper), Val Stanton (Postman), Alan Edmiston, George Leigh (Clerks), Charles Coleman (Man at Bonfire), Charles Knight (Maître d'), Charles Hall (Cockney Singer), Radford Allen, Murray Coombs, Harold de Becker, Jr., David Leland, Norman Wilnor (Boys), Wilson Benge, Jack Chefe, Eric Wilton (Waiters), Ted Billings, Bobbie Hale, Michael Jeffers, Pat McKee, Jack Tornek (Pub Patrons), Bob Burns, Steve Carruthers, James Conaty, Nestor Eristoff, Franklyn Farnum, Art Howard, Wilbur Mack, Count Stefenelli (Concertgoers), Roddy McDowall (Voice of Child), Kay St. Germain Wells (Singing Voice for Linda Darnell), Ignace Hilsberg (Piano Double for Laird Cregar).

Synopsis: Night in Fulham, 1903. A killer stabs an old antiques dealer named Ogilby and sets his shop afire. Shortly afterwards, George Harvey Bone, noted composer, who lives at Number 12, Hangover Square, London, S.W., comes out of one of his "dead moods," which are caused by any loud discordant sound. He's unable to remember where he was the previous night, has blood on his clothes ... and a knife in his pocket.

George and his lady friend, Barbara, go to

Scotland Yard, where criminologist Dr. Allan Middleton can find no proof that George is guilty of Ogilby's murder. George, meanwhile, is at work on a magnificent concerto, encouraged by Barbara and her father Sir Henry Chapman, who has offered to conduct the concert after George completes it. However, George runs afoul of his neighbor Netta Longdon, an ambitious chanteuse whose rousing pub rendition of "Have You Seen Joe?"—performed in panties and fishnets—captivates George. Netta dallies with the awestruck composer, seducing him into abandoning his concerto to write songs for her.

George eventually learns the truth, and the fact that Netta is engaged to Carstairs, a theatrical impresario. In a "dead mood," he strangles Netta with a cord, dresses her body as a "Guy" and carries the corpse to the Guy Fawkes bonfire in Cheyne Yard, where he places it atop the pyre and watches as the cadaver burns.

Free of Netta, George returns to his work. However, Middleton unravels the truth. On the night George plays his concerto at the piano, backed up by an orchestra, his crimes all come back to him. Middleton wants to take him away peacefully, but when the Scotland Yard inspectors arrive, George goes mad, starts a fire and runs to the balcony, where he watches his concerto played … and weeps. As Middleton, Barbara and Sir Henry run outside to safety, George, having resumed his place at the piano, finishes playing his concerto as the house burns around him, and the flames engulf him.

Production Notes: Patrick Hamilton (1904–1962) wrote the source material for such classics as *Gaslight* (1940), the saga of a husband who tries to drive his wife insane, and Alfred Hitchcock's *Rope* (1948), in which two young male murderers host a party with their victim's corpse inside a case in the room.

Linda Darnell, burned atop the Guy Fawkes bonfire in *Hangover Square*, strangely and tragically faced fires in her too-short future. During the filming of *Anna and the King of Siam* (1946), while being burned at the stake, fire singed her; during the shooting of *Forever Amber* (1947), a flaming roof fell and almost hit her; while filming *No Way Out* (1950), her car exploded. Fox dropped her in the early

1950s, and she went through a repertory of woes: three failed marriages, money problems, weight gain, hair loss and suicide attempts. Her final film: *Black Spurs* (Paramount, 1965), one of producer A.C. Lyles' westerns stocked with veteran players. Linda called it "a ten-day quickie no one will go to see."

On the night of April 8, 1965, Linda, staying with friends in Chicago, watched herself in *Star Dust* (1940) on the late show. A fire erupted in the house around 5:00 a.m., ravaging the actress' face and 90 percent of her body. In his biography of Darnell, *Hollywood Beauty*, Ronald L. Davis describes Darnell's adopted daughter Lola finding her mother in the hospital, hair and skin burned away, clad in a diaper, and whispering in "a horrible voice" (after a tracheotomy), "I love you baby, I love you."

Darnell died April 10, 1965, in Cook County Hospital, Chicago. Her ashes were kept at Memorial Park in Skokie, Illinois, for a time, then buried in her daughter's family plot at Union Hill Cemetery, Kennett Square, Pennsylvania. Her sister Undeen loved her dearly and during her final years, Undeen happily corresponded with fans of her sister.

As for George Sanders, one might have expected, after his outrageous defiance on *Hangover Square*, that Darryl Zanuck (and maybe Hollywood at large) would have blackballed him. Yet he prospered; indeed, he won the Best Supporting Actor Oscar for his superb performance as critic Addison DeWitt in *All About Eve* (Fox, 1950). The honor actually reduced the cynical Sanders to tears. "I can't help it," he wept backstage. "This has unnerved me."

He divorced his first wife Susan in 1949, and subsequently was married tempestuously to Zsa Zsa Gabor (1949–1954), happily to actress Benita Hume (1959 to her death in 1967) and disastrously to Zsa Zsa's sister Magda (1970–1971). An interesting Cregar connection: Sanders tried out in the musical *Sherry!* based on *The Man Who Came to Dinner*, with Sanders in the Sheridan Whiteside role that had been such a boon for Laird, Monty Woolley and Clifton Webb. The show opened at Boston's Colonial Theatre January 17, 1967; Sanders was panned, his wife Benita was ill, and he withdrew before the show opened on Broadway on March 27 with Clive Revill in the title role. *Sherry!* lasted only 72 performances. (Nineteen sixty-seven was a bad year for Sanders: Benita, his mother and his estranged brother actor Tom Conway all died.)

Sanders, who'd missed out on 1944's *Laura*, as had Cregar, appeared in two teleplay versions, both times as Waldo Lydecker: the "A Portrait of Murder" version on *The 20th Century–Fox Hour* (October 19, 1955, with Dana Wynter as Laura, Robert Stack as McPherson, and directed by John Brahm); and the TV movie *Laura* (January 24, 1968, with Lee Radziwill in the title role and Robert Stack returning as McPherson). One of Sanders' final films: *The Kremlin Letter* (1970), with Sanders as "The Warlock" in drag in a blonde wig.

April 25, 1972: Authorities found Sanders' naked body in his room at Rey Don Jamie, a seaside resort in Castelldefells, Spain. He'd taken five tubes of Nembutal, apparently washed it down with Vodka, and had left this note:

> Dear World:
> I am leaving because I am bored. I feel I have lived long enough. I am leaving you with your worries in this sweet cesspool—Good luck.

A second note, written in Spanish, asked that his sister in London be notified, and that there was enough money among his effects to pay for his funeral. Sanders was cremated and his ashes reportedly scattered over the English Channel.

Glenn Langan (Thomas Glenn Langan, 1917–1991) followed up at Fox in such films as *Dragonwyck* (1946), *Forever Amber* (1947) and *The Snake Pit* (1948). He did much television and won infamy as *The Amazing Colossal Man* (1957), Bert I. Gordon's 60-foot-tall, loincloth-wearing, mad-as-hell victim of radiation poisoning. His final film was an uncredited bit in *The Andromeda Strain* (1971), and he became successful in real estate. Langan was also successful in matrimony: His marriage to blonde actress Adele Jergens lasted from 1951 until his death. They had one son.

Faye Marlowe (born 1926) continued at Fox in *Junior Miss* (1945), *The Spider* (1945) and *Johnny Comes Flying Home* (1946). She starred in Republic's *Rendezvous with Annie* (1946), worked for John Brahm again in *The Thief of Venice* (1950), appeared uncredited

Hangover Square: **Linda Darnell, Laird Cregar.**

in the French-Italian-produced *The Bed* (1954) and wrapped up her acting career in several 1955 episodes of TV's *Conrad Nagel Theatre*. She also appears briefly in pin-up girl finery in the short subject *The All-Star Bond Rally* (1945). In later years, she has turned her interest to writing.

Alan Napier (Alan William Napier-Clavering, 1903–1988) was the cousin of British Prime Minister Neville Chamberlain, an alumnus of the Royal Academy of Dramatic Art, and a noted player on the London stage before coming to America in 1939. Among his films: *The Invisible Man Returns* (1940), *Cat People* (1942), *Lassie Come Home* (1943), *The Song of Bernadette* (1943), *Isle of the Dead* (1945), *House of Horrors* (1946, killed by Rondo Hatton's "Creeper"), Cecil B. DeMille's *Unconquered* (1947), Orson Welles' *Macbeth* (1948), the Bowery Boys' *Master Minds* (1949, as a mad doctor), *Julius Caesar* (1953) and *The Mole People* (Universal, 1956, as a Sumerian high priest). Napier did much TV, including three episodes of Boris Karloff's *Thriller* (1960–1961); he won his major fame, of course, as Alfred, the butler on TV's *Batman* (1966–1968).

Michael Dyne (1918–1989), who played Mickey, had been a candidate for Dorian Gray in MGM's *The Picture of Dorian Gray* (1945) before Hurd Hatfield landed the plum role. Dyne later became a writer, his credits including the screenplay for Disney's *The Moon-Spinners* (1964).

Joseph La Shelle (1900–1989), *Hangover Square*'s cinematographer, won an Academy Award for *Laura* (1944); he'd receive an additional eight nominations. A mainstream cameraman, he also was director of photography for *I Was a Teenage Werewolf* (1957).

As for director John Brahm, his final film for Fox was 1947's *The Brasher Doubloon* ("Some Women Can't Stand Cats.... *With Me It's Men!*"). In Europe, his credits included *The Thief of Venice* (1950), starring Maria Montez (and featuring *Hangover Square*'s Faye Marlowe). He returned to Hollywood horror with *The Mad Magician* (Columbia, 1954), starring Vincent Price, and directed over 190 TV episodes, including *Wagon Train, M Squad, Alfred Hitchcock Presents, Naked City, The Outer Limits, Gunsmoke, The Man from U.N.C.L.E, The Girl from U.N.C.L.E.* and many more. Brahm directed 12 episodes of the Rod Serling–hosted *The Twilight Zone*, including the famous "Time Enough at Last" (1959); he also directed 12 episodes of the Boris Karloff–hosted *Thriller*, including three of the show's most frightening episodes: "The Cheaters" (1960), "Well of Doom" (1961) and "A Wig for Miss Devore" (1962). His final feature credit: *Hot Rods to Hell* (1967), starring former Fox stars Dana Andrews and Jeanne Crain.

Brahm's final days and nights were frightening for him, in an unusual way: The cliff had been falling away from his oceanview home, 19419 Pacific Coast Highway in Malibu, and for safety's sake, he moved into the property's stable. He died there of cardiac arrest on October 13, 1982, at the age of 89, and was cremated on October 19, 1982, at the Grandview Crematory in Glendale, California.

Brahm's daughter Sumishta, who was 28 when her father died, told Marty Baumann in an interview in *Monsters from the Vault* #24:

A couple of days after my father died, I drove out to his house in Malibu and went down to the beach that used to belong to him before he was forced to sell it to the state for a nominal sum. I met up with Terry, one of the two men who took care of my father in the last two years of his life, and decided to go for a swim in the ocean my father loved to swim in for so many years. I started to swim out and in my anger kept going until Terry called out to me that perhaps it was time to return. I did so and cried a bit, then drove home along Sunset Boulevard to find that *The Lodger* was being screened that very evening at a little cinema, starting just five minutes after I stopped to find out when it was showing. I phoned my mom to tell her that I felt it was no coincidence. It was my father's way of saying not to worry, that he wasn't all that far from me. And here was a part of him to prove it.

Barré Lyndon followed up *Hangover Square* as co-scripter of Fox's *noir* spy thriller *The House on 92nd Street* (1945), for which he and his fellow writers Charles G. Booth and John Monks, Jr., won an Edgar Allan Poe Award. Lyndon's later credits included co-scripting Cecil B. DeMille's *The Greatest Show on Earth* (1952) and scripting George Pal's *The War of the Worlds* (1953); the film won a Hugo Award for Lyndon, director Byron Haskin and H.G. Wells (who'd died in 1946). Among Lyndon's TV credits: adapting Robert Bloch's "Yours Truly, Jack the Ripper" as an episode of Boris Karloff's *Thriller* (April 11, 1961).

On August 16, 1944, five days before *Hangover Square* began shooting, Louella Parsons wrote that Laird Cregar had told her at a party hosted by Sonja Henie that he'd agreed to do *Hangover Square*: "The reason I went back into the script is because it was rewritten." This isn't entirely true. Based on material in the John Brahm Archive at the University of Southern California, Nate Watt did a bit of uncredited rewriting (the scene in which George, Netta and Mickey walk drunkenly through the Square) on that date, August 16, 1944. Marian Spitzer did more extensive rewriting (again uncredited), including the scene at Perrino's Restaurant, the scene in which Bone and Netta snuggle in the coach, the episode in which Netta visits George at his study and seduces him, and the episode in which Bone attacks Carstairs in Netta's flat. These pages are dated between early and mid–September of 1944, after the film began shooting. Spitzer also wrote this scene for Netta and Carstairs in Netta's flat, date September 16, 1944; based on a still, it was apparently shot, but cut:

CARSTAIRS: You've come a long way in a little while, Netta.

NETTA (*preening*): And after *Gay Love* opens I'm going a great deal further....
She comes closer to him, smiling provocatively. But there is a decided difference between her attitude toward Carstairs and what we have seen to be her attitude toward George. Her coquetry is touched with eagerness, because she knows that, attracted though he is by her, the reins are in his hands.

NETTA (*looking up into his face*): ... Aren't I?

CARSTAIRS: I shouldn't be surprised, my dear.... Still, I'd be more comfortable if you'd get that other song from George.

NETTA (*perching on the arm of his chair*): Oh, bother George ... (*airily*) He's so tiresome.

CARSTAIRS (*regarding her quizzically*): He may be tiresome, Netta, but we need him ... (*he smiles knowingly*) You wouldn't be very much without his songs, you know.

NETTA (*pouting*): No?

CARSTAIRS (*going on*): Because you haven't any voice, and you can't sing, really...
Netta watches him, fascinated. She loves him for being on to her.

CARSTAIRS: You're just a very lovely, very clever creature who knows exactly what she wants...

NETTA (*tilting her face for a kiss*): Is that bad?

CARSTAIRS (*smiling intimately*): On the contrary, It's one of your chief attractions.
She leans down, eyes closed. He takes her in his arms and kisses her thoroughly. Then he releases her.

CARSTAIRS (*always the realist*): But you must get that song. We haven't much time.

NETTA (*rising*): Don't worry about that. I'll get it.
Carstairs reaches into his pocket and brings out a flat, velvet jewelers box. He opens it, revealing a beautiful diamond necklace.

NETTA (*her eyes sparkling greedily*): Oh!
She reaches for it but Carstairs pulls it out of reach.

CARSTAIRS (*mockingly*): After you've got the song.

NETTA: You mean that's my reward for being a good little girl?

CARSTAIRS (*tongue in cheek*): Well ... that's one way of putting it.

Marian Spitzer (1899–1983) also worked on such scripts as Fox's *Lifeboat* (1944) and *The Dolly Sisters* (1945). She was married to producer-director-writer Harlan Thompson and the mother of actor Eva Thompson.

Finally, there's Bernard Herrmann (1911–1975), who wrote *Hangover Square*'s "Concerto Macabre." Herrmann had scored Orson Welles' famed Halloween 1938 *The War of the Worlds* radio broadcast, and had won the Oscar for his score for *The Devil and Daniel Webster* (1941). Among his compositions were the scores for *Citizen Kane* (1941), *The Day the Earth Stood Still* (1951), *The 7th Voyage of Sindbad* (1958) and *Taxi Driver* (1976), which he reportedly finished recording just hours before his Christmas Eve death in 1975. Herrmann composed the scores for the Alfred Hitchcock films *The Trouble with Harry* (1955), *The Man Who Knew Too Much* (1956), *The Wrong Man* (1957), *Vertigo* (1958), *North by Northwest* (1959), *Psycho* (1960) and *Marnie* (1964). Hitchcock rejected his score for *Torn Curtain* (1966) and the two never spoke again. Herrmann also worked on television, including creating the original theme for *The Twilight Zone*. In September of 1999, Bernard Herrmann received commemoration on a 33¢ stamp, along with Hollywood composers Alfred Newman, Max Steiner, Dimitri Tiomkin, Franz Waxman and Erich Wolfgang Korngold.

While Herrmann composed *Hangover Square*'s concerto and the music for the song "Gay Love" (for which Charles Henderson wrote the lyrics), Lionel Newman wrote the music for the songs "Have You Seen Joe?," "Why Do They Wake Me Up So Early in the Morning?," "All for You" and "So Close to Paradise" (with Henderson writing the lyrics). Newman won an Oscar for adapting the score for *Hello, Dolly!* (shared with Lennie Hayton, 1969); among his many film-TV credits was supervising the music for TV's *Batman*.

Joseph Breen had enumerated his concerns about *Hangover Square* in an August 11, 1944, letter to Colonel Jason S. Joy at 20th Century–Fox:

- The present lyrics contain many objectionable lines that could not be approved...
- These opening scenes showing the method in which the fire is started and spread are certain to be deleted by some political censor boards...
- In accordance with the Association's agreement, the word "Fire" should not be shouted out ... this to avoid any possibility of panic in the theater.
- The costume of Netta described here and elsewhere must not be objectionably revealing.
- The attitude of George in wanting to come into Netta's apartment to play his new composition should not contain any suggestive inference. This is essential...
- There should be no close-up details of the thuggee cord...
- The dissolve of Netta and Carstairs seems suggestive of illicit sex. It must be revised to get away from any such flavor...
- George's line "I'll neither be held—nor be hanged" should be revised, to get away from any indication he intends to commit suicide.
- The cry of "Fire" by the butler is unacceptable, as explained previously.
- In the following scenes, please take care to avoid any playing up of the panic of the people, for the same reason of avoiding any mishap in the theater.

Fox took heed of most of these requests. However, George still said "I'll neither be held, nor hanged" and indeed committed suicide.

A 2009 film version of *Hangover Square* starred Mihran Konanyan as George Harvey Bone and Chloe Ginsburg as Netta Longdon. Ansel Faraj directed and adapted the story.

Finally, as for Darryl F. Zanuck.... At the Academy Awards ceremony on March 15, 1945, at Grauman's Chinese Theatre, Zanuck saw his prized *Wilson* lose Best Picture of 1944 to Paramount's *Going My Way*. He was bitterly disappointed, even though that night he won his second Irving Thalberg Award. Zanuck accepted the Best Picture Oscar of 1947 for *Gentleman's Agreement*; produced such acclaimed films as *The Snake Pit* (1948) and *Twelve O'Clock High* (1949); and received a third Thalberg Award on March 29, 1951, the same night he accepted the Oscar for Fox's Best Picture winner, *All About Eve*.

Zanuck, however, was destined to fall. His famous machismo overtook him. On January 18, 1954, he swung (bare-chested by one arm) from a trapeze at Ciro's night club; *Life* magazine photographer Loomis Dean got the shot, an embarrassment to Fox and the Zanuck family. By that time, Zanuck was involved in the infamous Bella Darvi scandal, starring Ms. Darvi (whose last name was a blend of his first name and his wife Virginia's) in *The Egyptian* (1954). Darvi, a colossal flop, eventually committed suicide in 1971. Meanwhile, Zanuck had left his wife, frolicking in Europe throughout the late 1950s with various mistresses, promising most of them stardom that never took root. He came back big as producer of *The Longest Day* (1962), and thereafter engaged in epically ugly studio politics at Fox with his son Richard. Meanwhile, Zanuck and wife Virginia had never divorced; he'd paid for her loyalty with Fox stock. Come the showdown between Zanuck and Richard, Virginia had her revenge on her chronically unfaithful husband—giving her stock to the anti–Darryl Zanuck group.

Burned out, personally and professionally disgraced, and suffering from Alzheimer's disease, Zanuck ultimately returned to his wife Virginia in Palm Springs, where he died from jaw cancer on December 22, 1979. The last of the Hollywood moguls is buried at Westwood Memorial Park in Los Angeles.

Review: "John Brahm's wildly stylized period *noir*.... Picture is odd in that we don't care if Cregar murders Darnell, because she's really a louse.... The enjoyment comes from watching heavy-set Cregar in his final film.... [He gives] one of his best psycho performances (in a role that Vincent Price, Victor Buono or Raymond Burr might have had fun with in later years); the wonderful period detail and Brahm's exciting, bizarre direction, especially impressive during the blackout sequences..." (Danny Peary, *Guide for the Film Fanatic*).

Theater Credits

Limelight Swing. Pasadena Playhouse, California. June 9, 1937. Laird Cregar as "A First-Nighter" and a Member of the Ensemble. No other credits available.

Miracle of the Swallows. Pasadena Playhouse, California. Opening Date, July 5, 1937. Play by Ramon Romero. Supervising Director: Gilmor Brown. Directors: William Williams, Lenore Shanewise, Frank Fowler; Assisted by Ray Arvedson. Art Director: Rita Glover. Technical Director: Fred C. Huxley. Production Manager: Frances McCune. Costume Director: Fairfax P. Walkup.

Cast: June Evans (Louisa), Emilie Johnson (Lola), Maude George (Josephina), Lola Montero (Juana), Earl Gunn (Padre Josef Barona), Robert Gillette (Manuel), Harry Bloom (Mendoza), Wesley Meredith (Aurelio), Dorothy Wegman (Maria), Henry Hinds, George Reading, Bert Johannes (Padres), James Westerfield (Padre Geronimo Boscana), Virginia Lykins (Dona Eulalia Fages), Laird Cregar (Pedro Fages), Catherine Feltus (Ana), Tom Seidel (Pedrito Fages), Joan Wheeler (Magdalena), Stevan Darrell (Augustin), Nicias Reckas, Claude Wisberg, Valerie Keith, Margo Snyder, Joe Helgesen, Fernando Torres, E. Marie Bullis, John Lansing Walsh, Thad Sharrets, Ann Clarey, Melcena Lafollette, Ellin Dunning (Neophytes), Richard Williams (Jordan), Victor N. Zimmerman (Jose Echeandia), Peter Veselich (Pancho), Gustave Tweer (Juan), Ian McDonald (Relief Guard), Charles Wood (Teofilo), Nicias Reckas (Mule-Train Driver), Herbert Thayer (Governor Jose Arrillaga), Robert Willey, Robert F. Stevens, Frederick Smith, Barton Booth, Benson Greene (Sailors), Sidney Sanner (Lt. Pacheco), Houseley Stevenson (Presidente Tapis), Laurence Van Mourick (Vallejo), Marguerite Snyder (Senora Vallejo), James Crow (Pio Pico), Elynore Dolkart (Senora Pico), Jack Noble, Hector Offenbach, George Bessolo, Gustave Schirmer, Ralph Tweer (Caballeros), Victor Mature (Hypolite Bouchard), Shiro Takahisa (Mateo), Richard Carpenter (Pedro), Carmen Morales (Kaya), Robert Hood (Alverez), George Tyrone (Salat), Jo Musacchia, Billy Scott, Mary Lee Jones, Nancy Ann Knettle, Lemyart Knettle, Harvey Knettle, John Eppolito, Nancy Snyder, George Snyder, Ernest Carlson, Patricia Callahan (Neophyte Children), Carmen, Jacque Poley, Martha Shaw, Gwen Horn, Nell Webb, Meg Wyllie, Gene Knudsen, Mary Alice Wrixon, Christina Welles, Lorraine Kelley, Esther Fromm, Ruth Jones, Lucy Gallegos, Florentina Valadez, Ruby Gallegos, Benita Espaza, Mary Porras, Consuelo Oreguera, Felicitas Hernandez, Magge Hernandez, Ramona Garces, Victoria Valadez, Alvina Mitchell, Kathleen Hinckley (Dancers).

The play, performed with musicians, had this "Author's Note" in the program:

> Most of the characters and incidents used in this play are historically true, but in order to embrace the glory of the Missions as well as their ruin, the Author has telescoped dates of certain happenings so that the dramatic continuity of the play may not be hampered. The play strives to combine the romantic legends of Capistrano with the political forces responsible for the downfall of the Mission's authority.

There were various players in the production on the eve of fame, or on its downslide. Victor Mature was still two years away from his first film. Catherine Feltus (1915–2004), who was married to Robert Preston from 1940 to his death in 1987, later had a film career under the name Catherine Craig. Maude George (1888–1963) had played the blonde-wigged Princess Olga in Erich von Stroheim's *Foolish Wives* (1922), and had retired from films. Houseley Stevenson (1879–1953) was a noted Pasadena Playhouse teacher, director and actor, had a prolific film career (memorable as the plastic surgeon in Bogart's 1947 *Dark Passage*), and was the father of actor

Onslow Stevens (whom many horror films remember as Dr. Edlemann in Universal's 1945 "monster rally," *House of Dracula*).

The Shoemaker's Holiday. Pasadena Playhouse, California. January 18, 1939. Play by Thomas Dekker. Laird Cregar as Cornwall.

Portraying the role of Simon the Shoemaker, who becomes a Lord Mayor of London in this Elizabethan comedy, was a 35-year-old Altadena dentist. Before 1939 had ended, he decided to become a professional actor, turned his practice over to his dentist wife, and went on to a prolific 35-year film and TV career. His name: Edgar Buchanan.

Where the Blue Begins. Pasadena Playhouse, California. Opening Night: February 21, 1939. Play by Christopher Morley. Supervising Director: Gilmor Brown. Director: Eva M. Fry. Technical Director: Fred C. Huxley. Production Manager: Frances McCune. Art Director: Edward Sheffield.

Cast: Herschel Daugherty (Mr. Gissing), Lila Eccles (Mrs. Spaniel), Dick Turner (Mike Terrier), Richard Barret (Groups), Billy Epp (Bunks), Jackie Foyil (Yelpers), George Baldwin (Mr. Poodle), Frank Ferguson (Bishop Borzoi), Eleanore Wilson (Miss Airedale), Norman Mennes (Mr. Beagle, Jr.), Frederick Blanchard (Mr. Beagle, Sr.), Ian McDonald (Mr. Hound), Iris Dornfield (Miss Whippet), Bea Hassel (Pom), Theodore S. Field (First Floorwalker), Chalmers Paulson (Second Floorwalker), Harry Lewis (Third Floorwalker), Ann Melvin (Mrs. Retriever), Radiana Pasmore (Mrs. Doberman-Pinscher), Edouard L'Esperance (Mr. Retriever), John Rogers (Mr. Doberman-Pinscher), Laird Cregar (Dane), Robert Stevens (Shepherd), Al Woods (Capt. Scottie), Edgar Nord (Mr. Pointer), Michael Ames (Setter).

Brother Rat. Pasadena Playhouse, California. Opening Night, March 7, 1939. Play by John Monks, Jr., and Fred R. Finklehoffe. Supervising Director: Gilmor Brown. Director: Victor Jory. Production Manager: Frances McCune. Technical Director: Fred Huxley. Art Director: Rita Glover.

Cast: Mary Greene (Mrs. Brooks), Gwen Gaylord (Joyce Winfree), Ollie Ann Robinson (Jenny), Frances Charles (Claire Ramm), Thomas Kelly (Bing Edwards), William Halstead (Harley Harrington), Charles Wood (Billy Randolph), Maxine Anderson, Jeanne Cagney (Kate Rice), Patrick Buell (Dan Crawford), Cliff Stone (A. Furman Townsend, Jr.), Paul G. Jones ("Newsreel" Scott), Michael Ames, Harry Lewis ("Tripod" Andrews), Teddy

S. Field ("Mistol" Bottome), Oliver B. Prickett (Slim), Laird Cregar (Lt. "Lace Drawers" Rogers), Tom Worth (Cadet Johnson), Paul Maxey (Colonel Ramm).

Brother Rat had opened on Broadway on December 16, 1937, and ran 577 performances. Eddie Albert played Bing, Frank Albertson played Billy, Jose Ferrer played Dan, and Vincent York played Lt. "Lace Drawers." In the Warner Bros. film of *Brother Rat*, released October 29, 1938, Albert reprised his stage role of Bing, and Priscilla Lane played Joyce, Wayne Morris was Billy, Johnnie Davis was A. Furman Townsend, Jr., Jane Bryan was Kate, Ronald Reagan was Dan, Jane Wyman was Claire, Henry O'Neill was Col. Ramm, and Gordon Oliver was "Lace Drawers." Warners produced a sequel, *Brother Rat and a Baby* (1940), with Albert, Lane, Morris, Bryan, Reagan and Wyman repeating their roles.

The director of this Pasadena Playhouse production was Victor Jory, saturnine Hollywood heavy and a devoted Playhouse member.

To Quito and Back. Pasadena Playhouse, California. Opening Night, April 18, 1939. Play by Ben Hecht. Supervising Director: Gilmor Brown. Director: Maxwell Sholes. Technical Director: Fred C. Huxley. Production Manager: Frances McCune. Art Director: Rita Glover.

Cast: Victor N. Zimmerman (Colonel Pizarro), Richard Claibourne (Howard Evans), Catherine Lewis (Lola Hobbs), Tom Skinner (Alexander Sterns), Victor Mature (Zamiano), Al Woods (Customs Officer), Maxine Chevalier (Florinda), Martha Collins (Maria), Clay Irwin (Alfredo), Laird Cregar (Capt. Stewart), Michelle Barney (Fifi Stewart), James Seay (Harold Frazer), Florence Bates (Countess Rivadavia).

To Quito and Back opened at Broadway's Guild Theatre on October 6, 1937, and ran 46 performances. Sylvia Sidney played Lola, Leslie Banks (Count Zaroff in 1932's *The Most Dangerous Game*) played Alexander Stern, Evelyn Varden was Countess Rivadavia, Joseph Buloff was Zamiano, and Horace Sinclair was Captain Stewart. The play took place in a railway station in the Andes and in the villa of Countess Rivadavia.

The play concerned a New York author who runs away from civilization to embrace the primitive world of Quito, South America. Victor Mature played Zamiano, leader of the revolutionaries. The *Los Angeles Times* wrote that Laird "won favor as Capt. Stewart."

The Great American Family. Pasadena Playhouse, California. Opening Night, May 2, 1939.

Play by Lee Shippey, dramatized by Robert F. Chapin and Charles King from Shippey's novel of the same name. Supervising Director: Gilmor Brown. Director: Frank Ferguson. Technical Director: Fred C. Huxley. Production Manager: Frances McCune. Art Director: Rita Glover.

Cast: Laird Cregar (Mr. Perkins), Frank Ferguson (Gregory Seymour), Mary Todd (Sylvie Seymour), Gene Love (Dr. Gillespie), Lisa Lawrence (Mrs. Maguire), John Long (Hank, younger), Richard Barrett (Chuck, younger), Billy Epp (John, younger), Jackie Foyil (John, younger), Grisette (Herself), Frank Rollinger (Postman), Lucia Sciarrino (Tina Gonzales), Domingo Ramirez de Arellano (Juan Gonzales), Robert Willey (Hank), Ward Wood (Chuck), Barbara Pitzer (Sylvia), Thomas Rucker (Frank), George Greene (John), Doris Brenn (Helen), Irving Judson (Forrest Jones), Chalmers Paulson (Driver), Robert Hancock (Driver's Helper), Margaret Kendall (Marion Gale), Julia Gage (Mrs. Gale), Leoline Sommer (Mrs. Fitch), Pierre Hathaway (Delivery Boy), Virgina Lykins (Mrs. Willis), Ella Crane (First Woman), Viola Gilberg (Second Woman), Chalmers Paulson (Radio Announcer), Marvin Alter (Milkman).

Lee Shippey claimed that showman Earl Carroll, playwright Sidney Kingsley and film directors Edgar Selwyn and Norman Taurog all wanted the rights to the play after its Pasadena Playhouse engagement. The play, which they hoped was Broadway-bound, opened at the Curran Theatre in San Francisco on August 14, 1939, with James Bell and Carol Goodner replacing Frank Ferguson and Mary Todd in the lead roles; Laird reprised his part as Mr. Perkins. The play failed and never reached Broadway.

Petticoat Fever. Pasadena Playhouse, California. May 25, 1939. Laird Cregar as Jason Foster. No other credits available.

Elizabeth the Queen. Pasadena Playhouse, California. Opening Night, June 26, 1939. Play by Maxwell Anderson. Supervising Director: Gilmor Brown. Director: Thomas Browne Henry. Technical Director: Fred C. Huxley. Production Manager: Frances McCune. Art Director: Rita Clover. Costumes: George Gullick.

Cast: Drake Smith (First Beefeater), Bill Wagner (Second Beefeater), Thomas Woolsey (Third Beefeater), James J. Manion (Fourth Beefeater), Ernest Perry (Fifth Beefeater), Marshall Irving (Captain of the Beefeaters), Vivian Cohn (Mary), Martha Nan Collins (Tressa), Pauline Davis (Ellen), Harold Lan-

don (Fool), Tom Skinner (Raleigh), Georgia Hawkins (Penelope), Byron Barr (Capt. Armin), George Baldwin (Cecil), Dave Hyatt (Bacon), Hal Furman (First Man-at-Arms), Everett Ball (Second Man-at-Arms), Harry Lewis (Third Man-at-Arms), Jack Joley (Fourth Man-at-Arms), Tom Isley (Fifth Man-at-Arms), Michael Ames (Sixth Man-at-Arms), James Seay (Essex), Sue Borden (First Lady), Lynne Sherman (Second Lady), Patricia Corelli (Elizabeth), Major Lorntsen (First Councilor), Paul Maxey (Burghley), Gordon Hayes (Second Councilor), Victor N. Zimmerman (Marvel), Robert F. Stevens (Courier), Arthur Gage (Courtier), Bill Erwin (Herald), Laird Cregar (Burbage), Tod Koch (Hemmings), Meg Wyllie (Poins).

The Wingless Victory. Pasadena Playhouse, California. Opening Night, July 10, 1939. Play by Maxwell Anderson. Supervising Director: Gilmor Brown. Director: Lenore Shanewise. Technical Director: Fred C. Huxley. Production Manager: Frances McCune. Art Director: Rita Glover. Costumes: Al Hamilton.

Cast: Laird Cregar (The Reverend Phineas McQueston), Betty Jane Bierce (A Girl), John Shade (Jared Mungo), Robert de Bruce (Winston Urquhart), Florence Bates (Mrs. McQueston), Herschel Daugherty (Ruel McQueston), Mildred Moore (Venture), Gwen Anderson (Faith Ingalls), Kirby Smith (Happy Penny), Fay Sappington (Letty), Frank R. Wilcox (Nathaniel McQueston), Joy Anderson (Durian), Muriel Elgar (Oparre), Julia Gage (Toala), Ian McDonald (Harry, a Bailiff), Robert Claborne (Van Zandt, a Sailor).

The Wingless Victory opened at Broadway's Empire Theatre on December 23, 1936, and played for 110 performances. Katharine Cornell produced this melodrama of witchery in 1800 Salem, as well as starring as Oparre, the beautiful Malayan, whose marriage to Nathaniel McQueston (Walter Abel) spikes racism and wild, wicked revenge. Portraying the fanatical Rev. Phineas McQueston was Kent Smith—perhaps a surprise to horror buffs, who recall Smith as the rosy-cheeked Oliver of *Cat People* (1942) and *The Curse of the Cat People* (1944).

Frank R. Wilcox (1907–1974), in the lead male role of Nathaniel, was billed in the *Wingless Victory* program as "Courtesy of Warner Bros." In 1939 he appeared at Warners in the shorts *The Monroe Doctrine* (playing Henry Clay) and *Old Hickory* (playing Lincoln). A prolific character actor, he acted in three Best Picture Oscar winners: *Gentleman's Agreement* (Fox, 1947), *All the King's Men* (Columbia, 1949) and *The Greatest Show on Earth* (Paramount, 1952). On TV, he played Eliot Ness' (Robert Stack) boss through several seasons of *The Untouchables*. Betty Jane Bierce, who appeared in this production as "A Girl," later took the professional name Jane Adams. Her most famous film credit: Nina, the hunchbacked nurse (in false eyelashes), in Universal's *House of Dracula* (1945).

The Wingless Victory was Cregar's final Pasadena Playhouse production, and it was fortunate that he ended his run there in so meaty a role.

Oscar Wilde. El Capitan Theatre, Hollywood, California. Opening Night, April 22, 1940. Play by Leslie and Sewell Stokes. Produced by Charles O'Neal and Arthur Hutchinson. Directed by Arthur Ripley. A Stage League Presentation, by Special Arrangement with Norman Marshall and Arthur Hutchinson.

Cast: Laird Cregar (Oscar Wilde), George Pembroke (Carson), Robert Heller (Lord Alfred Douglas), Earl Gunn (Frank Harris), Howard Johnson (Charley Parker), Wyman Kane (Eustace), Mervin Williams (Louis Dijon), Gordon Hart (Sir Edward Clark), Edward Cooper (The Solicitor General).

Review: "Laird Cregar has the stature to play Oscar Wilde and the voice to spin out his extraordinary witticisms. There is an easy grace about his readings as there is about his whole style of performance. As the poseur, as the vain and pompous Wilde, his work is remarkable. Especially in the trial scene, first superior, then fighting for his life, Cregar's characterization is outstanding." (Virginia Wright, *Los Angeles Daily News*)

The Man Who Came to Dinner. El Capitan Theatre, Hollywood, California. Opening Night, September 19, 1941. Play by Moss Hart and George S. Kaufman. Produced by C.E. Toberman and Matt Allen. Directed by William Atlee.

Cast: Laird Cregar (Sheridan Whiteside), Rose Hobart (Maggie Cutler), Doris Nolan (Lorraine Sheldon), Arthur Gould-Porter (Beverly Carleton), Sidney Melton (Banjo), Hugh Beaumont (Bert Jefferson), Renie Riano (Miss Preen), Eleanor Lawson (June Stanley), Mary Young (Harriet Stanley), Frank Jaquet (Doctor); Dora Clement, Dick Clayton, Paul Scardon, Ethel May Halls, Florence Short, Madoline Ashton, Boyd Irwin, George Meader, James Lord, Robert Macey, Eddie Crooke, Harry Benson, Arthur Wellington, Roger Hunt, George Reynolds, John Conway, Foster Hull, Bobbie Cooper, Douglas Cooper, Arthur Mason, Roderic Geddes, Robert Swanstrom, John Lancaster, Jerry Prosk, George Baker.

Review: "The fact that Laird Cregar decided to tackle the Whiteside characterization isn't surprising at all. As a matter of fact, it was inevitable. For by girth, by temperament, and by insight, Mr. Cregar is remarkably well-fitted to enact Whiteside.... He chews the scenery very little, he gesticulates just enough, grimaces just enough, snorts just enough, and in short, is practically perfect with his overbearing rudeness and fractious wit" (Carl Combs, *The Hollywood Citizen-News*).

The Man Who Came to Dinner. Strand Theatre, Stamford, Connecticut, July 10, 1944. Produced by Gus Schirmer, Jr. Staged by Rex O'Malley.

Cast: Laird Cregar (Sheridan Whiteside), Carol Goodner (Lorraine Sheldon), Rex O'Malley (Beverly Carleton), Teddy Hart, Margaret Hayes, John Archer, Ruth Gates, Harry Sothern, Roger Kinzel.

The advertising for this play read:

First Stage Appearance in East.
Famous Hollywood Star
LAIRD CREGAR
in Person in
THE MAN WHO CAME TO DINNER

Radio Credits

Hollywood Premiere. "I Wake Up Screaming," October 17, 1941. Hostess: Louella Parsons. Cast: Betty Grable, Victor Mature, and Laird Cregar.

The Bob Hope Show. March 17, 1942. With Frances Langford, Jerry Colonna, Betty Hutton, guest star Laird Cregar.

The Adrienne Ames Show. March 24, 1942. Laird Cregar, guest.

Lux Radio Theatre. "This Gun for Hire," January 25, 1943. Host: Cecil B. DeMille. Cast: Joan Blondell (Ellen), Alan Ladd (Raven), Laird Cregar (Gates), Jack LaRue (Michael), Charles Seel (Wilson), Gloria Blondell (Annie), Norman Field (Brewster/Ticketman), Arthur Q. Bryan (Baker/Drew), Jeff Corey (Tommy/ Mason), Fred MacKaye (Copy/Newsboy), Vickie Lang (Girl), Paula Winslowe (Pearl/ Ruby), Jane Bierce (Girl Operator), Leo Cleary (Fletcher/Second Copy), Boyd Davis (Senator), Earl Keen (Cat/Conductor), Torey Carleton (Waitress/Secretary).

Lux Radio Theatre. "The Maltese Falcon," February 8, 1943. Host: Cecil B. DeMille. Cast: Edward G. Robinson (Sam Spade), Gail Patrick (Brigid), Laird Cregar (Gutman), Charlie Lung (Cairo), Bea Benaderet (Effie), Eddie Marr (Wilmer), Fred MacKaye (Miles Archer), Warren Ashe (Dundy), Charles Seel (Polhaus), Leo Cleary (Bryan), Norman Field (Jacoby).

Lux Radio Theatre. "Once Upon a Honeymoon," April 12, 1943. Host: Cecil B. DeMille. Cast: Claudette Colbert (Katie), Brian Aherne (Pat O'Toole), Laird Cregar (Baron von Luher), Albert Dekker (LeBlanc), Charles Seel (Cumberland/Second Nazi), Bea Benaderet (Anna), Fred MacKaye (Cable/Attache), Regina Wallace (Elsa), Leo Cleary (Announcer/Manager), Denis Green (Radio/First Nazi), Norman Field (Fitter/Official), Stanley Farrar (First Voice/Steward), Griff Barnett (Second Voice/ Captain), Cliff Clark (Man/Waiter), Art Gil-

more (Attache/Aide), Ken Christy (Waiter/ Taxi), Barbara Jean Wong (Child Crying).

In the 1942 RKO film *Once Upon a Honeymoon*, Ginger Rogers played Katie, Cary Grant was Pat O'Toole and Walter Slezak played Baron von Luher. On the radio show, Albert Dekker recreates his role from the movie.

This Is Our Cause. July 25, 1943. Patriotic Revue, WINS Radio, New York. Performers: Nat Brusilof, Lulu Bates, Phil Brito, Alois Havrilla, the Barry Sisters, Mina Oravi, the Southernaires, Adrienne Ames, Elsie Hitz, Diane Courtney, the WJZ Victory Troupe, Laird Cregar, Kenneth Spencer.

This hour-long show was the twenty-sixth in this series, trying to rally a *Bundles for America à la Bundles for Britain*. It offered everything from Lulu Bates singing "Ta-Ra-Ra-Boom-De-Ay" to Kenneth Spencer singing "Old Man River" as the finale. Laird participated in a dramatic presentation in the show's second half, acting King Louis XI, watching poet Francois Villon go to the guillotine. (*The Billboard* claimed he'd played King Louis 14th, but the king in *The Vagabond King*, from which this scene derived, was Louis XI.) *The Billboard*, panning the show in general, noted, "Laird did a good job—but what it had to do with 'Bundling' is questionable."

Suspense. "The Last Letter of Dr. Bronson," July 27, 1943. Cast: Laird Cregar, George Coulouris, Harold Huber, Walter Kingsford, Helen Vinson, Theodore von Eltz, Ian Wolfe. Announcer ("The Man in Black"): Ted Osborne. Producer: William Spier. Director: Robert Lewis Shayon. Script: Leonard St. Clair (from the story by Richard Kreyke). Music: Lucien Morawek. Conductor: Lud Gluskin.

The Kate Smith Show. January 7, 1944. Guest star Cregar performs "Yours Truly, Jack the Ripper" by Robert Bloch.

Inner Sanctum. "The Death Laugh," January 8, 1944.

The Philco Radio Hall of Fame. January 9, 1944. Fannie Brice, Garry Moore and Laird Cregar, who appears in a drama titled "Moonlight."

Ed Sullivan. January 10, 1944. Sullivan interviews Cregar.

The Premiere of Lifeboat. January 11, 1944. For WQXR Radio, Cregar interviews celebrities attending the opening of Alfred Hitchcock's *Lifeboat.*

Molle Mystery Theatre. "The Most Dangerous Game," January 18, 1944. Laird Cregar plays Rainsford.

Star for a Night. "Dr. Jekyll and Mr. Hyde," January 19, 1944. Paul Douglas hosted and Cregar guest starred.

Inner Sanctum. "The Song of Doom," January 22, 1944.

The Kate Smith Show. January 28, 1944. Laird acted in a dramatic playlet, "Concrete Evidence."

Inner Sanctum. "Dealer in Death," February 5, 1944. Cast: Laird Cregar (Will Hare), Ruth Matteson (Mrs. Helen Hare), Ernest Cossart (Dr. Knox), Virginia Gilmore (Mary), George Karger (Mr. MacDougal). Announcer ("Raymond, Your Host"): Raymond Edward Johnson.

Stage Door Canteen. February 11, 1944. Laird Cregar, guest star.

Duffy's Tavern. February 15, 1944. Laird Cregar, guest star.

The Philip Morris Playhouse. "The Lodger," February 18, 1944. Laird Cregar and Wendy Barrie, guest stars.

What's New? February 19, 1944. Jim Ameche, Ed Gardner, Perry Como and Laird Cregar.

Suspense. "Narrative About Clarence," March 16, 1944. Cast: Laird Cregar, Hans Conreid, Wally Maher, John McIntire. Announcer ("The Man in Black"): Joseph Kearns. Producer-Directed: William Spier. Script: Dwight Hauser and Robert Tallman. Music: Lucien Morawek. Conductor: Lud Gluskin. Pitchman for Roma Wines: Frank Martin.

The Eddie Cantor Show. April 5, 1944. Laird Cregar, guest star. With Harry Von Zell, Nora Martin, Bert Gordon, Cookie Fairchild and His Orchestra, the Sportsmen.

The Groucho Marx Show (Blue Ribbon Town). April 15, 1944. Guest star, Laird Cregar.

The Abbott and Costello Program. May 18, 1944. NBC Network, 7:00–7:30 p.m. Pacific Coast Time. Starring Bud Abbott and Lou Costello. Guest star, Laird Cregar. With: Connie Haines, Artie Auerbach, Elvia Allman, Mel Blanc, Freddie Rich and His Orchestra. Announcer, Ken Niles. Songs: "Sweet Lorraine," "Since You Went Away." Sponsor: Camel Cigarettes.

Abbott introduces Cregar as "The screen's famous man of mystery," and Costello discusses the fact he's having trouble sleeping. A sample of the comic patter:

> LAIRD: Mr. Costello, after listening to you on the radio, I catalogued you in my mind as a congenital idiot; but now that I've come face to face with you, I am forced to concede that you are nothing but an apprentice moron!

Laird invites the comedy team to his house for a midnight séance. Costello protests, "I ain't goin' to his house—he played in that picture *The Lodger*—he cut off all those dames' heads!" They do attend, of course, complete with a wolf howl by Mel Blanc and Laird going into a trance:

> LAIRD: It's a message, Costello—coming to you from the Beyond! One of your aunts is going to leave you a million dollars!
> COSTELLO: A million! Hey, that's good!
> LAIRD: No! That's bad—because another aunt won't let her do it.
> COSTELLO: Hey—that is bad.
> LAIRD: No—that's good, because the first aunt won't pay any attention to the second aunt!
> COSTELLO: Oh, that's good!
> LAIRD: No, that's bad—because there's a third aunt who won't give the money to the second aunt, who was going to give it to the first aunt!
> COSTELLO: This guy's got aunts in his trance!

Additional Radio Shows, Without Specific Dates

Hello Americans. Episode No. 9. Orson Welles, Laird Cregar, Hans Conreid, Lou Merrill, Ray Collins, Agnes Moorehead. A scenario about Cortez and Montezuma in Old Mexico.

Soldiers with Wings. 1943. Frances Dee, Martha Tilton, Laird Cregar.

The Treasury Star Parade. "Address Unknown," Episode #21. Fredric March, Laird Cregar.

Unrealized Film Projects

In the biographical section of this book, there is coverage of various films in which Laird Cregar was set to appear but did not, such as *Sioux City* and *By Jupiter*. Here are others:

September 10, 1941: *Variety*, reporting on MGM's in-preparation production of John Steinbeck's *Tortilla Flat*, wrote, "Only casting done by studio is Spencer Tracy and Laird Cregar in the leads." Released in 1942, *Tortilla Flat* starred Tracy as Pilon, Hedy Lamarr as Dolores, John Garfield as Danny and Frank Morgan as "The Pirate." As Tracy and Garfield have romantic roles, one might guess that Laird was in line to play "The Pirate," a mentally enfeebled man followed by dogs, and who wants to buy a golden candlestick for St. Francis. Morgan's performance won him a Best Supporting Actor Oscar nomination.

August 4, 1942: Jimmy Starr wrote in *The Evening Herald-Express* that 20th Century–Fox was "so impressed" by Cregar's portrayal of Capt. Henry Morgan in *The Black Swan* that his "bosses today purchased *Captain Bartholomew Roberts*, a lusty adventure tale of a brutal pirate of the 17th century. It was director Henry King who suggested the idea, and now Mr. Cregar becomes the star. Undoubtedly King will direct." The film was not produced.

September 24, 1942: Jimmy Starr, *The Evening Herald-Express*: "Although the search for an actor to play Colonel Lanser in John Steinbeck's *The Moon Is Down* in no way resembles that of Scarlett O'Hara, it has, nevertheless, been long and varied. Laird Cregar today got the nod from 20th Century–Fox's new production boss, Bill Goetz, for the coveted part.

"Cregar recently completed the important role of Henry Morgan in the pirate thriller, *The Black Swan*. It was his excellent work in this that prompted the new assignment."

The character of Col. Lanser had inspired considerable criticism in Steinbeck's novel as being too intelligent and sympathetic for a Nazi. Prior to Starr's announcement that Cregar would play Lanser, *The Hollywood Reporter* (July 31, 1942) had written that George Sanders was scheduled to play Lanser, and later (August 20, 1942) that Orson Welles would direct the film and play Lanser. On September 17, 1942, a week before Laird was announced, *The Hollywood Reporter* claimed Otto Preminger would play Lanser. Also reportedly tested: Conrad Veidt, Paul Lukas, Fritz Kortner, Alfred Lunt and Charles Laughton.

The Moon Is Down began shooting November 18, 1942, and Sir Cedric Hardwicke ultimately played Col. Lanser.

May 24, 1943: James Francis Crow in the *Hollywood Citizen-News* wrote that 20th Century–Fox would produce a film based on the diary of William E. Dodd, ambassador to prewar Germany, who'd witnessed the rise of Nazism. No one had yet been set as "No. 1 Nazi Hitler," but cast as "No. 2 Nazi" and head of the Luftwaffe Hermann Göring: Laird Cregar. "The hulking Cregar," joked Crow, "is strong enough, the company figures, to bear up under the weight of all those medals Göring has given himself." The film was never produced. Erik Larson told the story of William E. Dodd in his book *In the Garden of Beasts: Love, Terror and an American Family in Hitler's Berlin* (Crown, 2011).

Chapter Notes

Introduction

1. Harrison Carroll, "Lights! Camera! Action!," *Los Angeles Evening Herald Express*, 9 September 1944.
2. Irene Thirer, "*The Lodger*, With Laird Cregar, Super-Shocker at Roxy Theatre," *New York Post*, 20 January 1944.
3. Anne Grosvenor and Art Smith, "Love for Film Idol Nets Runaway a Broken Leg," *New York Daily News*, July 1944.
4. Otis L. Guernsey, Jr., "The Playbill: Laird Cregar, Genial Villain Of the Films," *New York Herald Tribune*, 9 January 1944.
5. Letter from Joseph I. Breen to Colonel Jason S Joy, 20th Century-Fox, 8 September 1944, Motion Picture Producers and Distributors/Production Code Administration Collection, Margaret Herrick Library, Academy of Motion Picture Arts and Sciences.
6. "Fat Laird Cregar Suffers and 'Blows Up,'" *The Evening Sun*, 15 September 1944.
7. Louella Parsons, *Los Angeles Examiner*, 8 August 1944.
8. Erskine Johnson, "In Hollywood," *Moorhead Daily News*, 25 September 1944.
9. George Sanders, *Memoirs of a Professional Cad* (New York: G.P. Putnam's Sons, 1960), p. 41.
10. "Hollywood Film Shop," *The Daily Register*, 29 November 1944.
11. Sanders, *Memoirs of a Professional Cad*, p. 41.
12. *Photoplay*, January 1942.
13. Ella Wickersham, "Hollywood Parade," *Los Angeles Examiner*, 30 April 1941.
14. Author's telephone interviews with Henry Brandon, West Hollywood, CA, 19 and 26 April 1986.
15. Mason Wiley and Damien Bona, *Inside Oscar: The Unofficial History of the Academy Awards* (New York: Ballantine Books, 1986), p. 131.
16. Howard Barnes, "The Lodger," *New York Herald-Tribune*, 20 January 1944.
17. Death certificate for David Bacon. Thanks to Scott Wilson for providing me a copy of this document.
18. Hedda Hopper, "Hedda Hopper's Hollywood," *Berkeley Daily Gazette*, 3 November 1943.
19. Author's telephone interviews with Elizabeth Cregar Hayman, Penn Valley, CA, 12 and 17 January 2012.
20. Gene Brown, *Movie Time* (New York: Macmillan, 1995), p. 173.
21. Death certificate for Laird Cregar.
22. "Neal Gets One to 15 Years for Fatal Shooting of Wife," *New York Times*, 11 December 1965.
23. David Del Valle, "A Conversation with Vincent Price," *Video Watchdog*, no. 11 (May/June 1992): 38.
24. The author has visited Cregar's grave at Forest Lawn on several occasions, the first time on December 9, 1981.
25. Sanders, *Memoirs of a Professional Cad*, p. 41.
26. Louella Parsons, "Good News," *Modern Screen*, March 1945.
27. Harold Heffernan, "Heads Full of Secrets," *The Baltimore Sun*, 3 June 1945.

Chapter 1

1. Irene Thirer, "The Most Mountainous Mr. Cregar," *New York Post*, 31 December 1943.
2. My sincere thanks to R. David Schaaf, a noted architect and historian who is a member of the Philadelphia Historical Commission. He's also my second cousin—and by a quirk of fate, lives across the road from 629 Sedgwick Street. Mr. Schaaf patiently and enthusiastically provided invaluable information on the history of Philadelphia locales, arranged for me to visit Laird Cregar's birthplace on Cresheim Road, and directed me (and in fact drove me) to many sites mentioned in this book.
3. Dee Lowrance, "Man Of Many Faces—Laird Cregar," unsourced clipping, Laird Cregar File, Billy Rose Library of Performing Arts, New York City.
4. "Laird Cregar, 28, Film Actor, Dead," *New York Times*, 10 December 1944.
5. Thirer, "The Most Mountainous Mr. Cregar."
6. See *My Thoughts Be Bloody* by Nora Titone (New York, London, Toronto, Sydney: Free Press, 2010), p. 359. The author writes that Booth's "fiendish look and crouching walk were the well-known tricks of a theatrical villain."
7. There's a theory that Booth wed a woman named Izola Mills in 1859 ("in a fit of passion"), but the major Booth historians discount it. As Laird once explained it, the mother of John Wilkes Booth was his great-great-grandmother. On another occasion, he claimed (or the reporter who interviewed him did) that his great-great-grandmother was Ann Booth, the *wife* of John Wilkes Booth. Well ... Booth's mother was actually Mary Ann Holmes, mistress of his father, tragedian Junius Brutus Booth, who divorced his wife and wed Mary May 10, 1851—John Wilkes' 13th birthday. As for "Ann Booth," no Booth biographies mention such a woman, and most historians doubt that the assassin ever married.
8. Gladys Hall, "Outsize Hero," draft for magazine

feature, dated 7 September, 1942, p. 7. Margaret Herrick Library, Academy of Motion Picture Arts and Sciences, Los Angeles.

9. *Ibid.*, p. 4.

10. *Ibid.*

11. 1880 Census. Thanks to friends and colleagues Frank Dello Stritto, Scott Gallinghouse, and my son Christopher Colin Mank (a research librarian for Baltimore County, MD), all of whom provided valuable information from the Census records.

12. Some sources, including his death certificate, give his birth year as 1869 instead of 1868. However, records note he was baptized at Holy Trinity Episcopal Church, Philadelphia on October 20, 1869, which supports the 1868 birthdate.

13. Many thanks to Eileen Wolfberg, who not only proofread this book, but discovered this article by chance while performing Library of Congress research and shared it with me.

14. "Cregar's Death Accidental," *Philadelphia Inquirer*, 18 December 1890. Thanks to Scott Gallinghouse, an expert researcher, for locating this information.

15. "Damages for Son's Death," *Philadelphia Inquirer*, 19 March 1891. Thanks to Scott Gallinghouse.

16. Living on Woodland Avenue with Elizabeth in 1900 were her parents, her 21-year-old sister Viola, her 19-year-old brother Frank, her 18-year-old sister Eugenia, her nine-year-old brother James, Viola's baby daughter Clare, Elizabeth's grandmother Charlotte, and 28-year-old Mary Gibson, the Smith family's black servant.

17. Thanks to Scott Gallinghouse, who also provided the birthdates for Laird Cregar's five brothers.

18. Thanks to the City of Philadelphia's Department of Records for providing this birth certificate.

19. Gene Brown, *Movie Time* (New York: Macmillan, 1995), p. 27. This book covers Hollywood year-by-year and provides expansive information.

20. Thanks to the Division of Vital Records, New Castle, PA, for providing a copy of Edward Cregar's death certificate.

21. Emails to author 10 and 26 March 2014. Thanks to Lauren and Erica at the Woodlands Trust for providing the burial information on Edward M. Cregar.

Chapter 2

1. Theodore Strauss, "From the Ground Up," *New York Times*, 5 April 1942.

2. Harold Heffernan, "Hollywood's Heavyweight Star Eats 6-Course Dinner for Lunch," *Boston Daily Globe*, 19 April 1942.

3. *Ibid.*

4. Among the various sources reporting that Cregar attended Winchester College is "Larger Than Life," *New York Times*, 5 January 1941.

5. Email to author from Suzanne Foster, Winchester College, 16 May 2013.

6. Among the sources: Alexander Kahn, "Single Stage Role Opens Film Career to a Jobless Thespian," *The Washington Post*, 23 August 1940.

7. *Ibid.*

8. Email to author from Cassandra Keith, Episcopal Academy, 9 April 2014.

9. Gladys Hall, "Outsize Hero," draft for magazine feature, dated 7 September, 1942, pp. 4–5. Margaret

Herrick Library, Academy of Motion Picture Arts and Sciences, Los Angeles.

10. Inez Wallace, "Riches to Rags, to Screen's Peak, Is Laird Cregar's Story," *Cleveland Plain Dealer Pictorial Magazine*, October 1944, p. 15.

11. Hall, "Outsize Hero," p. 1.

12. Elizabeth Hayman, "Uncle Sam: Family Reminiscences of One of Hollywood's Most Beloved Character Actors: Laird Cregar," *American Classic Screen Magazine*, May/June 1982.

13. Hall, "Outsize Hero," p. 7.

14. *Ibid.*, p. 8.

15. *Ibid.*

16. *Ibid.* One anomaly with this story: Laird clamed Dorothy Arzner was set to direct *Young Eagles*. Perhaps she had been at some point, but the director was William "Wild Bill" Wellman, the Lafayette Escadrille veteran pilot who'd directed *Wings*.

17. *Ibid.*, p. 2.

18. The full details of Samuel Laird Cregar's actual schooling, despite the efforts of this author, seem doomed to the cavernous recesses of the City of Philadelphia's Student Records Center. He likely graduated from high school in 1932.

19. Hall, "Outsize Hero," p. 6.

20. Author's telephone interviews with Elizabeth Cregar Hayman, Penn Valley, CA, 12 and 17 January 2012.

21. Hall, "Outsize Hero," p. 9.

22. Author's telephone interviews with Elizabeth Cregar Hayman.

23. *Ibid.*

24. My thanks to Denise Fetterley, a devoted Cregar fan, who first brought this discovery to my attention. Strangely, the Merchant Marine records alternately give Cregar's height as 5'7" and 5'9", and since he was already 21 years old, some have doubted this Samuel Cregar was *the* Samuel Laird Cregar, who was 6'3". However, a perusal of the records shows no crew member listed at over 6' tall, which leads one to suspect the ship's doctor never took the time to measure each man and simply made up a height for each one.

25. Clarence Winchester, ed., "The Manhattan and the Washington," *Shipping Wonders of the World* 22 (July 1936): 678–682.

26. Author's telephone interview with Ellen Bailey, Pasadena, CA, 16 October 2014.

27. *Variety*, March 1937. In February of 1936, the Playhouse received a $100,000 bequest, to provide an executive office building, a new school hall, and a company shop.

28. In 2015, the club celebrated its 150th year in Philadelphia and is still committed to humanitarian and community causes.

Chapter 3

1. Eileen Creelman, unsourced interview, Laird Cregar File, Billy Rose Performing Arts Library, Lincoln Center, New York City.

2. Calvin Thomas Beck, *Heroes of the Horrors* (New York: Macmillan, 1975), p. 321.

3. *Southtown Economist*, 21 October 1937.

4. Edward Arnold was a heavyweight, and had played various leads (e.g., Universal's *Sutter's Gold*, 1936), but he was settling primarily into supporting roles. Of course, there were various comics, notably

Oliver Hardy, who stood 6'1" and weighed a publicized 250 pounds (he eventually considerably topped 300). Additionally, very few leading men were fully six feet tall: Gary Cooper, Clark Gable, Errol Flynn, Basil Rathbone, and Bela Lugosi. None wanted a towering co-player who made them appear short. All in all, a tall, heavy man faced a giant challenge in theatre and film, likely out of scale with his co-players.

5. Gladys Hall, "Outsize Hero," draft for magazine feature, dated 7 September, 1942, p. 11. Margaret Herrick Library, Academy of Motion Picture Arts and Sciences, Los Angeles.

6. Letter to author from DeWitt Bodeen, Woodland Hills, CA, 28 February 1979.

7. Hall, "Outsize Hero," p. 13.

8. Harold Heffernan, "Hollywood's Heavyweight Star Eats 6-Course Dinner for Lunch," *Boston Daily Globe*, 19 April 1942.

9. Thanks to the late Ellen Bailey, Pasadena Playhouse archivist, who welcomed me to the archives in February of 2011 and provided records of Laird Cregar's performances there, as well as copies of available programs from those plays.

10. David Stenn, *Bombshell: The Life and Death of Jean Harlow* (New York: Doubleday & Co., 1993), p. 236.

11. "Drama Festival to Tell 'Story of Great Southwest,'" *Los Angeles Times*, 31 May 1937.

12. Constituting the Playhouse's "play parade" would be Gerhart Hauptmann's *Montezuma*, Ramon Romero's *Miracle of the Swallows*, Maxwell Anderson's *Night Over Taos*, Franz Werfel's *Juarez and Maximillian*, David Belasco's *Girl of the Golden West*, Belasco and Richard Walton Tully's *Rose of the Rancho*, and Agnes Peterson's *Miner's Gold*.

13. Jonathan Mann, "Dramas Offered Writer Escape from World, Words of Movies," *Los Angeles Times*, 20 July 1981.

14. *Ibid.*

15. Ed Ainsworth, "Along El Camino Real," *Los Angeles Times*, 9 July 1937.

16. Tempe E. Allison, "Pasadena Does a Cycle," *New York Times*, 22 August 1937.

17. Hall, "Outsize Hero," p. 3.

18. *Ibid.*

19. James Robert Parish and Lennard DeCarl (with William T. Leonard and Gregory W. Mank), *Hollywood Players: The Forties* (New Rochelle, NY: Arlington House, 1976), p. 166.

20. Heffernan, "Hollywood's Heavyweight Star Eats 6-Course Dinner for Lunch."

21. Parish and DeCarl, *Hollywood Players*, p. 166.

22. Laird Cregar clippings file, Billy Rose Library for the Performing Arts, Lincoln Center, New York City.

23. *Ibid.*

24. Eddie Muller, Audio Commentary for "Fox Film Noir" DVD release of *I Wake Up Screaming.*

25. Thanks to Scott Gallinghouse for locating this information and the death certificate.

26. Inez Wallace, "Riches to Rags, to Screen's Peak, Is Laird Cregar Story," *Cleveland Plain Dealer Pictorial Magazine*, 8 October 1944, p. 15.

Chapter 4

1. Inez Wallace, "Riches to Rags, to Screen's Peak, Is Laird Cregar Story," *Cleveland Plain Dealer Pictorial Magazine*, 8 October 1944, p. 15.

2. Unsourced clipping, John Carradine Clippings File, Billy Rose Library for the Performing Arts, Lincoln Center, New York City.

3. Alta Durant, "Gab," *Variety*, April 1939, p. 3.

4. "Donlevy Recovering," *Variety*, 27 February 1939, p. 8. William A. Wellman, *Beau Geste*'s producer and director, described this saga in Richard Schickel's book *The Men Who Made the Movies* (New York: Atheneum, 1975, pp. 220–221), and seemed to find it all very funny. However, director Charles T. Barton, who appeared in *Beau Geste* as an actor, provided me a vivid account of the stabbing in a telephone interview (Toluca Lake, CA, 3 October 1980), claiming Wellman "was goddamn lucky it wasn't more serious than it was" and that Donlevy might have died.

5. Interview with author, Culver City, CA, 31 July 1976. She was previously Lillian Lugosi, married to Bela Lugosi from 1933 to 1953, when they divorced; she was the mother of Bela Lugosi, Jr. (born in January of 1938). Lillian wed Brian Donlevy in 1966. Donlevy died in 1972; Lillian died in 1981.

6. Gene Brown, *Movie Time* (New York: Macmillan, 1995), p. 147.

7. Helm, "Where the Blue Begins," *Variety*, 1 March 1939, p. 50.

8. Lee Shippey, "Leeside," *Los Angeles Times*, 12 December 1944.

9. *Ibid.*

10. "Play Reviews: 'The Great American Family,'" *Variety*, 3 May 1939, p. 3.

11. Shippey, "Leeside."

12. *Ibid.*

13. Warner Bros. was meanwhile shooting *The Private Lives of Elizabeth and Essex*, with Bette Davis and Errol Flynn in Technicolor in the title roles. The character of Burbage was not in the film.

14. The play had opened at Broadway's Empire Theatre December 23, 1936, and had run 110 performances. Katharine Cornell had stared as Oparre, with Walter Abel as Nathaniel. Playing the fanatical Rev. McQueston: Kent Smith, remembered by horror fans as the placid husband in *Cat People* (1942) and *The Curse of the Cat People* (1944).

15. John Russell McCarthy, guest columnist, "Theatre Chit-Chat" (by Enid Hart), *San Mateo Tribune*, 13 July 1939.

16. Arthur Miller, "The Great American Family," *Los Angeles Times*, 10 August 1939.

17. Lee Shippey was careful not to divulge her name when he related this story in his "Lee Side o' L.A.," *Los Angeles Times*, 19 September 1941. That night Laird, by now a star, opened at the El Capitan Theatre in Hollywood, starring in a revival of *The Man Who Came to Dinner.*

18. Shippey, "Lee Side o' L.A."

19. "Play Review: 'The Great American Family,'" *Variety*, August 1939, p. 4.

20. Author's telephone interview with Peggy Stewart, Valencia, CA, 17 June 2009.

21. Gene Brown, *Movie Time* (New York: Macmillan, 1995), p. 153.

22. "Grandmas Tote Firearms to Theatre to See Picture Free," *Showmen's Trade Review*, 28 September 1940.

23. *Ibid.*

24. Martin Murphy, "Weekly Status Pictures in Production Week Ending Fri., November 24," 25 November 1939, Universal Collection, University of

Southern California Performing Arts Library. All production information cited here on *Oh, Johnny, How You Can Love!* comes from that archive. Thanks to Ned Comstock.

25. Gladys Hall, "Outsize Hero," p. 14.

26. "Film Preview and Reviews," *Variety*, 16 March 1940, p. 3.

27. W.E. Oliver, *Los Angeles Evening Herald Express*, 8 May 1940.

28. Harold Heffernan, "Hollywood's Heavyweight Star Eats 6-Course Dinner for Lunch," *Boston Daily Globe*, 19 April 1942.

29. Author's telephone interview with Peggy Moran, Camarillo, CA, 12 August 1993.

Chapter 5

1. The quote is from Wilde's *Lady Windermere's Fan*, spoken by Lord Darlington in Act III.

2. John Tagliabue, "Walling Off Oscar Wilde's Tomb From Admirers' Kisses," *New York Times*, 16 December 2011.

3. Wilde's admirers had campaigned to move the body from its original place of rest, Cimetiere de Bagneux in Paris, to Pere Lachaise in 1909. The tomb's unveiling came in August, 1914. For the occasion, the angel's awesome testicles received a cover-up—a bronze plaque, shaped like a butterfly, no less. Epstein, outraged, refused to attend the festivities, hosted by Satanist Aleister Crowley, the self-proclaimed "Beast of the Apocalypse." A short while later, Crowley saw Epstein in a Paris café and showed off his new jewelry, worn around his neck. It was the bronze butterfly... presumably pilfered by "the Beast," to allow the angel to flaunt his testicular glory. As for Aleister Crowley, he and his "Scarlet Woman," Leah Hirsig, later lived at the Abbey of Thelema, where he performed Black Masses. Scandal ensued and Mussolini exiled Crowley from Sicily in 1920. Boris Karloff played a Crowleyesque satanic high priest in *The Black Cat* (Universal, 1934).

4. Bernard V. Kleinman, "Oscar Wilde's Grave" (Letter), *New York Times*, 20 December 2011.

5. Tagliabue, "Walling Off Oscar Wile's Tomb From Admirers' Kisses."

6. *Ibid.*

7. Brooks Atkinson, "Language's Lord: The Last Five Years of Oscar Wilde's Life Acted by Robert Morley," *New York Times*, 16 October 1938.

8. James Curtis, *Spencer Tracy: A Biography* (New York: Alfred A. Knopf, 2011), p. 374.

9. Brooks Atkinson, "The Play," *New York Times*, 11 October 1938.

10. Gladys Hall, "Outsize Hero," p. 14.

11. Author's telephone interviews with Henry Brandon, West Hollywood, CA, 19 April and 26 April 1986. All quotes from Mr. Brandon in this chapter come from those interviews. Another noted Brandon credit: Chief Scar in John Ford's *The Searchers* (1956).

12. W.E. Oliver, *Evening Herald Express*, 8 May 1940.

13. One of Ripley's strangest "gigs" had come in 1922, when he accompanied by train the print of Erich von Stroheim's *Foolish Wives* from Universal City, California, to its New York City premiere—cutting the film day and night to reach acceptable length. (Von Stroheim called the cut version "the skeleton of

my dead child.") See John McElwee's excellent book, *Sell It Hot!*

14. Among the El Capitan Theatre's later distinctions: The Hollywood premiere of *Citizen Kane* took place there in 1941, after the blackballing Hearst powers prevented Orson Welles from engaging a more prominent movie house. The El Capitan of 2017 is Disney's fully restored flagship theater in Los Angeles.

15. *Oscar Wilde* theatre program, author's collection.

16. *Variety*, 22 April 1940, p. 8.

17. In Hollywood, Price had impressed as the Duke of Clarence in Universal's *Tower of London* (1939, drowned in a vat of malmsey wine by Basil Rathbone's Richard III and Boris Karloff's executioner "Mord"), and *The Invisible Man Returns* (1940, playing the title role).

18. "Play Reviews: 'Oscar Wilde,'" *Variety*, 23 April 1940, p. 3.

19. Author's telephone interviews with Henry Brandon.

20. The song figured prominently in MGM's 1941 *Dr. Jekyll and Mr. Hyde*, sung by Ingrid Bergman, as the tragic barmaid Ivy.

21. The description is based on the *Los Angeles Times'* reviews of Cregar's performance.

22. Hall, "Outsize Hero," p. 14.

23. *Ibid.*

Chapter 6

1. Inez Wallace, "Riches to Rags, to Screen's Peak, Is Laird Cregar Story," *Cleveland Plain Dealer Pictorial Magazine*, 8 October 1944, p 15.

2. "Legit Grosses," *Variety*, 1 May 1940, p. 51.

3. "*Wilde* Slim $2,500, *People* $6,000 in L.A.," *Variety*, 8 May 1940, p. 59.

4. "'Town' Weak $8,500, 'Mice' Good 11G, L.A.," *Variety*, 19 April 1939, p. 59.

5. "Evans Stout $6,000 in L.A.," *Variety*, 15 May 1940, p. 51.

6. Gladys Hall, "Outsize Hero," p. 10.

7. "Chatter," *Variety*, 6 May 1940, p. 2.

8. "Evans Stout $6,000 in L.A.," p. 51.

9. Letter to author from DeWitt Bodeen, Woodland Hills, CA, 28 February 1979.

10. Author's telephone interview with Peggy Stewart, Valencia, CA, 17 June 2009.

11. Author's telephone interviews with Henry Brandon, West Hollywood, CA, 19 and 26 April 1986. All quotes from Brandon in this chapter come from those interviews.

12. "*Show Boat* Big $43,000 in L.A.," *Variety*, 22 May 1940, p. 59.

13. "Muni, $6,000, Slim in L.A.," *Variety*, 29 May 1940, p. 51.

14. Harry Crocker, "Behind the Makeup," *Los Angeles Examiner*, 22 May 1940.

15. "John Barrymore Due," *Variety*, 23 May 1940, p. 1.

16. "Moving?," *Variety*, 29 May 1940, p. 5.

17. Robert C. Roman, "Laird Cregar 1916–1944," *Castle of Frankenstein*, no. 9 (November 1966): 26.

18. "*Widow* Nifty $35,000 in L.A.," *Variety*, 5 June 1940, p. 43.

19. "Chatter," *Variety*, 3 June 1940, p. 2.

20. Hall, "Outsize Hero," p. 15.
21. Kurt Jensen's emails to author, 30 August and 23 October 2013. Thanks to Mr. Jensen who shared this information with me from his upcoming Rouben Mamoulian biography.
22. Warner Bros., "M-G-M Speed Plans for Production of Rival Calamity Jane Films," *The Fresno Bee/The Republican*, 19 June 1940.
23. Wood Soanes, "Curtain Calls New Star Rises in Oscar Wilde Role," *Oakland Tribune*, 9 July 1940.
24. The wake of *Oscar Wilde* bears mentioning. As Arthur Hutchinson hoped against hope on the *Oscar Wilde* issue, he and Arthur Ripley found a new play, *Every Man for Himself*, a farce about Hollywood. The star was Lee Tracy, who'd achieved infamy in 1933 when, during the location shooting of MGM's *Viva Villa!* in Mexico, he'd stood drunk and naked on a balcony during a parade and urinated onto marching Mexican cadets. (See Ronald Haver's *David O. Selznick's Hollywood*, New York: Bonanza Books, 1980, pp. 151–152.) Louis B. Mayer fired Tracy from Metro, replaced him with Stu Erwin, and Tracy's career had floundered. He'd since married a young woman who kept him sober, and *Every Man for Himself* would be Tracy's first New York show in five years. *Every Man for Himself* opened at Broadway's Guild Theatre Monday, December 9, 1940. The play canceled its Wednesday matinee and abruptly closed that night, after only three performances. Total loss: $22,000. (See "Four Flop Shows On Hollywood Meant Total Loss of Over $110,000," *Variety*, 18 December 1940, p. 49.)
25. "Reserves Decision On 'Wilde' Plagiarism Suit," *Variety*, 18 December 1940, p. 49.
26. Mason Wiley and Damien Bona, *Inside Oscar* (New York: Ballantine Books, 1987), p. 491.
27. There have been various biopics about Wilde, including *Oscar Wilde* (1960), based on the Leslie and Sewell Stokes' play, with Robert Morley repeating his stage triumph, and Sir Ralph Richardson as Carson. Also in 1960, Peter Finch starred in *The Trials of Oscar Wilde*, in which James Mason portrayed Carson. Stephen Fry, the 6'4" British actor who bears a resemblance to Laird Cregar, played the title role in the 1997 film *Wilde*, with Jude Law as a very unsympathetic Lord Alfred Douglas.

Chapter 7

1. See picture section of Marlys J. Harris, *The Zanucks of Hollywood: The Dark Legacy of an America Dynasty* (New York: Crown Publishers, 1989).
2. Lucie Neville, "Hollywood After Dark," *Montana Standard*, 3 November 1940.
3. This became the title of Mel Gussow's biography of Zanuck (New York: Doubleday & Co., 1971).
4. Henry Fonda and Howard Teichmann, *Fonda: My Life* (New York: Signet, 1982), p. 142.
5. Michael Buckley, "Alice Faye," *Films in Review*, November 1982, p. 515.
6. David Ragan, *Who's Who in Hollywood, 1900–1976* (New Rochelle, NY: Arlington House, 1976), p. 241.
7. Author's telephone interview with Kay Linaker, Keene, New Hampshire, 19 July 2000 and 23 January 2003.
8. Cobbett Feinberg, *Reel Facts: The Movie Book of Records* (New York: Vintage, 1978), p. 394.

9. Frank S. Nugent, "About *The Grapes of Wrath*: Twentieth Century–Fox's Magnificent Film...," *New York Times*, 28 January 1940.
10. See the various Zanuck biographies, including Harris' *The Zanucks of Hollywood: The Dark Legacy of an America Dynasty*.
11. It was also in 1940 that Fox released *Star Dust*, a Hollywood fairy tale, with Linda Darnell as a young hopeful seeking stardom. The finale showed Darnell placing her prints at Grauman's Chinese Theatre—a ritual that the actress did in fact perform at Grauman's on March 18, 1940. Fox's *Star Dust* took place at "Amalgamated Pictures," and featured William Gargan as a Zanuck-esque producer named "Dane Wharton"; while Zanuck habitually swung a polo mallet, Gargan wielded a cane. The climax showed Wharton firing a lecherous casting director (Donald Meek)—ironic, considering that Zanuck was a legendary seducer.
12. Author's telephone interview with Undeen Darnell Hunter, Lake Elsinore, CA, 17 June 2002.
13. Much of this information comes from the article "20th's Backlot" by George P. Erengis, published in the April 1962 *Films in Review*. Erengis wrote the article at the time that Fox had sold 260 acres to New York speculator/promoter William Zeckendorf, and Aluminum Co. of America was tearing down the back lot to build apartment houses and office buildings.
14. Irene Thirer, "The Most Mountainous Mr. Cregar," *New York Post*, 31 December 1943.
15. Although Carradine denied his early eccentric ways, many have claimed to have witnessed it. Veteran actor Fritz Feld, in an interview with the author (Brentwood, CA, 11 July 1987) provided me a colorful and convincing account of Carradine's Hollywood Boulevard "act."
16. Author's telephone interview with Kay Linaker.
17. John Carradine's contract, 20th Century–Fox legal files, UCLA Performing Arts Library.
18. Charles Hamblett, *The Hollywood Cage* (New York: Hart Publishing Company, Inc., 1969), pp. 217–218.
19. Laird Cregar 20th Century–Fox contract. Thanks to Julie Graham, curator of UCLA's Performing Arts Library, for providing access to the 20th Century–Fox Archives, making it possible for me to examine this contract, April 2010. All quotes from this contract come from this source.
20. John Carradine 20th Century–Fox contract, UCLA.
21. See Edith Gwynn's "Rambling Reporter," *The Hollywood Reporter*, 24 February 1942, and Barbara Berch's "Bold, Bad (Bluffing) Cregar," *Screenland*, January 1945.
22. 20th Century–Fox legal files.
23. Kurt Jensen's emails to author, 30 August and 23 October 2013.
24. Kenneth MacGowan production notebook, MacGowan Collection, USC Performing Arts Library. MacGowan produced *Hudson's Bay*.

Chapter 8

1. Hal Wallis and Charles Higham, *Star Maker* (New York: Berkley, 1981), p. 61.
2. Author's interview, New York City, 17 August 1978.

3. Charles Higham, *Bette: The Life of Bette Davis* (New York: Dell, 1981), p. 148.

4. "Legit Comes Back, Grabs Heavy Coin," *Variety*, 21 October 1940, p. 27.

5. Lucy Chase Williams, *The Complete Films of Vincent Price* (Secaucus, NJ: Citadel Press, 1995), p. 23.

6. "Pichel, 36 Thesps Off For Idaho Location," *Variety, 26* July 1940.

7. "Screen News Here and in Hollywood," *New York Times*, 1 August 1940 (Dispatch dated 31 July 1940).

8. Kenneth MacGowan's notebook, Kenneth MacGowan Collection, USC. Thanks to Ned Comstock.

9. "Cregar's Guinea Pig Taken by Abbott," *Variety*, 21 August 1940, p. 6.

10. "*Hudson's Bay* Offers Colorful Personages," *Los Angeles Times*, 16 January 1941.

11. Carl Combs, "*Hudson's Bay,*" *Hollywood Citizen-News*, 16 January 1941.

12. Harrison Carroll, *Los Angeles Evening Herald Express*, 14 September 1940.

13. *Photoplay*, December 1940.

14. MacGowan production notebook, USC.

15. *Ibid.*

16. Cal York, *Photoplay*, January 1941, p. 62.

17. "Tyrone Power Assigned Top Spot in 20th's *Ships* Remake," *Variety*, 27 August 1940. Fox later produced *Down to the Sea in Ships* (1949) starring Lionel Barrymore as the captain and Richard Widmark as the mate.

18. Among the autographed portraits on the wall: John Carradine (*Western Union*), Dean Jagger (*Western Union*), Maria Montez (Universal's 1942 *Arabian Nights*), Linda Darnell (Fox's 1944 *Buffalo Bill*), and Deanna Durbin (Universal's 1944 *Can't Help Singing*). The Frank Sinatra "Rat Pack" was there for the shooting of *Sergeants Three* (1963), as were Gregory Peck, Omar Sharif and Julie Newmar for *Mackenna's Gold* (1969). See James V. D'Arc's excellent book *When Hollywood Came to Town: A History of Moviemaking in Utah* (Gibbs Smith, Utah, 2010).

19. Jimmie Fidler, "Jimmie Fidler in Hollywood," *Los Angeles Times*, 14 October 1940.

20. Jimmy Starr, *Los Angeles Herald Express*, 22 October 1940.

21. Lucie Neville, "Hollywood After Dark," *Montana Standard*, 3 November 1940.

22. They'd already received an Academy nomination for "Always and Always" (collaborating with Edward Ward) from MGM's *Mannequin* (1938).

23. In 1934, Neal had become engaged to Inez Martin, ex–Follies mistress to gangster Arnold Rothstein, who'd been shot to death in the Park Central Hotel in 1928; Ms. Martin had collected $100,000 in life insurance and an extra $50,000 after contesting Rothstein's will. Neal's father had ended Tom's love affair with the twice-his-age Inez by threatening to disinherit him. Neal had made his Broadway debut in *If This Be Treason* (1935); in 1936, he appeared in *Daughters of Atreus*, with Eleonora von Mendelssohn and Maria Ouspenskaya. His film debut: *Out West with the Hardys* (1938).

24. Arthur Lyons, "Killer Career—Actor Tom Neal," *Palm Springs Life*. "Talitha cumi" are the words Jesus used to raise the dead girl to life in the Gospel of Mark, 5:41.

25. Hedda Hopper, "The Late Great Laird," *Chicago Daily Tribune*, 2 December 1945.

Chapter 9

1. "Film Notables Keep Up Old Year's' Spirit," *Los Angeles Times*, 2 January 1941.

2. "George Sanders," *Current Biography*, 1943.

3. L.F. R., "The Screen This Week," *The Albuquerque Journal*, 19 January 1941.

4. Harrison Carroll, *Los Angeles Evening Herald Express*, 16 January 1941.

5. *Ibid.*, 10 February 1941.

6. George E. Phair, "Retakes," *Variety*, December 1940, p. 2.

7. Harrison Carroll, *Los Angeles Evening Herald Express*, 13 March 1941.

8. Laird Cregar legal file 20th Century–Fox Collection, UCLA Performing Arts Library.

9. Charles Higham and Joel Greenberg, "Rouben Mamoulian," *The Celluloid Muse: Hollywood Directors Speak* (New York: Signet, 1972), pp. 160–161.

10. See Anthony Quinn's memoir, *One Man Tango*, written with Daniel Paisner (New York: HarperCollins, 1995).

11. See Harrison Carroll *Los Angeles Evening Herald Express,* 21 March 1941. Also, "Power, Cregar recover; *Sand* Nears Sked's End," *The Hollywood Reporter*, 4 April 1941.

12. Hal Wallis and Charles Higham, *Star Maker* (New York: Berkley, 1981), pp. 107–108.

13. Ken Morgan, "Hollywood Keyhole," *McKinney Daily Courier*, 23 May 1941.

14. Wallis and Higham, p. 107.

Chapter 10

1. Author's interview with DeWitt Bodeen, Woodland Hills, CA, 8 December 1981.

2. "20th Studio Club Party Clicks with Fun, Laughs," *The Hollywood Reporter*, 28 April 1941. Also, *Hollywood Citizen-News*, 28 April 1941, and "Fiesta Joyful Event," *Hollywood Citizen-News*, 30 April 1941.

3. "20th Studio Club Party Clicks with Fun, Laughs," *The Hollywood Reporter*.

4. *Ibid.*

5. "Fiesta Joyful Event," *Hollywood Citizen-News.*

6. Ella Wickersham, "Hollywood Parade," *Los Angeles Examiner*, 30 April 1941. Also, "Frolicsome Guests Enjoy Poolside," *Hollywood Citizen-News*, 30 April 1941.

7. "Frolicsome Guests Enjoy Poolside," *Hollywood Citizen-News.*

8. Wickersham, "Hollywood Parade."

9. Author's telephone interviews with Henry Brandon, West Hollywood, CA, 19 and 26 April, 1986.

10. John Truesdell, "Hollywood Personalities Revealed," *Oakland Tribune*, 26 May 1941.

11. Harrison Carroll, *Los Angeles Evening Herald Express*, 29 May 1941.

12. Carl Combs, *Hollywood Citizen-News*, 29 May 1941.

13. Hall, "Outsize Hero," p. 16.

14. Fred Lawrence Guiles, *Tyrone Power: The Last Idol* (New York: Doubleday & Co., 1979).

15. Cobbett Feinberg, *Reel Facts: The Movie Book of Records* (New York: Vintage Books, 1978), p. 394.

16. *Hollywood Citizen-News*, 26 June 1941.

17. Harrison Carroll, *Los Angeles Evening Herald Express*, 8 April 1943.

18. Unsourced clipping, Laird Cregar Clippings File, Billy Rose Library for the Performing Arts, Lincoln Center, New York.

19. Email sent to author 28 July 2015. Thanks to Gavin Murrell of Montgomery Management, Inc., West Hollywood, CA, for emailing me information about this address and photographs.

20. The information about Barney's Beanery comes from Domenic Priore, "The History of Barney's Beanery," www.barneysbeanery.com

21. The information about the tragic deaths which occurred at the addresses cited here come from Ken Schessler's book *This Is Hollywood* (Redlands, CA: Ken Schessler Publishing, 1987), an excellent source for locations with film-related history.

Chapter 11

1. Andy Lewis, "'Maltese Falcon' Statue Sells for Eye-Popping $4 Million at Auction," *The Hollywood Reporter*, 25 November 2013.

2. Steve Fisher, *I Wake Up Screaming* (New York: Bantam Books, 1960), p. 34. Fisher updated his 1941 novel to 1960 for this edition.

3. Thanks to Eddie Muller and his excellent audio commentary for *I Wake Up Screaming*, released by 20th Century–Fox DVD. The definitive biography of Woolrich is *Cornell Woolrich: First You Dream, Then You Die*, by Francis M. Nevins, Jr. (New York: Mysterious Press, 1988).

4. "The Film Scene," *Syracuse Herald-Journal*, 24 July 1941.

5. Muller, audio commentary.

6. *Ibid.*

7. Sidney Skolsky, "Watching Them Make Pictures," *Hollywood Citizen-News*, 13 August 1941.

8. Jeremy Arnold, *I Wake Up Screaming*, Turner Classic Movies online article.

9. Gladys Hall, "Outsize Hero," p. 11.

10. Hedda Hopper, *San Francisco Chronicle*, 24 October 1941.

11. Letter from the Production Code Administration to Colonel Jason S. Joy, 20th Century–Fox Film Corp., 23 July 1941.

12. Hall, "Outsize Hero," p. 15.

13. For information on Peggy Stack, I'm grateful to Denise Fetterley, a devoted Laird Cregar fan and valued friend and colleague.

14. James Francis Crow, *Hollywood Citizen-News*, 1 August 1941.

15. Dee Lowrance, "Acting Is a Painful Job," *The Washington Post*, 9 November 1941.

Chapter 12

1. Author's telephone interviews with Elizabeth Cregar Hayman, Penn Valley, CA, 12 and 17 January 2012. All quotes from Ms. Hayman in this chapter come from those interviews.

Chapter 13

1. Laird and Renie both had appeared in *Oh Johnny, How You Can Love!*, in the auto court episode: he as the mechanic, she as a mother who screamed for her bratty son with an ear-piercing "Jun-ior!"

2. Harrison Carroll, *Los Angeles Evening Herald Express*, 22 September 1941.

3. "Play Review: 'The Man Who Came to Dinner,'" *Variety*, 22 September 1941, p. 3.

4. Radie Harris, "Broadway Runaround," *Variety*, 18 July 1944, p. 4.

5. A photograph of this letter from John Barrymore survives in the Laird Cregar file at 20th Century-Fox.

6. Henry Brandon gave me a vivid account of this disastrous evening (author's telephone interview, 19 and 26 April, 1986); Brandon also knew Bob Neff, Cregar's stand-in, who told Brandon Laird's personal account of this debacle. Actor John Alvin told the story in Tom Weaver's book *Science Fiction Confidential* (Jefferson, NC: McFarland, 2002, p. 2). The story has widely circulated for many years; indeed, unfortunately, it's one of the most often-repeated anecdotes regarding Cregar.

7. Author's telephone interviews with Henry Brandon.

8. *Ibid.*

Chapter 14

1. Otis L. Guernsey, Jr., "The Playbill: Laird Cregar, Genial Villain Of the Films," *New York Herald Tribune*, 9 January 1944.

2. "The Screen," *New York Times*, 26 January 1942.

3. Author's telephone interview with Charles Bennett, Beverly Hills, CA, 29 October 1992.

4. "Trade Showings: 'Hot Spot,'" *Variety*, 17 October 1941, p. 3.

5. "'Dinner' $40,000 in 4 L.A. Weeks; Dante 15 G," *Variety*, 22 October 1941, p. 59.

6. Hedda Hopper, "Mickey Turns the Yule Tide!," *The Washington Post*, 30 October 1941.

7. Ethan Mordden, *The Hollywood Studios* (New York: Alfred A. Knopf, 1988), p. 81.

8. "Sad Story of Actor Wanting to Do Comedy," *Variety*, 12 November 1941, p. 6.

9. Hedda Hopper, "Musical Bon Bon Saves Starving!," *The Washington Post*, 1 November 1941.

10. Guernsey, "The Playbill."

11. James Robert Parish and Lennard DeCarl (with William T. Leonard and Gregory W. Mank), *Hollywood Players: The Forties* (New Rochelle, NY: Arlington House, 1976), p. 166.

12. Marc Lawrence, interview with Roger Hurlburt. Thanks to Roger, who had interviewed Lawrence and who emailed me this quote (31 December 2009).

13. "Cregar the Courtier," *The Baltimore Sun*, 30 November 1941.

14. Hedda Hopper, "Rubes on the Rogue!," *The Washington Post*, 8 November 1941.

15. Nelson B. Bell, "'Hot Spot' Deserves One Among Better Mysteries," *The Washington Post*, 14 November 1941.

16. Donald Kirkley, "'Hot Spot': Murder Mystery On Screen At New Theatre Has Double Twist At End," *The Baltimore Sun*, 29 November 1941.

17. Author's telephone interviews with Elizabeth Cregar Hayman, Penn Valley, CA, 12 and 17 January 2012. All quotes from Ms. Hayman in this chapter come from those interviews.

18. Kurt Jensen's emails to author, 30 August and 23 October 2013.

19. *Ibid.*

20. *Ibid.*

21. Parish and DeCarl, *Hollywood Players*, p. 166.

22. Kurt Jensen's emails to author.

23. Hedda Hopper, "Hedda Hopper's Hollywood," *Los Angeles Times*, 25 December 1942. In this Christmas day column, Ms. Hopper specified that the event described had occurred the previous Yuletide.

Chapter 15

1. Bill Wickersham, "Hollywood Parade," *Los Angeles Examiner*, 6 January 1942.

2. Gene Brown, *Movie Time* (New York: Macmillan, 1995), p. 164.

3. Paramount's all-star *Star-Spangled Rhythm* (1942) commemorated this joke with a skit in which a sugar daddy (Ernest Truex) wins the favors of a gold digger (Susan Hayward) by wooing her with a girdle.

4. David Carradine, *Endless Highway* (Boston: Journey Editions, 1995), p. 41.

5. Alta Durant, "Gab," *Variety*, 30 December 1941, p. 3.

6. Otis L. Guernsey, Jr., "The Playbill: Laird Cregar, Genial Villain Of the Films," *New York Herald Tribune*, 9 January 1944.

7. Peter Levins "What Has Happened to Justice? Death of Blueblooded Film Actor Remains an Embarrassing Mystery," *New York Sunday News*, 21 May 1944.

8. Thomas M. Pryor, "At the Roxy," *New York Times*, 5 June 1942.

9. Harrison Carroll, *Los Angeles Examiner*, 9 February 1942.

10. John Carradine Legal File, 20th Century–Fox Archive, UCLA Performing Arts Library.

11. Cobbett Feinberg, *Reel Facts: The Movie Book of Records* (New York: Vintage Books, 1978), p. 390.

12. Author's telephone interviews with Elizabeth Cregar Hayman, Penn Valley, CA, 12 and 17 January 2012. All quotes from Ms. Hayman in this chapter come from those interviews.

13. Mason Wiley and Damien Bona, *Inside Oscar* (New York: Ballantine Books, 1987), p. 120.

14. Sydney Greenstreet death certificate. Thanks to Scott Wilson for providing me a copy.

15. Scott Eyman, *Lion of Hollywood: The Life and Legend of Louis B. Mayer* (New York: Simon & Schuster, 2005), p. 4.

Chapter 16

1. Laird Cregar's 20th Century–Fox Legal File.

2. "A Mystery Play Is Due Here Soon," *New York Times*, 31 March 1942.

3. Theodore Strauss, "From the Ground Up," *New York Times*, 5 April 1942.

4. Neil Rau, "Joan of Paris," *Los Angeles Examiner*, 17 April 1942.

5. Harold Heffernan, "Movie Stars' Careers Shame Class Prophets," *The Baltimore Sun*, 19 April 1942.

6. "At the Roxy," *New York Times*, 24 April 1942.

7. Author's interview with Alan Napier, Pacific Palisades, CA, 15 May 1983.

8. *Ibid.*

9. Rudy Behlmer, Audio Commentary, *The Black Swan* DVD.

10. Author's telephone interviews with Elizabeth Cregar Hayman, Penn Valley, CA, 12 and 17 January 2012. All quotes from Ms. Hayman in this chapter come from those interviews.

11. Barbara Berch, "Bold, Bad (Bluffing) Cregar," *Screenland*, January 1945, p. 76.

12. *Variety*, 20 May 1942, p. 12.

13. Margot Peters, *The House of Barrymore* (New York: Alfred A. Knopf, 1990), p. 459.

14. Laird Cregar 20th Century–Fox Legal File.

15. Thanks to radio historian Bruce Forsberg, who made it possible for me to obtain a copy of this script.

16. Robert Louis Taylor, *W.C Fields: His Follies and Fortunes* (New York: Signet, 1967), pp. 251–252.

Chapter 17

1. Laird Cregar, guest columnist for Harrison Carroll, *Los Angeles Evening Herald Express*, 14 August 1942.

2. "Garden Party Awaited at Tyrone Power Estate," *Hollywood Citizen- News*, 24 July 1942.

3. Author's telephone interviews with Elizabeth Cregar Hayman, Penn Valley, CA, 12 and 17 January 2012. All quotes from Ms. Hayman in this chapter come from those interviews.

4. Cregar, *Los Angeles Evening Herald Express.*

5. Inez Wallace, "Riches to Rags, to Screens Peak, Is Laird Cregar Story," *Cleveland Plain Dealer Pictorial Magazine*, 8 October 1944, p. 15.

6. "Cabin in the Canyon," unsourced clipping, Laird Cregar Clippings File, Billy Rose Library for the Performing arts, Lincoln Center, New York.

Chapter 18

1. Gladys Hall, "Outsize Hero," p. 15. This interview, apparently never published, survives in Ms. Hall's Collection at the Margaret Herrick Library, Academy of Motion Picture Arts and Sciences. Thanks to Kristine Krueger for making it available.

2. Margo Peters, *The House of Barrymore* (New York: Knopf, 1990), p. 132.

3. Email to author from Scott Eyman, 22 March 2011. Eyman is the author of such excellent books as *Empire of Dreams: The Epic Life of Cecil B. DeMille* (2010) and *John Wayne: The Life and Legend* (2015). He had interviewed John Carradine near Cleveland when the actor was touring in Roy Radin's Vaudeville Show in 1981. Also in the show: Tiny Tim, and Zippy the trained chimp.

4. Email to author from Elizabeth Hayman, 18 January 2012.

5. Laughton's homosexuality is covered in his various biographies, as well as in Elsa Lanchester's memoir *Elsa Lanchester: Herself* (New York: St. Martin's Press, 1983).

6. The author examined this contract when describing it for the Entertainment/Memorabilia Catalog from Heritage Auctions, Dallas, TX, 2007.

7. For the most comprehensive coverage of Whale's life and career, see James Curtis, *James Whale: A New World of Gods and Monsters* (London: Faber & Faber, 1998).

8. Lyn Tornabene, *Long Live The King* (New York: G.P. Putnam's Sons, 1976), p. 20.

9. Stuart Jerome, *Those Crazy Wonderful Years When We Ran Warner Bros.* (Secaucus, NJ: Lyle Stuart, Inc., 1983), p. 223.

10. The story comes from the late Michael Fitzgerald, the author of the book *Universal Pictures*. In the late 1980s and 1990s, Fitzgerald organized a yearly reunion of Universal stars from the 1930s and 1940s. Fitzgerald recounted this story to me based on the reminiscences of some in recalling Ms. Allbritton, who wed Charles Collingwood in 1946 and who died in 1979. Another favorite Allbritton story among Universal's old guard: in *Son of Dracula*, when Robert Paige and other players were to open a coffin and discover Allbritton as a sleeping vampire, they found Louise, aside from her brunette wig, stark naked.

11. Author's telephone interview with Faye Marlowe, Cary, NC, 23 October 2007.

12. Harrison Carroll, *Los Angeles Evening Herald Express*, 27 August 1942.

13. Charles Higham and Roy Moseley, *Princess Merle* (New York: Coward-McCann, 1983), p. 160.

14. *Afternoon TV Showcase Exclusive: Hollywood Tragedies* (Englewood Cliffs, NJ: Dynasty Media Distributing Co., 1985), pp. 76–77.

15. "1600 Aboard Saved as Fire Spreads Through Ship at Sea: Witness Tells of Navy Grit as Transport Burned," *The Washington Post*, 10 September 1942.

16. "Beverly Hills Salutes Heroes and Buys Bonds," *Los Angeles Times*, 27 September 1942.

17. "Hollywood 'Goes to Town' for Uncle Sam's Warriors," *Los Angeles Times*, 5 October 1942.

18. Philip K. Scheuer, "Cregar to Play Javert in Victor Hugo Classic," *Los Angeles Times*, 8 October 1942.

19. Here are the *Film Daily* Poll results for the other categories of performers:

• Five Top Feminine Stars: (1) Greer Garson, *Mrs. Miniver*, (2) Joan Fontaine, *Suspicion*, (3) Bette Davis, *Now Voyager*, (4) Katharine Hepburn, *Woman of the Year*, (5) Teresa Wright, *The Pride of the Yankees*.

• Five Top Male Stars: (1) Gary Cooper, *The Pride of the Yankees*, (2) Walter Pidgeon, *How Green Was My Valley*, (3) Walter Pidgeon, *Mrs. Miniver*, (4) Monty Woolley, *The Man Who Came to Dinner*, (5) Fredric March, *One Foot in Heaven*.

• Five Top Supporting Actresses: (1) Teresa Wright, *Mrs. Miniver*, (2) Sara Allgood, *How Green Was My Valley*, (3) Betty Field, *Kings Row*, (4) Dame May Whitty, *Mrs. Miniver*, (5) Agnes Moorehead, *The Magnificent Ambersons*.

20. *Variety*, 30 December 1942, p. 9.

21. Hall, "Outsize Hero," p. 4.

22. Mason Riley and Damien Bona, *Inside Oscar* (New York: Ballantine Books, 1987), p. 128.

23. W.R Wilkinson, *The Hollywood Reporter*, 9 March 1943.

24. Riley and Bona, p. 131.

25. *Ibid.*

26. James Francis Crow, *Hollywood Citizen-News*, 8 March 1943.

Chapter 19

1. Harrison Carroll, *Los Angeles Evening Herald Express*, 5 April 1943.

2. "Price On 20th Termer," *Variety*, 14 December 1942, p. 2.

3. The most comprehensive Van Johnson biography to-date is Ronald L. Davis, *Van Johnson: MGM's Golden Boy*, Hollywood Legends Series (Jackson, MS: University Press of Mississippi, 2001).

4. Ned Wynn, *We Will Always Live in Beverly Hills: Growing Up Crazy in Hollywood* (New York: William Morrow and Company, 1990).

5. Ned Wynn's email to author, 7 March 2014.

6. Harold Heffernan, "Laird Cregar Advises Actors," *Miami Daily News*, 26 September 1943.

7. Author's interview with Fritz Feld, Brentwood, CA, 11 July 1987.

8. Thanks to the late John Conner, who told me this story, as told him by one of his Army colleagues.

9. Cal York "Inside Stuff," *Photoplay*, September 1943.

10. Elizabeth Hayman, "Uncle Sam: Family Reminiscences of One of Hollywood's Most Beloved Character Actors: Laird Cregar," *American Classic Screen* (May/June 1982): 28.

11. "Screen News Here in Hollywood," *New York Times*, 11 June 1943.

12. Sheilah Graham, *The Atlanta Constitution*, 16 June 1943.

13. Scott Eyman, *Lion of Hollywood: The Life and Legend of Louis B. Mayer* (New York: Simon & Schuster, 2005), p. 371.

14. Kay Proctor, "Mood Expert," *Motion Picture*, December 1945.

15. Joseph I. Breen, Letter to Col. Jason S. Joy, 20th Century–Fox Studio, 15 July 1943.

16. *The Hollywood Reporter*, 21 July 1943.

17. Barbara Berch, "Bold, Bad (Bluffing) Cregar," *Screenland*, January 1945, p. 77.

Chapter 20

1. *Film Daily*, 15 February 1931.

2. *Variety*, 8 December 1931.

3. Joel E. Siegel, *Val Lewton: The Reality of Terror* (New York: The Viking Press, 1973), p. 71.

4. Bodeen's research for the script involved visiting an actual devil-worshipping cult in New York City, where the Satanists invoked spells against Hitler!

5. See the MPAA/PCA File on *Hitler's Madman*, April 1943, Margaret Herrick Library, Academy of Motion Picture Arts and Sciences.

6. Rains had starred for Universal in several horror films: 1933's *The Invisible Man*, 1934's *The Man Who Reclaimed his Head*, 1935's *Mystery of Edwin Drood*, and 1941's *The Wolf Man*, playing Chaney's father in the last.

7. *Variety*, 5 August 1942, p. 2.

8. The British actor (1904–1988) had previously had two significant horror credits: *Svengali* (Warner Bros., 1931), in which he played Little Billee to John Barrymore's Svengali; and *The Mummy* (Universal, 1932), as Norton, the young archaeologist who, at the sight of Karloff's risen Mummy, goes stark-raving mad. Among his many theatre credits: Standby to Rex

Harrison as Henry Higgins in the original Broadway *My Fair Lady* (1956).

Chapter 21

1. Harold Heffernan, "Laird Cregar Advises Actors," *Miami Daily News*, 26 September 1943.

2. Rumbelow is the recognized expert on the Ripper, and author of the acclaimed book *The Complete Jack the Ripper* (London: Penguin Books, 2004). In July of 2010, the author joined his fascinating Ripper tour in Whitechapel, visiting the sites of the infamous murders.

3. The most complete (but partly suspect) biography of Oberon: Charles Higham and Roy Moseley, *Princess Merle* (New York: Coward-McCann, 1983).

4. Ray Hagen, Laura Wagner, Steven Tompkins, et al., "Movie Dubbers," credits for 674 movies, last updated: 24 June 2015. http://www.janettedavis.net/Dubbers/dubberslist.php

5. Letter from Joseph I. Breen to Col. Jason S. Joy, 9 August 1943. MPAA/PCA File.

6. Memo from Darryl F. Zanuck, 2 August 1943, John Brahm Collection, USC Performing Arts Library.

7. Donald Kirkley, "Film Notes," *The Baltimore Sun*, 15 August 1943.

8. Joan Fontaine, *No Bed of Roses* (New York: William Morrow and Company, 1978), p. 108.

9. Brahm Collection, USC.

10. Letter from Joseph I. Breen to Col. Jason S. Joy, 25 August 1943. MPAA/PCA File.

11. See the entry on *The Lodger* in the appendix, which explains how an editing decision made by Darryl Zanuck resulted in Pickard actually playing two roles in the film.

12. Joel Greenberg, "Writing for the Movies: Barré Lyndon," *Focus on Film*, no. 21 (Summer 1975): 48.

13. Leonard Maltin, *Behind the Camera* (New York: Signet, 1971), p. 171.

14. Marty Baumann, "Sumishta Brahm Remembers Her Father, John Brahm," *Monsters from the Vault* 13, no. 24 (Winter 2008): 53.

15. Author's telephone interview with David Frankham, New Mexico, 5 February 2014. Frankham worked with Brahm on TV's *The Alfred Hitchcock Hour* ("Murder Case," 6 March 1964), and, as he expresses it, "tormented" him with questions about Laird.

16. David Del Valle, "John Brahm: The Last Interview," *Video Watchdog*, January/February 1993, p. 50.

17. *Variety*, 3 September 1943, p. 9.

18. Author's interview with Frankham.

19. Barré Lyndon, Shooting script for *The Lodger*, 12 July 1943, author's personal collection, p. 78.

20. Greenberg, "Writing for the Movies."

21. "Laird Cregar Stalks Women as Hays Office Blushes Can-Can," *The Courier–Journal*, 23 August 1943.

22. Al Kilgore and Roi Frumkes, "Merle Oberon," *Films in Review*, February 1982, p. 90.

23. Higham and Moseley, pp. 160–161. In this biography of her, the authors spin an unsourced/suspect story that the star became so insecure during the shoot of *The Lodger* that she picked up a young carpenter on the crew, luring him home to seduce him, simply to boost her ego. It didn't work; the car-

penter informed the star he was religious and walked out on her. According to the book "...next day, he was missing from the crew."

24. *New York Times*, 20 January 1944.

25. Author's interview with Frankham.

26. Alton Cooke, "Jack the Ripper Spreads Terror on Roxy Screen," *New York World-Telegram*, 20 January 1944.

27. Louella Parsons, *Los Angeles Examiner*, 25 August 1943.

28. *Ibid.*, 5 October 1943.

Chapter 22

1. In researching the David Bacon murder and its aftermath, two comprehensive articles were very helpful: George O'Neal's "Hollywood's Real Thrillers Challenge Its Cleverest Movie Sleuths," published in *The American Weekly* Sunday magazine of the *San Antonio Light* (24 October 1943); and Peter Levins' "What Has Happened to Justice? Death of Blue-blooded Film Actor Remains an Embarrassing Mystery," published in the *New York Sunday News* (21 May 1944). Other sources include: *Variety* ("Socialite Film Actor Mysteriously Killed," 15 September 1943, p. 7); *The Los Angeles Times* ("Mystery Rider Believed Slayer of Actor Bacon," 14 September 1943); *The Boston Globe* ("Police Seek Hitchhiker Slayer of Bacon's Son," 14 September 1943; "Police to Quiz Bacon's Widow Concerning Her Doings on Murder Day," 16 September 1943; "David Bacon's Estate May Total $100,000," 17 September 1943; "Bacon Clew Seen in School Sweater Worn 5 Years Ago," 20 September 1943; "Tragedy Falls Again on Greta Bacon, Slain Actor's Wife," 24 September 1943); and *The Chicago Daily Tribune* (Hedda Hopper's "Looking at Hollywood," 2 November 1943).

2. My thanks to Scott Wilson, an unrivaled historian on the deaths of celebrities and on cemeteries, for sending me a copy of Bacon's death certificate.

3. Performing virtually all the action, behind a mask, was stuntman Tom Steele; dubbing his voice was radio actor Gayne Whitman.

4. For a peek at Greta Keller in this era, watch MGM's Joan Crawford–John Wayne 1942 release *Reunion in France*, in which she appears, briefly and uncredited, as "Countess von Steinkamp," the wife of a Nazi.

5. As the case festered, Police questioned suspect Erwin Shaum, whom Bacon had hired as a gardener nine days before the murder. Shaum, who turned out to be a deserter from Balboa Park Navy Camp at San Diego, was cleared of the crime. A man named Blakely C. Patterson confessed to the murder to two reporters, who hid him at Lake Sherwood, north in the San Fernando Valley, while they arranged exclusive publication to his story. Patterson turned out to be a crank.

6. Rezso Seress, who composed the song in late 1932, committed suicide in 1968. When his attempt to kill himself by jumping out a window in Budapest failed, he choked himself with a wire in a hospital.

Chapter 23

1. Otis L. Guernsey, Jr. "The Playbill: Laird Cregar, Genial Villain of the Films," *New York Herald-Tribune*, 9 January 1944.

2. Unsourced clipping, Laird Cregar Clippings File, Billy Rose Library for the Performing Arts, Lincoln Center, New York City.

3. Lucy Chase Williams, *The Complete Films of Vincent Price* (New York: Citadel Press, 1995), p. 84.

4. Barbara Berch, "Bold, Bad (Bluffing) Cregar," *Screenland*, January 1945, p. 76.

5. The day before, Basil Rathbone had emceed the Drive at the Shrine Auditorium in Los Angeles.

6. "The Most Mountainous Mr. Cregar," *New York Post*, 31 December 1943.

7. Guernsey, "The Playbill."

8. Radie Harris, "Broadway Runaround," *Variety*, 18 January 1944, p. 6.

9. Incidentally, the horror competition on Broadway was Universal's *Sherlock Holmes and the Spider Woman*, starring Basil Rathbone and Gale Sondergaard, and then in its second week at the Rialto Theatre. Its take that week: $7,500.

10. To describe the Roxy stage show: The Gae Foster Roxyettes opened with the Four Lyttle Sisters, segueing to emcee Milton J. Cross, the Paul Lavalle orchestra, comic Jack Durant, keyboardist Maurice Rocco, tap dancer Hal LeRoy, and singer Helen Forrest, who delivered "Besame Mucho" and a medley of her hits. *Variety* called the show a "heavy load of top talent" that "can't miss."

11. "Trade Showings," *Variety*, 5 January 1944, p. 3.

12. Thomas M. Pryor, "The Lodger," *New York Times*, 20 January 1944.

13. Kate Cameron, "Real Thriller Film On the Roxy Screen," *New York Daily News*, 20 January 1944.

14. Irene Thirer, "'The Lodger,' with Laird Cregar, Super-Shocker at Roxy Theatre," *New York Post*, 20 January 1944.

15. *Ibid.* Incidentally, *The Billboard*, which also reviewed the January 19 stage show, was less impressed by Laird's personal appearance: "Cregar's showing wasn't too hot. His act is geared to poke fun at his film killer roles. Material reaches out for laughs but has plenty of creaking moments. Obviously too little thought was given to what Cregar was to do and say after he had walked on stage and the result—very unfair to him—was in the style of oldie movie personal appearances. He deserves better treatment." Perhaps *The Billboard* reviewed a different presentation of the stage show that date; Thirer claimed Laird performed a scene from *The Lodger*, while *The Billboard* made no mention of it.

16. Thanks to Jonathan Dixon for discovering and sharing this recording of *Star for a Night*.

17. G.E. Blackford, *New York Journal-American*, 20 January 1944.

18. Howard Barnes, *New York Herald-Tribune*, 20 January 1944.

19. Kate Cameron, *New York Daily News*, 20 January 1944.

20. Alton Cook, *New York World-Telegram*, 20 January 1944.

21. "Picture Grosses," *Variety*, 26 January 1944, p. 13.

22. *Ibid.*, 2 February 1944, p. 11.

23. *Ibid.*

24. Fred Lawrence Guiles, *Tyrone Power: The Last Idol* (New York: Berkley Books, 1979), p. 171.

25. "Picture Grosses," *Variety*.

26. Laird Cregar Legal File, 20th Century–Fox.

27. "*Inner Sanctum*, Laird Cregar enacts role in one of radio's oldest horror programs," *Life*, February 1944.

28. "Picture Grosses," *Variety*, 16 February 1944, p. 11.

29. Radie Harris, "Broadway Runaround," *Variety*, 15 February 1944, p. 4.

30. "Song of Life," *The Billboard*, 26 February 1944, p. 10.

31. Robert C. Roman, "Laird Cregar 1916–1944," *Castle of Frankenstein*, no. 9 (November 1966): 60.

32. Irene Thirer, "The Most Mountainous Mr. Cregar," *New York Post*, 31 December 1943.

33. Author's telephone interviews, Elizabeth Cregar Hayman, Penn Valley, CA, 12 and 17 January 2012.

34. Cook, *New York World-Telegram*.

Chapter 24

1. The play would run in New York through a third year, playing until December 30, 1944, tallying 1,295 performances.

2. Nigel Jones, *Through a Glass Darkly: The Life of Patrick Hamilton* (London: Black Spring Press, Ltd., 2008).

3. Patrick Hamilton, *Hangover Square* (New York: Europa Editions, 1967), p. 12.

4. Jones, p. 216.

5. *Ibid.*, p. 272.

6. Hamilton, p. 24.

7. *Ibid.*, p. 275.

8. *Ibid.*, p. 250.

9. Joel Greenberg, "Writing for the Movies: Barré Lyndon," *Focus on Film*, no. 21 (Summer 1975): 47–58. All quotes from Barré Lyndon in this chapter come from this article/interview.

10. This script and all the other script drafts of *Hangover Square* are in the John Brahm Collection at USC's Performing Arts Library. Thanks to Ned Comstock for making them available to me.

11. An excellent account of *Laura*'s troubled production can be found in the chapter "The Mystique of *Laura*," in *The Cinema of Adventure, Romance & Terror*, edited by the late George E. Turner (Hollywood, CA: The ASC Press, 1989), pp. 244–253.

12. Rudy Behlmer, ed., *Memo from Darryl F. Zanuck: The Golden Years at Twentieth Century-Fox* (New York: Grove Press, 1993), p. 70.

13. From Clifton Webb's unpublished autobiography. The memoir was among Webb's memorabilia, which I reviewed for Heritage Galleries Auctions, Dallas, Texas, 2006.

Chapter 25

1. *House of Frankenstein* Production File, Universal Collection, USC Performing Arts Library.

2. David Carradine, *Endless Highway* (Boston: Journey Editions, 1995), p. 158.

3. *House of Frankenstein* Production File.

4. Laird Cregar 20th Century–Fox Legal File, UCLA.

5. Erskine Johnson, "Around Hollywood," *Pampa Daily News*, 10 April 1944.

6. Cregar Fox Legal File.

7. Thanks to Bruce Forsberg, who provided me a copy of the script for this show.

8. Cregar Fox Legal File.

9. *Ibid.*

10. John Brahm Collection, USC Performing Arts Library.

11. *Ibid.*

12. Author's telephone interview with Roger Kinzel, 1 July 2000.

13. Sam Zolotow, "New Lang Comedy Soon To Open Here," *New York Times*, 10 July 1944.

14. Rose had previously been married to Fanny Brice, 1929 to 1939.

15. See Robert A. Schanke, *Shattered Applause: The Eva Le Gallienne Story* (Fort Lee, NJ: Barricade Books, 1995). Also, Helen Sheehy, *Eva Le Gallienne: A Biography* (New York: Knopf, 2013).

16. "Shakespeare's Globe Theatre," www.shakespeare-online.com/theatre/globe.html.

17. "*Henry the Eighth* May Be the First of Billy Rose's Operas To Hit Main Stem This Fall," *The Billboard*, 29 July 1944, p. 30. This article also noted that Fredric March and Claude Rains were under consideration for the title role.

18. John Brahm Collection.

19. Joel Greenberg, "Writing for the Movies: Barré Lyndon," *Focus on Film*, no. 21 (Summer 1975): 56.

20. Anne Grosvenor and Art Smith, *New York Daily News*, July 1944.

21. John Brahm Collection.

22. Radie Harris, "Broadway Runaround," *Variety*, 18 July 1944, p. 4.

23. Sam Zolotow, "*Song of Norway* Nears Broadway," *New York Times*, 25 July 1944.

Chapter 26

1. See Antonia Fraser, *Faith and Treason: The Story of the Gunpowder Plot* (New York: Anchor Books, 1997). Also J. A. Sharpe, *Remember, Remember: A Cultural History of Guy Fawkes Day* (Cambridge, MA: Harvard University Press, 2005). Times change. In 2002, Guy Fawkes placed #30 in the BBC's 100 Greatest Britons List, voted for by the public. A Guy Fawkes Mask is a key feature in the 2005 film *V for Vendetta*, based on the DC/Vertigo Comic series.

2. Michael Buckley, "Richard Widmark (Part Two)," *Films in Review*, May 1986, p. 269.

3. Harrison Carroll, "Lights! Camera! Action!," *Los Angeles Evening Herald-Examiner*, 9 September 1944.

4. Louella O. Parsons, "Great Cast in *Home Again*," *Syracuse Herald-Journal*, 8 August 1944.

5. Louella O. Parsons, "Geraldine Fitzgerald Is Borrowed for *Hangover Square* Lead," *Waterloo Daily Courier*, 11 August 1944..

6. "News of the Screen," *New York Times*, 12 August 1944.

7. "Ethel Barrymore to Star for Guild," *New York Times*, 12 August 1944.

8. Sam Zolotow, "*Last Stop* Booked at the Barrymore," *New York Times*, 17 August, 1944. John Alexander had played "Teddy" in the original Broadway production of *Arsenic and Old Lace* as well as in the film version released in 1944.

9. Hedda Hopper, "Break for Geraldine," *The Washington Post*, 18 August 1944.

10. Author's telephone interview with David Frankham, New Mexico, 5 February 2014. All quotes from Mr. Frankham in this chapter come from that interview.

11. George Sanders, *Memoirs of a Professional Cad* (New York: G.P. Putnam's Sons, 1960), p. 41.

12. Charles Higham and Roy Moseley, *Princess Merle* (New York: Coward-McCann, 1983), p. 160.

13. Joel Greenberg, "Writing for The Movies: Barré Lyndon," *Focus on Film*, no. 21 (Summer 1975): 48.

14. Letter to author from DeWitt Bodeen, Woodland Hills, CA, 28 February 1979.

15. Barbara Berch, "Bold, Bad (Bluffing) Cregar," *Screenland*, January 1945, p. 77.

Chapter 27

1. Ronald L. Davis, *Hollywood Beauty: Linda Darnell and the American Dream* (Norman, OK: University of Oklahoma Press, 1991), pp. 177–182.

2. "George Sanders, Film Villain, a Suicide," *New York Times*, 26 April 1972.

3. George Sanders, *Memoirs of a Professional Cad* (New York: G.P. Putnam's Sons, 1960), p. 41.

4. Author's interview with DeWitt Bodeen, Woodland Hills, CA, 8 December 1981.

5. Jimmy Starr, *Los Angeles Evening Herald Express*, 4 September 1944.

6. Irene Thirer, "Screen News and Views: Picturized Thought a MUST For Good Films, Says Brahm," *New York Post*, February 1945.

7. Sidney Skolsky, *Hollywood Citizen-News*, 30 August 1944.

8. Edith Gwynn, "Rambling Reporter," *The Hollywood Reporter*, 13 September 1944.

9. On August 22, *Variety* had reported the casting of Reginald Gardiner; the trade paper didn't specify which role, but it was likely Mickey, Netta's pimp. Gardiner immediately began bitching about his lines; Brahm, anticipating enough trouble with Laird and the notorious Sanders, quickly replaced Gardiner.

10. Kay Proctor, "Mood Expert," *Motion Picture*, December 1945, p. 52.

11. Author's telephone interview with Faye Marlowe, Cary, NC, 23 October 2007. All quotes from Ms. Marlowe in this chapter come from that interview.

12. Author's interview with Alan Napier, Pacific Palisades, CA, 15 May 1983. All quotes from Mr. Napier in this chapter come from that interview.

13. Letter from Joseph I. Breen to Colonel Jason S. Joy, 20th Century–Fox, 11 August 1944, MPAA/PCA File.

14. "The New Pictures," *Time*, 12 February 1945, p. 52.

15. Douglas Gilbert, "Camera Softens *Hangover Square*," *New York World-Telegram*, 22 January 1945.

16. Author's telephone interview with Undeen Darnell Hunter, Lake Elsinore, CA, 17 June 2002.

17. "Two Streets Built for *Hangover Square*," *Variety*, September 1944, p. 14.

18. Sam Zolotow, "Rose's *Henry VIII* Off Till January," 8 September 1944, p. 16.

19. Leonard Lyons, "Looseleaf Notebook," *The Washington Post*, 31 August 1944.

20. Author's telephone interview with David Frankham, New Mexico, 5 February 2014. Frankham worked with Brahm on TV's *The Alfred Hitchcock Hour* ("Murder Case," 6 March 1964). All information from Mr. Frankham in this chapter comes from that interview.

21. Hedda Hopper, "Happy in 'Happiness,'" *The Washington Post*, 14 September 1944 (article dated 12 September 1944).

22. Hedda Hopper, "A Man of Acumen!," The *Washington Post*, 18 September 1944.

23. Hedda Hopper, "...Hunts a Headache!" *The Washington Post*, 20 September 1944.

Chapter 28

1. Erskine Johnson, *Moorhead Daily News*, 25 September 1944.

2. *Hangover Square* legal file, 20th Century–Fox Collection, UCLA.

3. Joel Greenberg, "Writing for the Movies: Barré Lyndon," *Focus on Film*, no. 21 (Summer 1975): 55.

4. Tyra Fuller, "Laird Cregar Hopes To Play Light Roles If He Can Reduce," *Worcester Sunday Telegram*, 17 September 1944.

5. *Hangover Square* legal file.

6. Irene Thirer, "Screen News and Views: Picturized Thought a MUST For Good Film, Says Brahm," 1945.

7. Author's telephone interview with Faye Marlowe, Cary, North Carolina, 23 October 2007. All quotes from Ms. Marlowe in this chapter come from that interview.

8. "Cregar's Pyre 10-Day Blaze," *The Baltimore Sun*, 10 December 1944.

9. Barbara Berch, "Bold, Bad (Bluffing) Cregar," *Screenland*, January 1945.

10. Author's interview with Alan Napier, Pacific Palisades, CA, 15 May 1983.

11. "New Film 'One-Puncher,'" *Los Angeles Examiner*, 11 October 1944.

12. John Brahm Collection, USC.

13. Rose Pelswick, "At The Roxy," *New York Journal-American*, 12 October 1944.

14. *Hangover Square* production file, 20th Century–Fox Collection, UCLA.

15. Jimmie Fidler, "Fidler in Hollywood," *Nevada State Journal*, 19 October 1944.

16. To add to the inanity, the synopsis Parsons provided sounds very similar to *The Frozen Ghost*, a Universal "Inner Sanctum" starring Lon Chaney, Jr. and Evelyn Ankers, filmed in the summer of 1944 and yet-to-be-released when this notice was published.

17. *Variety* (10 October 1945) would call *The Spider* a "neatly produced whodunit that will fill the second half of a double bill without boring the customers."

Chapter 29

1. Author's interview with DeWitt Bodeen (8 December 1981). Due to its nature, the story was presumably never printed, but spread nonetheless.

2. Author's telephone interview with David Frankham, Santa Fe, NM, 5 February 2014.

3. Author's telephone interview with Undeen Darnell Hunter, Lake Elsinore, CA, 17 June 2002.

4. Data for Bulletin of Screen Achievement Records, Margaret Herrick Library, Academy of Motion Picture Arts and Sciences.

5. *Hangover Square* production file, 20th Century–Fox Collection, UCLA.

6. Edith Gwynn, "Rambling Reporter," *The Hollywood Reporter*, 27 October 1944, p. 2.

7. *Ibid.*, 26 October 1944, p. 2.

8. *Ibid.*, 27 October 1944, p. 2.

9. Joel Greenberg, "Writing for the Movies: Barré Lyndon," *Focus on Film*, no. 21 (Summer 1975): 50–51.

10. Edith Gwynn, "Rambling Reporter," *The Hollywood Reporter*, 1 November 1944, p. 2.

11. Irene Thirer, "Screen News and Views: Picturized Thought a MUST For Good Film, Says Brahm," *New York Post*, February 1945.

12. Thanks to The Celebrity Archive, Scottsdale, AZ, which offers a large selection of celebrity wills, autopsy reports and divorce papers.

13. Lucy Chase Williams, *The Complete Films of Vincent Price* (New York: Citadel Press, 1995), p. 92.

14. Hedda Hopper, "The Late Great Laird," Chicago *Daily Tribune*, 2 December 1945.

15. Rudy Behlmer, interview with Maureen O'Hara, audio commentary, *The Black Swan* DVD.

16. "Hollywood Film Shop," *The Daily Register*, 29 November 1944.

17. Harrison Carroll, "Behind the Scenes in Hollywood," *The Wilkes-Barre Record*, 22 December 1944.

18. Hedda Hopper, "Looking at Hollywood," *Los Angeles Times*, 4 December 1944.

19. Edith Gwynn, "Rambling Reporter," *The Hollywood Reporter*, 4 December 1944.

20. "Price and Tierney," *Variety*, 5 December 1944, p. 4.

21. "Chatter," *Variety*, 6 December 1944, p. 2.

22. "Brahm Seeks New One," *The Hollywood Reporter*, 8 December, 1944.

23. "Laird Cregar, Film Star, Dies of Heart Attack," *Los Angeles Times*, 10 December 1944.

24. "Rain or Overcast, Week-end Forecast," *Los Angeles Times*, 9 December 1944.

25. "Actor's Condition Grave After Heart Attack," *The Washington Post*, 10 December 1944.

26. Laird Cregar death certificate.

27. Author's telephone interviews with Elizabeth Cregar Hayman, Penn Valley, CA, 12 and 17 January 2012.

28. Thanks to Ellen Bailey, Pasadena Playhouse archivist, who saw this production.

29. Memo from Lew Schreiber to George Wasson, 13 December 1944, Laird Cregar Legal File, 20th Century–Fox Collection, UCLA.

Chapter 30

1. *Photoplay*, January 1945.

2. Thanks to The Celebrity Archive, Scottsdale, AZ, for this information.

3. "Zanuck Goes East for Nobel Dinner," *Variety*, 6 December 1944, p. 2.

4. "Laird Cregar Rites," *Variety*, December 1944, p. 18.

5. David Del Valle, "A Conversation with Vincent Price," *Video Watchdog*, no. 11 (May/June 1992): 38.

6. "Warnings Ordered for Small Craft," *Los Angeles Times*, 13 December 1944.

7. *Variety* spelled his first name two ways: Harlan and Harley.

8. "Film Colony to Pay Final Respect to Laird Cregar," *Hollywood Citizen-News*, 11 December 1944.

9. Author's telephone interview with David Frankham, 5 February 2014.

10. Thanks to Scott Wilson, who provided a copy of Ms. Velez's death certificate.

11. "Cregar's Heirs—Mother, Aunt," *The Baltimore Sun*, 19 December 1944.

12. David Stenn, *Bombshell: The Life and Death of Jean Harlow* (New York: Doubleday & Co., Inc., 1993), pp. 241–242.

13. "Film Reviews," *Weekly Variety*, 17 January 1945, p. 14.

14. "The New Pictures," *Time*, 12 February 1945, p. 52.

15. "N.Y. Hot; 'Pirate' Record 45G, 'Square,' Berle Sockeroo 103G, 'Fear'—Long 73G, 'Vanities' Ups 'Gets Man,' Strong 35G," *Variety*, 14 February 1945, p. 11.

16. *Ibid.*

17. *Variety*, 21 and 28 February 1945.

18. Author's telephone interview with David Frankham, Santa Fe, NM, 5 February 2014.

Chapter 31

1. Hedda Hopper, "The Late Great Laird," Chicago *Daily Tribune*, 2 December 1945.

2. Louella Parsons, "Good News," *Modern Screen*, March 1945.

3. Margot Peters, *The House of Barrymore* (New York: Alfred A. Knopf, 1990), p. 377.

4. *Ibid.*, p. 428.

5. Neil Rau, "*Hangover Square* Full of Exciting Suspense," *Los Angeles Examiner*, 31 March 1945.

6. Nigel Jones, *Through a Glass Darkly: The Life of Patrick Hamilton* (London: Black Spring Press, 2008). Agate's review appears in this book on page 299.

7. *Ibid.*, p. 298.

8. Mr. Huston, "What the Picture Did for Me," *Motion Picture Herald*, 14 July 1945.

9. "Picture Grosses," *Variety*, 24 April 1946, p. 11.

10. On Broadway, the play was titled *Diversions and Delights: Being an evening spent with Sebastian Melmouth on the 28th day of November, 1899*. It opened at the Eugene O'Neill Theatre, April 12, 1978, and ran 13 performances.

11. Victoria Price was a guest at the Monster Bash Convention, Mars, PA, where we chatted 19 June 2015.

12. "Film Industry May Pass the Hat for Pasadena Playhouse," *Variety*, 31 December 1952, p. 11.

13. In this production, Eva Le Gallienne played Katherine of Aragon, Walter Hampden played Cardinal Wolsey, June Duprez played Anne Boleyn, Eli Wallach played Cornwall, and Margaret Webster appeared as "Old Lady." In the repertoire, Webster also directed *John Gabriel Borkman* (with Victor Jory in the title role) and *Androcles and the Lion*; Jory directed *A Pound on Demand*.

14. Thanks to Scott Wilson.

15. "Mrs. Cregar Autobiog Is Optioned by Metro," *Variety*, 17 October 1945, p. 5.

16. Author's telephone interviews with Elizabeth Cregar Hayman, Penn Valley, CA, 12 and 17 January 2012.

17. Elizabeth Cregar's death certificate.

18. A comprehensive Raymond Burr biography is *Hiding in Plain Sight: The Secret Life of Raymond Burr*, by Michael Seth Starr (Montclair, NJ: Applause Theatre and Cinema Books, 2009).

19. Tom Weaver, *Bride of the Gorilla*, script from the Crypt #3 (Albany, GA: BearManor Media, 2015), p. 164.

20. Robert C. Roman, "Laird Cregar's Successor, Victor Buono," *Castle of Frankenstein*, no. 9 (November 1966): 27–30, 58.

21. Fry has written three memoirs: *The Fry Chronicles: An Autobiography* (New York: The Overlook Press, 2012), *Moab is My Washpot* (New York: Soho Press, 2014), and *More Fool Me: A Memoir* (New York: The Overlook Press, 2016).

22. Thanks to Denise Fetterley for this information.

Bibliography

Books

Beck, Calvin Thomas. *Heroes of the Horrors*. New York: Macmillan, 1975.

Behlmer, Rudy. *Inside Warner Bros. (1935–1951)*. New York: Viking Penguin, 1985.

_____, ed. *Memo from Darryl F. Zanuck: The Golden Years at Twentieth Century–Fox*. New York: Grove Press, 1993.

Benson, Jackson J. *The True Adventures of John Steinbeck, Writer*. New York: Penguin Books, 1984.

Billips, Connie, and Arthur Pierce. *Lux Presents Hollywood*. Jefferson, NC: McFarland, 1995.

Brown, Gene. *Movie Time*. New York: Macmillan, 1995.

Carradine, David. *Endless Highway*. Boston: Journey Editions, 1995.

Curtis, James. *James Whale: A New World of Gods and Monsters*. London: Faber and Faber, 1998.

_____. *Spencer Tracy: A Biography*. New York: Alfred A. Knopf, 2011.

Eyman, Scott. *Lion of Hollywood: The Life and Legend of Louis B. Mayer*. New York: Simon & Schuster, 2005.

Feinberg, Cobbett. *Reel Facts: The Movie Book of Records*. New York: Vintage, 1978.

Fonda, Henry, and Howard Teichmann. *Fonda: My Life*. New York: Signet, 1982.

Gussow, Mel. *Don't Say Yes Until I Finish Talking*. New York: Doubleday, 1971.

Hamann, G.D. *Laird Cregar In the 40's*. Hollywood: Filming Today Press, 2012.

Hamblett, Charles. *The Hollywood Cage*. New York: Hart Publishing Co., 1969.

Harris, Marlys J. *The Zanucks of Hollywood: The Dark Legacy of an America Dynasty*. New York: Crown Publishers, 1989.

Higham, Charles. *Bette: The Life of Bette Davis*. New York: Dell, 1981.

_____, and Joel Greenberg. *The Celluloid Muse: Hollywood Directors Speak*. New York: Signet, 1972.

Higham, Charles, and Roy Moseley. *Princess Merle*. New York: Coward-McCann, 1983.

Hirschhorn, Clive. *The Universal Story*. New York: Crown Publishers, 1983.

Jerome, Stuart. *Those Crazy Wonderful Years When We Ran Warner Bros.* Secaucus, NJ: Lyle Stuart Inc., 1983.

Jones, Nigel. *Through a Glass Darkly: The Life of Patrick Hamilton*. London: Black Spring Press, 2008.

Lanchester, Elsa. *Elsa Lanchester: Herself*. New York: St. Martin's Press, 1983.

McElwee, John. *Showmen, Sell It Hot!* Charlotte, NC: Paladin Communications, 2013.

Maltin, Leonard. *Leonard Maltin's Movie Encyclopedia*. New York: Plume, 1995.

Moshier, W. Franklin. *The Alice Faye Movie Book*. Mechanicsburg, PA: Stackpole Books, 1974.

Parish, James Robert, and Lennard DeCarl (with William T. Leonard and Gregory W. Mank). *Hollywood Players: The Forties*. New Rochelle, NY: Arlington House, 1976.

Peary, Danny. *Guide for the Film Fanatic*. New York: Simon & Schuster, 1986.

Peters, Margo. *The House of Barrymore*. New York: Knopf, 1990.

Quinn, Anthony, and Daniel Paisner. *One Man Tango*. New York: HarperCollins, 1995.

Rumbelow, Daniel. *The Complete Jack the Ripper*. London: Penguin Books, 2004.

Sanders, George. *Memoirs of a Professional Cad*. New York: G.P. Putnam's Sons, 1960.

Schessler, Ken. *This is Hollywood: An Unusual Movie Guide*. Redlands, CA: Ken Schessler Publishing, 1987.

Schickel, Richard. *The Men Who Made the Movies*. New York: Athenaeum Books, 1975.

Siegel, Joel E. *Val Lewton: The Reality of Terror*. New York: The Viking Press, 1973.

Stenn, David. *Bombshell: The Life and Death of Jean Harlow*. New York: Doubleday, 1993.

Taylor, Robert Louis. *W.C Fields: His Follies and Fortunes*. New York: Signet, 1967.

Titone, Nora. *My Thoughts Be Bloody*. New York: Free Press, 2010.

Tornabene, Lyn. *Long Live The King*. New York: G. P. Putnam's Sons, 1976.

Turner, George, ed. *The Cinema of Adventure, Romance & Terror*. Hollywood: The ASC Press, 1989.

Wallis, Hal, and Charles Higham. *Star Maker.* New York: Berkley, 1981.
Wiley, Mason, and Damien Bona. *Inside Oscar: The Unofficial History of the Academy Awards.* New York: Ballantine Books, 1986.
Williams, Lucy Chase. *The Complete Films of Vincent Price.* Secaucus, NJ: Citadel Press, 1995.
Wynn, Ned. *We Will Always Live in Beverly Hills: Growing Up Crazy in Hollywood.* New York: William Morrow, 1990.

Interviews

Bennett, Charles. Beverly Hills, CA. October 29, 1992.
Bodeen, DeWitt. Woodland Hills, CA. December 8, 1981.
Brandon, Henry. West Hollywood, CA. April 19 and April 26, 1986.
Feld, Fritz. Brentwood, CA. July 11, 1987.
Frankham, David. Santa Fe, NM. February 5, 2014.
Hayman, Elizabeth Cregar. Penn Valley, CA. January 12 and January 17, 2012.
Hunter, Undeen Darnell. Lake Elsinore, CA. June 17, 2002.
Kinzel, Roger. Sarasota, FL. July 1, 2000.
Linaker, Kay. Keene, NH. July 19, 2000, and January 23, 2003.
Marlowe, Faye. Cary, NC. October 23, 2007.
Moran, Peggy. Camarillo, CA. August 12, 1993.
Napier, Alan. Pacific Palisades, CA. May 15, 1983.
Stewart, Peggy. Valencia, CA. June 17, 2009.
Wynn, Ned. March 7, 2014.

Archives

Billy Rose Library for the Performing Arts. Lincoln Center. New York City, NY.
Enoch Pratt Free Library. Baltimore, MD.
Margaret Herrick Library. The Academy of Motion Picture Arts and Sciences. Los Angeles, CA.
Pasadena Playhouse Archives. Pasadena, CA.
University of California, Los Angeles. Performing Arts Collections. Los Angeles, CA.
University of Southern California Film and Television Library. Los Angeles, CA.
University of Southern California. Warner Bros. Archives. Los Angeles, CA.

Magazines, Newspapers and Trade Journals

The Albuquerque Journal
American Cinematographer
The Atlanta Constitution
Baltimore Sun
Berkeley Daily Gazette
Billboard
Boston Daily Globe
Castle of Frankenstein
Chicago Daily Tribune
Cleveland Plain Dealer
The Film Daily
Filmfax
Films in Review
Films of the Golden Age
Focus on Film
Harrisburg Daily Register
Hollywood Citizen-News
The Hollywood Reporter
Independent Exhibitors
Film Bulletin
LIFE
The Lima News
Los Angeles Daily News
Los Angeles Evening Herald Express
Los Angeles Examiner
Los Angeles Times
McKinney Daily Courier
Miami Daily News
Midnight Marquee
Monsters from the Vault
Montana Standard
Moorhead Daily News
Motion Picture Herald
Nevada Sate Journal
New York Daily News
New York Herald Tribune
New York Post
New York Sunday News
New York Times
New York World-Telegram
Oakland Tribune
Philadelphia Inquirer
Photoplay
Salt Lake Tribune
San Antonio Light
San Francisco Chronicle
San Mateo Tribune
Screenland Magazine
Showmen's Trade Review
Southtown Economist
Syracuse Herald-Journal
TIME
Variety
Video Watchdog
The Washington Post
Waterloo Daily Courier
Worcester Sunday Telegram

Index